W9-AZI-158

LETHAL MARRIAGE

Nick Pron

SEAL BOOKS
Toronto

Copyright © 1995 by Nick Pron

All rights reserved. No part of this publication may be reproduced or
transmitted in any form or by any means, electronic or mechanical,
including photocopying, recording, or by any information storage and
retrieval system, without permission in writing from the publisher.

Seal Books and colophon are trademarks of
Random House of Canada Limited.

LETHAL MARRIAGE
An Original by Seal Books

If you purchased this book without a cover, you should be aware that
this book is stolen property. It was reported as "unsold and destroyed"
to the publisher, and neither the author nor the publisher has received
any payment for this "stripped" book.

ISBN 0-7704-2710-3

Seal Books are published by Random House of Canada Limited.
"Seal Books" and the portrayal of a seal, are the property of
Random House of Canada Limited.

Visit Random House of Canada Limited's website:
www.randomhouse.ca

Cover photo of Paul Bernardo courtesy Canapress/Frank Gunn
Cover photo of Karla Homolka courtesy *The Toronto Star*
Cover design by Melody Cassen

PRINTED AND BOUND IN THE USA

OPM   15   14   13   12   11   10   9

To John Pearce for his guidance, to my family for their support, and to Dave Ellis and Steve Tustin of The Toronto Star *for their backing.*

TABLE OF CONTENTS

AUTHOR'S NOTE

The most disturbing aspects of the Paul Bernardo and Karla Homolka saga concern the videotapes the couple made of the rapes of four young women. Two of those victims, Kristen French and Leslie Mahaffy, were then murdered. Their families hired a lawyer and fought hard to keep the tapes from ever being shown in public, out of respect for the dignity of the slain teenagers. The families didn't even want the public to hear the dialogue on the tapes. Their legal motions were opposed by major Canadian media outlets.

The families won a partial victory from the courts when Associate Chief Justice Patrick LeSage ruled that the public could hear, but not see, the gruesome videos at Bernardo's trial. LeSage's shrewd decision was an attempt to strike a balance somewhere between the rights of the victims and freedom of the press.

The transcripts of those videos were clearly upsetting, and were never reproduced in full or verbatim by any of the 60 or so media outlets that covered Bernado's murder trial. Newspapers and television and radio stations all tried to stay within the bounds of what is described as good taste. Even so, their reports were usually prefaced with warnings. At the *Toronto Star*, for example, senior editors often agonized over how much detail to relay.

A book, however, is different. Except for some minor editorial changes, the mind-numbing transcripts of the rapes and beatings of the four teenagers have been reproduced here on the premise that they are a necessary component of the narrative. Because of their significance as evidence, they have been reproduced virtually verbatim, despite the high degree of offense readers may feel. As with the news reports, this book comes with a warning. Undoubtedly, there will be criticism over such graphic descriptions of the brutal rapes of minors. "Aren't you guilty of writing child pornography?" was the loaded question from a magazine writer who had listened to the tapes in court. "Surely the families, and the public for that matter, deserve to be spared further grief?"

It is a compelling argument, but I disagree with it for one simple reason: the tapes detail the full involvement of Homolka in the despicable actions of her husband. The full horror of what they did has to be told somewhere. In a case notorious for bumbling police investigation, secret deals, and secret trials, Homolka's role in the murders and sex crimes has probably been the most contentious and hotly debated issue. Was she really a victim of wife abuse, as she claimed, or was she essentially Bernardo's accomplice?

In exchange for testifying against her husband, Homolka was sentenced to 12 years in jail — four years in reality with parole. There are those who say a dozen years is insufficient punishment for her part in three sex killings and at least one other rape. A public outcry has already started against her deal. Legally, it cannot be overturned. Morally, it should be, argue the critics, myself included.

John Rosen, Bernardo's defense lawyer and one of the finest criminal lawyers in Canada, succinctly summed up Homolka's role in the criminal proceedings against her husband during a pre-trial hearing: "The police investigation turned out to be a big fat zero until Karla Homolka came along, and then things started to fall into place." But although Homolka's testimony helped put her husband behind bars, her version of the truth was laced with contradictions, perhaps even lies. Large chunks of what she said differ completely from Bernardo's recollection of events. Not all the discrepancies can be blamed on one person pointing an accusing finger at the other. And that presents another problem for the chroniclers of this case.

Since, among the living, Bernardo and Homolka were the only ones present for many key events in their relationship, the truth of what really happened probably lies somewhere between what each testified. In describing various scenes, particularly the murders, I have generally followed what I feel to be the most likely account. Occasionally, I have let the contradictions stand by recording what both of them said.

But there is one truth that cannot be disputed: the brutal rapes and beatings of the two schoolgirls recorded on videotape. Just as prosecutor Ray Houlahan presented all the videos to the jurors at Bernardo's trial before they sat in judgment of him, I feel an obligation to give readers the fullest account possible to help them decide if justice was served, particularly in the case of Karla Homolka. But a similar consideration applies to Paul Bernardo. Since Canada does not believe in putting its killers to death, Bernardo could one day be eligible for parole. Although I have not seen the tapes, I have heard them enough times, and I shudder at the thought of what those two unfortunate teenagers went through. Even though there seemed to be saturation coverage of Bernardo's trial, the public has the right to know all the gruesome aspects of this case before there's any debate on whether Bernardo should ever be released.

My special thanks to two people who did not want their real names used, for different reasons. One has been identified as Renya Hill. A bright, intelligent woman, she, along with her parents, was deeply troubled by the role of their one-time family friend Karla Homolka in the deaths. She hopes Homolka can one day explain all the apparent discrepancies in her behavior. Hill has chosen to remain anonymous because she does not want the hassle of becoming too close to such a notorious case.

And then there is Eddie Grogan, the police officer. Over the past 20 years working the crime beat for the *Toronto Star*, I have enjoyed my daily contacts with members of law enforcement. Their job is difficult and dangerous, and opinion polls suggest that the general public has a far greater respect for police officers than for, say, journalists. In many cases I have covered over the past two decades, the police — whether the Ontario Provincial Police, the Toronto or Niagara forces — have done a tremendous job of solving crimes. Unfortunately, the Paul Bernardo case is not one of those successes. To say otherwise would be a lie, even though some very fine, dedicated officers spent three hard years working on what was a very difficult case. Journalists are often criticized for focusing too much on the negative, and overlooking some of the more positive aspects of what is going on in society, such as police work. Often that claim has some validity. But not in this case.

Eddie Grogan was an officer who recognized early on there were aspects of the case that were being handled very poorly by the various forces. In a military-style organization, such as the police, criticisms like these are not encouraged or rewarded. For those reasons, Grogan's true identity will have to remain secret.

Toronto
August 1995

Prologue
Sharing the Blame

The letter Karla Homolka received that day was different from the others. Hate mail, that's all she had been getting after settling into her new home, a correctional institution in Kingston, Ontario, called the Prison for Women. The censors at P4W, as the prison was known, were intercepting the letters, but Homolka had heard about the venom directed her way.

Total strangers from all over the continent had been writing to her, people disgusted by what she and her husband, Paul Bernardo, had done to a pair of schoolgirls, Kristen French and Leslie Mahaffy. The two teenagers had been abducted and held captive at the couple's fashionable home in St. Catharines, where Bernardo had used them as sex slaves, repeatedly raping and sodomizing them. Not only did Homolka videotape the assaults for her husband's later enjoyment but she also took her turn having sex with each of the girls. Then she watched, and did nothing, when her husband strangled them to death.

By the time police investigators finally caught up to Bernardo, ending his six-year spree of rape and murder, Homolka had turned on her husband and offered to help the authorities. Although this act of contrition had earned Homolka a reduced jail sentence of 12 years, it had not won her any favor with an angry public. As she was driven off to jail after her trial, a pensioner had held up a handwritten sign that summed up the feelings of many: "Rot in Hell — bitch!"

Unlike her other "fan mail," the return address on this particular envelope came with a familiar name that evoked pleasurable memories from her younger years. It was from an old friend, perhaps one of the precious few she had left in St. Catharines, a blue-collar automobile-manufacturing city right next to the honeymoon capital of the world, Niagara Falls. Homolka took out the letter and a photograph.

There were two girls in the faded snapshot, both about eight years old, one a blonde, the other a brunette. They were sitting on some wooden crates stacked in front of a garage. Between them was a dog named Max. The girls looked happy; the dog didn't. The blonde had a mischievous look on her face and a pretty good grip with her left arm around the neck of Max, who looked ready to bolt, given the chance. Her luxuriant hair flowed well past her shoulders. Homolka had always been proud of her hair, and now one of her biggest worries was that she wouldn't be able to keep up her grooming while serving her time at P4W.

Nearly half of the prison's 120 inmates were there for murder or manslaughter. And many of those women had been abused, had been dumped into foster homes in their early teens, only to run away to an uncertain and violent life on the streets.

But Homolka's upbringing had been nothing like that. She came from a privileged background, a comfortable middle-class home, with doting parents and many good friends. Homolka wasn't treated like "one of the girls" at P4W. Other inmates called her Skinner, a derogatory term reserved for sexual offenders. For her own protection, she had been given a segregated cell. She wanted to tell them she was just as much a victim as they were. Her only sin, she once said, had been to pick the wrong man for a husband. But the women in P4W didn't see it that way. One had threatened her. Another had pitched a telephone at her head. They weren't buying her story that her abusive husband forced her into committing the crimes.

Homolka had always been horrified of going to prison, being locked up like some zoo animal in a cage. Her husband had kept preying on that fear to ensure her silence. "If you tell the truth you'll go to jail, and everybody will hate you," he often warned. It was ironic that, despite her apprehensions, life in jail wasn't so bad after all, she wrote to her friends. She was catching up on her reading and working out in the gymnasium to get back into shape, Homolka said in a letter to a former co-worker, Wendy Lutczyn. "I feel great," she enthused. There was always something happening, like the prisoner who tried to commit suicide by setting her cell on fire. Homolka said she too had thought of taking her own life over her feelings of guilt. But that had passed, and she was looking forward to the future once more.

She had her color TV to help pass the time. And no one to nag at her for spending hours watching cartoons. Her parents had promised her a microwave oven for Christmas, so she could have her popcorn while she watched the afternoon soaps. She told friends she was determined to better herself during her incarceration. You had to think of a prison term, Homolka wrote, as if you were going off to college.

She enrolled in correspondence courses from Queen's University, taking sociology and psychology. Having a degree would help her at the parole board hearing when she applied for release after serving a third of her sentence. Besides, she had always wanted to go to university, only Paul had talked her out of it after they met. She was also learning a trade — earning four dollars a day making name tags for government employees.

When she got out, she planned to spend more time with her family and try to start a career. She talked to friends about working with abused women. She yearned to start over fresh, once again become confident, find another husband, settle down, have children. Only the next time she would be more careful in selecting a mate. Life without Paul was going to be great, she wrote to a friend. They had been together for six years, and she still had feelings for him, despite all the times he had beaten her up and anally raped her whenever she was "bad." Signing the divorce papers had been wrenching. But slowly, she was severing herself from him emotionally. There was only one big hurdle left.

She had to testify against him at his coming trial. Only when she had put Paul away for life, she felt, could she break free from their twisted love. She had once dreaded facing him in court, but now she was anxious to tell her side of the story about everything, even about her part in the death of her younger sister, Tammy Lyn.

A publication ban, meant to ensure that Bernardo received a fair trial, had prevented the public from knowing most details about Homolka's trial, including her version of events. Homolka knew that everyone hated her after learning of her involvement in the two killings and the way she had acted like a Judas Goat in setting up her younger sister. But Homolka desperately wanted people to know that she was not that bad a person, to realize that she was the victim of an abusive husband. To her friend Lutczyn, she wrote: "A big fear of mine these days is that the people I care the most about will have the wrong idea of me, or the things I say. I don't want you to hate me — I want you to understand me. I feel sad because I don't have the power to make you understand. I'm afraid . . . without answering that very important question of 'why,' you'll find it impossible to continue our friendship.

"I know you're feeling all kinds of conflicting emotions. If only I could tell you *my* side, perhaps it will make it easier for you. You *will* have a much greater understanding when you hear my testimony at his trial. I wish you could get inside my head and see and feel everything that happened."

Several psychiatrists had tried just that and they all come away with the opinion that she was an enigma, a *diagnostic mystery*. If her friends were confused about her role in the murders, the psychiatrists were having just as much difficulty. There wasn't much doubt that Homolka had been battered and brainwashed by an abusive husband, but this was a highly-intelligent woman, with an I.Q. that put her in the top 2 percent of the population. And she was a strong-willed individual, not the type of person to be easily manipulated by a spouse.

Homolka reread the letter from her old friend Renya Hill. It reminisced about their days together in public school back in St. Catharines. All the good times when they played with Homolka's Barbie and Ken dolls, the nights when they camped out in Renya's back yard and talked about their futures. Homolka took out her very special stationery, the one with the cartoon of the smiling cow wearing sneakers.

"Your letter made me laugh, it made my cry," she wrote. "Thank you so much for being kind and sweet enough to write it."

"I got accepted at Queen's University. I'm taking correspondence courses. I just started my first, Introduction to Sociology. Hopefully I'll be able to finish my degree while I'm here. I'm eligible for parole in four years and intend to be out of here — for sure!

"Anyway, I want you to know that life in here isn't as bad as most people think. I want to thank you — deeply — for not judging me. There are some people, like you, who know that this horror is not of my own making. Thank you for bringing back many happy memories, many fun times, loving times that we shared together. I need that now. If only we could turn the clock back."

Paul Bernardo was furious. He wrapped towels around his knuckles to cushion the blows as he punched the concrete walls of his cell at the detention center in the east end of Toronto. The latest development in his case was right there on the front pages of the morning newspapers in bold headlines: his wife of nineteen months had made a cozy little deal for herself with the prosecutors. He was facing first-degree murder, yet she had been charged only with manslaughter in the two schoolgirl killings, had pleaded guilty, and been given twelve years in jail.

To save her own skin, she was going to testify against him, help put him away for life, while she got off with jaywalking. Isn't that how it worked? First one in to rat on the other always got the deal.

"Fucking system!" Bernardo screamed as he hit the wall again with his fist. "Bitch is sicker'n me and she's gonna get off."

A prison guard heard the outburst, went over to his cell, and peered in through the small flip-down opening through which the inmate was passed his tray of food. Bernardo was staring out the lone window of his cell, rubbing his sore knuckles as he looked down at the parking lot.

"Enjoy the view," the guard said, "because that's all you'll see of the outside world for the rest of your life."

Bernardo ignored the jailer's attempt to goad him. He gave the man his trademark smile, then looked back out the window.

Bernardo knew that his lawyer, Ken Murray, had in his possession evidence that would have killed Homolka's deal and likely put her in the prisoner's box alongside him had its existence been revealed to the prosecutors: six tiny film cartridges that showed the two schoolgirls being raped. But if the prosecutors ever got hold of those videos, it would be all over for him. Bernardo knew that.

Since he couldn't get back at Homolka through the tapes without incriminating himself, he would have to wait until his trial. His lawyer would make sure she endured a good grilling about her part in the killings. Discrediting her was the key to his defense. If the jury was left with any doubt about who did the killings, it might even mean a reduced sentence for him. Maybe he could get second-degree murder? It would mean ten fewer years in jail. Since there were no witnesses to the murders, it would be her word against his. And Homolka, already a convicted killer, was not the world's most trustworthy witness.

In the meantime, Bernardo had to be content with riding the prisoner in the next cell. The man had killed his male lover in a fit of passion and was still mourning the loss. But Bernardo had no sympathy for the inmate.

"Hey, faggot!" he screamed through the air vents that connected their cells. It was a daily ritual of abuse that went on for hours. "C'mon, queer boy, tell me why you did it. Couldn't he get it up?"

"Shut up!" The man screamed back. "Just shut up!"

"Hey, pervert, I bet you were a momma's boy," Bernardo continued. "You want your momma now, queer boy?"

All that day, Bernardo kept up the taunting, until his fellow prisoner started to cry. Only then did Bernardo stop. But not because he felt sorry for the man. Bernardo simply grew tired of the exchange, and lay down on his cot to rest.

PART ONE:

LOOKERS

1

The Princess of Garden City

She was easily the prettiest girl in the class.

Who else had such beautiful hair? Long blond locks that swirled so delicately around her shoulders. Or who wore nicer clothes? Pink dresses, usually, and plenty of frills. But there was something else about her: she seemed almost *majestic*. Renya Hill was convinced that the six-year-old blond-haired girl sitting near her had to be a princess. Imagine that, right there in their Grade Two class at Parnell Public School in St. Catharines, someone royal. Renya was intrigued. She desperately wanted to be the Princess's friend.

The Princess, if she really was one, was always drawing houses. Before school started, she was at her desk, pencil in hand, sketching out frames. She was the first one back from recess, the first to carry on with her work. Picking a topic for art class was never a problem for the Princess. And she was so fussy and precise with her coloring, making sure everything was inside the lines. Coloring for the roof never blended into the sky; green stayed on the grass and never strayed onto the walls of her homes.

Renya had been quietly watching the Princess ever since school started that fall of 1976. She was fascinated with the girl's intensity as she busied herself on her houses, hardly ever taking her eyes off her drawings. One day, Renya walked over and complimented her on work, praised her for her neatness.

If the Princess heard her, she never said anything. She never even turned her head to acknowledge the compliment. She just did a strange thing with her eyes, shifting them sideways to glance quickly at the girl standing beside her. Then she went back to the task of completing her house. Renya, embarrassed at being ignored, returned to her own desk.

Later, at recess, Renya watched the Princess on the playground swings. She was by herself, as usual, and she was staring at a group of boys who were peering at something on the ground. One of them had a stick in his hand and was poking at whatever it was that was crawling through the grass. The Princess got off the swing and approached the boys. So did Renya. The boy with the stick was toying with a large black beetle, flicking it onto its back as it tried to scurry off. And then one of the boys held up his foot, ready to stomp on the tiny creature and end its misery. But the Princess stepped in front and pushed him away.

"You shouldn't kill it," she admonished. "It's wrong to kill anything."

She was the lone girl and they were four or five boys. But the Princess held her ground, and they backed off, muttering. Renya walked up to the Princess and tried once more to praise her for her drawings. This time the Princess was more receptive. She seemed pleased with the tribute, and smiled.

"Would you like to be my friend?" she asked, beating Renya to the question that had been on her mind for days. "My name is Karla. Karla Homolka. What's yours?"

Renya told her, and then asked her what later seemed such a dumb question. "Are you a princess?"

Karla giggled. "No," she replied. And Renya never, ever mentioned that word again, at least not to Karla.

Karla said she wanted Renya to give her a push on the swings. When Karla was finished swinging, she wanted to play on the slide. Renya dutifully followed her, first to the slide and later to the see-saw. Finally Karla wanted to know what Renya was doing that weekend. She wanted Renya to come to her house and play.

Renya had previously thought the blond-haired girl was shy and withdrawn. She was now beginning to think that she might have been wrong. Karla was bossier than Renya would have liked, but she still wanted to be her friend.

The Homolkas lived in a townhouse near Linwell Road, in the north end of St. Catharines, not far from Lake Ontario. Karla had two sisters. Tammy was the baby in the family, just one. And Lori was four, two years younger than Karla. They had moved from Toronto to Garden City, as St. Catharines liked to call itself, in the past year. Karla's mother Dorothy was Canadian but her father Karel was from Czechoslovakia, which was under Communist rule when he had left with his parents, small-time entrepreneurs who wanted to live in a country where free enterprise was not a crime. The family had a motto: *Better to work for yourself than someone else*.

Her dad, Karla explained to her new friend that Saturday afternoon, was an art dealer, well known in the city. He sold black-velvet paintings outside shopping malls. Portraits of Elvis Presley were a big seller, she said.

"My parents just love Elvis Presley," Karla went on. "They play his music all the time. 'Love Me Tender' is my favorite. Do you like Elvis Presley?"

About the only song Renya listened to with any regularity was the national anthem that was played before hockey games. The Toronto Maple Leafs, who played in the Big City across the lake, were *her* team. Her favorite game was road hockey, and she wasn't afraid of the rough stuff when she played with the boys in the parking lot of a nearby church.

It seemed like an unlikely friendship. Karla, with her blond locks and frilly pink dresses, was prissy. Renya, on the other hand, hated dresses and looked very much the tomboy with her blue jeans and short brown hair. Unlike most girls her age, Renya didn't have any dolls — she didn't *want* any. So when Karla asked her if she wanted to play dolls, Renya reluctantly agreed, even though she would have preferred to do something else that afternoon. But she liked Karla, and didn't want to upset her.

"Good," said Karla, taking Renya to her bedroom to show off her Barbie and Ken collection.

Karla had more than a dozen Barbie and Ken dolls. They and their accessories and outfits took up one wall of her room. "Here," she said to Renya, passing her a Ken figure. "You can be Ken because you have short hair. I have long hair like Barbie. I always play Barbie."

Karla liked the dolls, she explained, because everything about them was just so perfect, from Barbie's hair to her house — even her underwear. It was a wonderful pretend family in a beautiful pretend world. Someday, she said, she would have a lovely house just like Barbie, with her own fabulous kitchen and a handsome husband just like Ken.

Karla could have played all day in her imaginary world, but Renya soon grew tired. There wasn't enough action for her. And besides, Karla controlled the game: Barbie going here, doing this, playing with that. Everything was too nice in the make-believe world of Barbie, Ken, and Karla. Renya had an idea for something different. She got together some of the cars, put Barbie in one and Ken in the other, and then fashioned an intersection with the houses.

"Here," she said, handing Karla the car with Barbie behind the wheel. Renya took the Ken doll and his vehicle.

Karla had lost control of the game and she wasn't sure she wanted to go along with whatever her friend was planning. Even at that age she always had to be the leader, happiest when she was the one in charge. She was so strong-willed that she didn't want anyone, neither her parents nor her school chums, to tell her what to do. But Renya was insistent. "We're going to have a Barbie and Ken car crash," she said, searching through Karla's collection for an ambulance.

Karla's eyes reddened, she was so upset. Quickly, she scooped up all the dolls. "You must never, ever hurt Barbie or Ken," she said as she put them carefully away. "I don't want to play anymore."

They went into the living room and watched cartoons. Soon it was time to go: Renya's father was there to take her home. Renya was sure the Princess would never want to see her again. She had barely spoken while they watched television.

But Karla was smiling as she walked Renya to the door. She handed her a small, smooth stone. "Our friendship," she said, "will last forever. Just like this rock."

Nobody in the Hill household could believe it. The family dog, Buster, the ill-tempered, cantankerous mongrel who was friendly toward no one, least of all his own masters, and who went after everybody — the postman, the kid next door — took to Karla Homolka, right from her first visit. It was as if Renya's best friend had some magical power over the poor dumb creature.

The Hills lived on Geneva Street, not far from the Homolkas. They had lived there for years and knew just about everybody on the street, including Doug and Donna French and their children. Renya always had friends over, but she was particularly excited this weekend because her best chum was spending the day.

Buster didn't growl when Homolka petted him. Donald Hill was impressed. He didn't talk much about it in front of his daughter, but he had been thinking of putting the dog down. He was afraid the animal was going to bite someone and the family would end up on the losing end of a big lawsuit. Half in jest, he wondered if his daughter's best friend would like a pet.

"I already have a dog," replied Homolka. "His name is Lester."

That drew some quizzical looks from the Hills. They knew she didn't have a dog.

The two girls played Barbie and Ken with some of the dolls Homolka had brought with her, but Renya was soon ready for something more. She had a tent and asked if her friend wanted to set it up in the back yard. They could play house there.

Homolka wasn't so sure. "Will I get dirty?" She had on a frilly white blouse and good slacks. "I've never put up a tent."

Homolka tried helping, but she broke a fingernail and hit her hand banging in one of the pegs. Finally, Renya asked her brother, Eddie, for help.

"I don't like her," he whispered to Renya as they raised the tent. "There's something strange about her."

"What?"

"I don't know. She's just weird."

Later, when the two girls were alone in the text, Homolka confided she had a secret she wanted to share. There was something she liked to do — *talk dirty*. "My dad won't let me because girls aren't supposed to. But I just love to swear." As if to prove her point, she suddenly fired off a whole string of expletives, getting louder and louder, throwing her head back and laughing uproariously after each cussword. Renya was shocked that her friend had such a foul mouth. Homolka told her to join in.

In the two years the girls had known each other, Homolka had firmly established herself as the leader of the duo. When they got together, it was never Renya, the mouthier of the two, who got her way. Homolka was the better conniver, always scheming to get Renya to do whatever she wanted.

It was no different on this day, and soon both girls were cursing like two angry motorists at a fender-bender. They stopped only when Renya's dad, who had heard them from the kitchen, came rushing outside to see what was wrong. Renya flushed, but Homolka just smiled. She was having a great time shocking the hell out of everyone.

The two girls went to Renya's room, and it was Homolka, again, who came up with the idea. Renya, as usual, went along.

For a long time, Homolka had been eyeing Renya's pet hamster, George. Homolka was excited about her plan, and was characteristically persuasive. Eventually Renya agreed to help, providing George didn't get hurt. Homolka was offended by the very thought. She promised — guaranteed! — that nothing bad would happen. After all, wasn't she the animal lover? The one who wanted a career one day as a vet? She would never intentionally hurt anything, especially not George, Homolka said.

She got a pillowcase and told Renya they would need some string. Renya got some, then took George out of his cage and held him in her lap, warily eyeing Homolka, who went about her task with the same intensity with which she drew her houses. At last, Homolka finished her preparations and proudly held up her project — a parachute.

"Nothing will happen to George," Homolka repeated as she tied the strings of the parachute to the hamster. "I promise."

She then took George to the window of the second-floor bedroom, opened it, and looked out. "Are you going to help or not?"

The two girls leaned out the window, checking again to make sure no one was there. Renya suddenly changed her mind — but Homolka had the hamster in her hands, and she flung him out the window.

At first the parachute billowed in the air, and for an instant George hung there, high above the ground. But then the pillowcase collapsed, and George crashed to the lawn below. Renya shrieked and ran down the stairs and out into the back yard. Homolka was close behind.

George was lying on the grass, not moving but still alive. Renya, close to tears, gently picked up the dazed animal. Homolka was smiling.

"That was mean," Renya told her. "We never should have done that."

Homolka seemed to think it was fun. Renya didn't see the humor in it. She took George back to her bedroom, laid him carefully into his cage. Two weeks later, he was dead.

Renya put George in a shoebox, and her father gave the hamster a proper burial in the family's back yard. He said George had probably died of natural causes — hamsters never lived that long anyway. Renya knew otherwise, but didn't tell her dad. George was going to Hamster Heaven, her dad said, where he would get all the food and water he wanted.

Several weeks later, Homolka came up with another idea. She had to do some real persuading before getting Renya to agree. They would have to do it when no one was home, their best chance being on a Saturday, when Renya's parents went shopping and her brother was out with friends.

Renya thought the whole idea a bit ghoulish and let Homolka do the digging. The tiny grave was near the flower-bed.

"I wonder what he will look like," Homolka said over and over as she dug into the soil. "Probably all puffy and bloated," she continued when Renya didn't reply. Finally she reached the top of the tiny casket.

Homolka dropped to her hands and knees, anxiously brushing away the dirt from the top of the shoebox. Renya pressed tight against Homolka's shoulder as her friend lifted the lid from George's cardboard coffin.

"Ugh," Renya said, pulling back in disgust after peering inside the box. "Oh, that's awful."

George's body was flat and stiff, the legs straight out, the black eyeballs looking up at them from the grave. Tiny worms crawled over his body. Renya went to put the lid back, but Homolka stopped her. She stared at the hamster for several more moments.

"You're right," she said at last. "It's awful."

"I never want to do that again," said Renya, tossing dirt back onto the tiny grave.

After supper, when they were alone in Renya's room waiting for Homolka's parents to collect her, Homolka pulled out a pin.

"Give me your hand."

"Why?" Renya asked, somewhat leery.

"You'll see."

Homolka grabbed her friend's thumb, squeezed it, and pricked the end with the pin. Renya yelped, and a speck of red appeared. Homolka did the same to her own thumb. Then she pressed the two thumbs together, mixing the blood.

"We're blood sisters," she said. "We'll have to keep each other's secrets until we die."

2
The Secret of Youth

There were some who called the three-block stretch of
Linwell Road the Avenue of the Churches. There were nine
holy houses on, or near, Linwell. That was just one reason
why St. Catharines was such a good place to live. For its
130,000 residents it offered all the conveniences of a large
urban center, yet there was still that cozy, small-town feel
about it. But when Renya Hill went to Grace Lutheran at the
end of her street, it was not to worship.

What Renya liked most about Grace Lutheran was
the size of its parking lot. It was about as big as a skating rink,
and well back from busy Linwell Road. And, except for
Sundays, it was usually empty. In other words, the church lot
was the ideal site for a pick-up game of road hockey.

On weeknights and holidays, just about any free time
they had, Renya and her friends, mostly boys, gathered at the
Grace Lutheran lot for a game. Road hockey for them was like
a national sport, and for Renya, Grace Lutheran was the
Maple Leaf Gardens of St. Catharines. What more could a
hockey-mad 10-year-old ask for?

Karla Homolka didn't particularly like hockey — or
any other sport, for that matter. In her fantasy world, when
Barbie engaged in a physical activity it was always tennis, so
much nicer a game than the roughhousing of hockey. But her
best friend loved hockey, and so Homolka made concessions.

If Homolka went to watch her friend play at Grace Lutheran, Renya could always be persuaded to do what Homolka wanted to do later. But on this particular Saturday afternoon in the fall of 1980, the bounds of her friendship were really being stretched.

Homolka had been standing watching them play for what seemed like hours. Renya and her pals were having fun, and she was bored. Worse, her friend was showing no signs of getting tired. Renya had brought along a hockey stick for her friend, but Homolka was not the least bit interested in *mixing it up* with the boys in their dumb game.

Renya didn't want to stop playing, but she felt sorry for her friend. She knew what Karla wanted to do — as always, play house with Ken and Barbie. Renya had more fun going to the dentist. But they were buddies, so she dropped out of the game. They were supposed to play at Renya's house that day, and Homolka had been looking forward to it all week. Renya's dad had also just bought an eight-millimeter camera, and Homolka couldn't wait to see herself on home movies.

The two girls were playing dolls in Renya's bedroom when her father came in with the new camera. Homolka bounced to her feet in joy, giggling as she stuck her face in front of the lens. She gave the camera a toothy grin, picked up one of her dolls, and pranced around with it as Renya's dad followed her with the camera. Renya finally joined in, still sulking because her heart was back at Grace Lutheran. Homolka jollied her into smiling, got her to prance around, and then stepped between her and the camera, blocking her out. That was Karla. Always the Princess at center stage.

Later, when they were watching themselves on film, Homolka leaned over to Renya and whispered into her ear, "Someday I'll be famous too."

Renya had been in the news that year, many times, on the front page of the local paper. She had wanted to play ice hockey with a team of boys at the community center but had been turned away because she was a girl. Girls weren't supposed to play contact sports with boys, or so the coaches had told her. Renya's parents had taken the case to the human rights commission. It seemed that everyone in the city was talking about it. And, later that night, when Homolka's mother, Dorothy, arrived to take her daughter home, it was on the evening news.

"Your daughter is so famous," Dorothy said to Renya's father as everyone crowded around the set. "Must be nice to have a celebrity in the family."

"Give me your hand." It was a request, but coming from Homolka, it was more like an order. And then, as an afterthought: "Please?"

Renya hesitated, remembering when Homolka had pricked her finger with the pin a few years earlier. The two friends were spending the weekend at Homolka's house in Merritton, a suburb of St. Catharines to which her family had recently moved. It was another townhouse, only bigger. The area was nicer, there were plenty of parks and, nearby, a cemetery, Victoria Lawn. The two 12-year-olds had remained friends, but they didn't see each other as often, usually just on the weekends, alternating between homes. It was Homolka's turn to play host on that weekend.

"C'mon, don't be silly," Homolka persisted. "I'm not going to hurt you."

They were playing in Homolka's bedroom in the basement, next to the den. She was proud of her bedroom, along with her collection of dolls, her books, and the wooden hope chest that she would fill with household items for when she got married. Homolka had recently developed a new passion — mystery novels. She was an avid reader of the *Hardy Boys* and *Nancy Drew* stories, her nearly complete collection prominently displayed on a shelf along one wall, right up there beside the prized dolls.

That afternoon, Homolka had brought out her Hardy Boys crime-fighting kit. It included a fingerprint set, along with the prints of famous criminals. Homolka wanted to match up Renya's prints with those of gangsters like Al Capone. Renya failed to see the humor.

"How can we play if I can't take your fingerprints?" said Homolka. To show it was safe, Homolka dipped her thumb in the ink pad and rolled it across the blank piece of paper, leaving behind a perfect impression. She held up the paper for her friend.

Resigned, Renya stuck out a hand. What was the point of fighting her? Homolka was only comfortable being the dominant partner in the relationship. It was better just to go along with her, and Renya usually did, even though at times she could be just as forceful and determined as her friend, as with her insistence on playing hockey with the boys.

Homolka dipped the ends of Renya's fingers into the ink pad. First one hand, then the other. Renya couldn't see the point. Only bad people got their fingerprints checked. Besides, she had to scratch an itchy nose, and pretty soon there was ink all over her face.

Homolka laughed at her friend's splotched features and went for a towel. Renya was cleaning herself up when they heard the tinkling of a small bell. Homolka quickly left the room.

The sound was coming from the bedroom of her younger sister, Lori. She was ill with the flu and Karla was looking after her while her parents went shopping. The bell had been Homolka's idea. She told Lori to ring it whenever she needed anything. And that had been often. Homolka never seemed to mind, though. She was enjoying the role of the elder guardian.

Lori really only wanted some company. Homolka sat down on the edge of the bed and put her hand on her little sister's forehead.

"You're so hot, poor baby," she said, and headed for the bathroom. She came back with a damp towel for her sister's forehead. "There, this should help the fever."

Lori smiled weakly as her big sister fussed about her, propping up her pillow, adjusting the bedcovers. Homolka had been looking forward to playing junior detectives with her friend that weekend, but she wasn't about to leave her ailing sister unattended.

Later, after supper, Homolka wanted to go back to the fingerprint game, but on earlier visits Renya had seen the boys playing baseball in the field behind the house, and she had brought her glove along, hoping for a chance to get into a game. Anything was better than Barbie and Ken.

Karla's other passion, playing amateur sleuth and spotting the clues in the Nancy Drew mysteries, wasn't very exciting either. Renya had tried reading one of the books, but her friend kept interrupting, giving away the story, telling her what clue was vital to solving the crime. Karla remembered every single twist in every one of the books, and would remind Renya when she missed one — like a detective in training, that was Karla.

Homolka wanted to stay and play detective, and she made a big performance about doing what Renya wanted to do, but this time Renya won. In the field behind the house, half a dozen teenage boys were playing soft-toss. The outfielder who caught the most flyballs became the next hitter. Renya caught enough flyballs to get a turn at bat.

After taking a few swings, she glanced over at her friend, who was standing off by herself, sulking. Renya had seen that expression before. It was pasted on Karla's face every time she went out to the arena to watch Renya — who had won her human rights case — play hockey. Renya called her over, held out the bat.

"What do I do with *that?*" Homolka said, staring at the piece of wood as if it had just fallen from a passing spaceship.

"Hit with it, of course."

Homolka rolled her eyes but took the bat. Renya showed her how to hold it. She swung at, and missed, the first half dozen pitches. Finally, Homolka connected. The ball dribbled toward the pitcher, who made a great show of fielding the ball, which ran out of steam before it reached him. Homolka dropped the bat from her hands, as if it were on fire.

"It stings," she whined to Renya, staring at her fingers. "I don't want to play this anymore."

Renya took back the bat, and soon the outfielders were busy chasing flyballs again. Homolka just stood there and watched, rubbing her fingers, doing her best to look miserable. Soon her attention shifted to a group of children kicking around a soccer ball. Homolka began staring at one of them, a girl about her age, 12.

It took a few minutes for the girl to realize she was being watched. She turned and smiled, but Homolka didn't acknowledge the gesture. She continued to stare at the girl, whose arms were about half the normal length and ended in hands that flopped against her chest. Despite her handicap, she was having a great time. Her legs were strong. She tried to ignore the stares; being gawked at was nothing new for her. But Homolka persisted. Finally, the girl tried to placate her with yet another smile.

Homolka said something to her. Renya, who had stopped her hitting to watch, thought it sounded like "freak."

The girl went back to her game. But she played for only a few more minutes before abruptly leaving the field. The other children stopped kicking the ball as they watched her go. Homolka went up to one of them, a boy her age.

"Your sister is a freak!" she stated.

"Is not," he replied.

"She's creepy looking."

"Shut up!" the boy yelled back. "Shut-up-shut-up!"

"She's got seal arms," Homolka continued. "Seal arms. Seal arms. Your sister's got seal arms."

"She's better than you," the boy retorted.

"She belongs in a zoo."

That one made him cry, but it spurred on Homolka. She started to slap her palms together and make noises like a seal begging for food. Some of the other children thought that was clever and joined in, imitating Homolka. Renya was one of them. Homolka liked that, and gave her friend a smile.

It took her a few moments, but Renya suddenly felt ashamed and stopped clapping. Karla poking fun at a handicapped girl? And teasing the brother who spoke up for her? This was a side to Karla she hadn't seen. Renya was more mad at herself than anything. Every time she was with Karla, she let herself be manipulated.

The boy ran from the field and down the same path his sister had taken. The other children stopped chanting and eventually went back to their game. Homolka headed for home, Renya dutifully following.

"That wasn't nice," Renya said when they were back in Homolka's bedroom playing Barbie and Ken once more.

"But it's true," Homolka replied. "She is freaky looking."

"I know. But you shouldn't have said it."

"You said it too."

"I know I did. But it was wrong."

"So what if it was?" Homolka gave her friend that little sideways glance as she brushed Barbie's hair. "Who cares?"

Renya was playing road hockey at Grace Lutheran one summer afternoon when a visitor dropped by. Renya hadn't seen Homolka for nearly a year, although they still chatted regularly on the phone. Homolka had discovered the opposite sex, and she already had several boyfriends. As for Renya, hockey remained her only true love. Although they had even less in common than before, Renya was still glad to see Homolka, though somewhat surprised by her appearance.

The Princess had changed over the past year. She wasn't wearing anything frilly. There was no pink dress, no delicate blouse. Black had become her color of choice, from jeans to T-shirt. But what Renya noticed first was the hair. The beautiful blond mane was streaked with other colors, browns and reds. Gone, too, was that mischievous grin. As they walked toward Renya's house, Homolka blamed her bad teeth on the medication she was taking for asthma. It embarrassed her, and she didn't smile that much. One thing remained the same, however. Homolka was still playing with her Barbie and Ken collection.

When Homolka had called earlier, to say she was coming over and wanted to play dolls, Renya had almost told her they were getting too old for that at 14. But Homolka had brought along the toys from her fantasy world, and Renya didn't want to hurt her friend's feelings, so she did her best to fake interest.

But Renya soon grew tired of her charade. She started to talk about hockey, a topic that drew a glazed look from her friend. There was something different about Karla, Renya thought, aside from her hair and the clothes. She didn't seem to be as happy anymore; she was moody, distant. The Karla she knew was always excited about something. Renya asked her if anything was wrong, but Homolka shrugged it off. Then Homolka had an idea.

"We should make a time capsule," she said, "and when we're really old, like forty, we can dig it up and see what we were like as kids."

They would stuff it full of their most treasured mementos. It seemed like more fun to Renya than stupid Barbie and Ken, so she got a jar from the kitchen and looked around her room for something to put inside. A hockey puck didn't fit, and she settled instead on a plastic ring from a cereal box. Part of a program from a hockey game at Maple Leaf Gardens was next, along with a wood chip from her first hockey stick. She glanced over at her friend, and was shocked.

Homolka was doing the unthinkable to one of her precious Barbie dolls — cutting off a lock of hair. Renya recalled a time when she had tried to cut Barbie's hair and Homolka had freaked, ripping the scissors from her hands. No one, not even her closest friend, was allowed to hurt Barbie in any way. Now Homolka carefully wrapped the hair in tissue and put it inside the jar. Then she had another idea, and handed a sheet of paper to Renya.

"We'll each write something," she ordered. "Anything you want. But we won't tell each other what. It will be our secret."

Homolka sat down on the floor in a corner, thought for a moment, then started to scribble. Renya wrote about her coming game against a team from Niagara Falls. They put the letters into the jar and took it out into the garden. Renya dug a hole and buried the jar. Homolka made a treasure map of where it was hidden.

"Someday when we're both famous we'll come back and dig it up," Homolka said, and let out a hearty laugh. Years later Renya would spend a weekend digging up her parents' backyard, but never found the time capsule.

3
Barbie Meets Ken

Although she was one of the most popular girls at her school, Homolka never seemed to be happy. Her friend Donna gathered that part of the problem was with boys. It was a dilemma Donna wished she had. Donna was totally baffled by Homolka's anguish over the opposite sex: the girl had everything going for her.

Homolka was easily one of the prettiest girls at Winston Churchill High School. She had the total package: blond hair, great looks, a knock-out body. Homolka just had to snap her fingers, Donna figured, and all the boys in school would flip over on their backs and wag their paws in the air. She was even brainy, her I.Q. probably one of the highest in the school. She had always been an honors student, but recently her marks had been slipping. Homolka told Donna she was getting bored with school. Boys, it seemed, were her main interest. Along with getting married.

There was no doubt Homolka was erratic. There were days when she never stopped prattling, gushing on about going to university and studying to be a veterinarian. But at other times she barely spoke, except to say that she was sick of high school, couldn't wait to graduate. On that day, following a particularly bad stretch when she had hardly spoken for ages, Homolka brought up her *little problem* while the two of them were alone in their "smoke hole," the special meeting place at Winston Churchill where, sometimes along with three or four others, they chatted about life over a cigarette. They were "The Outsiders," the group of friends who weren't part of any clique.

Homolka butted out her cigarette, rolled up her sleeves, and held out her wrists. There were small scars across each one. "I tried to kill myself," she said. It was more of a pronouncement. There had been other attempts, she admitted, with sleeping pills. "Sometimes I just don't want to live."

When it came to suicide, Donna didn't take a back seat to anyone. She rolled up her own sleeves. She had scars of her own to brag about. Only hers were a lot bigger — red, and inflamed. Homolka's marks of distress were like little scratches made by a kitten.

Homolka was shocked. For the moment, she forgot about her own troubles and revealed a caring side that Donna had never seen before. She should, cautioned Homolka, get help before it was too late.

Homolka was truly concerned, and Donna didn't understand how one minute there was all this talk of death, the next about how precious life was. Donna doubted Homolka was ever serious about killing herself. Her feeble efforts had to be more for attention than anything. Would anyone so worried about how she looked ever want to take her own life? And Homolka could be really vain. She was forever in the washroom, fussing with her hair. She should have been a hairdresser; she was forever changing the color of her flowing locks, tinting them black one day, red the next. As if she was searching for the color of happiness. But the boys weren't interested in her hair, Homolka lamented. "All they want is sex," she said.

Homolka was between boyfriends again, after breaking it off with a senior boy at the school who had been "just perfect" when they met. Maybe that's why she has been so quiet lately, Donna thought. But Homolka often just listened to others. She was like that in school, too, shying away from being the center of attention. The one time she had tried out for the school choir, she had made everyone in the class turn the other way, not stare at her when it was her turn to stand up and sing. If she had a passion at all, it was the one for drawing houses. There were times when she spent all day doodling, sketching her dream homes.

At the smoke hole, when she *did* talk, it was often about the latest horror movie she had seen. She had some favorites. One was *Friday the Thirteenth*. She liked the way the virgins always got the deranged killer, Jason, in the end.

"What kind of sleeping pills did you use?" Donna asked, half-kidding that she might try them herself.

Homolka was alarmed by her friend's question. She begged Donna not to kill herself. After school, Homolka wrote something out, and she read it to Donna the next day, when they were alone at the smoke hole. It was a poem entitled "Suicide."

> Suicide is not an act of selfishness.
> It is only an escape, the only escape I can see.
> People say that if I take my life
> I'm thinking only of myself.
> But it is my life, isn't it?
> Why should I live in pain, just to spare the pain of
> others? What if, after carefully thinking?
> And remembering? And hurting?
> I come up with only one answer. Suicide.
> Then I am considered "selfish."
> What is selfishness anyways?
> Caring about me? Thinking about me?

Wasn't I taught to have pride in myself?
My work? My play? Pride is me thinking of me.
And me caring about me. And me liking me.
I don't like me. I am no longer the person I used to
be. I am different.
Pride is just another word for selfishness.
I have reached the end. I have nobody to turn to.
I am thinking and nothing makes sense.
I end up with one thought. Suicide.
This is the one thought that makes sense.
The only one.
It is hard to take a life, yet so easy.
Life is so fragile, yet so strong.
It all depends on which way you want to go.
I have tried. Unsuccessfully.
I've also tried to get it out of my mind.
I have willed it to leave.
But even when I'm happy, and those times are far
and few, the thought is always there. In the back of
my mind. It will never leave.
I wish I could turn back time.
To the days of my simple, yet happy childhood.
I was so carefree. So happy. I had no problems.
But I must face facts.
I am caught up in this world, a nightmare.
Where hundreds of thousands of teenagers, like me,
kill themselves every day.
Not out of selfishness. Or anger.
But simply, out of pain. Pain.
Such a little, simple word for a big, complicated
emotion. An emotion strong enough to kill.
I can understand. Will I end up a statistic?
Only time will tell.

Some advice to you who have not yet let the thought
pass your mind:
Don't let it — once it's there, it's there for
good.
You can try and try, but it will refuse to leave.

Donna was moved by what Homolka had read. She
swore that she wouldn't try to kill herself.

"Let's make a pact right now," Homolka said, "that
neither of us will talk about suicide again, ever."

The two girls gave each other a hug, promised to
remain friends forever. Then they butted out their cigarettes
and headed off to class.

"Have you ever tried suicide?" Homolka asked.

Renya Hill was stunned by the question. "No. Of
course not." Renya couldn't believe her friend would contemplate something so drastic. The Karla she knew had never
been unhappy: bossy, mischievous, curious about life, always
searching for new experiences, but never depressed. Had
things soured that much for her in the past few years?

Homolka explained that she was upset because her
boyfriend had moved away to Kansas City. She had wanted to
marry him, she said, and she missed him terribly. The other
boys she had dated before him just wanted a cheap feel in the
back seat of a car. But he was special, and she had dreamed
about staying with him for the rest of her life. Earlier that
summer she had gone to Kansas City on her own to visit him.

Renya wanted to know what her parents had thought
about that, and Homolka told her they had refused because
she was only seventeen. But she had secretly saved up the
money for the ticket from her part-time job in a pet store, and
had gone anyway, openly defying her parents. She had called

a limousine and sneaked out of the house with her suitcase, not calling her parents until just before she boarded the plane so they couldn't stop her.

Renya thought that sounded more like the Karla she had known — bent on getting her own way, determined to do what she wanted, no matter what. Though she loved her parents, Homolka said, she wasn't going to let them run her life.

The two friends were waiting in the ticket line outside the movie theater in St. Catharines late that summer, in 1987. Homolka had been full of surprises that day. Most of all, in her appearance: she had gone totally black, in her clothes, her face; there were even black streaks in her hair. The last time they had met there had been hints of change. A bit of black here, more of the old frilly stuff there. But the new version of Karla was nothing like the old model Renya had known for years.

Her hair was teased, sloppily piled up to one side of her head. Renya tried counting the number of colors in it — red, black, green, perhaps orange, something else she couldn't name. Black was the only color anywhere on Karla's body: black tank top, undershirt and bra, torn black leggings, black skirt, black Doc Martens boots. Her lipstick was black. Even her eyeshadow.

Homolka said that she had been squabbling badly with her parents over the trip and over her school marks, which were just average, and the punk-style clothing was her way of rebelling against their authority. She was on the Pill, she boasted, but hadn't told her parents because she knew they wouldn't approve.

Renya had not seen her one-time best friend for almost two years, and it took her a few minutes to get over the shock. She wondered what had happened to the Princess who played with dolls and listened to bubble-gum songs like

"Billy, Don't Be a Hero", a song Karla used to love. It was pure teenybopper music; the words were about two doomed lovers: Billy, the soldier who died a useless death in some unknown war; and his fiancée, left behind to live out a lonely, bitter life. Renya had never been sure whether it was the lyrics or the supposed message in the song that Karla had loved.

However, now all that seemed light-years away. Karla's new favorite group was the Beastie Boys, with their song "You Gotta Fight for Your Right to Party." Homolka said she still wanted to go to university and become a vet, but her marks hadn't been that great. School, she said, was b-o-r-i-n-g.

Homolka loved any kind of horror flick, the scarier and bloodier, the better and she had wanted to see one of the *Friday the Thirteenth* movies, but Renya preferred an adventure film. While they were deciding, Homolka had started talking about witchcraft, demons, and curses. God didn't really exist, she said, but there was a devil, an evil in the world that people worshipped. However, Homolka changed the topic as quickly as she had started it when she noticed that Renya wasn't a believer and was giving her a doubting look.

They settled on a movie that was perhaps midway between their interests. It was called *The Explorers*, a film about two boys who built a spaceship in their back yard. Renya thought it might be too much of a kiddie flick for them, but she went along with her friend's choice. Some things just never changed.

Afterwards, they went out for coffee. They chatted pleasantly, mostly about what they had done years back, like playing Barbie and Ken. Homolka said how much she missed those simple, carefree days. Life was getting too complicated, she said. Soon they ran out of things to talk about: Homolka still wasn't interested in sports and Renya didn't follow punk bands.

Homolka said she was looking forward to a weekend trip to Toronto the following month. She was going with her boss from work and some friends, and they would be staying at a hotel in Scarborough to attend a convention of pet-store owners. But the real reason she was going, Homolka said, was to party.

Scarborough had been in the news that summer, Renya remembered. Several women had been sexually assaulted there while walking home at night, and the police believed at least two of the attacks might have been perpetrated by a man they had dubbed the Scarborough Rapist. A manhunt was under way, but since neither victim had seen his face, the police didn't have much to go on.

It was late October when Homolka rang up Renya to say she had met "the most perfect man in the whole world." He was a bit older — she was 17 and he was 23 — but that wasn't a problem. Besides, she said, she was tired of all the immature boys she had been dating. He was a University of Toronto graduate who came from a solid middle-class family in Scarborough. He was so ambitious, she enthused. He wanted to go into business for himself and hoped to become a millionaire. For the time being he was training to be an accountant with Price Waterhouse. They had been out on several dates and were having a scintillating time of it in bed, she giggled. They had so much in common, she went on. He, too, was looking for a permanent relationship and was tired of dating. In fact, she said, laughing, they even liked the same horror movie, *Friday the Thirteenth*. "He's just gorgeous looking. I think I'm in love with him. He's so different from those jerks I've gone out with. I can't wait for you to meet him."

Homolka's voice was animated, just like the Karla that Renya used to know. She was so happy for her friend, glad that she seemed to have finally found that perfect man to help her build that perfect life, the fantasy life of the world of her dolls.

"This Prince Charming," Renya interrupted, "what's his name?"

"Paul Bernardo."

"You know what it sounds like to me?" said Renya. "I think Barbie just met Ken."

4
Audience of One

Mr. B. was smiling, his eyes glistening with pride. He had a cooing new baby in his arms, a boy barely a year old, and he was just about the happiest man around that day as he sat by the backyard pool in the enclave of middle-class homes in the east end of Kitchener-Waterloo. Mr. B., that's what everybody in the neighborhood called him — Mr. B., Frank Bernardo, the Tile Man. The immigrant laborer who had come to Canada in the 1920s from his native Portugal and had made his mark in the new country laying terrazzo and marble in rich people's homes in Kitchener-Waterloo, the twin Ontario cities renowned for their annual beerfest.

On that warm summer day in 1965, Mr. B. couldn't help being just a wee bit melancholy. Recently retired, he and his wife, Mary, lived quietly, talking to neighbors, socializing at the nearby Roman Catholic church, tending the garden at their modest split-level home. They had once lived in a far bigger house, in the ritzy part of town, but he was more comfortable in these new surroundings. Mr. B. looked back on his years in the tile business with a feeling of pride and accomplishment. For more than three decades he had worked hard to build up the tile company that bore the family name, and the Bernardo name had become synonymous with quality craftsmanship. The marble compass he had built into the basement floor of one of his homes was perhaps meant to symbolize that none of his kin were going to lose their way in the world.

And right now, as he sat by the pool of his neighbor's house, what he was most proud of was his family, particularly his brand-new grandson.

The boy had been christened Paul Kenneth Bernardo, the third child of Mr. B.'s son Kenneth and his wife, Marilyn. Kenneth and Marilyn's two other children, David and Debbie, were frolicking in the shallow end of the pool, while their parents and grandfather looked on. Mr. B. and Mary treasured these weekend visits from Kenneth and Marilyn and the kids. They had just moved from Kitchener-Waterloo to Scarborough — only a two-hour drive away, but just far enough that their visits now had to be on the weekends.

Mr. B. cradled the baby close to his chest, gently rocking the boy to sleep, thrilled there was yet another grandson to carry on the Bernardo name. True, there had been some disappointment when his sons, Kenneth and Raymond, hadn't followed him into the family trade; after nearly four decades, there was no longer a tile company in the city bearing the Bernardo name. He understood, though, that his sons had their own lives to lead. Kenneth had chosen accounting. He had done well and had a devoted wife and three lovely children. That afternoon, Mr. B. told his neighbor, with a tiny, uncharacteristic hint of boasting, that he foresaw only the best for the coming generations of Bernardos, and especially Baby Paul.

After all, the child had been born of hard-working immigrants on one side; on the other, the Canadian establishment, Marilyn's family being part of the city's upper crust. She was an Eastman, and the Eastmans had a long tradition in Kitchener-Waterloo, and in Canada. They were descendants of the United Empire Loyalists, a family of British stock whose roots in Canada dated back to the birth of the nation. Marilyn's father, Lieutenant-Colonel Gerald Eastman, had been a hero of the Second World War, a major who had distinguished himself in the Italian campaign. After the war he resumed his law career at one of the city's most prestigious firms. He was active in the community, holding posts on the board of education and the Chamber of Commerce and being a founding member and director of the city's art gallery and a past president of the local bar association. Every year he had twenty-six lines in *Who's Who in Canada*.

Kenneth and Marilyn had met when their families were neighbors for a brief time. They fell in love in 1957, a year when the Russians and the Americans were threatening each other with nuclear oblivion, and the year in which Kenneth and Marilyn mourned, like so many other movie fans, the death of Humphrey Bogart. Three years later they wed; the society pages of the local newspaper had a big story on their marriage at St. John's Anglican Church.

Shortly afterwards, the first of their three children was born. Meeting the bills was difficult at the start for the newlyweds. Kenneth was just beginning his career as an accountant, and Marilyn stayed at home with the babies. But it would be nearly a decade before Kenneth ran into his "emotional difficulties."

On that afternoon by the pool, with a new baby in the family, there was only joy in the Bernardo clan.

"He's such a beautiful child," Mr. B. boasted to his neighbor. "I just hope I live long enough to see him grow up and marry."

Kenneth Bernardo knew it was wrong. What he was doing, it was against the laws of man and God. But he just couldn't stop himself.

And for him, of all people, to be committing such an immoral act. He was, after all, a respected member of his community: a regular churchgoer, a family man, nine years married, with a good wife and three lovely children, a professional with a good career. And now he was risking everything. He could end up in jail, destroying himself and his family, bringing embarrassment and shame to the Bernardo name. And what of his father? His dad would be mortified. He would think his son abhorrent and disown him.

Yet despite all of that, he was not deterred. It was just something inside him, some despicable sickness he didn't understand. It had started in 1969, on the first day of the new year. There had been so many changes in Kenneth's life over the past decade: a move to the big city, the pressures of his career, the financial demands of his family. And then there was the trouble with his youngest, Paul. The boy was nearly five and he had barely spoken a word, he was still pointing and grunting. The doctors said Paul was suffering from a form of aphasia. There had been a lack of oxygen to the brain during his birth, but the boy would talk in time. The doctors were confident there was no permanent brain dysfunction. It was upsetting, though, when your youngster couldn't speak.

But it was this other trouble that caused a rift with Marilyn. As the decade came to a close, women were making headlines around the world through their attacks on traditional beliefs about roles in the family, especially the prevailing attitude that a woman's place was in the kitchen. Marilyn Bernardo was not one of those rebellious females. She felt that her place in life was to be at home for her children, to have freshly baked cookies ready for them when they returned from school, and to look after her husband.

Recently, she had put on some weight, sure, understandable after three children and being a full-time housewife. But it wasn't right that he told her in front of the children how heavy she looked, even made jokes about it. She had tried to make their family life as pleasant as possible, but it was difficult because of that business with her husband. It was too unpleasant to talk about, even think about. Perhaps, in time, it might go away.

The girl had been barely nine. She was a trusting child — vulnerable, especially with an adult. It began with just a single touch in the girl's forbidden zone, and after that, it became easier for him.

Those first few times the child seemed to welcome his touches. Girls of eight or nine were more aware of their bodies than boys, more willing to experiment, he wanted to believe. There was never any violence or struggling. It was all done with gentleness. It had been a pleasurable experience for both parties, he believed. As if that somehow justified his actions. But he had no control over himself. He had urges, needs, that had to be satisfied.

The boy, just nine, was off by himself in the crowded school-yard when the group of children his age surrounded him. He looked up, saw what he thought were happy, familiar faces in the circle, and returned their smiles.

The ring of children tightened around the boy. But their smiles weren't for him. And they weren't smiling: it was more like sneering — nasty little expressions of derision on every one of their faces.

"Barnyard. Barnyard," they chanted in unison. "Look at the dirty barnyard. Barnyard. Barnyard. What a smelly barn-yard."

The smile on the boy's face vanished. He dropped his head, and tears started to roll down his cheeks. His distress didn't faze the other children in the least. They were having too much fun. The target of their disdain pushed at one or two of them. They just pushed back and carried on with the chant-ing, the tempo quickening.

"Barnyard-Barnyard-look-at-the-dirty-barnyard.
Barnyard-Barnyard-what-a-smelly-barnyard." Over and over.
Louder and louder. Those words he just loathed.

Finally, one of the teachers waded in, shooed the
children away. The young boy was sobbing as he watched
them retreat to a safe distance, where they kept up the chant.

"Why do they always have to tease me?" Paul
Bernardo asked the grownup. The adult had no answer to give
him. "Why is everybody so mean to me? I hate my name. I
just hate it!"

The two pre-teen boys were having fun that summer afternoon. Paul and his good friend Kenny were doing something
they weren't supposed to be doing in the pool, and that's why
it was all the more exciting.

The Bernardos had a swimming pool behind their
home on Sir Raymond Drive in Scarborough. And that made
them, at least with many of the children in the neighborhood,
and especially on these muggy summer days, one of the most
popular families around. The youngest Bernardo, at the age of
10, had many friends on his street, and they often went over
to his house for a swim. Of the three Bernardo children, Paul
was seen by neighbors as being the friendliest. He had two
older siblings, David and Debbie.

He was always happy. A young boy who smiled a lot.
And he was so cute, with his dimpled good looks and sweet
smile, that many of the mothers just wanted to pinch him on
the cheek whenever they saw him. He was the perfect child
they all wanted: polite, well mannered, doing well in school,
so sweet in his Boy Scout uniform. His speech impediment
had gone, and now he spoke well, save for a slight stutter.
There had been, however, that one unfortunate little incident.

One of the women on the street had caught him at it. He had been skulking in some bushes near the back of her house, not far from the bedroom window of a neighbor's house. The young girl getting ready for bed that evening didn't know that she was taking off her clothes for an appreciative audience of one. A very young, and very aroused, little boy had his hands over his crotch as he stared up at the window. Paul Bernardo, the Little Angel of Sir Raymond Drive, a Peeping Tom.

The woman had surprised him, scared the daylights out of him, and chased him quickly away. He had seemed embarrassed and later she had just put it down to normal childhood curiosity, harmless really. The woman never mentioned the incident to Marilyn Bernardo. Why bother her with this little prepubescent indiscretion? There seemed to be tension enough in the Bernardo household. Some of the neighbors felt Kenneth was perhaps harsher than he should have been with his children. He never struck them, but he was often heard yelling at them.

The youngest of the Bernardos climbed up onto the roof of the shed near the pool that warm summer day. He waved his friend Kenny up, daring him to follow. Paul had been warned by his parents about the danger of what he had in mind. But he loved the excitement of doing something forbidden, perhaps even slightly dangerous, in defiance of his parents.

He clasped his hands over his head, looked down at the pool, then dove. It was a clean dive, but he just missed the side by inches. Eventually he talked his friend into trying it and they spent the afternoon plunging from the roof.

Then around suppertime they had to leave: Paul's father would be home soon to take his swim, and Kenneth Bernardo didn't want anybody else in the pool when he went for his dip — especially not a bunch of neighborhood kids. Before Kenny went home, Paul asked his mother if he could stay over for supper.

No, he was told, not this time. Perhaps another day. But Paul knew that would never happen. None of his friends were ever allowed over for supper. They weren't even welcomed in his house, though he regularly went over to their homes. Other close friends were Van Smirnis and his brother Steve. As he was growing up, Bernardo spent more time at their house than his own, often telling his friends how much he envied them their home life. It wasn't like that at his house, he lamented. It seemed like his parents were always arguing.

Later it would come out in court that his father had been assaulting a young female, who cannot be identified under a court order. When Paul was about 10, he realized what was happening. The effect was devastating.

5

The Night Crawler

It was a tradition at Wabacon, a favorite outing for the children at the summer day camp just outside Kitchener-Waterloo. Daily they broke into groups of a dozen or so, then headed across a farmer's field to the town of Heidelberg, about a mile away, for ice-cream cones.

Each group was led by one of the teenage counselors who lived in the camp bunkhouse. Working at Wabacon was a much-coveted summer job, and the camp sought out responsible teenagers who liked working with children. And that particular summer one of the most popular counselors was a 16-year-old from Toronto with long sandy brown hair and a winning smile.

Everyone wanted to be in Paul Bernardo's group for the daily excursion. The children adored him. He never scolded any of them when they misbehaved. He would stop to let them climb trees, look at birds, explore animal tracks. He was so patient. People who worked at the camp said that some day he would make an excellent parent, he was so good with the kids.

That afternoon one of the children in his group, an eight-year-old girl, got tuckered out midway through the trek. Crying, she went to the head of the line and tugged at the sleeve of the counselor. He smiled at her, then knelt down and tenderly wiped away her tears.

"I'm tired," she said. "I can't walk anymore."

"That's okay," Bernardo replied as he gently scooped up the girl in his arms. He then carried her the rest of the way into town.

That evening Bernardo led everyone in a sing-along at the campfire. The daily ritual was a favorite with both the children and the counselors. Sometimes, while everyone else gathered around the pile of burning logs, several of the counselors would sneak off into the woods and have a cigarette at the nearby lookout point. Smoking, of course, wasn't permitted at the camp, especially not by the teen leaders, but that lent excitement to skulking off for a clandestine puff. The lookout was also a secluded place where the teen counselors sometimes went to neck. Make-Out Hill they called it.

Bernardo didn't smoke. He thought it a disgusting habit and wasn't shy about preaching to others about the dangers of tobacco. He had a good physique, long and lean; he was healthy, and he wanted to stay that way. There were times at the camp when he had trouble tearing himself away from the mirror, seeming so enthralled that he just couldn't get enough.

He stood up and began with "Home on the Range." He had a high, almost childlike, voice and, although his rendition of the cowboy tune was a bit off-key, he received a good round of applause when he finished. Indeed, that summer Bernardo was adored by everyone at the camp. When the people who ran the operation talked about what qualities made for a model leader, they always used Bernardo as their benchmark, the standard everyone else was measured against.

His soft, almost angelic face, accentuated by a total absence of facial hair — due to a genetic trait — gave him the aura of someone who was special, even destined. His manner was quiet, almost shy, his laugh infectious. Even his vanity could be charming. He blushed when teased about it. Most of the girls in the camp fell in love with him, so captivated were they by his high cheekbones, delicate lips, and dimpled smile, and his easy, laid-back personality. One of the other teens nicknamed him the King of First Impressions. He was fun to be with, and always so cheerful. But despite all this, there was something about him that seemed a little off, even slightly disturbing.

It seemed to some that there wasn't much else to him, nothing of substance behind the pretty face. He was intelligent enough, but there was almost a coldness to his eyes. Everyone at the camp was friends with him, but no one was truly his friend. It was as if he wouldn't let anyone get close to him.

He never talked much about himself, or his family. Except to brag. He had been a top Boy Scout. He was always the smartest one in his class. None of his friends would be going to university because they weren't as bright as he was. The haughty attitude seemed an incongruous trait. But at the summer camp that year, no one really cared much: they just wanted to have a good time and, at the end of the day, go to Make-Out Hill. But not Bernardo.

He had a girlfriend in Toronto, a brunette called Nadine, and he stayed faithful to her. When he was with Nadine, who was his first love, he was happy, and that was more than he could say about his life at home. There his parents were always quarreling. They had separate bedrooms. His dad yelled too much. His mother was depressed, and it had to be over his father's secret problem, which nobody in the family dared talk about.

The couple on Make-Out Hill had just finished their cigarettes and were starting to neck when they heard a noise from the bushes. It wasn't unusual for local residents to cut through the camp; several footpaths led from the nearby road to

some of the surrounding farms. But this noise was from someone hiding in the bushes, not a passerby. The boy jumped up.

"Who's out there?"

The couple saw a dark shape, someone running. It
looked like a teenager, about their age, with long hair to the
shoulders. The boy gave chase, but the bushes were dense,
and in the darkness he lost him without getting a good look.

"It's funny," the boy said when he returned, "but I
could have sworn it was Bernardo who was spying on us."

Bernardo was tucked in behind the bush that evening, waiting
for the late show. He had his usual front-row seat, just beneath
the bedroom window. The trademark bright smile was pasted
on his lips, and his hands were positioned near his crotch. He
didn't have to wait long. The brunette in her early twenties
walked into the bedroom and flicked on the lights. She
glanced out the window at her back yard, then started to undo
her blouse. Bernardo leaned forward, his breath quickening as
she took off the blouse and reached behind her for the clasp
on her brassiere. His hand moved for the stiffness in his pants.
The woman was naked from the waist up when Bernardo got
the angry tap on the shoulder.

Startled, he jumped to his feet, looking around for an
escape. The man who had grabbed his shoulder was a neighbor.

"Goddamn pervert! What the hell are you doing, you
sicko!" he railed as the teenager cowered. The neighbor
glanced over at the bedroom window, where the brunette had
discreetly covered her chest as she pressed close to the glass
for a better look at the disturbance outside. "Get out of here!"

Bernardo was already heading toward the street. But
the neighbor, one of the few not enthralled by Bernardo's
good looks and easy charm, was right behind him, shaking a
fist, cursing. He plain didn't like this kid. He was annoyed by

the way Bernardo and his friend Kenny took their girlfriends to the trailer in the back of Kenny's yard He had heard that Bernardo might be a Peeping Tom, but he had never believed it until now. "You're sick," he told Bernardo. "You should get help."

Out in the safety of the street, Bernardo's demeanor changed. He gave the neighbor a smirk, as if he had done nothing wrong. It was too much for the neighbor, who rushed at Bernardo and grabbed him by the head. Someone called the police.

Const. Eddie Grogan was on the "snooze and cruise" detail that evening, patrolling in his scout car around the middle-class homes in the southeast end of Scarborough known as Guildwood. Not much ever happened here. Drugs, muggings, murder rarely disturbed the serenity of the citizens of Guildwood, with its half-million-dollar homes overlooking Lake Ontario. Here, women weren't afraid to go out alone at night. Dogs that used the area's forty parks as their own private toilets were a bigger problem than house burglaries.

And that's why Eddie Grogan had transferred to a division here. He had grown weary of battling criminals in the downtown Toronto housing projects. Shaking down doorknobs, that was his new job these days, checking for insecure premises, doors left open by shop owners at the end of the business day. Life was slow for Grogan, and that's the way he wanted it.

When he got the call for the disturbance on Sir Raymond Drive, Grogan had to check the map for directions. He couldn't recall ever going to a trouble call on Sir Raymond. By the time he pulled up in his cruiser, a crowd had gathered. There appeared to be two combatants. On one side of the gathering, a middle-aged man with tousled hair and a wild look in his eyes. On the other, a frightened teenager shielded by an older woman, likely his mother. But there were no bloody noses or black eyes. And no one appeared to be drunk. In the old days, in the downtown core, Grogan would have been ready with his gun, looking for a flying beer bottle or a knife. But this was one of the prettiest streets in Scarborough. Sensible people lived here, good, law-abiding citizens who handled their problems responsibly. It looked like the dispute had already been sorted out.

Grogan asked questions, but no one seemed anxious to press for any police involvement. It had just been a misunderstanding, he was told. The boy may have been looking in the window, but the middle-aged man couldn't be sure anymore. Perhaps he had overreacted. In any case, he didn't want to pursue it. He just wanted to forget the whole thing.

The boy seemed frightened out of his wits. He probably had been peeking in the window, but the embarrassment of being caught in the act was probably punishment enough. Now everyone in the street knew that the kid was a Peeping Tom.

Grogan got back into his cruiser and jotted down the time of the disturbance in his notebook. Then he called his dispatcher and said he was clearing the scene. Grogan liked Scarborough. Problems had never been settled so easily in his former haunts. He missed the overtime, but he liked getting home to his wife on time. It would only be years later, and in the context of one of the biggest criminal cases in Canadian history, that Grogan would recall the incident on Sir Raymond Drive.

6
Bloodlines

He was in his bedroom when his mother burst in. She looked angry, confused, distressed; she had just been arguing loudly with his father. In his mother's hand was a photograph. Bernardo sat up as his mother came toward him, holding the picture out for him to see. He was just 16 at the time, still in high school and planning for university. On the outside he seemed like a pleasant enough teenager who did well in school and had plenty of friends. But there were demons rattling around inside his head, filling his mind with all sorts of ideas about the sexual urges he was feeling. He didn't need the added confusion his mother was about to bring into his life.

Van Smirnis was watching television when his friend came running over, barely stopping to knock at the door. Bernardo was crying. More than likely something again with his family, Smirnis figured. His buddy was always saying how he wished his family was like others, like the Smirnis family. Smirnis felt sorry for him.

"What's wrong?" he asked.

Bernardo blurted out: "My father isn't my real father!"

"What?"

Bernardo said his mother had just told him his real father was another man.

Smirnis didn't know what to say. What *could* he say?
Was it even true? Paul was still close to his dad; he planned to
be an accountant just like him. That was the Bernardo household, though — nothing but turmoil.

After that incident with the picture, when Bernardo's
mother got mad at her son, she would often yell at him that he
was the "bastard child from Hell." It's impossible to tell how
greatly this affected the young Bernardo, but it is safe to say
he became utterly confused about his bloodlines. He grew to
hate his mother, even more than his father, with whom he was
already upset because of the senior Bernardo's prolonged sexual abuse of the young woman.

What was developing, psychiatrists later speculated,
was the beginning of Bernardo's hatred toward society, and
his anger toward his mother and women in general. That rage
would later come out in some of his writings — documents
released later at his trial — that he wanted to turn into rap
songs. One verse went:

Gettin' even, gettin' back at society
for what it owes you,
Gettin' back at people who crossed you,
Only those who truly dare.

Another said:

You want to battle us, you get beat down
The establishment is saying to the people
You want to battle us, you get beat down
By the beat-down law

Bernardo had been in several fights at high school
with other guys who thought he looked "too pretty." So he had

had to learn how to fight; and along with the fisticuffs came a taste for violence. He took courses in self-defense, and began to lift weights, and along with the new physique came a more self-assured young man. He still smiled a lot, but he was ready to fight at any time. He became proud of the way his appearance fooled people: the sweetness on the outside masking the anger on the inside. Later this self-definition became his theme. He called it "Deadly Innocence" and described it in his crude rap music:

> You think I'm innocent?
> But behind this I'm packing a lot of deadliness
> So come at me, come at me
> I got a fucking nice face
> I look like a pretty boy
> Why don't you come at me, man?
> Take your best shot
> See what happens to you, pal
> You're outta here, man
> You come at me with your beer belly
> And you think you're really tough
> I come back, looking like I'm 13 years old
> I'll kick your ass
> I'll kill your parents
> Then I'll shoot your girlfriend
> And fuck your wife
> That's me, Deadly Innocence.

Psychiatrists have theorized that his growing hostility, and a variety of emerging aberrant sexual cravings, later combined into an explosive mixture that led to kidnapping, rape, and murder. By his mid-teens, one of Bernardo's sexual tastes was already quite pronounced — his voyeurism. But his desires soon expanded beyond the Peeping Tom stage, although he would continue hiding in bushes watching bedroom windows right up to his arrest. In his later teenage years, his sexual fantasies became more violent, and featured him dominating women.

Pornography fueled those lusts. It started from the seemingly innocent saving of the brassiere ads from the Eaton's and Simpson's catalogues. Over time he accumulated a huge collection of glossy pictures of women in their underwear, a fetish he kept secret, hiding the pictures in his bedroom, taking them out and masturbating into his pillow whenever he felt the urge. If the pictures he saved were an indication, Bernardo found underwear ads featuring prepubescent girls, as young as 10, just as stimulating as pictures of adult women. But, eventually, still pictures weren't enough to satisfy his sexual desires, which were beginning to dominate his thoughts, almost controlling his life. It was as if the switch to his libido was jammed in the "on" position.

From catalogue ads he moved on to X-rated videos, especially ones in which women were being raped, tapes that could be bought or rented in stores in downtown Toronto. In time he began to see women not as people but as sexual objects for the gratification of men. Bondage movies titillated him the most. It was the master/slave relationship he found appealing, and the suffering — though simulated — of the female victims.

Bernardo's sexual interests were not limited to sadism or voyeurism, though. Psychiatrists would later note that he was a veritable catalogue of kinkiness. His other perverted desires included coprophilia, arousal while watching someone defecate, and urophilia, excitement from watching someone urinate.

The pornographic videos that he bought were fine for a while. But soon he grew bored watching simulated sex performed by actors. He was 19, just entering a Bachelor of Arts program at the University of Toronto's Scarborough campus, focusing on commerce, when he met Lucy, a woman whose real name and identity can't be revealed under a court order. He had broken up with Nadine. He wanted a woman with whom to explore kinky sex, and that wasn't Nadine. But Lucy was different. He saw in her the chance to explore the outer reaches of his sexual imagination. She was just 16, still in high school when they met, a virgin and sexually naive. She was also a young woman of marginal intelligence. Since Lucy knew little about sex, she assumed the rough way he treated her was normal. Bernardo let her think that way for the three years they were together. Their dates were usually just trips in his Capri to deserted parking lots behind factories.

The sex between them started off with vaginal intercourse, but gradually Bernardo wanted mostly fellatio, followed by anal intercourse. After a time, he wanted to tie Lucy up. Then he began calling her names while they had sex. Just before she ended the relationship, Bernardo was particularly rough during one of their trips behind a factory. Years later she recalled the incident to the police. He had been annoyed that night because she had told him she didn't feel like having sex. He drove to the factory anyway, parked in the shadows, and killed the engine.

"Get in the back seat, bitch!" he demanded.

She took off her jeans and underwear as always. She had seen the wine bottle on the floor but had no idea it was going to be a sex prop. He climbed into the backseat, picked up the wine bottle, and handed it to her.

"Stick it up your cunt."

At first she refused, but he was insistent. She put it in slowly, and he grew impatient.

"Deeper!" he demanded.

It aroused him, and he took his pants off, rubbing his erection. "Get on your knees," he ordered her. As she did so, he grabbed her arms and held them behind her back, tying the wrists together with twine.

"Paul, don't," she protested. "That hurts."

But he wasn't listening. All she heard was his excited breathing as he shoved her head to the floor.

"Arch your back!" he yelled at her, recalling a line he had heard in one of the porn films he had rented. "Get your ass in the air."

Although she loved him, or thought at the time she did, she was terrified of him that night. Gone was the sweet smile and delicate voice. He was cold and demanding as he penetrated her anally. And the worst was yet to come.

He had another piece of twine and he grabbed her long, brown hair, trying to shove it out of the way as he placed the twine around her neck. "Fucking hair is in the fucking way," he complained. When he got the cord around her neck, he drew it tight. He eased up on the twine only when she started gagging. She remembered her extreme discomfort, and the pain of the anal rape.

"Stop, please," she begged him, and began to cry. "No, you're hurting me."

"I'm the king," he said. It was another line from one of his rented videos. "And you're the servant girl. You deserve to get fucked up the ass.

"You're the servant girl," he repeated, and when she didn't reply: "Aren't you!"

"Yes."

Helpless and vulnerable, she hoped it would soon be over. She had never consented to being so roughly handled by him. But she was still flattered that someone so handsome was paying so much attention to her. He was her first boyfriend, and she was anxious to please him, afraid he might lose interest and move on to someone prettier. She enjoyed the way her schoolfriends fawned over him whenever he came to pick her up after classes. She knew they were jealous, and she enjoyed that. And he wasn't mean with her the rest of the time, only when they were having sex.

"I'm the best, aren't I?" he asked.

"Yes," she said, her face pressed against the floor, "you are."

She knew he was close to climaxing when he dropped the cord and started pulling on her hair.

"You were really great tonight," he told her, climbing off. "I can't believe how good you were."

Her cheeks were streaked with tears, but he either never noticed or never cared as they got into the front seat. He started the car and flicked on the radio, as if nothing had happened. "I'll take you home," he said pleasantly.

That was all he ever wanted to do with her, have sex behind a factory and then take her home. Infatuated as she was, she was beginning to think something was wrong with their relationship. But she never told anybody. That night, though, she didn't stop crying as he drove home. Eventually he got annoyed.

"Will you shut up," he demanded. "Stop fucking crying."

She brushed away the tears and took out a mirror. There was a red mark on her neck from the twine.

"You look terrible," he told her. "Can you fix your makeup or something? You parents see you like that and they'll wonder what happened."

Lucy didn't want her parents to find out they were having sex. But she also knew that her father, who was a policeman, would be doubly furious with Bernardo if he ever found out what had just happened. So she kept her little secret, hoping that the sweet person she remembered would return. But Bernardo was even rougher the next time, and she eventually broke off their relationship. It would be years before she had the courage to tell anyone what he had done.

7

Deadly Innocence

Bernardo liked what he saw in the mirror. He spent a lot of time in his bedroom looking at himself, flexing his muscles, admiring his physique, getting lost in his fabulous baby blues. His reflection always set off another vanity trip. Every mirror led to a personal orgy of indulgence, a regular ritual of self-worship. He was always fussing with his naturally sandy hair and had taken to tinting it blond. Someone had called him a California beach boy once, and it was an image he wanted to develop.

Nobody made fun of Paul Kenneth Bernardo any more, or dared ridicule his surname. He still hated his name, and he vowed that one day he would change it. He had thought of dropping the "o" to make it sound less ethnic. He wanted it more Anglo and hip, not the handle of some immigrant just off the plane. Of course, at 6' 1" and a solid 180 pounds, no one would be so stupid as to mess with him. He was a specimen of a man, a superior organism, he liked to say. Not someone who hung his head in shame at the jibes of lesser mortals.

The pudginess of his teenage years was gone. He had bulked up his frame through weightlifting and had taken martial-arts training. It gave him such a lift, knowing that he could quickly incapacitate an opponent. A sudden karate chop to the face, for instance, was effective; so was a choke hold, immobilizing the enemy into submission. Anybody dumb enough to mess with him could expect the appropriate punishment, a mouthful of knuckles for their error in judgment. But no one taunted him anymore.

That summer of 1987 Bernardo was in his last year of university. Some days he took time out from his studies to glance around his bedroom. Over the years he had decorated it the way he liked. The poster of a Caribbean beach dominated one wall, that of a red Porsche another, the two giant posters representing his definition of success: wealth and pleasure. On a third wall were sayings that guided his life, each adage neatly printed out in rows on white bristol boards. Most were borrowed from movies and songs, or were the utterances of famous people. Many centered on making money and succeeding in life.

"Poverty is self-imposed," said one. "Time is money," and "Money never sleeps." Others: "There are winners, and there are whiners." "You'll never make the grade by playing it safe." "The game is won in the final quarter." "Poverty sucks." "Think big. Be big." "Self-denial leads to self-mastery." "I don't meet the competition — I crush it!" "The facts don't count when you have a dream."

Some of the sayings were more personal and telling: "My private life is strictly taboo," read one. "Don't tread on me" was another, followed by "No more Mr. Nice Guy." "I regret I only have one life to give for my country." "Give me liberty, or give me death." "Walk softly, and carry a big stick." And one line was from the movie *Angel Heart*: "A bad ass makes a woman's heart beat faster."

He did see himself as a bad ass. He said so in his writings, which he saved in his secret Blue Book. One day he planned to set his creed to music and put out a rap album. He already had his title: *Deadly Innocence*. He liked to think of himself as a dangerous man, and was proud that nobody knew it, not even his best friends. He was the Rebel Hype. The definition was in his Blue Book: "A rebel is a person who resists authority, who opposes the lawful government by force of arms." And for hype: "International excess verging on deception."

He even had his own logo: a broken religious cross, with two handguns crossing each other over it. Below, the words "Deadly Innocence." And above, the words "Young Hype." Psychiatrists would later say the words offered a fascinating peek into his mind. In his Blue Book, Bernardo described how rap music had influenced his life. "A large percentage of the records sold over the last few years have been to white, middle-class kids and college students such as myself . . . You cannot help but be affected by them. They become part of your life.

"What I rap about is what I know. Being competitive, love, parties, picking up girls. But I also talk about issues that I've faced through my life, such as relationships, breakup, stealing, vandalism and death. I mean, I don't profess to have all the answers. I just tell it like I see it. I rap about what I know."

And it was his plan, he wrote, to market those thoughts one day in the form of his rap record. He got the idea for the title after describing how someone supposedly tried to push him around in a bar and take away his girlfriend, only he pushed back harder. He wrote:

"The jealous chump don't like that because he's all alone so he wants to be the tough guy. You know it's the only way he can show his machoism. So if he steps on me cause I look non-threatenin', it's his biggest mistake. It's a case of misjudging or underestimating. It's a case of Deadly Innocence."

His writing would prove prophetic. Over the coming years many people would misjudge Bernardo in similar fashion. Crown prosecutor Greg Barnett would eventually state in pre-trial arguments that Bernardo "started to develop this theme of Deadly Innocence as a teenager . . . He gives the impression of being a pretty boy, but underneath he's full of violence . . . willing to kill. It's the projection of the image of deception." Ironically, some of the people who would badly misjudge Bernardo would be usually cynical police officers, their suspicions sidetracked by his soft looks and polite manner. Others would be women fatally drawn to his soft smile and deadly charm, not realizing until it was too late how dangerous he was.

Given that a raft of psychiatrists would later analyze Bernardo's writings as a way to understand his inner thoughts, it is possible that Bernardo himself may have done the same, perhaps in a bid to understand himself. That might explain one passage from his Blue Book:

> Life has played me out
> Taken its toll and laid me out
> Makes me want to scream and shout
> What it's really all about
> Look at what's become of me
> I seemed to have lost reality
> Endless search for possibilities
> Why was I so hard to please?

If his writings were a view into his soul, then it's possible Bernardo may not have liked what he saw. He defined himself as the "solo creep," barely able to keep his anger in check. But he also wanted to explore that facet of his personality. That could explain why one of his favorite expressions was from the German philosopher Friedrich Nietzsche, who wrote, "Whoever fights monsters should see to it that in the process he does not become a monster. And when you look long into the abyss, the abyss looks back at you."

By 1987 Bernardo knew what he liked and was ready to take it, even if it was against the law. Perhaps he realized that he couldn't stop himself, and so the best way to avoid prosecution when the authorities came looking for him was to be ready with his practiced smile.

He had done things to Lucy that should have got him in trouble, but he was confident it was his charm that had stopped her from complaining to the police, even after they had split up. Psychiatrists later said that Bernardo was "fully in touch with reality," well aware that what he did to women like Lucy was "legally and morally wrong." He simply did it for his own sexual gratification.

"She pissed me off," Bernardo said one time to his friend Van Smirnis, after describing one assault on Lucy. "And I had to rape the bitch."

Bernardo's writings in the Blue Book perhaps reflected his state of mind at the time, and perhaps what he was planning. But no one ever read his book until after his arrest, when it was analyzed by psychiatrists and prosecutors. "Deep in the Jungle" might have predicted his behavior. Like many of his other verses, it was borrowed but revised to fit his feelings.

> I am going deep, deep, deep into the jungle.
> deep in the jungle, a burning desire
> Lost in the crowd, but my heart is on fire
> Stalk like a wolf, and you are my prey.
> I'll be on you before the break of day
> I am going deeper and deeper into your jungle.

Prosecutor Greg Barnett later said that the lines revealed Bernardo as a man who stalked women and wrote about it. But Bernardo may have anticipated such scrutiny. All his writings, he seems to suggest in another piece from his Blue Book, are musings that mean nothing.

Fooled by innocence
This is not a confession
It's just an artistic vein
So you have no case
And I'm laughing in your face.

There had been a time when he wanted to be with only one woman, but that was long ago. He now enjoyed the adulation he received from the many women who found him attractive. They loved his face and his skin was smooth as a baby's cheeks. As he said in the Blue Book, he had a "fresh and funky style, that drives the girlies wild." While he believed that women should be monogamous, he didn't think such a restriction applied to men like him.

People who knew Bernardo dated the dramatic change in his personality to the incident with his mother. Gone was the shy, smiling kid who used to deliver the paper and play road hockey. Smiles and bashfulness were now just an act to get the women.

Bernardo's vanity went with some pretty weird ideas.

"There's something in my brain that keeps telling me how good I am" was a favorite line of his.

"We are all organisms, and some organisms are better than others" was another.

Bernardo believed he was a special person with special needs. Everyone else was just an inferior organism that would be run over while clogging up the slow lane of life. Friends like Van Smirnis suspected there were malevolent personality traits inside Bernardo's head, mysterious quirks he kept tucked deeply away in the recesses of his mind. Plenty of people knew Bernardo, but nobody ever got truly close to him.

Bernardo had some favorite movies that fascinated him. Several were *Friday the Thirteenth* slasher flicks. Their theme never varied: Jason, the crazed killer with the hockey mask who terrorized the summer camp, killing all the beautiful teenaged girls who were being bad, having sex with their boyfriends when they shouldn't because they were too young. The scenes that most aroused him almost always ended in some horrid, barbarous death: the young girl with the large breasts suntanning topless just before Jason plunged the machete into her belly, the camera lingering on her writhing body as she died; the naked blonde about to reach a moaning climax on top of her boyfriend as the gleaming blade ripped through her back and out through her chest, blood spurting all over her horrified lover's face.

Jason usually waited until the young lovers were having sex before he administered his *coup de grâce*. If anyone survived his murderous assault, it was the virgins who were left to mete out revenge for their slain comrades, dispensing capital punishment on the deranged killer in an equally appalling fashion just before the final credits. It was the virgins of this world, symbols of justice and purity, who always won. A true Hollywood ending. And, although Jason always died at the conclusion of each flick, that didn't mean it was the end of him. Somehow he managed to spring back to life, machete in hand, poised to kill and kill again.

The Jason movies may have been where Bernardo developed his theory of life. He called it looping. It was like reincarnation: people never died — they just went away for a while before returning. But you came back as yourself, to live again in a different place and another time. Perhaps there should be a television show about it, he once kidded: *Lifecycles of the Rich and Famous*.

Bernardo's appetite for soft-core pornography and slasher movies didn't last long. He soon moved on to the titles they kept on the top shelves at the back of the video store:

Debbie Does Dallas, Hot Lust, Writing Bodies, and so forth. These hard-core videos featured anal sex and plenty of oral exploration. But soon not even those were enough. They were too contrived, the moaning too phony. Besides, Bernardo felt the women in those videos, mostly in their late twenties and thirties, were old, used up. He wanted flicks with younger girls, kiddie porn that was sold only at the specialty stores in downtown Toronto, the establishments with big Xs on their signs.

Along the way, he developed a taste for homemade smut. In the underground these films were known as "raised-skirt videos." For those tempted to peek through bedroom windows, it was much safer to get your jollies in the privacy of your living room. The technique for shooting a raised-skirt movie was simple: set up a camera hidden at ground level to shoot up a woman's dress as she walked down the street, with the lens zeroing in on her underwear. The ones Bernardo bought were crudely produced, the women seemingly unaware of how they were being violated. It was the amateurish quality to the jerky film that made the flicks so titillating, the idea that the viewer was doing what a real Peeper would be doing. For some, that was more of a turn-on than watching the staged couplings on some sound set.

While he was going to university, Bernardo supplemented his income with a little cigarette smuggling, loading up the side panels of his Capri with cheaper American cigarettes that he brought across the border at Niagara Falls, then selling the smokes in bars throughout Scarborough. Soon he developed a regular clientele.

One customer was a stripper named Suzie. After each of them had taken some clothes off in his car one night, Bernardo tried his bondage trick. Suzie, streetwise and tough, shook him off and jumped from the vehicle. The next time he was around the bar, Bernardo was stopped by Suzie's boyfriend, a member of a local motorcycle club.

The biker backed Bernardo up against a wall. "Who the fuck are you, and why are you fucking around with my old lady, man?"

"Hey, man," Bernardo replied, flashing his innocent smile, "I'm just a wheeler-dealer guy."

"Well, Mr. Wheeler-Dealer Man, you keep away from my old lady if you want to keep that pretty face."

Bernardo, a tough guy when it came to pushing women around, did not want to mess with the biker. He apologized and left quickly, skipping the bar for a time and selling his cigarettes elsewhere.

Karla Homolka was having a great time that Friday night in October 1987. She and her friends had booked in at the Howard Johnson hotel in Scarborough, for the pet-store convention, but all Homolka wanted to do was party. She and a friend had gone out to a local dance club and brought two men back to their room. Later, though, they had regretted their move and tried to rid themselves of the pair, eventually threatening to call the management before the would-be suitors got the message and left.

It was well after midnight and Homolka was hungry. She and her friend called for room service, but were told that it was now closed. Homolka, who had already changed into her pajamas, then made a decision that would forever change her life. "Let's go downstairs to the restaurant," she said.

The pair were eating their grilled cheese sandwiches in the hotel's all-night eatery when two men walked in and went right up to their table. The blond was the more forward, and he focused on Homolka, teasing her about being in the restaurant in her pajamas. They made small talk and exchanged names. Smiling at Homolka, he said, "My name is Paul Bernardo." His friend was Van Smirnis.

The foursome chatted in the restaurant for an hour, but Bernardo and Homolka might as well have been alone. The King of First Impressions pulled out all the stops, dishing out the charm with a large spoon. Homolka was enthralled by the handsome six-footer, nearly a foot taller than her, and at 23, six years her senior. All her other boyfriends suddenly seemed to her so immature. Later she would tell friends she had never met a man with such "animal magnetism." He, on the other hand, was attracted to her body and the prospect of scoring that night. But he liked the way she did that neat little thing with her eyes, glancing sideways at him without turning her head.

The two women invited the guys back to their room, and as the foursome walked to the elevator, Bernardo had already paired off with Homolka. An hour later the two were in bed, making love.

Years later psychiatrists would try to analyze that fateful evening at Howard Johnson's in their bid to understand why the two mated so quickly. Bernardo, of course, saw himself as a ladies' man, believed he could get any woman he wanted. And as a fledgling cigarette smuggler, he may perhaps have been intrigued by Homolka's address in the border town of St. Catharines.

But most psychiatrists felt there was another, deadlier reason for Bernardo's attraction to the blonde high-school student. He needed a compliant female with whom he could act out all his oft-criminal sexual fantasies, someone he could control to the point of having the power of life and death over her. He was uncomfortable around women with forceful personalities. He had dated one woman for two weeks, never going any further than kissing her, before he broke off the relationship. She was too aggressive for him. Lucy was not worthy of being his mate. Though compliant, she was simply not beautiful enough for him. He knew that his latest conquest was captivated by him, and he perhaps sensed the rest would follow in time.

Homolka's motivations were, paradoxically, both easier to understand but difficult to fathom. According to the psychiatrists, Homolka, living in a houseful of women, was looking for a strong man who exuded a sense of dominance. Homolka would have found Bernardo's decisive, self-assured and successful image particularly appealing. She suffered from a sense of insecurity, and with her conciliatory, self-doubting nature, hoped to draw out assurances and directions from a stronger, male partner. It was almost as if she believed the stereotypical view that, for a relationship to succeed, the woman needed a domineering male partner. It was a perfect match, Homolka believing she needed a forceful man in her life, and Bernardo searching for a vulnerable woman he could control. But the nature of Bernardo's particular lusts would set it on a course toward murder.

In other respects Homolka baffled the psychiatrists. She had been a feisty, forceful woman all of her young life, and in other relationships, so it seemed inconsistent that she was so willing to be compliant to her new mate. They would also be baffled by her apparent lack of any sense of moral judgment, difficult to understand in a highly intelligent, well-read, and seemingly ambitious young woman. She had just met, and fallen for, a completely amoral man. He was about to open for her the door to another world, one the trusting young woman found exhilarating, and dangerous. She eagerly followed him along his path of sexual depravity, and the abuse she was about to suffer at his hands would never fully justify her later actions.

PART TWO:

TERROR
BY NIGHT

8
The Usual Suspects

There was still snow on the ground when she saw him, lurking behind the bushes, a bottle of beer in his hand. That was enough to set off the warning bells, drinking beer outside on a frosty April night in 1987. But it didn't look as if there was anything wrong with him. Just the opposite, Mary Lawson thought, as she watched from the window of her kitchen in the townhouse complex in southeast Scarborough. The lad in the shadows looked more like every mother's dream. A healthy and handsome six-footer, late teens, maybe early twenties. Dirty blond hair parted in the middle and so good looking. The soft, sweet face of an angel.

He wasn't from the townhouse complex, Lawson was sure of that. She made it a point to know her neighbors, was almost the unofficial superintendent of the cozy little cul-de-sac of row houses. When she moved there, she had sought the peace and quiet that only a residential area near the end of the bus line could bring. There was none of the madness or crime of downtown Toronto. She liked her little community. What she didn't like was some pervert sneaking around in the bushes near her home.

She was sure she had seen him before in those very same bushes beside the brick enclosure where the homeowners put their garbage. It was a neat little hiding spot. People walking by on the street wouldn't see him. Is that what he was, a mugger? Waiting to pounce on some poor unsuspecting pensioner? Maybe she was some thirty years his senior, but Mary Lawson liked to think of herself as one tough old broad. No punk kid was going to pull off any shenanigans where she lived. She walked outside and over to the garbage compound, where Pretty Boy was peering through the bushes.

As she got closer, she noticed another empty beer bottle on the ground.

"You there," she called out. "What do you think you're doing?"

Sweet Face had his back to her, so he was startled by her challenge. "I . . . I don't want anyone to see me," he replied, rather honestly, she thought. He looked a little embarrassed, and he was shaking, but that was probably more from the cold; all he had on was a thin black jacket.

"Where do you live?"

"Over there," Angel Face replied, pointing vaguely toward nearby Lawrence Avenue and the big homes overlooking the lake.

"What business do you have here?"

"I'm . . . waiting for someone."

"Well, go wait somewhere else. Go on. Get out of here." And when it didn't look like he was moving, "Before I call the police."

"I'm going," he said, dropping his unfinished beer. "I'm leaving right now. To get warm."

He scurried off across Centennial Road, going west toward the new subdivision they were building, Highland Ridge.

As she picked up his beer bottles, Lawson had this image of the raccoons with their bandit-like eyes slinking into the night when she chased them away from the garbage. She thought for a long time about calling the police, but let it pass.

Since Bernardo and Homolka had gone to bed within an hour of meeting each other, there wasn't much doubt as to how their first official date would end. The following weekend, Bernardo traveled to St. Catharines and the couple went to see a movie, *Prince of Darkness*, ironically about an evil spirit being unleashed into the world. Afterwards they went to her parents' house. Dorothy was an administrator at the Shaver Hospital at St. Catharines. Karel was running a lighting business out of his house. He was a gracious host. Even though his English was bumpy, he was friendly, and popular with everyone in the neighborhood.

Homolka and Bernardo arrived with some of her friends, and they had a party.

"He's just gorgeous," one of her friends gushed as they gathered in the basement den. "You're so lucky."

Bernardo and Homolka were anxious to resume their sexual explorations and, with the party still going on, they went into her adjoining bedroom, locking the door behind them. She had a jean jacket on the back of the door, with a set of handcuffs sewn onto a pocket as an ornament. Bernardo's eyes lit up when he saw the cuffs.

"You can use them on me," she teased.

That's exactly what he did. He positioned her on the bed, cuffed her hands to a bedpost, then took off her jeans and panties. "Your big bad businessman wants to fuck you so badly," he told her, using the pet name he had given himself after taking the job as a junior accountant at Price Waterhouse. In the ensuing months there would be many more names.

Their relationship was moving along at a brisk pace: they were into bondage the second time they were in bed. But he was gentle with her, seemingly satisfied with vaginal sex. He took to calling her his Little Princess, bringing gifts for her and wine for the family whenever he visited. His easy charm, bright smile, and generosity made him an instant hit with the family.

Several days after their first date, Homolka had written what would be the first of several hundred cards and letters to him during their courtship. On some days she wrote him two or three cards, mailing them to his house in Scarborough.

The first card said: "Dear Paul. You're always on my mind. I miss you. Karla." The first letter: "Hi Paul. I'm cleaning up my room just waiting for your call . . . I hope you want to spend the weekend with me. I can't wait to see you. Karla."

Bernardo began to do a lot of driving in those first few months. He visited Homolka on Fridays after finishing work, staying late before driving back to his home in Scarborough, about a three-hour round trip. Then he would return to St. Catharines on Saturday, and leave on Saturday night before returning on Sunday and staying late into the evening.

But soon weekends weren't enough for Homolka. She wanted Bernardo to start visiting during the week. So every Wednesday night after he finished at Price Waterhouse, he got on the expressway. She always had a little love note ready to hand him whenever he walked in.

"To my Prince," read one. "Call or visit me anytime. Love from your Little Princess."

On that visit, he gave her some flowers and wrote her a card of his own: "You are the best."

Often he took her out for dinner, at first with her friends from school, but later alone.

After dinner, they usually went to Lake Gibson. They had a favorite spot just off Beaverdams Road. Although a popular fishing hole during the day, at night it was deserted. They parked far enough back that the car was hidden behind some bushes so passing motorists wouldn't see them making love in the back seat of Bernardo's white Capri.

Soon Bernardo moved beyond vaginal intercourse, and he wanted Homolka to spend more time giving him fellatio. Once he even shoved her head — albeit gently — down between his legs. Although she had known him only for two months, Homolka was already desperately in love with her handsome junior accountant, and was ready to do anything for him. One of her letters showed the depth of her affection:

"Dear Paul, how I miss you . . . all I really want to do is cuddle with you. I care for you. I'm really starting to fall for you. I can't wait to cuddle again. And I don't believe that's all I want to do with you."

Bernardo was fond of driving, but the round trips were starting to wear him out. Homolka began pestering her mother to let her boyfriend stay the weekends. "Paul could fall asleep behind the wheel, and crash," she fretted. He could sleep on the couch in the den, she said. Dorothy, somewhat reluctant at first, agreed that it wasn't fair Bernardo had to do so much driving.

So soon after they met, Bernardo was spending his weekends at the Homolka household, sleeping on the chesterfield. At night he and Homolka would wait until everyone had gone to bed before he snuck into her bedroom. But with each successive round of their sexual intimacy, it was taking him longer and longer to reach a climax. On one occasion he couldn't ejaculate and seemed frustrated by his inability. They often talked about ways to improve their sexual performances. "I'm always the one initiating everything," he complained. "You should be more aggressive." He also wanted more fellatio, to the point of where she was spending almost all their intimate time making him happy by using her mouth and hands to stimulate his penis. After their nightly sessions Bernardo always went back to the chesterfield because they knew her parents would otherwise be upset. She was only seventeen and, with two younger girls in the house, Dorothy and Karel didn't want their eldest daughter setting that kind of an example.

One night, after Homolka had fallen asleep after sex, Bernardo quietly got out of bed and went outside to the rear of the house. The bedroom of Homolka's youngest sister, Tammy Lyn, overlooked the back yard, and once Bernardo had seen her undressing while he was lounging beside the pool. Though Tammy Lyn was only 12 the sight had aroused strong sexual urges in Bernardo. He climbed a fence at the side of the house for a better view into her bedroom. Since there was an empty field behind the house, he had to worry only about the Homolkas or their neighbors. Though Tammy was asleep that night, there would be plenty of other chances.

As 1987 came to a close, Bernardo was still commuting between Scarborough and St. Catharines. But there were other places he liked to drive. On the days he wasn't in Garden City, he would cruise around Scarborough, usually ending up at shopping malls. He sometimes spent hours there just sitting behind the wheel of his Capri, secretly watching women leaving the stores with their parcels. Other favorite spots of his were the ends of bus routes. There was one in particular, just a little to the east of his house, where he often parked, checking out each bus as it went by. Frequently there would just be the driver and a lone female passenger, or two.

The woman, 22, had just stepped off the Lawrence Avenue bus near the end of the line and was walking north, toward her home, on that December night in 1987, keeping on the west side of the street because it was better lit. It was just after 2 a.m., and Centennial Road was deserted. Though wary of being out so late, she was in her neighborhood and she felt safe. That part of Scarborough was known as West Hill, a comfortable enclave of middle-class homes, mostly with big homes, mostly with big lots and two-car garages, the kind of community where you waved to all your neighbors.

She had just passed the townhouse complex when a figure tackled her from some bushes near the sidewalk, knocking her face first to the ground. There was no time to react or fight back as he dragged her between the two houses. Before she knew it, she was on her stomach, her arms pinned by her sides. He straddled her, held her down with a strength far greater than her own.

"Don't look at me," he warned, "or you're dead."

She obeyed, though he punched her anyway on the side of the face. The blow nearly knocked her unconscious. Then he had the cord out, and he was pulling it so tight around her neck that she couldn't breathe. She was gasping for air when he ripped her pants and her underwear roughly down her legs. First he wanted oral sex. Then he penetrated her anally while she lay on her stomach, helpless, the madman on her back panting, his disgusting breath in her ear. "What's your name!" he demanded. When she told him, he said, "Tell me that you love me!"

"I love you," she replied obediently.

"Again! I want to hear it again."

"I – love you."

Please dear God, she thought, don't kill me. She had heard that another woman had been raped in the area not two weeks earlier, and tried to recall the details. She remembered that the woman had been attacked after getting off a bus, as she had just done. Why hadn't she taken a cab?

Just don't kill me, she kept thinking. I don't want to be lying here, half naked, for everyone to see. She closed her eyes and tried to pretend she was somewhere else. She kept her eyes shut for the longest time, but it didn't work. He was deep inside her and there was nothing she could do. She wanted to scream, but was afraid he might kill her if she made any noise. And then he was finished.

She didn't move, stayed flat on the ground, half naked, sore and shivering in the cold. She had followed his orders. He didn't have to kill her. Why hadn't he run away? What more did he want? He was coming around in front of her. She didn't look up. He knelt down and again gave the warning not to look at him. She wouldn't. Oh dear God, she wouldn't. He just had to believe that. His voice was controlled, calm. He was enjoying himself.

Oh God, she thought. He isn't satisfied. He wants more. Oh God, no, not that. He was shoving his penis toward her mouth. She wanted to die.

Later, when he dragged her toward a fence, she didn't fight him as he tied her hands to a picket with her own belt. She kept her eyes down, looking away as he went through her purse. He started to leave and then, with an evil afterthought, he hoofed her in the ribs. She waited a long time before freeing herself, going for help.

At the hospital, they were compassionate. A counselor from a rape crisis center was there. Everyone was doing their best to be kind, but all she wanted to do was go home and take a hot bath, cleanse her body of the filth from that animal. Tests had to be done, however. Samples were needed for the crime lab. They had to swab her mouth. Her anus. She worried that she might have caught some disease from him. Syphilis. AIDS.

After the doctors it was the police. A nice detective brought her a coffee, was sympathetic about her half shut, bruised eye. Could she describe the attacker? She told what she could: he was white, maybe six foot, 180, and that was about it. She never saw his face. It was a good description of half the men in Scarborough, the detective thought, but kept that to himself. The rapist wore gloves, so it was unlikely he had left behind any prints. And there were no witnesses to either attack. So far, all the odds favored the rapist. As with so much police work, they would have to plod along and hope for a break.

Mary Lawson was annoyed with herself. She should have called the police. Two rapes in her neighborhood, and maybe the culprit was that nice-looking man she had seen. He certainly fit the description.

Scarborough had seen better years than 1987. A whole string of rapes, including those two in her end of the city. Then there was the jogger, Margaret McWilliam, raped and murdered in a park. Had the whole place gone mad? Lawson dialed the police and a detective was there later that day.

He had some photos for her to look at, a selection of the usual suspects, known rapists, molesters and other sexual deviants. She studied each mug shot, but none was the pretty boy with the beer bottle. All the men in the photos looked scruffy, dirty, mean and ugly.

Her boy had sweet features, she told the detective, and knew right there she had lost his interest. Perhaps the police wanted only the rapists from central casting, the ones with knitted eyebrows, hair growing out of their ears and knuckles dragging on the ground. Why ignore someone, she wondered, just because he looked so nice?

"Our boy is missing a few sandwiches in his picnic basket," the detective said as he packed up his mug shots. There wasn't much more the police could do with her tip, he explained. They would have a scout car patrol the area and keep an eye on the bushes in case the good-looking man ever came back. She told him the man had gone west, along Lawrence. That figured, said the detective. More than likely he had been parked farther along and was just watching the well-lit buses, waiting for one with a lone female on board. Then he would drive ahead of it and wait for her to get off.

The detective gave her his card, told her to call if she saw the man again, then got up to go. As she walked him to the door, Lawson made a suggestion. Why not get a sketch artist to do a composite drawing of the man she had seen? She had a real good look at him and remembered his face clearly: high cheekbones, a delicate curve to his nose, a smooth complexion. If the police posted the sketch in the neighborhood, perhaps other witnesses might come forward.

The detective said he would check with his superiors and get back to her. But it was wrong, he cautioned, to jump to conclusions about the good-looking young man. The fact that he was acting suspiciously didn't mean he was their rapist. He might have had a legitimate reason. Lawson couldn't think of one, but she didn't feel it was her place to question the professionals. Didn't the city have the finest police force in the country?

Homolka was so proud whenever he picked her up at Winston Churchill after school. The big city boyfriend with the white car. She liked the way everyone stared at her as she walked up to his car. She was just so cool when she was with him. The world seemed right with Paul by her side. He was everything she had ever wanted. Life was great again. There were no more thoughts of suicide.

Although Bernardo found her attractive, he didn't want her tinting her hair so many colors; she should let it go back to its natural blonde. And he didn't like her wearing such short skirts. She complied, and her appearance began to change. Homolka's new look was popular with her parents, who had never liked her punk style.

One weekend when Bernardo discovered she had gone out with friends to a bar, he got angry. "I don't really like you talking to other men," he admonished. "Maybe I'm too jealous, but I'd prefer that you didn't go out without me. Look, I'll do the same. I haven't seen any other women since we met, Kar."

She knew that was a lie. He had taken a former girlfriend to his university graduation, but she didn't challenge him. She was in love and wasn't interested in seeing other men. And if he didn't like the way she dressed, then that too was a small enough change to make for a man who was so good to her.

Although she tried to take the sexual aggressor's role more often, that wasn't enough to please him. He wanted her to start calling herself dirty names while she gave fellatio. There were three he had in mind: cocksucker, cunt, and slut. And in that order. Once when she got the order reversed, he called her stupid. But he did it in a joking way, and apologized right after, so she forgave him almost immediately.

"My name is Karla," she always said when starting off their sex by Lake Gibson. "I'm 17." Then she would fondle his penis, begin oral sex, and say, "I'm your little cocksucker. I'm your little cunt. I'm your little slut."

Later, he wanted her to add a fourth part. It also bothered him that she hadn't been a virgin when they met. There had been other boyfriends, she had admitted, just as he had had other girlfriends. One had been Doug, who had moved with his family to the States. She had stopped writing to him, but Bernardo remained jealous. In addition to calling herself demeaning words, he wanted her to denounce her former boyfriend. She didn't see the point. But Bernardo got mad, and since she didn't think it was that big a deal, she went along. So then the routine became: "I'm your cocksucker, your cunt, your slut. And I love only you. I hate Doug. I never want to see him again."

That seemed to please him for a time, but around Christmas 1987 he wanted more again.

"Since you weren't a virgin when we met," he told her one night, "we should, like, you know, do it up the ass."

"No, Paul!" She found the idea abhorrent.

It was the first time she had denied him anything, but rather than accept her refusal, he persisted. "C'mon, Kar," he kidded, "it would be like a first experience we could share."

Bernardo didn't think that he could force Homolka into something she didn't want to do, since he thought of her as being strong-willed, unlike Lucy. But he planned, in time, to persuade her. He could wait.

She kept sending him cards, but instead of the cute ones with animals and hearts, the pre-printed cards started to get racier. One read: "Roses are red, violets are blue, nothing's more fun than a pervert like you." Another: "You're such a disgusting sexual pervert — I like that in a man!" A third: "Oh please, don't take off my clothes and throw me on the bed and ravage me for an hour — do it all day!" She signed most of the cards with the same line: "Thanks for making me so happy. Love, Kar."

Although thoroughly infatuated, Homolka still wondered about their relationship. While telling her friends how much she loved Bernardo and wanted to marry him, privately she had some doubts. In one letter to him, she wrote: "I'm just sitting in bed listening to a depressing song by Elvis Presley, 'I can't help falling in love with you.' Some things were meant to be, like me and you. I trust you completely now. I'm not even afraid that you'll take my trust and fuck me up. I trust you one hundred percent. But I still worry sometimes that we're going too fast. It just feels so right, though. I just love you so much. You're wonderful. You're the best. My Prince. I love you. Kar."

She followed up with a pre-printed card that expressed her love, and doubt, in the same message. On the outside was a heart. "A crystal heart signifies fragility," the card read. "Take it, but don't break it." And then she wrote: "I haven't seen you since Sunday. I can't stand it any longer. Why do I need you so much? Don't forget, I love you. Kar."

On the two-month anniversary of their meeting: "Happy anniversary, sweetheart. It's been the best two months ever of my life. You're my prince. Je t'adore. I want to give you a kiss. I want to go with you to an obscure cul-de-sac. I love you, my fantasy prince. Don't ever let me go. I want to marry you."

9
The Missing Face

Bathgate Drive was always at its prettiest just before Christmas. That year, 1987, almost every house along the street that wound north from Lawrence Avenue was lit up for the festive season: big homes, plenty of lights, one of the nicest streets in the West Hill area of Scarborough. Some of the choicer properties on Bathgate were at its south end, near Lawrence, palatial homes with three-car garages and wide lots. Bathgate had character and charm. And at the bottom end, near Lawrence, it had scenic wooded ravines where creeks had once flowed into nearby Lake Ontario.

The young woman, 17, had been out buying gifts that evening, two days before Christmas. It was just after midnight when she got off the Lawrence Avenue bus at her stop, Bathgate Drive. Like everyone else in her community, she knew about the Scarborough Rapist, who had struck three times as 1987 came to a close. Two of the attacks had been on Centennial Road, just one street east from Bathgate. His third and latest victim, a girl aged 15, had been raped a week earlier in the Guildwood area, a little to the west.

If he kept to the pattern of attacking in twos, people in her neighborhood had speculated, it was likely he would strike again soon, but probably in Guildwood. At least, that was what the residents of West Hill were thinking.

One of the houses she passed on Bathgate had a nativity scene for its Christmas decorations. It wasn't right that women had to worry about being raped on this holiest of Christian holidays, the girl was thinking, when suddenly she heard footsteps behind her. The street had been deserted; instinctively she turned to see who it was. But he had a gloved hand over her mouth before she could turn around. And then she felt the blade of the knife against her throat.

"Don't scream," he warned. "If you do I'll kill you."

He shoved her toward some bushes between two big houses. He threw her to the ground, face first, and started ripping at her clothes. She felt the sharp pain of the knife probing her anus. She heard his zipper go down, and he was inside her vaginally first, then anally. When he was finished, he held the knife to her throat.

"Give me one good reason," he said, "why I shouldn't kill you right here."

Sobbing, she pleaded for her life. She hadn't seen his face, she didn't know what he looked like, she wouldn't be able to give the police his description. It wasn't what he wanted to hear. He warned her not to go to the police at all. He had been through her purse, he reminded her, and he knew her name, where she lived. "If you go to the police, I'll come back and kill you." He told her to lie on the ground, and not move, for half an hour. And then he was gone.

Long after he had left she lay there, sobbing, too afraid to move. There were houses all around. Someone should have heard something and come to her rescue. How long had she been lying there? Fifteen, twenty minutes? She didn't know. Finally she got up and looked around for her clothes. They were scattered all over the grass.

She was reaching for her underpants when he lunged at her from the bushes. The fist came up too fast for her to react. It struck her in the jaw, knocking her backwards. She fell to the ground, dazed, as he moved onto her.

"Bitch," he said, rolling her onto her stomach. "I told you not to move."

And then he was in her again. "Arch your back," he screamed, punching her on the shoulders. She looked up at the house and saw a light. Had someone called the police? She waited for the help that never came while she drifted in and out of consciousness. Once she thought she heard him say "my fucking mother." And then he was gone, this time for good.

Const. Eddie Grogan was in his mid-forties and had long since given up any thoughts of making the rank of detective. Once he had been quite ambitious, but that drive had dulled. He still liked the job, but hated the politics involved in being promoted. His wife was expecting their first child, and he had promised her that he would spend more time at home. But here it was Christmas Day, and he was on overtime, a stake-out detail, watching bus stops. The "eye and die" of police work: keep an eye out for anything suspicious, and die waiting for something to happen. And on this Christmas Day, absolutely nothing was happening.

Grogan was one of a team assigned to watch bus stops in the rapist's hunting grounds. But there were hundreds of bus stops in the bottom half of Scarborough. What were the chances that one of the team would nab the rapist in action? Winning that week's lottery seemed like a better bet. But the community was outraged, and the police had to do something.

Dressed in his civvies, slunk low behind the wheel of a rather beat-up Chrysler, Grogan stared vacantly at a bus stop on Lawrence Avenue nearly half a block away. At least a dozen other police officers were doing the same at bus stops from Guildwood to West Hill.

It didn't figure that the rapist would strike again so soon after the last assault, two days earlier. There seemed to be a pattern to the attacks, two in May, two more in December; more than likely, he would take a break for the rest of the holiday season. But of course the police didn't know that for sure, and so Grogan sat there eyeballing a bus stop, looking for a rapist who was probably at home enjoying his Christmas dinner.

He had a great description to work with. Male, white, 20, 180 pounds. He had seen at least a dozen guys who looked like that this evening. What the police needed most was a face. So far, they had only a mind.

Psychiatrists had told the police they should be looking for a psychopathic rapist, a sexual predator who felt no remorse for his deeds. If they were right, thought Grogan, then the predictable pleas they were making through the media were probably pointless. "Turn yourself in," Insp. Joe Wolfe, in charge of the investigation, had said through reporters. And then this gem: "He obviously needs help, and if he surrenders we can see that he gets it." Save your breath, Joe, thought Grogan. If the shrinks are right, a psychopath with no conscience isn't going to turn himself in for doing something he enjoys.

The police had set up a hotline for tipsters, but it was mostly bringing in calls from scorned women ratting on former boyfriends. There was also a team of detectives poring over the files of known sex offenders who lived in the area. That avenue of investigation, though, was based on the large, and not necessarily accurate, assumption that the man they were looking for had a history of sexual offenses.

But what if he was a first-timer? Or so clever that he had never been nabbed? Still, they had to eliminate the known offenders first. It was what Grogan hated about police work.

So predictable and plodding. Eliminate the world before you zeroed in on your man. The same went for this mind-numbing stakeout.

An old lady in a house across the street had been peering through her curtain at him for hours, probably wondering what he was doing. As the night wore on, he thought about knocking on her door, telling her he was a cop. He couldn't tell her what he was doing, of course, but at least she wouldn't have to worry that he was a pervert waiting for a chance to jump her.

As he glanced over at the old lady, Grogan thought about the severity of the attacks on the four women: the gratuitous violence with each assault, that extra punch in the face, the kick in the ribs. The shrinks had a fancy name for that category of rapist. Grogan had seen it in one of the reports: paraphilia. Translation: he was a sexual sadist who enjoyed hurting his victims as much as he savored the sex. A sick bastard who was aroused by pain; the more they suffered, the better he liked it. The paraphiliac, according to what Grogan had read, was a lot more devious than a psychopath, and therefore harder to catch.

Neither felt any guilt, but the paraphiliac was better at masking his aberrant sexual tastes. The psychopath could be a self-centered jerk, breaking the rules whenever it suited him, not concerned that he was bringing too much attention upon himself. The paraphiliac was just the opposite. He passed himself off as a law-abiding citizen, appeared normal, and might be the boy next door. Maybe they should go to the nearest high school and grill the captain of the football team. Or haul in the local chapter of the Boy Scouts and give a rubberhosing to the one with the shiftiest eyes.

Even those closest to the paraphiliac, like a wife or a girlfriend, could apparently be deceived by him, at least at first. Paraphiliacs were not only mean but manipulative. There were cases where wives and girlfriends had been molded into sex slaves. Grogan had read a paper on that by Special Agent Roy Hazelwood of the Federal Bureau of Investigation.

Women with low self-esteem were the best victims. Easily swayed, they were taken in by the charm of the paraphiliac, who kept his oddball lusts tucked well back behind the glitzy smile. Only later came the abuse. First physical, then sexual, and finally a psychological hammering of the woman into submission until she was no better off than one of his victims. It was at that point the deviant risked capture; when the women feared for their lives, sometimes they fled to the police.

Good speculation, all of it, thought Grogan. But none of it was helping them catch this particular culprit. And so he sat there on Christmas Day, in his beat-up Chrysler, waiting for the villain without a face to strike again. It was going to be a long winter.

Bernardo lavished expensive gifts on Homolka that Christmas, including a gold necklace and a watch. But there was one present in particular she liked: a white teddy bear she named Bunky. She cuddled it every night in bed because it made her feel good.

After Christmas, there were more demands from Bernardo for anal sex. When she refused, Bernardo became angry with her for the first time. "You weren't a virgin when we met!" he challenged. "And I deserved a virgin. I don't love you anymore."

When Homolka broke out in the painful skin rash known as shingles, Bernardo, rather than feeling sorry for her, grew angry with her, afraid that she was going to give the skin irritation to him. It was not the way she had wanted to start off

1988, squabbling with the man she loved. When he didn't come one weekend early in January she was upset. She sent him a letter, attempting to apologize.

"I'm so sorry for what I've done," she wrote, a reference to her sexual encounters before meeting him. "I hate myself. I know I don't deserve it, but I want a second chance. Hearing you say you didn't love me was one of the worst days in my life. I guess I really screwed things up. There are no perfect people in this world. One day you may find your virgin. Kar."

"I also want to apologize for my stupid insecurities," she wrote in a second letter. "I wish to God I wasn't such a stupid idiot. Sometimes I feel just so useless. Please let's not fight again. Your furry little creature, Karly Curls."

He called her soon afterwards and they made up. She cried most of the time on the phone, then told him what he had been waiting to hear — that she agreed to anal sex. He visited her the next day, bringing flowers for her, a bottle of liquor for her father, and wine for her mother, all the while acting like the concerned boyfriend as he commiserated about the shingles. When they were alone, he told her of his plan. His parents were leaving on a weekend trip in February, and he wanted her to go to his house.

"My parents would never let me go," she said, recalling the grief she had endured over visiting her boyfriend in the U.S.

"Silly," he replied. "Just say that my parents will be home."

She gave him fellatio that evening in their usual hiding spot off Beaverdams Road. He had told her to think up a name for his penis, and she came up with Snuffles.

"I love having Snuffles in my mouth," she told him, pausing for a moment.

She had become very proficient at fellatio but, good as she was, it sometimes took her up to 20 minutes to bring him to ejaculate. He leaned his head back, moaning in pleasure.

"And what are you?"

"Your little cocksucker," she replied.

"What else?"

"Your little cunt. Your slut. I want to suck on Snuffles all the time," she continued as his breathing quickened.

This time, when he ejaculated, Bernardo held her down, telling her to swallow his semen. She was happy to oblige, thankful he had come back to her. In him she saw a sexually dynamic, exciting person, a man of destiny, she once said, someone who was going to do great things in the world, and she wanted to be there, by his side.

A flurry of notes led up to their secret weekend of lust at his parents' house. There was the Love Coupon, which stated: "The bearer will receive one cute little blonde 17-year-old to put on her knees between his legs and satisfy his wishes."

Then there was another card: "Dear Paul, You're a dream come true. You are the best, my Big, Bad Businessman. I've been fantasizing what playful things to do with your body all day. Your strong chest. Your muscular arms. Your beautifully shaped legs. Your hard, flat stomach. And Snuffles, oh wonderful Snuffles. The pleasure I get from touching, from licking, from sucking Snuffles, is indescribable.

"You know what I love? Having you stick it inside me and making me gasp for air while my parents are in the next room. I love it when you shoot it into my mouth. I want to swallow every drop, and then some. The power you wield over me is indescribable. When we sit together on the couch I have to use all my strength to keep from ripping off your clothes. You make me so horny. Your send tingles with your touch.

"I love you an amount I never thought possible. Words can't even come close to expressing my feelings. With you in my life, I feel complete. Whole. With you by my side, nothing can go wrong. You have opened my eyes to a new way of thinking and being. I will love you forever, no matter what. Karla. XOXOXO."

10
Kinky Urges

They were going to be alone together all that weekend in February 1988 at his parents' Scarborough house. Homolka had been excited all week: she had already set up the lie with her parents, telling them that Bernardo's parents had invited her over to get to know her better. They were barely in his house when he started taking off her clothes.

"What's that for?" she asked, pointing at the Polaroid camera on a chair near his bed.

"Just to take a few pictures. You don't mind, do you?"

She began, as usual, with fellatio after Bernardo had set the automatic timer on the camera. Then he took out his set of handcuffs and locked her arms around a bedpost while they had vaginal sex. Next he took out a wine bottle, uncuffed her, and told her to push it into her vagina. She was hesitant.

"C'mon," he said, peering out from behind the camera.

"What are you going to do with the pictures?"

"Nothing. Just save them. Something to look at when we're older."

She complied, and he snapped away with the camera. Then came the part he had been waiting for. Down on her hands and knees, she raised her buttocks in the air. He set up the camera, then penetrated her anally. She yelled out in pain, and he withdrew, solicitous of her discomfort. He asked to try it again, and she agreed. Only this time he took a black electrical cord off his dresser and slipped it around her neck as he penetrated her. He then yanked on the cord, so hard that she started clawing at it to get some air. He released the cord, worried that he might have hurt her. She said she didn't want him to use the ligature, but when he promised to be careful, she let him.

Later he took out a knife. It was in a sheath, and had an eight-inch blade. It frightened her at first, but he said he wouldn't hurt her. Using the knife during sex, he told her, excited him. He entered her anally, put the cord around her neck, then pressed the tip of the knife to her throat. He tugged on the cord, but not as tight as before, grunting in pleasure as he thrust away. Within a few minutes, he climaxed and rolled off.

"You were just great," he exclaimed, lying on his back. "Just great."

She loved him and wanted to marry him, but she later said that this was the point at which she became concerned about his sexual fetishes. Still, she found him exciting and, while she didn't like everything they did, she was ready to subordinate her personal desires. They were more his little fantasies than hers, and she thought that, as long as she went along, he would "get them out of his system." She couldn't know that his kinky urges were only going to get worse.

The 19-year-old had just got off a bus in Scarborough and was walking along Markham Road when he grabbed her from behind one night in April 1988. She was returning from her job at a restaurant, and later told police she thought the attacker had been hiding in some bushes. She had read about the Scarborough Rapist but had felt safe because she lived in the city center and the previous four attacks had all been in the southeastern end.

He wasn't going to take her without a fight, though. She struggled, and he punched her hard on the head, momentarily stunning her. Then he dragged her off the sidewalk and began tearing at her pants. He wanted fellatio first, then he raped her vaginally, all the time holding a knife to her neck and warning her not to look at his face.

"Get your ass in the air. Arch your back," he then yelled at her, pounding her on the shoulders as he penetrated her anally. "Say your name." She told him.

"You're a cunt, aren't you?" When she didn't respond: "Aren't you!"

"Yes."

"Say it!" he yelled, pounding on her back. "Say it!"

"I'm a cunt."

"And a cocksucker too."

"A cocksucker," she repeated.

The attack seemed to go on forever and, despite her screams, no one had come to her rescue. Finally she heard him zipping up his pants.

"Don't ever go to the police," he warned. "I know your name. I'll come back, and I'll kill you." And then he was gone.

She pulled her clothes back on and ran to the first house, pounding on the door until someone came. But, by the time the police arrived, her assailant was long gone. Not long after, the police organized a public meeting in the gymnasium of a high school in West Hill. Three hundred concerned and angry residents attended to grill the authorities.

In addition to the Scarborough Rapist's fifth assault, there had also been a recent attack in Mississauga, where a woman had been pulled into some bushes after descending from a bus. There were some uncanny similarities between that assault and the ones in Scarborough, but, unlike the attacks in Scarborough, in Mississauga, the woman had seen the rapist's face. A sketch had been released of a man in his early twenties, with fine features and wavy blond hair, and about six feet tall.

It was turning into a bad year for violence against women in the greater Metropolitan Toronto area. Sexual assaults were up, to an average of more than four a day. And at least three serial rapists were on the prowl. The residents at the meeting wanted to know what the police were doing about it.

"Spending less time at the donut shop," Const. Eddie Grogan, who was standing at the back of the auditorium, felt like yelling out, but it didn't seem the appropriate time for levity. Really, though, what could the police do when they didn't even know what the culprit looked like?

Five attacks in Scarborough, and not one woman had seen the face of the man in his early twenties with dirty blond hair. The woman in Mississauga had seen enough of her attacker to generate an artist's sketch. But although the description of the rapist in Mississauga was close to that of the man they were hunting in Scarborough, Grogan's bosses doubted it was the same person. Why not go with it anyway? thought Grogan. Put the face out there. If it was the same man, they might get some names to work with. But the brass didn't see it that way – the location didn't fit the pattern — and Grogan didn't have the rank to question their judgment.

He was one of about 30 officers hunting for the rapist. He wanted to tell the angry citizens about all the hard work, the tedious all-night stakeouts at transit stops, the women decoys riding the buses. But he couldn't disclose any of that. That was the trouble with police work: you had to be so secretive, and when you didn't make the pinch, you had to take your lumps. This evening it was Insp. Joe Wolfe's turn to sit in front of the gathering.

Wolfe was doing his best to put a positive spin on the investigation. The team was bringing in a computer program from Britain, something the coppers had used to catch Peter Sutcliffe, who had murdered 13 prostitutes in Yorkshire. Grogan was skeptical; he had yet to see a computer interrogate a suspect.

Some detectives had been calling other forces in Canada, looking for similar-type rapes. But Grogan was sure their boy lived right here, in the community. Each of the women had been stalked. That meant a great deal of patience waiting around for just the right victim. Some drifter passing through wouldn't have gone to all the bother.

The team of investigators had also gone south of the border for help, to the FBI, who had put together a psychological profile of the rapist. According to the FBI's crime profilers at Quantico, Virginia, the guy they were looking for probably showed some signs of "extreme anger" and an abusive attitude toward women, either physically or verbally. Any abusive husband, boyfriend, or male friend could be a potential suspect, and the attacks could have been sparked by an angry confrontation with a female boss, a wife, a lover, or even a mother.

What a great help to the case, thought Grogan. According to the FBI, they were looking for an angry young man who hated women and would probably strike again. "Well," said Grogan to one of the other officers, "I never figured he'd be a feminist." What the FBI needed, Grogan felt like saying, were psychics on the payroll who could give them a description of the rapist. That was the key.

Window-dressing, that's what the good citizens of Scarborough were getting, thought Grogan. Computer this, FBI that. Why not just tell the public the truth? They were no closer to making a pinch that evening than a year ago. All those

7,000 posters the police were handing out weren't going to be much help if there was no face for the attacker. If anything, the "fink money" might work; $50,000 would put a severe test on anyone's loyalty, especially a wife on the receiving end of a few backhands from a woman-hating spouse.

The man they were looking for could be the least suspicious guy in the neighborhood. In time, he would slip up; they all did. But the specialists were warning it had better be soon. The rapist had been getting more violent with each attack, clubbing, slashing at the women he assaulted, toying at their sexual organs with his knife. He was sadistic enough to kill. And the next time he just might.

Grogan headed for his stakeout post near the bus stop. He had been there for so long that the people on the street were starting to wave at him, suspecting he was a cop. Even the old lady across the street had guessed what he was doing. Once, she had brought him out a coffee. Just great, he thought; he had turned an undercover stakeout into a spectator sport.

Bernardo knew they were staring at him. He loved the way his presence flushed out all the little teenyboppers on the street where Karla lived. On Dundonald Street they called him the neighborhood heartthrob, the Big City Boy with the killer good looks. Some of the teenyboppers were friends of Karla's sister Tammy, and they always found an excuse to visit her whenever he was there.

Bernardo enjoyed their adulation; he encouraged it, always talking to them, at times even flirting with the girls who were at least 10 years younger than him. Paul and his harem, that's what one of the neighbors had said, teasing him about cradle robbing. He laughed it off.

He stripped off his shirt that warm June afternoon as he washed his white Capri. If they were going to watch him from their yards, then he wanted to give them something to talk about. Tammy sat on the front steps of her house staring at her sister's boyfriend while he scrubbed the tires of the car. A friend walked over from across the street.

"How do you keep your hands off him?" she whispered to Tammy. "He is such a hunk."

"I know," replied Tammy. "He's really a terrific guy."

In the year Bernardo had been dating Homolka he had quickly become the house favorite. Karla's parents seemed enthralled with him. Paul, her mother was fond of saying, had become their "weekend son." It was a good thing they liked him because their eldest daughter had really fallen for the accountant trainee.

He was all she ever talked about — Paul this, Paul that — as if nobody else in the world mattered. And it's true, he had been good for her. There were no more bouts of depression. There was no more talk about suicide. Still, it worried them that her school marks had started to slip, and they hoped she hadn't lost interest in everything except Paul. He had become the focus of her life, and at times they wondered if that was healthy. And then there were those long-distance phone bills! During the week, when he was back in Toronto at his job, the two of them gabbed for hours on the phone, like lovesick puppies. Karel Homolka had a chat with his daughter after she rang up a bill of $300.

Homolka could have moved to Toronto, but Bernardo had started to rave about St. Catharines. He liked it because it was so handy to the U.S. border.

Although they had just met, Homolka had already started to think about marrying Bernardo. He liked the idea of her staying at home. "Since I'm going to stay at home after we get married and raise a family, going to university would be a waste of money," she often told her parents.

She thought his protectiveness neat, but there were times when he could be too jealous. He didn't have to worry about her affections. There had been other lovers, but they were long before she met him. She never talked about them anymore. Sometimes he didn't even like her seeing her school friends. She had wanted him to meet Renya Hill for lunch that afternoon, after he washed his car. Bernardo agreed to take her there, but then told her he just wanted to drive around, enjoy the sights of the city.

Renya was waiting for them at the Pen Center, the biggest shopping mall in St. Catharines. Bernardo was polite to her, asking a few questions before he hurriedly left.

"Isn't he just great?" Homolka said over lunch. "There's just nobody else in the world that I want."

Renya had noticed her friend was back to the Karla of old, none of that moody talk like the last time. Afterwards, they went shopping. Homolka headed for the lingerie section of the department store, looking for a frilly push-up bra and matching panties.

"Not that you need it," kidded Renya.

"Do you think Paul will like it?" Homolka asked, giggling.

Bernardo often liked to cruise through the streets of St. Catharines. Once, he told Homolka, he had even been pulled over by the police, who thought he was acting suspiciously as he parked near a bus stop. He laughed off the incident and Homolka put it out of her mind. One area that Bernardo liked to drive around was Port Dalhousie, at the north end of the city. Originally a sailor's town, Dalhousie, as it was called, was now a quiet community of middle-class homes, several of them overlooking Lake Ontario.

Bernardo drove across the bridge to Henley Island. The parking lot was crowded that day. Everywhere he looked,

Bernardo saw young women. He strolled around, smiling at them, enjoying himself on the pleasant summer afternoon.

11
Beyond Belief

They were driving back from Lake Gibson one fall evening in 1988 when Bernardo told Homolka he wanted her to wear a dog collar while they were having sex. She thought the idea stupid, and told him so. That made him angry and he slapped her across the face. Almost as soon as he had hit her, he apologized. It was the first time he had ever struck her.

"Kar, I'm really sorry," he said, pulling off the road. "I didn't mean to do it."

He hadn't hit her hard, and she was more surprised than hurt. But he was so upset with himself that he began to cry. She started to feel guilty, and immediately began blaming herself: it was just a harmless little fantasy he wanted her to try. Soon after the incident, she bought the collar. Bernardo was pleased, and the next time they had sex in her bedroom, she put it on her neck and he tugged at it while he entered her anally and called her his "little mutt."

Soon, however, he wanted something different again—anilingus. As always, she complied. And as with any new sexual act, he found that it satiated his desires—at first. He made her add to the vocabulary she recited: cocksucker, cunt, slut, and now, asslicker.

The next time he hit her, he wasn't as apologetic. He had persuaded her to take a trip with him to Florida that fall, again telling her to lie and say they were going to stay with his grandparents on Georgian Bay. While in Florida, he bought a Sony Camcorder and was like a child with a new toy, taping everything: scenery on the road ahead, other cars, each other. One evening, at a motel, he called out to her, "Tape me in the shower." She walked into the bathroom and asked him to open the curtains. He got mad, said, "Gimme that," pushed back the curtain and grabbed for the camera. "I'll do it myself."

But she dropped the camera as she was passing it, and the lens smashed. He was furious. He lunged at her from the shower, kicked and punched her, knocked her to the floor. He kept hitting her for several minutes.

"You really are a stupid cunt, you know that?" he told her, when he finally helped her up. "You're nothing without me."

He had started calling her a bitch and cunt in front of friends. When they talked on the phone, he called her a bitch almost all the time. These were words they had previously used only during lovemaking. But now he had struck her twice and the verbal abuse was getting worse. The only way she could improve herself, he began to say more often, was to write herself reminders of how dumb she was. She taped one note to the door of her bedroom. It read: "Remember, you're stupid. Remember to think before you speak."

But she still kept mailing him cards, and giving him notes whenever he visited. Read one: "I'm your little cocksucker, cunt, slut, asslicker, and I want to marry you." "Your wish is my command" was another. It's hard to know whether she was repulsed by the abuse or whether she wanted more, believing that their relationship was something special. Certainly, the more he called her a bitch and a cunt in front of her friends, the more she loved him. Taking his abuse was the price she felt she had to pay to keep his love. All that fall, the letters continued. Nearly every second day she wrote him.

"Thank you for making my life so wonderful," she wrote in September. And the next day: "I want to lick you all over, you furry creature. The things that I'm going to do to your body the next time we meet."

He kept each titillating letter in his bedroom desk. One of his favorites arrived at the end of September. "Hi Paul. I'd like to lick you and kiss you and suck you all over. I long to labor lovingly over your beautiful body. I want to suck Snuffles and get him so hard that he can't take it anymore. And then I want to ease your pulsating penis into my tight little cunt. Your little girl wants to be abused. She needs her Big Bad Businessman to dominate her the best he can. Love, Kar."

On the one-year anniversary of their meeting, she sent him a card: "Thanks for the best year of my life. You have enriched my life beyond belief." Much later, in court, her actions would be described in the same way—as beyond belief.

Joe Cosantino had been talking about giving up smoking for months. Smoking didn't make sense for him, a 52-year-old man with a bad pumper and a little extra weight around the middle. The doctor warned him about those little pains he had been feeling in his chest. And what better time for a New Year's resolution than just three days before the end of 1988? Cosantino was the superintendent of an apartment building just off Lawrence Avenue in Scarborough. It wasn't a bad job. The only heavy work was moving around the dumpsters, and that's when he felt it the most, that sharp jabbing around his heart. He lit up a cigarette as he thought about it, and it was then that he heard the woman's screams, just outside his apartment, late that night.

Cosantino jumped from his chair, butted out his cigarette, and ran out of the building in his stocking feet to where the woman was screaming. There she was, in the flower garden near the building, lying on her side, with her hands up over her head in a defensive position. Straddling her was a man with a rock in his hands, who looked as if he was about to club her head. Cosantino got just the briefest look at the man when he turned his way: in his early twenties, with wavy, dirty blond hair to the shoulders, and a smooth complexion, almost angelic. A choirboy, that's what Cosantino thought in that instant. What in hell was a choirboy doing beating up a woman with a rock?

"Stop that, you son-of-a-bitch!" Cosantino yelled, but the man had already put down the rock and had turned to go. Cosantino kept running toward him. Was it possible, he thought, that he had just foiled an attack by the Scarborough Rapist? There had now been six assaults, and five had been in the area near his apartment building. One of the attacks had been near Markham Road, just several streets over. "Come back here, you bastard!" Cosantino yelled at the man, who by now had quickened his pace.

Cosantino knew no one had ever got a good look at the Scarborough Rapist's face. The bastard isn't going to get away, not this time, not from me, he thought. He had been a hunter most of his life, but he had just given away his collection of rifles because his wife said he was too old to go traipsing through the bushes trying to kill Bambi. If only he had his rifle... A creep like this one didn't deserve to live.

Cosantino picked up his pace. If only he could get close enough for another look at the face. The man had not turned to him again and all he could see was the back of his head. It wasn't enough.

But Cosantino wanted to do more than just get a better look. Bad ticker or not, he wanted to catch him. The reward had nothing to do with it. A monster like that should be locked up. The man in front of him was at full stretch now, and Cosantino wasn't far behind.

Variety, that's what he liked about this case, thought Eddie Grogan. No longer was he watching bus stops south of Lawrence Avenue. He had been moved farther west and north, away from the lake, the same direction the rapist seemed to be taking.

Watching a stop on Markham Road, one night he thought he had hit paydirt. A young man with dirty blond hair had been hanging around the bus stop for what seemed like an hour. Grogan had been ready to call it in when the bus arrived and a woman got off and walked straight over to the man: a worried boyfriend, that was all. The Scarborough Rapist had done that to the city: changed the way people lived. Fewer women seemed to be going out at night these days.

One thing for sure, thought Grogan, they better catch the guy before my health is totally shot. Every night he was on stakeout all he did was eat junk food: bags of chips, chocolate bars, pop, and far too much coffee. He was starting into his second bag of chips when the call came over the two-way radio.

It was a "hot shot," meaning a serious occurrence still in progress. A woman had been attacked just north of Lawrence Avenue. She had managed to get away and call for help. The suspect was being pursued by a neighbor and the dispatcher asked the closest scout cars to respond.

Grogan was maybe four minutes away. A chill of excitement ran through his body. Was it possible it was their boy? He had always known they would need a lucky break to crack the case.

Two scout cars were already on the street just north of Lawrence when Eddie Grogan pulled up. Then another cruiser came roaring around the corner behind him and there were more sirens in the distance. All along the street people were gathered in small groups, many in their nightclothes.

Grogan walked over to where one of the officers was interviewing a woman by an apartment building. She was just getting the beginning of a real good shiner around one eye, Grogan noticed. He also spotted one of the detectives from his squad. "Did we get the pinch?" Grogan asked. The officer shook his head. "Was it our boy for sure?"

"Probably. Maybe. Who knows?" The detective nodded toward the woman. "She didn't really get a good look at his face. She was lucky, though. Neighbor came out just in time. She might have got brained with a rock. The big fella there's a hero." The detective was pointing at a heavy-set man in stocking feet. Joe Cosantino was bent over, puffing from exhaustion, one hand against a tree for support. He had a cigarette in the other hand.

"Sure," said Grogan. "But did he get a look at the face?"

"Not really. Just our luck. First time someone gets close to that bastard, and he's got a bad heart."

"A hero with a bad heart," Grogan commiserated, turning to leave. "We needed a sprinter, and we got a shotputter."

"Hey," the detective called after him. "Where do you think you're going?"

"Back to my bus stop."

"Nice try, Eddie." The detective pointed to a nearby wooded ravine. "We need some help searching. That's where he was last seen."

The woman who walked into the Scarborough police station that day was nervous. At the front desk the duty sergeant was glancing through a report.

"I'd like to make a complaint," she said to him.

"About?"

"There's this man, and he's bothering me." She was a blonde, about 18. Her red fingernails matched the color of her earrings. Weren't all good-looking blondes, the sergeant thought, bothered by men? "I want him to stop."

"And what has he done to you?"

"Well, nothing. I guess. But he's written me this nasty letter." She showed it to the sergeant. "He's threatening me in it."

The sergeant read the letter. Then he read it again. He gave the young woman a quizzical stare. "There's no threats in here," he said finally. "He sounds lovesick. Is he a boyfriend?"

"That's just it. I don't know him. I mean, I only just met him through some friends. I've never gone out with him. I don't even like him. But he keeps calling me to go out. I think he was even following me around."

"Do you know that for sure, that he was following you?"

"Well . . . I think it was him I saw. And here." — she pointed to a line.— "here he says we should go out because it would be best for me. Isn't that a threat?"

The sergeant looked at the letter again. "Maybe," he ventured. To him it was just a minor squabble between a young couple. When the woman said she didn't know the guy, was she telling the whole truth? "What do you propose we do? Should we bring him in for a little chat?"

"I don't know. I just don't want him bothering me anymore."

"I'll have somebody look into it," the sergeant said, reaching for a sheet of paper. Last time he checked, being in love wasn't a crime. "This fellow, what's his name?"

"Paul Bernardo."

The sergeant took down the particulars, promised her again that the police would look into it, then stapled the letter to the report and put both away in a drawer at the front desk.

About a week after that the sergeant was rummaging through the drawers at the front desk. Had anybody in the station seen that report he had made out on the complaint by the blond-haired woman? The question drew several shrugs. Was it important? he was asked.

He thought for a moment. "Guess not," he replied. "She never came back. They probably settled it between themselves."

When Bernardo found out later, through a friend, that the woman had complained to the police, he stopped sending her letters and never spoke to her again.

Bernardo was astounded when Homolka told him of her changed plans for the future. She was graduating that year, 1989, and she now wanted to go to the University of Toronto to study criminology. "I eventually want to become a police officer," she said. All her life, she had been fascinated with crime, from her early childhood reading of the *Hardy Boys* and *Nancy Drew* to her teenage years when she read nothing but crime novels by Lawrence Saunders, Elmore Leonard, Mickey Spillane, and others.

Bernardo was adamantly opposed. "That's too dangerous a job," he said. "I'd worry all the time that my wife would get killed."

Eventually he convinced her that it was not a good idea for her to become a cop. To show his true love, Bernardo bought her a pre-engagement, or promise, ring. For days she went around showing it off to her friends. Soon she forgot about university, reverting to her plans to get married and start a family.

It was early in 1989 that Bernardo decided that he

needed a new vehicle, one that befitted a young accountant who was soon going to be a millionaire. He sold his white Capri and leased a brand-new gold Nissan 240SX, license plate 660 HFH, and equipped it with a cellular phone. He got a standard transmission, even though he knew Homolka could drive only an automatic. If she had to go anywhere, he was going to take her there. At that stage in their relationship, his control over her was almost absolute. He virtually dictated what she wore, who she saw, and what they did. For her part, she seemed happy to have such a strong man guiding her life. Her turn, she told friends, would come when they got a house: that was where women were truly in control.

All through that year her notes to him continued: "It's true, I love you more now than I ever did." "You're the smartest, sweetest, cuddliest boy in the world." "I love you. I love you. I love you." As always, some of the cards were quite racey: "Dear Paul, you are cordially invited to fuck the shit out of me. Go for it. Love, Kar."

He began to write her a few notes of his own. "Karla," read one, "every time I think of you I get a lump in my throat, not to mention other places. Paul." And "I'm your Big Bad Businessman. On your knees, bitch."

That summer, Homolka's mother finally confronted her over something that had long been troubling her: had her daughter and Bernardo been sleeping together? It was upsetting, she told Karla, to think her daughter had violated her trust. Homolka denied that she and Bernardo were having sex. Her mother didn't believe it, and for a week the two barely spoke. Homolka's inability to confide in her mother would later prove disastrous.

Patti had always considered Bernardo a friend. She could tell that he liked her, but although she was slightly attracted to him, she just didn't see a relationship working out. She already had a boyfriend and she knew that he had a girlfriend, someone from St. Catharines named Karla. Indeed, from what she had heard around the office Bernardo probably had several others as well. That wasn't surprising: he was good-looking and easy to talk with. But there was something about Bernardo that made her feel queasy.

It was the way he kept staring at her. And then there was that time when she had spotted him on her street late one night, watching her house. It gave her the creeps to think he was spying on her, but she had never mentioned it to him. She didn't want to cause trouble for him at the Scarborough office. They might have fired him, and she didn't want that because he seemed such a nice guy, maybe just a bit oversexed.

One of the men in the office had told her how Bernardo was always bragging about his sexual exploits, the weird, kinky sex he was having with the girls he dated. She found that kind of locker-room talk disgusting — nor did she want her intimate life the topic of conversation around the office coffee machine. Already other workers were assuming the two had a relationship because he had driven her home a few times after work. That wasn't true. They were just friends. Strictly platonic.

Today he had asked her if she needed a ride home, but she had said no; she was going out with her boyfriend tonight. He had to work late, and to save time she was going to meet him at the subway station on Lawrence, then go for supper and a movie. Bernardo had seemed disappointed, then offered her a ride to the subway station instead. She knew it was out of his way, but he said he wasn't doing anything tonight anyway.

"Have a good time," he said when they reached the Lawrence subway stop.

That's what she liked about him, he could be considerate and not pushy. She thanked him, watched as he drove off in his Nissan sportscar, went into a restaurant, had a coffee, then later went back out onto Lawrence. She was scanning the street for her boyfriend's car when she spotted the Nissan, Paul Bernardo behind the wheel.

At first she thought nothing of it. Perhaps he was just cruising around Lawrence looking for something to do. She pretended not to see him as he turned into a lot farther up and parked so that his car was facing her. She almost expected him to get out, perhaps go into one of the stores. But he just sat behind the wheel, staring in her direction, watching her. What on earth was he up to?

When her boyfriend, Stan, finally arrived she quickly got into his car. Quiet at first, she later asked him if they were being followed by a man in a Nissan. He checked the rearview mirror. "There is one," he said, "a few cars behind. What's going on?"

"Nothing," Patti replied, wanting to forget about it. "Just thought I recognized someone."

Stan checked again. The Nissan was still there.

"It's him, isn't it," he said. "The guy from work."

"Who?"

"That Bernardo creep. Is he still always watching you?"

"He doesn't do that anymore."

"I think you should go to the police."

"And tell them what? He hasn't done anything wrong."

"At least mention it at work."

"And get him fired for just being a horny guy, like most guys? No thank you."

"If you won't do something, I will." He pulled the car over.

"What are you doing?"

"I'm going to stop Mr. Nissan Man and mash his face into the steering wheel."

She grabbed his arm. "No, Stan," she pleaded. "Forget it. Just forget it."

While she was tugging on his arm, the Nissan roared by. It ran the light at the next intersection and disappeared around a corner.

"I don't think you should ignore it," said Stan.

"If he does it anymore, I'll say something to him."

"Okay. But don't go accepting any more rides from him either."

"I won't."

12
The Darker Half

"You just watch," Insp. Joe Wolfe was saying to reporters in the squad room, "a wife or a girlfriend will be the key to breaking this case."

It was the fall of 1989 and the hunt for the Scarborough Rapist was in its third year. Three years and seven rapes later the police were no closer to catching him. Wolfe, tough, remained optimistic. The police had made a lot of progress, he told a reporter that day.

A special unit, the Sexual Assault Squad, had now been formed to catch the culprit. It had a fancy new office at police headquarters in downtown Toronto. All the thousands of tips pouring into the office were being categorized in the HOLMES computer program they had imported from Britain that had proved its worth in the capture of Peter Sutcliffe. Someday something might match up.

Then the "fink money" had been increased to $150,000. That staggering amount of cash was bound to loosen a few tongues: it was the third-highest reward ever offered in the history of Metropolitan Toronto.

And even though they didn't know what their man looked like, the police had a pretty fair idea of how he thought. And that's why a wife or a girlfriend might be the key to the case. Eventually, Wolfe said, he might brag to them, even take them to the place where he had raped one of his victims, or perhaps abuse them so badly they would go to the police. Meanwhile, the detectives would keep on checking out tips and interviewing suspects.

Eddie Grogan got brain cramps when he thought about it. Grogan had followed his boss when he moved from Scarborough to the special unit's new office at headquarters. He was beginning to regret it. The pressure to catch the Scarborough Rapist had been intense, the progress minimal.

For months Grogan had been part of the team trailing a man they were convinced was the rapist. He looked like the culprit. Same height, hair, age. The police had become suspicious of him after he had been given a parking ticket on a street not far from one of the rapes. After a time, investigators facetiously started to call him the "Million Dollar Man" because that's how much it seemed they had spent following him around. The Million Dollar man was a bouncer in a bar in Scarborough. After a while it became pretty clear to all the undercover officers that he had about a dozen girlfriends; as soon as he hopped out of one of their beds, he was off into another the next night. Why would such a man want to go around raping? Eventually, they hauled him into the station to find out.

The bouncer was genuinely shocked at their accusations. He had a record, but it was for non-violent crime, burglary, car theft. "Maybe I'm a crook, but I would never go around hiding in bushes and doing *that* to women."

Would he mind, then, taking a lie-detector test and giving the officers some fluid samples? Anything, he said, if it would help convince them they had the wrong man. They let him go and, not surprisingly, the tests came back negative. And so it was back sifting around for fresh suspects.

Although Grogan was skeptical the computer would ever spit out their rapist, he had to agree with Wolfe that if their man was as good looking as they had been led to believe, then he probably had a girlfriend, maybe was even married. And it had to be just a matter of time before the woman realized what kind of man she was living with. They were certainly dangling enough cash out there to tempt her to talk. But here's what Grogan didn't understand. Three years had passed since the first rape. *What in hell was taking her so long?*

That evening in 1989 was supposed to be a special one for Homolka. For weeks she had been looking forward to her high-school graduation party aboard the *Garden City*, a boat moored at Port Dalhousie. It was one last chance for her to show off her boyfriend before everyone from Winston Churchill went their own ways, either to university or into the working world. It had started so romantically, the two of them sneaking away from the party, leaning over the railing of the boat, and gazing into the distance at the lights of Port Dalhousie as the *Garden City* slowly made its way along the waterfront.

If Homolka could have her choice of a place to live in St. Catharines, it would be Port Dalhousie. She was pleased Paul felt the same way, and they often drove through Dalhousie, looking at property and imagining how wonderful it would be to raise a family in the community by the lake. But homes there were so expensive. How could they afford it?

"I've got some business ideas in mind," Bernardo said, but never elaborated.

They had been talking about maybe getting engaged soon. He wasn't proposing, but Bernardo told her it would be wonderful if they settled down and had children while he set up his business. He could do his accounting from their new home. He didn't want to work any longer for Price Waterhouse. He didn't like the long hours. He wanted his evenings free, so he could spend more time with her. There were plenty of opportunities for a freelance accountant in St. Catharines, he said, especially at income-tax time.

Homolka thought it was time to mention something she had been worried about: his spending habits, the way he was always treating everybody. Now that they were a couple, he had to start thinking about *their* future and not always pay for everybody when they went out. One supper with friends had been particularly extravagant. The bill had been nearly $500. No one had been expecting him to pay, but he had picked up the tab, *and* left a $100 tip.

Often he did a little trick with his wallet that always got laughs. At first she too had thought it funny. But not anymore. He would hold his wallet upside down and let all the plastic envelopes come flopping down like dominoes, each one holding a charge card. It seemed like 30 pieces of plastic.

"Don't worry so much," he told her. "When one card gets filled up, I'll just use another."

She didn't understand that logic, but found it hard to get mad at him. And especially not tonight. They went back inside to join some friends she wanted to chat with. She hadn't been avoiding them; just spending the evening with Paul.

She said hello to one group by the bar. She had dated one of the boys standing there, but long before she had met Paul. Bernardo watched her from the other side of the main dining room. She was laughing with her friends and maybe, from a distance, it might have seemed she was flirting too much. But why shouldn't she talk to other men? He was always making eyes at other women. She knew how jealous he got, but she had always liked the way he was so possessive. This time, though, there was a look on his face she had never seen before. More than just annoyance, it was anger, almost hatred.

Although she sensed his hostility, she didn't feel like ending the conversation with her friends. She was finishing high school, moving on, and it was her night to say good-bye. He was scowling as he walked toward her and the group of boys she was chatting with.

"Are you trying to hustle my girl?" he asked one of them, a teen about his size with a brushcut.

"No, Paul, we —" Homolka tried to interrupt, but he pushed her aside.

"You've been hitting on her all night."

Homolka's friend was confused. He didn't know what to say, so he shrugged, and tried to explain they had just been talking. But Bernardo wasn't placated. He asked again, there was some shoving, and then the fight started. Other than Homolka, Bernardo didn't know anybody on the boat. He was the outsider, a guest at their function, an older man, 25, who was trying to wreck their night. Nobody was taking his side in the dispute.

In no time, Bernardo was surrounded by half a dozen or more of the boys at the party. Some were from the football team, but it didn't matter to Bernardo that they were bigger. He knew how to fight; he had taken courses in self-defense. He threw some quick punches, knocking one or two of them down.

"C'mon. C'mon," he challenged the others.

There was a mocking leer on his face as he bounced around on the balls of his feet like a boxer, his fists clenched in front of his face. All evening he had been so friendly with everyone, buying drinks, smiling. Despite being badly outnumbered, Bernardo now was dishing out as much as he was receiving. The brushcut teen nailed him in the nose with a punch, but that just seemed to excite him more. In the midst of an ugly brawl, Bernardo was the only one with a smile on his face.

Homolka jumped between the combatants, screaming at everyone to stop, swinging her purse wildly at anyone who got near her boyfriend. And then, as quickly as it had started, the melee was over, broken up by other classmates and the boat crew. A police cruiser was waiting for them when the boat docked.

"I want you to charge them," Bernardo demanded of one of the police officers, pointing to several of the boys he had been fighting with.

"We'll do the investigating here," the officer replied, and started taking names and statements. After talking to everyone, the police officers decided not to lay any charges, sending people on their way with a lecture.

It was well after midnight when Bernardo and Homolka got back to her house. All the way home Bernardo complained about how the officers had handled the investigation. It seemed to him that the Niagara Region cops had been playing favorites, sticking up for the "hometown boys."

With each passing day, Homolka was seeing more and more of the "other Bernardo," a man who could be kind and considerate one moment, abusive, mean, and even vicious the next. His anger seemed to be percolating just beneath his smiling exterior. He wanted to know what she was doing all the time. Once he couldn't get her on the telephone because she had accidentally knocked off the receiver. "You're such a fucking idiot, Kar," he said when he finally got through. She tried to explain that someone else had knocked off the receiver, but he didn't care. She vowed in a letter to a friend that the relationship was finished.

"Paul can get mad at me for fucking ridiculous reasons," she wrote, explaining the phone incident. "He called me a fucking idiot. Who the fuck does he think he is? He yelled at me and hung up — the asshole! He said he wasn't going to call me ever again. Well bo-fuckin-bo. I'm not going to call him again either."

But shortly afterwards Bernardo apologized, claiming that he had been working too hard taking night school courses for his accounting degree. He took her out for dinner and was contrite. As she wrote to a friend, "He was so sweet and romantic, saying how much he loved me and how he wanted to get married." He was upset, though, that she had told a friend about their argument. "You shouldn't be airing our dirty laundry with your friends," he said. "If we have an argument and you tell your friends, they'll always hold that against me." And then he made what she later recalled as a telling statement, though she never realized it at the time. He said he didn't want her friends to know the true state of their relationship because that was something between just him and her.

She followed up his apology with a flurry of notes. She had just got a job at a veterinary clinic in Thorold, south of St. Catharines, but instead of trying to impress her new boss with her good work habits, she often spent time writing Bernardo love letters.

"Hi sweetheart," read one. "Just a little note to tell you how much I love you. I love you tons honey bunny. Come and see me soon." Next to a picture of a puppy on the inside of the card she wrote: "He's just like the dog I am — the fucking dog."

In the two years they had known each other, a definite pattern had emerged. He was clearly the aggressor, and kept pushing her to new limits sexually, at the same time as he abused her verbally. She found the sex exciting, and seemed willing to become his doormat, without challenging the abuse. What this conveyed to Bernardo was that she was placing no restrictions on his actions.

"It has been two wondrous years," she wrote on the second anniversary of their meeting. "On that night a little girl met and fell in love with the man of her dreams. Their eyes met and they were driven to each other. The spark of love they felt that first night burst forward into a flame that will be an everlasting glow in their lives."

Less than two months later they became engaged at Niagara Falls. Homolka was so proud that she entered a contest sponsored by the *Toronto Star* that called on readers to describe the most romantic moment in their lives. In her entry she wrote:

"Paul took me to Niagara Falls, and we walked hand-in-hand, gazing out at the red and green lights bating the falls. There were other couples out strolling, but when we were alone Paul pulled out a small box. He whispered words of love in my ear. It was a music box, and it played the Impossible Dream. And then with a shaky voice, he asked me to marry him. I threw my arms around him and cried tears of joy. Every night I wind up the music box, gaze at the ring, gaze at the photograph of the most wonderful man in the world and remember the most romantic moment of my life."

Homolka's entry didn't win the contest.

As 1990 drew on, Homolka started planning for her wedding: she would be a traditional June bride. It would be a huge wedding, and Homolka didn't care how expensive it was.

"My life is going great," she wrote to a friend. "Paul and I are happier than ever. We're spending our time planning our wedding, and everything is going well. The dinner is going to be $45 a plate. I'm glad I don't have to pay for it. My mom and I have already been out looking for wedding dresses. It was great. Paul was really enthused. He's being so great, so romantic, but that's typical of my honey."

But her honey was getting bored with their sex life. She had become as proficient as any streetwalker at giving fellatio, and anilingus was the latest act in their sexual repertoire. But this was all just between the two of them, and Bernardo had started dropping hints early that year that he wanted to go further afield.

"It's okay," he said to her one night, "for a man to have more than one woman." If he went away on a trip, for instance, and had a fling, that would be all right. Homolka, fresh from looking at wedding dresses, was opposed to any such idea. "No way," she told him. "If you do that then I'm out of the relationship." He kept pushing her and pushing her.

Bernardo tempered his comments somewhat. What if the second woman joined them in a threesome? Homolka wasn't ready for that. So what if when they had sex she pretended to be someone else? Homolka wanted to know whom he had in mind.

Your sister, he replied. Tammy Lyn.

It was after midnight one Saturday in May and the woman had a decision to make. She could wait there, on Sheppard Avenue, for the Midland Avenue bus that would take her the seven city blocks to her friend's house. Or she could walk.

She would be safe waiting by the bus stop on Sheppard. Even at that time of night, the six-lane road was busy with traffic. But as she looked north up Midland, she also felt it would be fairly safe to walk. She had a transfer for the Midland bus, but it might be a long wait. It had been nearly nine months since the last of the seven attacks by the Scarborough Rapist. There hadn't even been much in the paper lately about him. Had he moved on? Quit? Most of the attacks had been in the eastern end of the city, around Lawrence, well south of where she was. There had been only one attack off Sheppard, a few blocks to the west. But that had been nearly two years ago. She looked around for the Midland bus, didn't see it, and started walking.

That night he had picked Sheppard Avenue to do his trolling. It was his time of night, the time when he got those urges he never could control, never really wanted to control. He had seen her there, by the bus stop, and she was perfect. Late teens. Good looking. Out by herself. Walking up that lonely, deserted street. He couldn't ask for more. As if he had just ordered her up from room service. And it had been such a long time between meals.

It was likely, the police believed, that he drove quickly off Sheppard, parked at the back of a church lot near the corner of Midland, killed the engine. He took the keys from the ignition and hid them under the driver's seat. He couldn't risk them falling out of his pocket while he was having his fun. From under the seat he grabbed his knife with its eight-inch blade in a leather sheath and tucked it into the waistband of his khaki shorts, then got out of the car. He had to hurry. She had a good head start, and she was walking fast.

She didn't know exactly what made her turn around so suddenly. Maybe it was the passing headlights of a car reflecting off a window. Maybe she heard his footsteps. Whatever. She looked back, and that's when she saw him, just a few feet behind.

"Oh, you scared me," she said to the good-looking man with the wavy, dirty blond hair to the shoulders. "I didn't think there was anybody else out."

He appeared to be just as startled as her. He was casually dressed in shorts, sneakers with no socks, and a blue windbreaker. Although she was alone with him on a desolate street, she wasn't frightened. He had such delicate features, a smooth, sweet face, high cheekbones, and bright, blue eyes. Not at all what you'd expect a sadistic rapist to look like.

"It's a nice night, isn't it?" he commented, glancing along the street. "You live around here?"

"Just going to a friend's house," she said.

He had to think fast. She had seen him, talked to him. It was a mistake he had never made before. Until now he had a perfect record. None of the others had seen his face. But she had turned and looked into his eyes just as he was about to make his move, and now he ran the risk of being identified. He had eluded the police for three years. This time it would be safest, of course, to leave her alone, just keep on walking, look for another victim. But there were urges he couldn't control. Making an instantaneous decision, he grabbed her and forced her into a nearby schoolground.

Later the woman would tell police what he had said, the signature remarks so reminiscent of the previous seven attacks. "What's your name?" "How old are you?" "Tell me you love me." "Arch your back." As in the other rapes, he used the ligature, drawing it tight around her neck. He forced her to turn her head to the side, as if he had to see her face while he took his pleasure. She was afraid he was going to kill her, but when he was finished, he disappeared into the night.

"Hi, Tam," Bernardo said.

He was lying on the bed in his fiancée's bedroom, smiling at the person who had just walked in. Everyone else in the Homolka household had gone to bed.

"Hi, Paul," Karla replied.

Homolka had on a new outfit, a short black skirt and white blouse — clothes that belonged to Tammy Lyn. She climbed onto the bed, pulled off Bernardo's clothes and began to perform fellatio. Every so often she stopped to look up at him. There was some scripted dialogue he wanted to hear.

"I'm your 15-year-old virgin. I love you."

"I love you too, Tam," he replied.

"You're the best, Paul. You're the master. You're the king."

"And what else?"

"I love Snuffles."

"And what do you want to do to Snuffles?"

"I want to suck him. I want him to come in my mouth. I want to swallow every drop."

"And who do you love, Tam?"

"I love you, Paul."

"And what do you want to do, Tam?"

"I want to marry you."

For a while in the summer of 1990, Homolka's role playing satisfied Bernardo. To help in their little game, he stared at one of Tammy Lyn's photographs during fellatio. But soon it wasn't enough. Bernardo now wanted them to have sex in Tammy's bedroom. As always, Homolka went along.

And then came something even more bizarre. Bernardo started going into Tammy's room on his own, masturbating on her pillow while staring at one of her photos. Then late one night, as he later told Homolka, he sneaked into Tammy's room while she was sleeping and stood over her at the side of the bed, rubbing his crotch. He unzipped his pants and he masturbated, ejaculating on the pillow beside her head. She never awakened.

That summer the number of love cards Homolka gave Bernardo dropped off considerably. Earlier she had been mailing him one nearly every day. Now she sent him only about half a dozen a month. But they still showed the deep affection she had for him, along with the scripted words he liked to hear. "Dear Paul," read one. "How are you? I can't describe how deeply and intensely I love you. You better come to see me this weekend. We have to snuggle and give hugs and kisses all weekend. It's the rule. Signed, your furry little creature. Your princess. Your cunt, slut, asslicker, and cocksucker. And most of all, the little girl who loves you so madly."

To her friends, Homolka continued to rave about her fiancé. "Paul is just great," she wrote in one letter. "Our relationship gets better every day. He'll make the perfect husband. I can't wait 'til it's official."

That summer, while Bernardo went on unemployment insurance, she was hired at the Martindale Animal Clinic in St. Catharines as a technician's helper at a salary of $8.25 an hour. Her duties included working on the reception desk and feeding the animals and cleaning their cages. She also had to prepare the animals for surgery and was training to anesthetize them with an ether-like substance known as halothane, and keep track of the drugs used at the clinic.

One day when they were at the Pen Centre shopping mall, Bernardo went into an appliance store for an item he had wanted to buy for a long time. He walked over to the camcorder section.

"We'll need one for our wedding," he told Homolka, "and for other memories."

13
The Short List

Eddie Grogan was at home that Sunday changing the diapers on his baby girl when he got the call from a detective on the squad. Grogan had had enough of the Scarborough Rapist and put in for his transfer. Three years on an investigation was long enough. But the detective who called him had great news about the case.

"We finally got his face," he said, briefing Grogan about the attack the night before off Sheppard Avenue.

"Yes!" Grogan shouted, punching a fist in the air, surprising himself with his exuberance.

The detective said every available body was needed for the next while, including Grogan, even though his transfer request had been approved. Metro police artist Bette Clarke was putting together a sketch for release to the media, and they were expecting a flood of calls from the public.

"Is the sketch that good?"

"One of the best I've ever seen. It almost looks," the detective added, knowing this was a sore point with Grogan, "like that guy from the Mississauga attack."

Grogan was still sure the Mississauga rapist was the same man they had been hunting in Scarborough. But the composite from Mississauga had never received wide circulation in Scarborough. Grogan's bosses were never convinced it was the same man.

When a Toronto newspaper ran a story wondering if there was a connection, Metro police took pains to say they didn't believe the attacks in the two cities were related. But, apparently, the police may have been wrong. Three years later Bernardo was charged with rape in the attack in Mississauga.

Certainly Clarke's sketch and the one released earlier in Mississauga looked eerily similar. The Metro police could have had a composite sketch a lot sooner, perhaps two years sooner, had they only turned to their colleagues in the neighboring force for help. It was, perhaps, an understandable oversight, one of those things that happens from time to time in police work. But it was a harbinger of what was to come for beleaguered investigators.

"What'd I tell you?" Stan said to Patti as he held up the front page of the tabloid paper with the color sketch of the man police were calling the Scarborough Rapist. "I knew there was something weird about that Bernardo guy. It's gotta be him. Just look. Look!"

The story described the man as the "boy next door" type: clean shaven, blue eyes, fair complexion, feathered hair.

"You gotta call the police," he insisted.

Patti acknowledged that some people around the office had been teasing Bernardo about the composite sketch that was in all the papers, on television, on billboards, at bus stops. Just about everywhere you looked there was that face, as if he was a movie star, not a rapist.

Bernardo had recently changed his hair style, Patti said. He now had a feathered cut, as in the composite sketch. But he had laughed about the comparison, she said. And it just didn't seem possible.

"If you won't call the police, then I will," Stan said. "I never liked that son-of-a-bitch."

"No, Stan," she pleaded. "I have to work with him."

Renya Hill kept staring at the newsbox as she approached it on her way to the grocery store. There was a huge sketch on the front page of the Toronto tabloid. That face, she thought, dropping in some change and taking out a paper, looked awfully like Karla's boyfriend.

She read the story. The police said the man they were seeking was between 18 and 22. He was six feet tall, with a good build, and clean shaven. That was certainly Paul, but wasn't he a lot older? What had Karla said, 25? Anyhow, it couldn't be Paul. He was a really nice guy.

The teller at the Canadian Imperial Bank of Commerce was on her lunch break when someone handed her a copy of the newspaper. She had seen that face before, she was almost positive. What was his name again? It was on the tip of her tongue. He had just been at the bank the other day. He was so polite, friendly.

She went back to work early, asked one of the other tellers if she remembered the name of the good-looking young man who always had a nice smile on his face.

"Paul Bernardo, isn't that who you're thinking about?"

Yes, that was it. Should she call the police? It really didn't seem possible such a sweet-looking kid could be such a maniac.

Bernardo didn't speak much to the other "bankrupts" at the round-table meeting that afternoon in uptown Toronto in 1990. He had spent thousands of dollars on his charge cards, always buying meals and drinks for his friends. Finally, hopelessly in debt to credit-card companies, airlines for trips to Florida, gas companies, and department stores, he had declared bankruptcy, listing as his only asset his cellular phone.

None of the other bankrupts gathered at the government office said as much, but it was clear that several were thinking it shouldn't have happened to him: he was a trainee accountant, and accountants are supposed to know how to handle money. The seminar was a meeting to share tips on how to avoid getting so badly in debt again. Everyone had to discuss their problems. When it was his turn, Paul Bernardo, who owed his creditors some $25,000, confessed, "Charge cards have been my undoing." In his brief speech Bernardo said he had been overly generous with his friends.

"Were you hoping too much to win their affection?" a woman ventured.

"Maybe," he replied.

After the meeting broke up, one of the women in his group followed him onto the elevator, and stood at the back of the car to get a better look at his face. She couldn't be sure, but the quiet young man looked a lot like the composite sketch of the Scarborough Rapist. Almost on a whim, she looked around for a police car as they walked from the building. She didn't see one, and when she turned back, the young man had disappeared into the evening rush-hour crowd.

During the summer of 1990, Bernardo's fascination with Tammy continued. Every time he and Homolka had sex, he wanted her to pretend that she was her baby sister. Homolka saw no harm in that. But Bernardo had started flirting with Tammy as well. The two of them often drove Tammy to her soccer games, and Bernardo videotaped her there, joking with her about how she was a good athlete while her big sister was so clumsy. Homolka was almost jealous over the attention her fiancé was paying to Tammy.

Once that summer Bernardo and Tammy went on a trip across the border to buy some liquor. They were supposed to be gone only for an hour, but on the way back they parked in a secluded lot and began petting. When they finally got back Homolka was furious because she thought they had been in an accident. Bernardo told her they had just gone driving. Later Homolka confronted him about what had really happened. Homolka may have been the submissive partner, but there were times when she showed her teeth. She accused Bernardo of "fooling around" with her sister. He denied it at first, but later admitted he and Tammy had indeed been necking. Really jealous now, Homolka lashed out. At one point she said about Tammy, "She's a virgin. She wouldn't know what to do with Snuffles."

What Homolka had done was to give Bernardo an opening. He had been waiting for the right time and now he made his pitch.

"Maybe I should have sex with Tam and teach her the proper way," he said. "Wouldn't it be great if Tam got to feel Snuffles inside of her? Wouldn't it be great if I took her virginity?"

Homolka refused to consider the idea. She was afraid of her parents' fury if they ever found out. It would be the end of her marriage plans. But rather than just being repulsed and perhaps breaking off her engagement, Homolka weighed the suggestion in terms of what would happen to her. Her response was an example of what psychiatrists would later call her "moral vacuity." Though highly intelligent, she seemed to lack the personality skills necessary to make moral judgments, even one involving her younger sister.

Although she refused, Bernardo persisted, and their relationship became strained. That July was the first month in nearly three years together that she didn't send him a single love card. Bernardo began to use what was later described as emotional blackmail: "If you were a good enough girlfriend, I wouldn't need Tammy."

They began to argue more, and one night fought about which movie they were going to see that weekend. Bernardo punched Homolka on the shoulder, and for the first time she hit him back, on his arm. Bernardo left in a fury, vowing never to return. She chased after him, catching up to him just as he was stepping into his car.

"I'm sorry," she said, "I didn't mean to hit you."

He motioned for her to get in, and they went out driv-ing. They passed the deserted parking lot of a factory, and Bernardo turned in and stopped the car.

"Get out," he ordered, even though it was raining, pushing her to show he meant it. He followed her out. "So you think you can hit me, eh?" Then he started kicking her, knock-ing her to the ground in the worst beating she had ever received from him. She fell into a puddle, covering her white jeans in mud. He kept kicking her until she apologized. All the way home, she kept apologizing. He told her to sneak into the house, and not let her parents see the mess on her pants.

"This is just between me and you," he warned. "If your parents find out that we fought, they'll never talk to me again."

He drove back to Scarborough, but returned the fol-lowing day, with more demands that he wanted to have sex with Tammy Lyn. His plan was to drug her unconscious and he promised to use a condom. He insisted he wanted to have sex with her only the one time. "It'll be all over in five minutes." If Homolka agree to go along with him, it would make up for all the times she had disappointed him with her behavior.

Bernardo had been secretly experimenting with sedatives that summer on some of Tammy's friends when they came by for a swim. He had ground up Valium and laced their drinks with various amounts, gauging how long it took to make them drowsy. But he stopped his research when one of

Tammy's friends noticed some white powder in her glass and complained that the drink tasted bitter. To drug Tammy they would have to try another type of sedative, he told Homolka, as if she had already agreed to the scheme.

He told her that if she didn't go along with his plans he was going to secretly videotape Tammy while she undressed. And that's what he did one night, standing on the fence, while Tammy got ready for bed. Bernardo had jimmied the blinds in her room so that she couldn't close them all the way.

All that fall, and into the winter months, Bernardo kept pressuring Homolka to go along with his scheme. Homolka kept refusing, but never told anyone else. She kept making plans for her wedding, as if hoping Bernardo would forget about his wild idea. She started sending him love cards again: "To my one and only love, happy three years together. Just think, in eight months I will be ecstatic." "I wuv you Paul. To my one and only Number One Guy in the world. Your snuggly wuggly, honey bunny. Kar."

She kept sending him the cards right up until Christmas.

The man worked in the freezer end of the beer store on Lawrence Avenue, unloading cases from delivery trucks into the storage room, then onto the conveyor belts for the customers. The job involved a lot of heavy lifting, and as Eddie Grogan remarked to his partner as they pulled into the parking lot, strength was a key trait of the rapist.

In the weeks after the release of the composite sketch, Grogan and the other officers on his squad had been sorting through the hundreds of tips phoned in to their office every day, each caller claiming to know the identity of the elusive rapist. Men were being pulled off planes, stopped as they were leaving work, girlfriends were turning in boyfriends, wives ratted on husbands. It seemed every good-looking man with dirty blond hair in Metropolitan Toronto was under suspicion.

More than 16,000 calls were logged by the police that summer after the release of the composite. The force had to lay on extra help just to answer the calls that came in every day — on one day 2,500, a new tipster every 30 seconds. With that much help from the community, the public expected to see some results. An "A List" of suspects had been compiled: more than 500 deemed the best bets for being the rapist. For a short list it was a little on the long side and it would have to be pared down to a workable number, say 30 or 40. There was also a "B List" of men the detectives were less sure about. Grogan was beginning to think they would have to question everyone in Toronto since, despite all the help, they still hadn't zeroed in on that one good suspect.

That's why Grogan wasn't so excited about the beer-store candidate, a blond who strongly resembled the sketch, or so the tipster had claimed. Grogan and his partner identified themselves and the man came out of the cooler. As soon as Grogan saw him, he turned to his partner and snickered.

"Just how tall are you?" he asked the employee.

"Six-foot-seven," the man replied. And in a deep growl: "What's your problem?"

"Nothing," answered Grogan. "You just dump a girl-friend or something?"

"What's it to you?"

"Skip it," said Grogan. "Go back to work."

It was November of 1990 before detectives got around to checking out Bernardo from the list of hundreds of potential suspects in the Scarborough Rapist case. Bernardo was asked if he minded going to the downtown Toronto headquarters of if he minded going to the downtown Toronto headquarters of Metro Police one afternoon for an interview. It was just routine, he was told. Someone thought he looked like the composite sketch, and the police wanted to check it out. The interview would take only a few minutes.

14

The Christmas Present

If there was one thing people said about Paul Bernardo, it was that his face always lit up for everyone. He had, it seemed, the sunniest of dispositions. When he was young, women always wanted to hug the boy with the angelic face. And as an adult, the smile was an integral part of his charm. But as he sat in the Sexual Assault Squad Room, his smile wasn't earning him any points. He was grinning, as always, but there was a distinct lack of humor in the eyes of his two interrogators facing him across the table.

Since the release of the composite sketch that summer, several callers had given the police Bernardo's name: there was the woman teller from the bank; a man claiming to be a friend; someone else who had met him in a bar. Too many tips for the police not to be suspicious.

"You understand that we have to check out these tips," Det. Steve Irwin said.

"Sure, of course," Bernardo replied. "Look, whatever I can do to help. It's not me. I want to clear this up."

"Do you know why you're here?" Irwin continued.

"Because I look like the composite," Bernardo replied earnestly.

The sketch was pinned to the wall. Irwin glanced at it. Irwin was about the same height as Bernardo, around six feet, but he had a sturdier build. And the hooded, penetrating stare of a suspicious cop. "You do look a lot like the sketch."

"I've got a baby face," Bernardo replied, "sort of like that picture. But it's not me."

Irwin then asked for Bernardo's date of birth, the key information the police need when they check the computer to see if a person has a criminal record. Bernardo had none.

They wanted to know where he worked, the car he drove, how long he had lived in Scarborough. One of the earlier attacks was only a few blocks away from his house. Had he seen anything suspicious in his neighborhood? Was he following the case? Did he have a girlfriend?

Bernardo told Irwin about his girlfriend in St. Catharines. He said he spent most of his time with her. They planned to get married. He knew about the case only from the media.

What about an alibi? Irwin asked. Where had he been the night of the last attack? Probably at home with his family, he replied. Or out with his girlfriend.

Had people mentioned to him that his face, hair, eyes, build, and height all bore a striking resemblance to the composite sketch? If there was a discrepancy, it was over age. They wanted a younger man, somewhere between 18 and 22. Bernardo was 25. But he had the smooth, peachy complexion of a teenager, and it was easy to see how the victims could have mistaken his age.

Yes, he said, people had been teasing him all the time about his likeness to the drawing. And that's why he was so anxious to co-operate with the authorities, put everyone's suspicions to rest, clear himself.

Did he mind, Irwin asked, giving them some hair and fluid samples for the crime lab? They had some samples from the victims. If the tests came back negative, he was in the clear.

"No, why would I mind?"

A technician was called in. Bernardo was given a sanitized comb and ran it through his hair several times, collecting some loose strands. Then he was given a test tube, asked to spit into it. A pinprick gave police the drops of blood they needed for the lab. The samples were for DNA analysis, Irwin explained. DNA, or deoxyribonucleic acid, is the genetic material found in human cells. Except for identical twins, everyone's DNA is unique. The DNA taken from a person — from samples of blood, saliva, semen, and hair — is reduced in the lab to a series of lines that look like supermarket bar codes. Bernardo's sample, the detectives told him, would be compared with the DNA samples taken from the rape victims.

What the detectives didn't tell Bernardo was that the DNA samples taken from at least three of the rape victims matched perfectly with each other, which meant the same man had raped all three. All the police had to do was find a sample to match those DNA lines, but checking out each suspect took time. Especially in Toronto in 1991.

DNA analysis, or genetic fingerprinting as it is commonly called, had been pioneered by scientists in Great Britain in 1985. It was being hailed as foolproof. So precise, the geneticists were saying, that the odds of a DNA match in a criminal case being wrong were nearly a billion to one. Aside from establishing guilt, it could also help to clear a suspect if the DNA strands didn't match.

But it had been three years later — 1988 — before law authorities in Canada started using the new technology as an investigative tool in criminal cases. And in the two years since then, only a few crime labs across the country had been set up for DNA testing. Bernardo's sample was analyzed in Toronto at the Centre of Forensic Sciences. But in November 1990, the lab had only one scientist who was qualified to do DNA work. Others were upgrading their skills, but it would take months before they got the proper certification enabling them to testify in court.

Because they were short of qualified technicians, the Toronto crime lab had to put police requests for DNA testing on a priority list. And the cases that got preferential treatment weren't rapes. Top billing went to investigations dealing with murder. Even if the lab were to start working on Bernardo's — or any other rape suspect's — sample that afternoon, it would take a minimum of three months to finish the testing. And with Christmas coming up, it would be March of 1991, at the earliest, before investigators with the Sexual Assault Squad could even think of getting back some results.

The many suspects in the Scarborough Rapist case weren't the squad's only concern, though. They were hunting at least two other serial rapists that year, another prowler in Scarborough and a third who had assaulted six women in the High Park area of Toronto. These and numerous other incidents kept the squad bogged down with work. Bernardo was just one of hundreds of men the detectives were checking out.

Doing a thorough investigation of each man was impractical — there just weren't enough officers — and the squad badly needed the crime lab to narrow down the list. But even though Bernardo was one of hundreds, something about his behavior merited a closer look.

He didn't have a criminal record, so presumably he had never dealt before with the police. Yet he had been so confident with them, his manner bordering on brazen, smarmy. "He talked like a used-car salesman," one of the detectives said. For most people, being grilled by the police for the first time is intimidating. Perhaps for a university graduate with a good job, plenty of friends, a steady girlfriend, and a solid family background it was different. But he also looked so much like the composite. Maybe they should be keeping a closer eye on him.

That evening after his interview with the police, Bernardo made a surprise visit to Homolka's house in St. Catharines. It was a Wednesday, and she wasn't expecting him until his usual visit that weekend. He got there well after dark, but he didn't go inside, rapping instead on the window of her basement bedroom. He had a frightened, worried look on his face, she would later remember.

She opened the window. "What are you doing here, Paul?"

"I gotta talk. Alone. You and me. It's important. Don't tell your parents I'm here."

"Okay." It was unusual for him to keep his visits a secret. Always in the past he had come with gifts, flowers, cartons of pop, or bottles of wine for her family. She joined him outside. "What's going on?"

He didn't answer at first. He drove aimlessly through the streets. She could tell he was extremely upset, but she had no idea about what.

Finally, he said, "I've just been questioned by the police about the Scarborough Rapist case."

"But you didn't do those rapes."

"What if they charge me with it anyways?"

"They won't."

"But what if they decide to arrest me because they can't find anyone else? What if they arrest me just because I look like that picture?" He explained how the police had taken hair, blood, and saliva samples from him, reasoning they would do that only if they had indeed intended to charge him. She tried to calm him down, but he wasn't listening.

"Don't worry," she said. "If you're not the man they want, they won't charge you. The police don't do things like that."

"*But they took my forensics!*" he snapped. "What if they charge me?"

He turned to her when they were stopped at a red light. "What if I am the Scarborough Rapist?" he said, and, for the first time that evening, he smiled.

Like all their friends, Homolka had noticed his similarity to the composite sketch. And she had been out with several friends one evening when they had teased her about it. But it wasn't Paul, she had told them; she was sure he had been with her on the night one of the women was raped.

"Oh, stop," she said now, tapping him on the shoulder.

"Okay, I'm not," he said. And then: "But what if I am?"

"Don't, Paul."

"Maybe I am, maybe I'm not," he continued, trying to be funny, but there was just enough anxiety in his voice to make her remember that evening for a long time afterwards.

One day Bernardo noticed that someone was following him. It was after his interview with the police. They weren't even discreet — as if they didn't care if he saw them. Finally he had had enough. He drove to the nearest police station.

"I've got a complaint," he told the desk sergeant. "I'm being followed around by someone, and I think they're police officers."

"Oh?"

He explained that although he looked like the composite sketch of the Scarborough Rapist, he wasn't the man the police wanted. "I've talked to the detectives, and I've been cleared."

"Is that so?"

He wanted the surveillance to stop immediately or he would file a complaint. The desk sergeant promised he would look into it. He waited until Bernardo left the station, then he checked to see if any officers were free. One was just about to go on the road.

"There was a guy in here who looks a lot like the sketch of the Scarborough Rapist," the desk sergeant said to the officer. "He's just leaving. Tail him for a bit. I got a funny feeling about him."

The officer followed Bernardo as he drove home and, parking farther up the street, watched him as he went inside. A few minutes later, it seemed someone was peering out at him from behind the curtains. The officer watched the house for a while, then left for other duties.

Although Homolka had known Bernardo for three years, there were times when she didn't understand him at all. He had always been so ambitious, yet he had given up his plans to become a chartered accountant, dropping out of the night-school courses he needed for his accreditation. And he had quit his accounting jobs, never happy with any of them. They expected too much of him, and he needed his free time, he told her.

Then there was the money situation, which was always a sore point between them. He had been discharged from his bankruptcy, his outstanding loans had been forgiven, and he didn't have to pay anything back. But rather than being more frugal with his money after the experience, he was tossing his money — and hers! — around more than ever.

She knew that irritated her parents. Over the past three years, the Homolkas had begun to see a different side to the junior accountant from Scarborough. He had always been so friendly, so polite, so considerate and generous. But he could also be a showoff and a braggart. He was only 26, yet he was the one wearing the $150 silk ties, the $1,000 Giorgio Armani suits, the Gucci loafers, and the argyle socks.

Sometimes it was embarrassing the way he made her flaunt her $4,500 diamond engagement ring to her friends while he commented on its price. He kept telling people that he was going to be a millionaire one day, but when anyone asked him how, he referred vaguely to his business ventures. His only enterprise, though, was smuggling cigarettes.

Homolka, however, remained ready to do just about anything for him, even, as it turned out, setting up her baby sister.

"If you really loved me, you would do it," he told her one time. "Now that would be a great Christmas present for me."

"I just can't," Homolka replied. "I just can't."

But finally, after months of denying Bernardo what he made to sound like his right, Homolka changed her mind and agreed. It was a fateful decision that she would regret for the rest of her life. Some psychologists later argued that Homolka was forced into her decision as a victim of what is known as the battered-wife syndrome. Taken in by Bernardo's charm, overwhelmed by his good looks, she had been conditioned by his constant verbal and physical abuse into pleasing him. Other psychologists, however, scoffed at the notion. Most notable among the skeptics was Dr. Nathan Pollock at the University of Toronto. Homolka just didn't fit the usual profile of battered women, he wrote in an evaluation prepared for Bernardo's defense team. They tended to be women in their late thirties who had been married for almost nine years. Most had been physically abused as children.

Homolka fitted none of those categories. She was just 20, still single, and had never been abused as a child. Most battered women who became involved in acts of violence, wrote Pollock, were socially isolated by their abusive parents. At the time of her decision Homolka was living at home with her parents.

All her life she had dreamed of the day when she would live in her pretty house with the white picket fence, and when she finally found the man she believed could give her that, she seemed to close her eyes to everything else, with disastrous consequences.

PART THREE:

LAST BREATH OF LIFE

15

Sleep in Heavenly Peace

It was a yearly tradition in the Homolka household. Every December 11, Dorothy and Karel celebrated their wedding anniversary with a weekend away from the family. And that year, 1990, was even more special. It marked their 25th anniversary. Since the date fell on a Tuesday, they waited until Friday before driving to the American side of Niagara Falls and renting a room at the moderately priced Comfort Inn Hotel. The following night they had four visitors. Bernardo, Karla, Lori, and Tammy had made the short drive from St. Catharines to offer their congratulations.

"Surprise!" Paul Bernardo yelled out as Dorothy opened the hotel-room door to see her future son-in-law with his ever-present camcorder pointed at her face.

"Don't do that," Dorothy said in annoyance, shielding her face. "Put that thing away."

Ignoring her protestations, Bernardo walked right past her and went to the balcony, his camera focusing on the nearby festively lit buildings. In the distance, the mist was rising off the cascades of Niagara Falls.

"Oh, isn't it pretty," Bernardo said. "I love those lights. I just love this time of year."

The three sisters chatted with their parents for a few minutes, while Bernardo stayed on the balcony, his camera panning the Christmas lights, and immediately below him, a playground. Carols were being played on a loudspeaker outside. "Silent Night" could be heard from the balcony.

When Bernardo walked back into the room, Dorothy scowled at him again as he pointed the camera at her and Karel. Bernardo scanned the room with his camera and then stepped into the bathroom, taping the toilet and the shower before waving at himself while he pointed the camera at the mirror.

"Okay, Mr. B.," Karel said to Bernardo as the foursome was leaving, "take good care of my girls."

As they left, the closing lines of "Silent Night" sounded over the loudspeaker: "Sleep in heavenly peace, Sleep in heavenly peace."

Bernardo kept the camera on for the ride down the elevator, filming the sisters as they filed out through the lobby, past the inquiring stares of other guests. The three smiled at Bernardo as he directed them to stand by his Nissan sportscar. The camera lingered on each blond sister for a moment before Bernardo commented, "Three lovely women. Look at those bodies — I mean the bodies of the cars."

And then Bernardo giggled to himself just before he switched off the camera.

Days later, Homolka wrote her lover a note apologizing for her earlier refusal of his request to have sex with her sister. She now agreed to help him. She couldn't bear the thought of losing the best thing that had ever come into her life. Tammy had always flirted with Paul, and Karla felt she probably would have gone to bed with him if asked. Now Homolka decided to let him satisfy his curiosity, "get it out of his system." Then maybe he would forget about it and think more about the two of them.

Bernardo was delighted. He told her to check the pharmaceutical compendium at her animal clinic for the best sedative to use on Tammy. Homolka looked up several before deciding on the sleeping sedative Halcion, which she ordered from the nearby drugstore, telling the pharmacist it was for the clinic. Bernardo wanted backup, to ensure that Tammy Lyn stayed under while he was having his sex. He asked Homolka what the vets used at the clinic to knock out animals before surgery, and she told him halothane, an ether-like substance.

"Steal some," he told her, and she did. Then she waited for him to pick the day.

"We're going to do it tonight," he told her suddenly. It was two days before Christmas, 1990, and they were alone in her room.

She was reluctant.

"We're going to do it, and that's it," he replied, then went for a hammer.

He began crushing some of the pills on her desk with the hammer. But he was making a lot of noise.

"What's going on down there?" Dorothy yelled from the tope of the stairs.

"We can't do it here," Bernardo said.

They drove to the parking lot of a nearby store and finished the job there, crushing the blue sleeping pills into a fine powder. When they returned, the rest of the family was relaxing. Homolka made a round of drinks for everyone, slipping some of the blue powder into the rum and eggnog she made for Tammy Lyn.

It started snowing heavily that evening, clogging many of the city streets, leaving them barren of traffic. Like many of the residents of Garden City, the Homolka family, along with their houseguest, stayed home for the night. After a light supper of macaroni and cheese, some of them drifted down to the basement recreation room to watch TV while they munched on Christmas cakes and cookies. It was warm and cozy in the house that night, while outside the blizzard still raged. Around 8 o'clock Bernardo got out his camcorder.

"Aha!" Bernardo said to his fiancée, filming her ironing in the kitchen. His camera and a finger were pointing to a wrinkle in his shirt that was on her board. "There's lots of wrinkles. Here's another one."

Homolka gave him a patronizing smile and went back to her work.

"You're my little girl," he said. "You do your ironing and you never complain."

Then Bernardo turned his attention toward Dorothy, who was cleaning up around the kitchen. "And here's the elusive Mrs. H. in her kitchen."

She scowled at him, tried to shoo him away.

"How about an extreme close-up, Mrs. H.?" he asked, moving in even closer in the small galley kitchen, and blocking her exit.

"Go on," she said gruffly as she brushed by him.

"There goes Mrs. H. again, running away from the camera," said Bernardo.

"Do it, Mom, do it," her eldest daughter shouted, imploring Dorothy to smile for the camera. "Do it! Do it!"

Her mother glanced back, but wouldn't smile for Bernardo.

He then headed down to the rec room, Karla close behind. Her father was lying on one of the couches after his evening bath, naked except for a towel around his waist.

"And there's Mr. H.," Bernardo said, panning the camera across his body, "lying on the couch with only a towel."

"Get out of here," Karel snapped, trying to wave Bernardo away.

But Bernardo kept the camera on him for a few more moments, before turning to the brick fireplace, beside which stood a Christmas tree, surrounded by presents, then back to Karel. "Extreme close-up. Extreme close-up." It was a line from the comedy skit "Wayne's World" on the TV show *Saturday Night Live* in which characters went around videotaping their friends with the camera close to their faces. But Bernardo's future father-in-law didn't see the humor in what he was doing. Nor did his wife when she walked into the room.

Bernardo then turned the camera on Tammy Lyn, who was seated by herself on another sofa, a drink in one hand. She waved.

"Hi,Tam, how ya doin'?" Bernardo asked.

"There should only be one camera there," Tammy replied, holding up her drink as she leaned forward, weaving slightly.

She was the athlete in the family, one of the city's top female soccer players who also excelled in track and field. She seldom drank, but it was the festive season, and her parents hadn't objected when she had a couple of glasses of rum and eggnog. Tammy smiled at Bernardo, then flopped back against the couch, a glassy look in her eyes as she stared at the camera.

"Are you into the Christmas cheer?" Bernardo asked her.

Still smiling, she held up her glass.

"Are you drinking it up? What are you drinking?"

"It's just ice," she answered, looking at the drink he had made for her.

"One ice baby to go," he said.

Only he and his fiancée knew what was really in the drink: more powdered Halcion that he had slipped into the glass. Bernardo then swung the camera around to the others.

"Le Karla, drinking," he said. "Le Lori, not drinking. Extreme close-up. Extreme close-up."

As if on cue, the two sisters put their arms around each other and shoved their faces toward the camera as each shouted "Whoooaaa . . . whoooaaaa," wide grins on their faces.

"This is Christmas 1990, everybody," Bernardo declared. "We've got the tree, and the presents. We're all having a good time. What we need are some Christmas hugs."

Then he flicked off the camera, and there was a round of hugs. A little later, Lori looked over at her younger sister to see if she was okay. Tammy was groggy, sipping away and giggling to herself.

"Don't give her anything more to drink," Lori said.

Then she went up to her room for the night. The parents said their goodnights not long after.

"You look so tired," Dorothy said to Tammy Lyn. "Why don't you go to sleep? You look like you're about to pass out."

Earlier that day, Tammy had been out shopping with her mother. Tammy had met one of her school friends there and told her how anxious she was to get home that evening. Her big sister and her fiancé wanted her to stay up late, watch a movie, and have a few drinks. Just the three of them. Tammy had been looking forward to it for days, she told her friend. She was the youngest in the family, and staying up late and having drinks with her big sister and her future brother-in-law made her feel older than her 15 years.

"I want to stay up, Mom," she said, "and watch the movie with Paul and Karla."

When the three of them were alone, Bernardo put the film he had rented into the VCR. It was called *Lisa*, and it was about a disturbed young woman who killed her male victims after treating them to candlelight dinners and drinks.

Tammy weaved about on the couch. On the other couch her sister and Bernardo were staring more at her than the television. After sipping at a glass of orange juice that Bernardo had spiked with yet more sedative because he was impatient for her to pass out, Tammy put the glass down, then slumped sideways on the couch.

A few moments later, Bernardo turned to Homolka. "Go poke her and see if she'll wake up."

Homolka did so. When Tammy didn't move, she turned back to Bernardo, as if waiting for him to make the next move. He went over for a closer look.

"She's out," he declared.

Bernardo helped Homolka lay her sister on the floor of the den, next to the Christmas tree. Homolka then got the brown flask of halothane from her room, poured some onto a cloth, and pressed it against her sister's mouth. Bernardo unbuttoned Tammy Lyn's blouse, shoved up her bra, and fondled her breasts while Karla took off her own clothes. He was breathing heavily as he pulled down her blue track pants and her underwear.

He got the camcorder, switched it on, and positioned it on the floor beside him as he took off his pants. Then he spread Tammy's legs and prepared to mount her.

"Put on a condom," Homolka urged him, afraid that her sister would get pregnant.

Bernardo ignored her as he began thrusting his pelvis.

"Paul, hurry up," Homolka now urged, her voice just a whisper, yet sounding desperate.

"Shut up!" he snapped back, a little louder.

"Please hurry up," Homolka pressed. "Before someone comes down."

"Shut up," Bernardo repeated. "Keep her down."

Homolka poured some more halothane onto the cloth. The substance was twice as potent as chloroform, and four times stronger than ether. When administered with a vaporizer in operating rooms, its use is closely regulated. But in the basement den on Dundonald Street that evening, Homolka was slopping the pungent liquid onto a rag and haphazardly pressing it against her sister's face while Bernardo was raping the girl.

Since she worked in an animal clinic, Homolka would have known that the volatile substance could induce nausea and vomiting. It was dangerous to use on someone who had been drinking or eating because that increased the risk of vomiting and the possibility of choking. There was also a warning that came with the pills, cautioning that overuse could induce a coma, or even death. A second warning, printed in bold letters on the side of the package, advised against taking the pills with alcohol. But in the heat of passion that night, none of those dangers were paramount in the minds of the two as Bernardo withdrew.

"Put something on," Homolka implored him as he began intercourse again.

"Shut up, Karla," he snapped.

"Put something on," she pleaded, her voice now louder. "Do it."

"You're getting all worked up."

"Fucking do it. Just do it."

But he didn't put the prophylactic on. The sphincter muscles of Tammy Lyn's anus were relaxed because she was unconscious, so Bernardo didn't have much trouble penetrating. For nearly a minute he pounded away while Homolka looked on. Then he withdrew and turned to the woman he was going to marry.

"Do you love me?"

"Yes," Homolka replied, her unconscious sister lying at her feet.

"Will you blow me?"

"Yes," she replied, but Bernardo wanted her to do other tasks first.

"Suck on her breasts," he ordered.

"I can't," Homolka protested.

"Suck on her breasts. Suck-suck-suck."

Homolka did so. "Hurry up, please," she urged, glancing up at him and the doorway.

"Lick her cunt," he demanded.

Tammy Lyn was having her period, and her sister didn't want to perform oral sex on her.

Bernardo grabbed Homolka by the back of the head and pushed her face down between her sister's legs. "Lick," he ordered. He watched for a moment, still not satisfied. "You're not doing it."

"I am so."

"Do it. Lick her cunt. Lick it. Lick it up clean. Now put your finger inside."

"I don't want to."

"Do it now. Quick, right now. Put three fingers right inside."

"No."

"Put it inside. Inside! Inside!"

Homolka started sobbing, but eventually did what he wanted. After probing inside Tammy's vagina for several moments, Homolka took away her hand. A look of disgust crept over her face as she stared at the forefinger. There was a red smear at the top, some of her sister's menstrual blood. Bernardo turned the camera to her finger.

"Okay, taste it."

She refused.

"Taste it. Inside . . . inside."

"I did. I . . . did!" she cried out, after finally doing what he wanted. But even now he was not satisfied.

"Now do it again, deeper. Inside. Deeper."

Homolka repeated the act, but Bernardo still wasn't satisfied.

"Deeper, deeper," he urged. "Right inside. Okay, taste good? Taste good?"

"Fucking disgusting," she replied.

Bernardo turned off the camera and slugged her in the arm. It was not the response he wanted. She was supposed to say how much she enjoyed it. He picked up the camera, turned it on.

"Taste good?" he asked her again.

But she still wouldn't comply. "No."

Bernardo gave her the camera to hold while he again had vaginal and anal sex with Tammy Lyn. He still hadn't climaxed when he suddenly stopped and withdrew. She put down the camera, turned it off.

"I don't know why," he said, "but I think there's something wrong."

Tammy Lyn's face had turned blue. While Bernardo was anally raping her, her neck had been crimped to the side, probably blocking her air passage and causing her to vomit. Homolka got a makeup mirror from her room and held it under her sister's nose, checking to see if the glass would fog.

"Oh my God!" Homolka shrieked when that didn't happen. "She's not breathing! Tammy's not breathing! Oh my God, I think I just killed my sister!"

Carolyn Homolka was having trouble getting to sleep that night. No matter how many blankets she put on her bed, she still felt cold. She lived with her parents on Georgian Bay, in the region of Ontario known as Muskoka. It was cottage country in the summertime, but desolate when the lakes froze over in the winter. For some reason, she later told an acquaintance, she kept thinking about her cousin Tammy Lyn. The two girls had always been close.

Carolyn was drifting off to sleep when she heard a noise. There was someone near the foot of her bed, coming toward her, calling out for help. The figure came closer, emerging from the shadows. Finally, she saw who was there.

"Tammy," Carolyn called out, jerking upright in her bed.

But her room was empty. As she rubbed the sleep from her eyes, it took Carolyn a few moments to realize that she had just been dreaming.

16

And It Makes Me Wonder

The emergency crews hurrying to Dundonald Street just before 2 o'clock that Christmas Eve morning were responding to a 911 call about a possible sudden death. David Weeks, a rookie constable with the Niagara Region police, was in the home stretch of his 12-hour shift when the dispatcher called. He ended up following an ambulance as it plowed its way through snow-clogged roads. The fire truck arrived just as Weeks and the ambulance pulled up to the semi-detached home. The lanky officer followed the emergency crews in and down to the basement, where they were told a young girl had stopped breathing.

The teenager was lying on her back in a bedroom. The first observations he made, Weeks later recalled, were the gray pallor of her skin and the baseball-sized reddish mark around her mouth. A handsome blond couple were in the small room, and, since they seemed to be in the way, Weeks asked them to leave while the crews tried to revive the child. The couple went upstairs into the kitchen.

"No, no, no, no, no!" Bernardo wailed, as Dorothy, Karel, and Lori came rushing down the stairs. "I should have been able to save her. She can't be gone. She just can't."

Karla threw her arms around her mother's shoulders and cried as her parents, still half asleep, tried to figure out what was happening.

"What's going on, Karla?" Lori asked.

"It's Tammy. She's not breathing."

"Oh my God. What happened?"

Officer Weeks joined the family in the kitchen and told them what he could: the crews were trying to revive Tammy and would soon be taking her to hospital. Now he wanted to know what had happened. Bernardo and Homolka gave their version of the events while he took notes.

The three of them had been in the basement watching a movie, they said, when Tammy Lyn complained about having trouble seeing. They just assumed blurred vision from the drinks and didn't ask her if she was feeling ill. Partway through the movie the two of them fell asleep in each other's arms, they said. They awoke to the sound of Tammy Lyn gagging. Bernardo said he tried to revive her with mouth-to-mouth resuscitation. When that didn't work, they called for help.

Although new to the force — seven months on the job — Weeks already had a policeman's cynicism. He didn't believe he was hearing the complete story. If the three of them had been watching TV in the den, then why, he wondered, was Tammy in the adjoining bedroom suite when the crews arrived? And how did she get that red mark around her mouth? A quick thought came to mind. Had they, he wondered, been freebasing cocaine? Was that how she got burned? Was this a cocaine overdose? Those were questions he would ask them later. For the moment, they were upset, and he wanted to give them a chance to compose themselves.

Tammy Lyn was carried up the stairs on a gurney, and taken out to the ambulance. Though her skin was no longer so gray, Weeks wasn't optimistic about the teenager's chances. But he kept his thoughts to himself, watching and listening as the family clung to the slim hope that she would survive.

Weeks took a closer look at the red mark on the teenager's face as she was taken away. Once a security guard in a housing project in Toronto, he had been to many fires, and the mark reminded him of the soot around the mouth and nose of someone fleeing a burning building.

Dorothy and Karel dressed and followed the ambulance. Weeks went down to the basement to obtain a more detailed statement from the couple. Lori joined them on the couch.

"I want you to know that there was absolutely no drugs involved in this incident," Bernardo abruptly volunteered to the officer.

"I never said there were," Weeks replied, somewhat surprised. "But we'll get to that later." For the moment, he wanted just the basic information — names, ages, what had happened that evening, where everybody was when Tammy was in distress. He was still taking statements when the telephone rang. The hospital was calling for Weeks.

"How is she?" asked Bernardo.

Notification of death is probably the worst part of a police officer's job. There is no easy way to break the bad news to next-of-kin. Weeks wanted to be as compassionate as possible. He shook his head solemnly as he put down the phone. The doctors had been unable to revive Tammy; she had died without regaining consciousness. The reactions of the threesome were instantaneous.

Bernardo's was the most extreme. He banged the back of his head against the wall and screamed "No, no, no!" Then he hugged his knees to his chest and rocked back and forth on the couch. "No! No!" he yelled again, then began pulling at his hair.

The two sisters, though more subdued, were just as distraught. They hugged each other and sobbed quietly.

Weeks kept a respectful distance, waiting until the initial shock had passed. Lori then unexpectedly went to her bedroom to make a phone call. Weeks followed her upstairs, listening at the door while she told a friend her sister had just died. Satisfied she was okay, and there was nothing suspicious, he returned to the basement. But when he got there, Homolka was gone.

"Where is she, Paul?"

Bernardo pointed to another part of the basement. Weeks approached a room at the end of the hall and heard a washing machine. He came upon Homolka just as she was shoving the comforter, which had been on the floor in the den, into the machine. Politely, but firmly, Weeks stopped her. "Everything in the room has to be in the condition it was when we arrived, until the investigation is over. That's just standard procedure."

Homolka didn't try to argue. The officer carried the comforter back into the den, where he resumed the interview. He was curious, he said: why had they moved Tammy from the den to the bedroom?

"The lighting in the rec room was too dark," Bernardo answered. "The light in the bedroom was quite bright. I thought that would be better so we could see what we were doing."

Weeks was not entirely satisfied with that answer, but let it pass for now. Later, on his own, he tested both sets of lights. To him, they seemed to have equal candlepower. But perhaps, since it wasn't Bernardo's house, he may have been unfamiliar with how the lights in the den worked. The bedroom had a simple on/off switch, whereas the den had a dimmer switch. In times of duress, people react differently, sometimes inexplicably. Perhaps that explained the decision to move the girl. At the moment, though, the officer was more concerned about the cause of the mark on Tammy's face.

"How could she have gotten that burn?"

Homolka said nothing. Bernardo had a ready explanation. The mark, he explained, was probably a rug burn, made as he moved Tammy from the den to the bedroom.

Weeks thought about that one. The only explanation for a mark like that, he thought, was if she had been dragged face down from one room to the next. And if that's what happened, it was an odd way for an apparent rescuer to handle a person whose life he was trying to save.

Weeks's occurrence report on the sudden death of Tammy Lyn Homolka contained some troubling questions about the mark on her face, the moving of the body from one room to the next, and the attempted washing of the comforter. Weeks wasn't entirely satisfied with the couple's answers, but his role was restricted to filling out a report, noting any concerns he might have, and turning the case over to senior officers.

That part of the investigation started immediately. Bernardo and Homolka were told they would have to go to the police station to make a formal statement. The couple repeated what they had said to Weeks. In his statement, Bernardo reiterated that he had tried to revive Tammy after waking up and finding her choking. When he was unsuccessful, they had immediately called 911. For now Bernardo wasn't pressed about moving her into the bedroom. Investigators were puzzled, though, by the burn mark.

At one point, the detectives speculated amongst themselves that it could have been caused by a flash fire from freebasing crack cocaine. But since the hairs on her cheek weren't singed, they concluded the cause had to be something else, perhaps an acidic burn from the vomit in her stomach.

Long after Bernardo and Homolka had given their statements, they were still at the police station while the detectives awaited word from the hospital on what could have caused the burn mark. Around daybreak, Bernardo started getting agitated.

"I know my rights," he suddenly bellowed. "You can't hold us here if you're not going to charge us with anything. So either charge us or we'll leave."

There had never been any talk of charges. The detectives were simply trying to figure out how a healthy 15-year-old girl could suddenly choke on her vomit and die. They were looking for answers, not pointing fingers. The couple was told that if they wanted to leave they were free to go. Bernardo called for a taxi, and he and Homolka headed back to the somber household on Dundonald where they had to explain, one more time, what had happened in the basement.

The detectives had also questioned Karel that night. He had told them of Tammy's asthma, a condition suffered by all three of his daughters. They had wanted to know more about Paul Bernardo. How long had he been dating Karla? Did he get along with the family? Had there been any disputes? Had he ever been in trouble with the law? He was liked by everyone in the family, Karel said, and had been especially close to Tammy.

Later, when they were alone, Bernardo and Homolka looked for the tape they had hidden in the basement, behind a shelf of preservatives. But they couldn't find it right away.

"It's gone," he told her. "The cops have got it." Then he held his forefinger to his mouth. "Shh. The house is probably bugged."

They kept searching and finally found the tape at the other end of the shelf. Bernardo sighed with relief. "It's a good thing they didn't find this, or we would have been screwed."

Homolka never responded. She didn't say much at all. She was in a daze, and felt numb, guilty, ashamed at what she had done. Tammy's death marked a turning point for

Homolka. While she had gladly walked through the doorway into Bernardo's world because she found it exciting, her life had suddenly turned into a nightmare befitting any of the horror movies of which they were both so fond.

Although there had been no visible signs of trauma, an autopsy was ordered because of the unusual circumstances of Tammy Lyn's death. No charges were being considered, yet the death was still listed as suspicious in nature.

Karla Homolka and Paul Bernardo stood beside the casket, holding hands, solemnly greeting the Boxing Day mourners who filed into the funeral home. Although the investigation wasn't completed, the body had been released to the family for the service. An athletic teenager who played soccer, participated in gymnastics, track and field, and cross-country running, a girl who was never, ever sick, except for her slight asthma condition, was dead, and everyone in Garden City who knew the Homolkas wanted to know why. Since Tammy wasn't a drinker, even a few libations might have been sufficient for her to pass out. And both Bernardo and Homolka seemed sincere in their recounting of events; they had done their best to help her. It all sounded so reasonable, yet people were still suspicious.

Among the mourners that day was one of Karla Homolka's oldest friends, Renya Hill. The two women hugged each other tearfully, and Homolka volunteered some details of her sister's death.

"It all happened so fast," she explained, using a line she had repeated over and over, to her parents and relatives, to the police, to doctors at the hospital, to friends, to the many acquaintances who had called the house. "Paul tried to save her. He gave her CPR, but it was too late. There was nothing we could do."

As if on cue, Bernardo stepped forward. He had been standing a respectful distance away at the foot of the open casket, staring at a picture of Tammy that was framed in a wreath. He put an arm around Homolka's shoulder and she gazed at him, perhaps searching for some kind of reassurance.

"It was an unfortunate accident," he said, as if he was equating the death to a traffic fatality. "We tried to save her, but there was nothing anyone could have done."

Although the police were calling Tammy's death an accident, whispers would continue to circulate through St. Catharines after the funeral. Why were the police still involved? And what was that mark on Tammy Lyn's cheek, and the smaller blotches around her mouth? One mourner said the tiny marks looked like cigarette burns. Years later, the cause of the burn marks would still be a mystery. Pathologists speculated that the skin may have been discolored from a chemical reaction between the halothane and whatever other substance was on the rag Homolka had held over Tammy Lyn's mouth.

At the funeral service Bernardo sat with the family at the front of the chapel, between the two remaining daughters and their parents. Karla kept fussing with her hair, running her fingers through it, brushing it off her ears, at one point even combing it. That behavior drew some curious looks from the mourners seated behind her.

Tammy Lyn was buried near her home, in Victoria Lawn Cemetery. A soccer ball was carved on the tombstone, together with the words "You were loved so very much. And now you've gone away. Memories will keep you near. We miss you every day."

Bernardo and Homolka had each written notes that they quietly placed in the casket before it was closed for the final time. Bernardo wrote:

Dear Tammy,
My dearest little sister, words cannot express the deep sorrow and regret that I now feel. You gave me your love, and trusted me like your big brother. We shared a lot of good times and you touched my heart in a way no one else ever could. I love you, Tammy. I always have, and will. I miss you so much and my life will never be the same now that you're gone. If I ever caused you any harm or pain, Tammy, please forgive me. I only wanted the best for you. Just for you to be happy and to experience the joys of this world. Please forgive me, Tammy. I'll love you from now. I'll love from now 'til eternity and I'm looking forward to seeing you once again when I die.
Love,
Your brother, Paul
XOXOXO

In hers, Karla told her sister:

Dear Tammy,
I have so much to say to you that words cannot express. I've talked to you every night and you know how I feel about everything. I want to give you these thoughts to carry with you. I love you deeply and will hold you in my heart forever.
Your big sister,
Karla
XOXOXO

There was a wake at the Homolka house for a hundred or so mourners. Bernardo greeted the guests at the door, graciously taking their coats, offering them beverages. Though the Homolkas put on a brave face for their visitors that evening, inside they were hurting terribly. "Part of me," Dorothy Homolka would say later, "died with her." For weeks afterwards Karel lost all interest in his business and just moped around the house, grieving the loss of his child. But at the wake, both parents had nothing but praise for their future son-in-law.

"I don't know how we would have got through this if it weren't for Paul," Dorothy said to one visitor. "He's so upset, yet he's handling it so well."

At one point Bernardo and Homolka excused themselves, telling everyone they wanted to be alone in their grief. They went down to the basement and closed the door to the den. Bernardo put a tape of Tammy Lyn playing soccer into the VCR. He then cranked up the volume on the TV set.

"If you ever tell anybody," Bernardo said, grabbing Homolka roughly by the arm, "I'll kill you, and I'll kill your other sister, and then I'll kill your parents. Do you understand what I'm saying? I'll kill your whole family if you ever open your mouth. Don't ever forget that I've got the tape. And we're both on it." If either one of them talked, Bernardo said, both of them would go to jail for the rest of their lives.

Homolka's uncle, Calvin Seger, had watched them leave the gathering. He hadn't liked Bernardo from the first time he had met him. Like many others, he had his suspicions about Tammy's death, but no proof of any wrongdoing. A little later, he went downstairs to the basement, stood outside the closed door for several moments, and listened. He couldn't be sure, but he thought he heard Bernardo cursing his niece. He didn't know why, especially on that of all days, but it just confirmed his impression that the guy was a Grade A jerk.

Homolka's actions after her sister's death were to be confusing and contradictory. She often wrote letters to friends, describing how excited she was about her upcoming marriage. In one she even described her parents as assholes because they didn't want her to get married so soon after her sister's death. Homolka would later blame Bernardo, telling the police he had forced her into marriage under the threat of death. The truth probably lay somewhere in between. She certainly didn't want to go to prison and, still in love with Bernardo, believed — foolishly, she would later say — he would change after they got married. She was right. He did change. He got worse.

Many of Tammy's friends had missed the funeral because they had been away over the Christmas break. The staff at Sir Winston Churchill High School, where she was a Grade 10 student, later held a memorial service in the gymnasium, and the Homolka family, along with Bernardo, were invited. But he didn't go, and his future wife made excuses for him, saying he was too distraught. It wasn't quite the truth.

He had told her the night before that he wanted to know what Tammy Lyn had gone through, and so he took the same number of sleeping pills that he had put into her drink. He also took a whiff from the bottle of halothane. The sedatives had knocked him out, and he was still groggy the following morning as the family prepared to go to the school. He stayed in bed all that day.

Tammy's favorite song, "Stairway to Heaven," was played over the loudspeakers as the students filed in. One line from the song — "and it makes me wonder" — was on the minds of many of the students that day when they talked about the sudden death of one of the school's most popular students.

In the weeks after Tammy Lyn's death, neither Bernardo nor Homolka went out much. Both lost weight. Their obvious grief over Tammy's death garnered a lot of sympathy from their friends. But their real worries concerned evidence of rape and the fact that Tammy Lyn's body was full of barbiturates that were sure to be detected when the tissue samples from the autopsy were sent to the crime lab. When the police found out, they would be even more suspicious. It would mean a renewed investigation.

Bernardo feared that if the detectives leaned on Homolka, she would crack. And that's when his abusive behavior toward her really began, in these weeks just after Tammy's death. He did it to ensure her silence. Time and again he told her that if she ever confessed, she would go to jail, and her family and friends would despise her forever.

And then early in the new year, the results of the post-mortem arrived in the mail.

17
Fifty-Seven Bayview Drive

and the eyes. Bernardo spent more time in the bathroom brushing his hair than Tammy had in caring for the whole of her body. Homolka also noticed that just once when she wanted the camera somewhere her words just were not the same. Homolka put the tape to shame. It made her shiver just to remember it, but she knew she would survive in dealing with Karla. And there were days in the life later on, on tape.

Dorothy Homolka anxiously tore open the letter. Tammy Lyn's death, according to the findings of the autopsy, was due to aspiration, or fluid in the lungs. She had vomited after passing out, and in her unconscious state she had swallowed enough of the vomit to choke to death. Dorothy worked at a hospital. She knew how quickly a person could die from aspiration.

The report, signed by Dr. Joseph Roslowski, noted traces of just a small amount of alcohol in the blood, an amount consistent with one, or perhaps two, drinks. The findings reaffirmed what Bernardo and Homolka had been telling everyone. "She couldn't hold her booze," Bernardo had said once. All night she had complained about feeling woozy. Bernardo even had her on video talking about seeing double. He didn't belabor the point, however. Lori was still angry at them for giving Tammy too many drinks.

The post-mortem found no visible signs of trauma. Although Tammy Lyn had been violated four times by Bernardo, twice each anally and vaginally, the pathologists had noticed nothing unusual about her orifices. The only aspect of her death the authorities found troubling was the red mark on her face. Had the acid in the girl's vomit discolored her skin? More than two years later, when the body was exhumed in a new investigation, the mark was still visible on what remained of her face.

Dorothy Homolka seemed almost relieved when she told friends about the findings, leaving unspoken any fears that there may have been more to Tammy Lyn's death than even she cared to admit.

The detectives with the Niagara police force reviewed the report and decided Tammy's death was an accident; no foul play was suspected. Case closed.

Soon afterwards, life in the Homolka household returned to a semblance of normality. Dorothy resumed her administrative duties at the Shaver Memorial Hospital. Her husband continued with his business selling light fixtures. Lori returned to her job at McDonald's, and Karla went back to work at the animal clinic. Bernardo seemed to be handling the death, publicly at least, the worst of anyone. He was still on unemployment insurance after quitting his job at Price Waterhouse and then at a second accounting firm the previous fall. And while he talked about establishing businesses in St. Catharines, such as a lighting company, like Karel Homolka's, or even a limousine service, the truth was that all he wanted to do was smuggle cigarettes and cruise the streets for women.

For the first time in three years, there was growing resentment toward Bernardo's presence at the home on Dundonald. Both parents, along with Lori, wanted a period of mourning for just the family members, some time alone to get over their grief. They were getting on each other's nerves. Although Bernardo was engaged to Karla, he was still an outsider. Though they had once told him he could live there until the wedding, they now wanted their houseguest to leave. Nobody dared bring it up with him, though, or with Karla.

The family was also upset over the way he was treating Karla. Ever since Tammy Lyn's death, Bernardo had been hovering around Karla, seldom leaving her side. When she sat down to talk to her mom or dad, he was there, eavesdropping, butting in, taking over the conversation. It bothered them that he had taken to ordering her around, always having her fetch him a drink or make his food. He was treating her, they felt, like his personal servant. She didn't want to do anything without checking with him first. But the couple seemed happy, and with the family still going through a period of pain, nobody felt like saying anything to Karla. It would just get her upset.

In mid-January, Dorothy and her husband went on a seven-day trip; Karel was going to display some of his lighting fixtures at a home show. Lori was going to spend that week with relatives.

One evening, after everyone had gone, Bernardo and Homolka locked all the doors to the house, went down to the basement, and had sex in front of the fireplace. He taped it, telling Homolka the home movie was something they would enjoy in later years. Afterwards, they went upstairs to Tammy Lyn's bedroom. It had been left untouched since her death; her clothes were still hanging in the closet, her dolls neatly piled against the pillows on her water bed.

Bernardo set up the video camera so that it pointed at the bed. He looked around for one of Tammy Lyn's school pictures, and chose the last one taken before her death. Homolka went to her sister's closet, took out the outfit Bernardo liked the most—Tammy Lyn's black miniskirt and black blouse—and put it on.

"Remember," Bernardo warned her as he adjusted the camera, "don't say anything stupid that will ruin the tape."

Ever since Tammy Lyn's death he had been mad at her for ruining the tape by saying she wasn't enjoying herself. "It's my only tape of Tammy," he often reminded her, "and you fucked it up. Don't make that mistake again."

To reinforce his admonition, he had taken to punching her arms and chest, and sometimes the side of her head, but never in the face because that left bruises that couldn't be covered up with clothes. No one in her family suspected anything, and she felt she couldn't tell them because then she would have to explain why he was hitting her. Trapped, she suffered his abuse in silence. Some psychiatrists later said that Homolka developed survival technique strategies, that is, she turned off her mind to much of what Bernardo said or did and tried her best just to please him, hoping to improve their relationship; she developed something akin to the Stockholm Syndrome, taking the side of the person who was holding her prisoner, agreeing with him even though he was abusing her. But other psychiatrists said that, knowing what would happen to her if she told the truth, she put her personal comfort first, and lied about everything else to protect it. She had no conscience about her role in her sister's death, they said. Only later did she show any grief because that helped her situation with the authorities.

He now flicked on the camera, climbed onto the bed, and lay on his back, staring at the picture of Tammy Lyn. Homolka climbed onto the bed with him. She brushed her long hair over the top of her head so that it covered her face.

"Here's my little virgin Tammy," Bernardo said, staring at her picture, which he held close to his fiancée's face as she began performing fellatio. "Fucked by me. I broke the hymen."

"Tammy was a virgin," Homolka said.

After a few minutes of oral sex, Bernardo then turned over onto his hands and his knees while Homolka performed anilingus, rubbing his penis at the same time.

"I love licking your ass," she said. "I love sucking your cock. I love you. I love to be fucking you so much."

Bernardo moaned in pleasure as he stared at the picture of Tammy Lyn. He turned on to his back again, then adjusted Homolka's hair so that it completely covered her face while she resumed the oral sex.

"I love you so much," Homolka said.

Bernardo held the picture of Tammy Lyn near Homolka's head while she continued the fellatio.

"I love you too, Tammy," Bernardo said.

"I want your cock in me," Homolka said, pausing. "I'll give you the best orgasm of all. Together we're perfect. I want to lose my virginity to you."

"You didn't know I was filming you, Tammy, when you were in your room, undressing. But I was watching you through the window."

"Can you ever stop thinking of me? Can you ever stop coming in my face? Take my virginity, Paul. Take it."

"I will, Tammy. I love you, Tammy."

He shifted Homolka to a new position, on her hands and knees. Then he pulled up her short black skirt and entered her anally. She moaned with pleasure.

"Take my virginity, Paul," she said. "Take it."

"I love you, Tammy," he said, still staring at the picture.

"Oh," she moaned, "I'm losing my virginity. I love you, Paul. I love you so much."

Later, Bernardo wanted more oral sex. "Suck me, Tammy," he said. "Suck me, Tammy, hard."

Homolka did so, as Bernardo lay there, holding Tammy Lyn's picture in the air. A short time later, he wanted to try yet another position. He told her to go to the side of the room and wait while he positioned the camera so that it was aimed at the side of the water bed. Then he lay on his back near the edge of the bed, his legs apart and resting on the bed frame. When he was ready, he looked toward the camera, smiled, and directed Homolka to walk up to the bed.

"Hi, Tam," he said to her.

"Hi, Paul," Homolka replied.

"Gonna make me happy?"

"I love sucking you."

"You're better than Karla," he said, "that's for sure."

"I love you. Will you fuck me, Paul?"

Homolka got down on her knees at the side of the bed and started massaging his penis while he pushed her hair so that it again covered her face. Then he lay back, staring at the picture while Homolka began fellatio.

"I'm a virgin," she said.

"Oh, Tammy." He moaned with pleasure. "Oh, I love you. Yes. Yes. Yes, my little virgin. Yes."

"I love you, Paul. I'm your virgin."

For the next 20 minutes, Bernardo moaned as Homolka worked feverishly to get him to climax. Every now and then she stopped to look up at him. But he was dreamily fixated on the picture of Tammy Lyn. Finally, he climaxed. At this point, Bernardo presumably saw Homolka as just another prop in his sexual fantasy world, one he could do anything he wanted with because of their joint secret. For the moment he was content to have Homolka role-play in their sexual encounters. Later he would put new demands on their partnership.

Homolka slumped to the floor, exhausted. Bernardo rolled over onto the water bed and fell asleep, the picture of Tammy Lyn by his side.

The next night Bernardo went out driving. He told Homolka that if he came back with anyone she was either to hide or to lie and say that she was his sister. He returned several hours later with a girl about 16 years old. Homolka hid behind the living-room drapes as the two went down into the basement. They stayed there for several hours, and then Bernardo drove her home.

"I fucked her ass off the whole time," he said when he returned.

"You're the king," Homolka replied. "You deserve it. You deserve the best."

Lori began pushing her parents. "Could you just ask him to go?" she said to her mother one night near the end of January 1991. "Could he please leave?"

Both parents wanted Bernardo to leave, but it was Lori who was the most vocal. Her mother said she would broach the subject as soon as possible.

Karla cried when her mother told her one night it might be best for everyone if Bernardo left the house and went back to his home in Scarborough. She knew Bernardo would be upset, and she knew what that meant — another beating. However, she couldn't tell her parents that, so she begged her mother to change her mind. But the family held firm. They needed time alone. Bernardo was her fiancé, but he wasn't part of the family. Several days later, Homolka finally got up the courage to tell him.

Bernardo was furious, cursing her and her family. "That's just earned you five," he told her. It was his latest expression of anger; it meant he was going to hit her five times. "I'll never come back to this house," he said. "Never."

Soon after, he returned to his parents' home in Scarborough. But he couldn't take the chance of leaving Homolka alone with her family for long. If he wasn't around, she might weaken and tell them the truth. He had been gone for two days when he called her and said he wanted her to move out with him. Until they found a place they could stay in a motel. Homolka's parents were upset when she told them, but she went anyway. She felt, she would later testify, that she had no choice.

The next day, she and Bernardo went looking for a place to stay. One area of St. Catharines that Bernardo liked was Port Dalhousie. What attracted him most about the lakeside community were all the young female athletes who belonged to the rowing club and often jogged through the streets.

In Dalhousie one home they both liked was a cheery Cape Cod–style house on a corner lot on Bayview Drive. The home had been built at the turn of the century, and exactly a dozen families had lived there, but none of its latest owners, a syndicate of three couples, had any intention of becoming number 13.

The couples had bought the property strictly as an investment, negotiating a purchase price of $164,000. They hired a contractor, who gutted the two-story home, and over the next several months 57 Bayview was turned into something that belonged in *Home and Gardens*. The renovated masterpiece, with its center-hall plan, featured a living room with fireplace, and a door to the attached garage. Also on the main floor was a den or spare bedroom and a brand-new galley kitchen. The second floor had a master bedroom with "his" and "her" walk-in closets. Next to it was a new bathroom with Jacuzzi tub, and a spare room. The basement was unfinished, but there was a large room off one wall that could be converted into a wine cellar.

After the renovations were completed, the house was put back on the market in the summer of 1990 and listed at just under $300,000. It was an ideal home for a young, professional couple — if one came along in the middle of a nationwide recession. Unless they found a buyer, the six owners would be stuck with $1,300 a month in mortgage payments on their "can't miss" investment. So when the handsome couple in the gold sportscar came along, it seemed almost too good to be true.

Paul Bernardo said he and his fiancée were planning to get married and needed a place to live. But the couple couldn't afford to buy, at least not yet. They were interested, though, in renting with an option to buy.

What a sensible young couple, thought Brian Delaney, who headed the syndicate. He liked Bernardo's firm handshake and pleasant smile. A monthly rent of $1,200 was agreed upon which didn't even cover the mortgage payments, but which was all the market could bear, and the couple signed a year's lease. Since the house was unoccupied, the couple said they wanted to move in on February 1, 1991. Bernardo said he would drop off six months' worth of post-dated cheques.

"I've just come into an inheritance," he said, explaining that his grandmother had recently passed away.

At this point Bernardo had moved full-time into his cigarette-smuggling business and was making almost daily trips across the border. The introduction of a new tax in Canada, the Goods and Service Tax, was proving good for his business because the cost of a pack of cigarettes had gone up to just over $5. With no shortage of customers, Bernardo was making at least $1,000 a week tax-free. But he was spending it just as fast.

Dorothy and Karel were upset when their daughter told them she was moving in with Bernardo. He didn't have a job, and she was making only a clerk's salary. Did they have to pick such an expensive place to rent? But Bernardo was insistent that he wanted to live there and that Homolka was going with him.

It would also be a good place to bring two young girls he was particularly interested in, he told Homolka. He wanted Homolka to convince them to go to bed with him. One was called Jane, and the other Margaret. Because they were minors, neither can be fully identified under a court order.

By the beginning of 1991, scientists at the Centre of Forensic Sciences had received 224 samples from the A List in the Scarborough Rapist case.

"Wouldn't it be quicker just to bring in the phone book?" quipped a homicide detective, who had only three samples needing analysis to find *his* suspect.

Investigators with the Sexual Assault Squad had been collecting the samples since June of 1990. The fluid samples had been sent over to the crime lab in batches and there were some late arrivals. The saliva, blood, and hair samples taken from Paul Bernardo in November 1990 was one.

At the crime lab there were still only one scientist and one technician qualified to do the work. And neither, as yet, was fully certified in the area of DNA testing.

It would take months just to do the preliminary testing, then a further 90 days to complete the work. Detectives would have to wait at least until the fall before all the results were in.

Murder cases still took precedence, since it was thought more important to get a killer off the street than a rapist.

"But what if the rapist now kills someone?" Det. Steve Irwin, one of the recent additions to the squad, wondered out loud. It was a continual concern for investigators. Officials at the forensics lab were sympathetic, but they were backed up with homicide requests from other police forces around the province.

Although Homolka would say later she never wanted to marry Bernardo, her letters to friends at the time said otherwise.

"I finally have some good news in my life," she said in one. "Paul and I are moving in together. Yes, we'll be living in sin. We've got a beautiful house in Port Dalhousie. It's an all-new kitchen in white. Three bedrooms, two bathrooms, a Jacuzzi. The master bedroom is pretty big. There's a huge walk-in closet. And plenty of room for my furniture — and my hope chest! I fell in love with the house and so did Paul when we saw it. It's got a fireplace and central air. There's a big backyard, and green window shutters. It's really going to be my house!"

As soon as they moved in, Bernardo and Homolka went out to buy furniture: a washer and a dryer, coffee tables, chesterfields, area rugs. They put everything on her charge cards. Homolka seemed happy, out shopping, planning for her wedding.

Bernardo moved in all the furniture from his bedroom at his parents' house. He put his desk, along with the collection of women's underwear ads, into the second-floor spare room. There, he told Homolka, he would work on the rap album that would make him famous and them rich. Although he had no formal training and had a poor voice along with a limited, confused imagination when it came to songwriting, Homolka wanted to believe him. Bernardo had other possessions which he moved in, including a collection of tools he had received from his grandfather, Gerald Eastman. One was a power saw.

Homolka resumed writing her love letters in early 1991. In February she gave him a card which said: "Happy Valentine's Day to my Number One Love on our first Valentine's Day in our new house. All my love, Karla."

The letters to her friends also continued. "Living with

Paul is great," she said — lied? — in one. "I can't believe we're finally together in our own house. It's lots of work getting it the way we want it, but we're having a great time."

18
The Big Lie

They were putting away the dishes after having dinner at their new home when Bernardo suddenly got angry at Homolka. She never knew what would spark one of his outbursts, but they were happening with increasing frequency. Often he blamed her for Tammy Lyn's death. Other times, he got mad when she went several days without saying how much she loved him. Tonight he was angry because she hadn't completely turned off one of the faucets.

"You're so fucking stupid," he yelled, then hit her on the arm, one of his favorite punching spots, one she could cover with a long-sleeved blouse.

"I'm sorry."

But it didn't appease him. He shoved her toward the wall, finally pushing her out the French doors at the rear of the house. She fell onto a woodpile on the deck, and a nail in one of the boards made her cry out in pain.

His demeanor suddenly changed, another aspect of him she was learning to live with: enraged one moment, placid the next. He apologized and helped her to her feet, later watching while she cleaned up the wound.

She went to bed early that night because she had to get up around 7 a.m. for her job at the veterinary clinic. But Bernardo was on unemployment insurance and usually stayed up late, drinking and listening to music. Often, he replayed the tape he had made of Tammy Lyn, masturbating while he watched it.

That night, he wanted sex. He went upstairs, awak-ened Homolka, and demanded fellatio. When she told him no, he slugged her in the head, and she began to cry. Then she did as she was told. He climaxed, crawled into bed, and fell asleep.

Although they had a queen-sized bed, Bernardo was always shoving her to one side, complaining that the bed was-n't big enough. That night, he was particularly restless. He kept kicking her, telling her to move over. Finally, he pulled back the covers, put his foot against her back, and shoved her onto the floor.

"Could you sleep on the floor tonight, Kar," he said.

Homolka got some blankets from the closet and made herself a bed on the floor. She hated what was happen-ing to her, but she didn't see a way out. Her husband-to-be was turning into a monster, and she didn't know how to stop him. Bernardo enjoyed the extra room so much that the next night he asked her if she would mind sleeping on the floor again. Since it made him happy, she agreed. Later, he bought her some foam to use as a mattress.

Although barely a month had passed since Tammy Lyn's death, Bernardo had decided they were still going ahead with the wedding they had planned for June. "A wife," he was fond of telling her, "cannot testify against her husband."

Homolka's parents were surprised by these wedding plans so soon after the funeral, and had been quietly lobbying their daughter to scale back on what was going to be a lavish affair. The two had booked one of the nicest hotels in nearby Niagara-on-the-Lake and planned to invite more than a hun-dred guests. But Bernardo wasn't going to change his plans for anybody. He had certain standards to maintain, he told Homolka. He was a successful young man, with a lovely wife and a nice home. A cheap wedding just wouldn't fit his image.

Though he had vowed never to return to the Homolka house, they went there one night to discuss their wedding plans.

As they talked in the basement den, her parents expressed concern about the expense, and said they didn't have enough money to pay the anticipated $10,000 for the wedding. Most of their savings had been used up on Tammy Lyn's funeral. But Bernardo still refused to cut back on any of the items, such as hiring a hansom to take them from the church to the reception.

"If you don't have the money," he told the Homolkas, "then remortgage your house."

The Homolkas were flabbergasted. They turned to their daughter for support, but she said very little. She didn't even want to get married, but she felt she had no choice. It wasn't just her parents she was fooling. She was living the Big Lie with everybody, pretending she had the perfect relationship with the perfect man. And if she didn't agree with Bernardo that night, she knew he would beat her later.

It was finally agreed that the Homolkas would pay for most of the wedding but would split the rest of the expenses with Bernardo's parents.

"Your parents are cheap," Bernardo told her as they were driving home. Afraid of getting him even more upset, she agreed with him. He dropped her off at home, then went out driving by himself. She assumed he went trolling for young girls; he often talked about bringing one home and using her as a sex slave.

She was sleeping on the floor when he got home that night, and it bothered him that she hadn't stayed up.

"I have to get up for work tomorrow," she protested.

"You know I wanted you to stay up," he said, and kicked her in the ribs. "You were supposed to stay up."

"I'm sorry."

"I'm hungry," he complained. "Go and make me something."

She went downstairs and put a frozen pizza in the oven. Then she sat on the living-room couch and tried to stay awake while he described how he had followed a woman home and, from the bushes, watched her undress. He held up his palm when he finished his story. It was a little ritual they had. She slapped it with hers.

She stayed up with him until he fell asleep on the floor, then she got a blanket, covered him, and went back upstairs to bed. She was getting dressed in the morning when he burst into the bathroom, furious.

"Why didn't you sleep beside me?" he demanded. "Why did you leave me alone?"

She tried to apologize, but he punched her on the side of the head before she could finish. The blow knocked her down, made her dizzy. She couldn't go to work that day, and phoned in sick.

Renya Hill noticed the bruises on her friend's arms when she visited her for the first time at her new home. She asked Homolka what had happened.

"Oh, that," replied Homolka. "It's nothing. Some of the dogs at the vet's were getting a little rough."

What were they wearing, wondered her friend, boxing gloves?

Homolka quickly told her news. "We're going to get married," she said, making her best effort that day at a smile. "I'm going to be a June bride."

Renya gave her friend a hug of congratulations. "I'm sure it will be a wonderful wedding," she said.

"Maybe some good can come from all this sadness," Homolka remarked, a veiled reference to the death of her sister.

Renya wanted to congratulate Bernardo and asked where he was.

"He's gone to Florida," replied Homolka, and then smiled. "One last fling as a bachelor."

"Aren't you jealous?" Renya asked, half in jest.

Homolka just smiled, but there was no joy there.

What better place to be in mid-March than Fort Lauderdale? Students from across the United States and Canada flooded into the city for the annual spring break and a week of partying by the ocean. Bernardo had been excited about it as a holiday spot where there would be "wall-to-wall babes." It would be his last fling before his marriage and it would also mark the end, he said, of his mourning.

Van Smirnis had felt badly for his friend, the way he was practically blaming himself for Tammy Lyn's death. He seemed so distraught. The two had become close again. It was good to see his old friend back in character again, chasing the skirts, the Bernardo he remembered. And yet Smirnis felt it was in bad taste that Bernardo was using Tammy Lyn's death as a come-on line to women they met on the beach. As in: "I'm here because I'm trying to get over the death of my sister, Tammy Lyn." But in poor taste or not, the line worked. The women they met felt sorry for Bernardo and his friend. And, over drinks, they tried to cheer him up.

Once when they were walking along the beach Bernardo saw a blonde in a string bikini and his body started quivering, shuddering as if he had just been hit with a charge of electricity. And then, when she was barely out of earshot, he made that comment, the one Smirnis had heard many times before. Bernardo threw it out as if testing his friend, trying to gauge his reaction.

"How'd you like to knock the bitch down," he asked, "and rape her?"

Smirnis did what he always did whenever Bernardo asked him that question. He ignored it, shrugged it off, kept walking. Bernardo never pushed it, and Smirnis was glad. Why would Bernardo even think of raping anybody? He never had a problem meeting women. Bernardo had to be kidding, yet something about the way he said it always made Smirnis wonder.

As they walked along the beach, Bernardo got onto a favorite topic, his hair. He wanted to dye it totally blond, shave it on the sides in a cut like that white rap singer Vanilla Ice. It was all he talked about ever since some women had yelled at him from the balcony of the hotel, calling him Vanilla Ice. Bernardo had been flattered. Vanilla Ice was the hottest singer around and Bernardo had become obsessed with the idea of changing his appearance to look like the singer.

Bernardo could be so vain: one night at the hotel he had stared at himself in the mirror for three hours, just talking about his hair and how he planned to sculpture it. But he had no trouble getting women. That night, in fact, they had a couple lined up who were coming over to their hotel room for a drink.

By March 1991, three months after the last of the 224 bodily-fluid samples had been given to the Centre of Forensic Sciences, scientists there still hadn't begun the DNA testing — the government-funded facility just didn't have the staff — and with a backlog of murder cases taking priority, it was starting to look as though it would take years.

What the scientists could do soon was serology tests on the samples, to eliminate those suspects whose blood type didn't match the semen found on the rape victims. It wasn't what detectives with the Sexual Assault Squad had in mind, but at least it would reduce their 224 suspects to a more manageable number. On the other hand, only if they could narrow their suspect list down to a dozen or fewer, might there be the resources to do all the genetic fingerprinting they needed.

Paul Bernardo was in one corner of the hotel room, naked from the waist up, groping with a young blonde in an equal state of undress. The woman had her arms wrapped around him, and she was raking her fingernails across his bare back. Suddenly Bernardo screamed out in pain and threw the woman to the floor. He went to a mirror, twisting around to get a better look at the scratch marks. Smirnis, who was at the other end of the room, looked over.

Bernardo turned back to the blonde and began swearing at her. There was a small kitchen in the hotel room. Bernardo went to a drawer, took out a knife, and turned back to the blonde. She had hurt the King and would have to pay.

"No bitch is going to scratch me," he said, stepping toward the terrified woman, who was clutching some of her clothes to her chest. The man with the pretty face had turned into something sinister.

Smirnis jumped to his feet and quickly got between Bernardo and the woman. "What the hell's wrong with you?" he said. "Have you gone crazy?"

"I'll kill the bitch," Bernardo vowed.

"Jesus, gimme that knife," Smirnis pleaded, reaching for it.

Reluctantly, Bernardo handed it over. "Goddamn bitch," he said, sneering at the blonde as she quickly got dressed and left the room with her friend.

"What the hell got into you?" Smirnis asked later. But Bernardo was back in front of the mirror, checking his hair, too busy with his grooming to respond.

Although they had known each other for a long time, Smirnis was beginning to believe there was something very wrong with his friend.

She had been jogging along Main Street in Port Dalhousie that April morning before turning onto the winding road that led to Henley Island and the rowing club. It was early, not even six, and although there were no other joggers in sight, there had never been any attacks in the area, and the 15-year-old felt safe as she followed the road that led onto the island, which was connected with the mainland by a short bridge. Ahead of her the safety of the clubhouse was only a few minutes away. And behind her, the traffic was already building on Main Street.

That part of the road was winding and surrounded by thick bushes. There were no lights, and she picked up her pace just a little as she approached the most desolate section. The road bent and dipped slightly, so that there was a blind spot where you couldn't see back to Main Street or ahead to the clubhouse.

He had been hiding in the bushes in just the right place. He pounced on her from behind, clamping a gloved hand over her mouth and the other arm around her waist as he dragged her into the bushes. There wasn't a chance to protect herself, or even scream. He was powerful, and, even though she was a rowing athlete, she was no match for his strength.

"Make any noise and I'll kill you," he threatened as he shoved her face to the ground and ripped off her jogging pants and underwear.

And then he was inside her, violating her anally in an animalistic rage, pounding her on the back with his fists as he shoved her head into the icy water of Richardson's Creek. When it was over, he warned her not to call for help or he would come back and kill her. Then he ran away through the bushes.

It was then that she heard the voices. They were nearby, walking along the road, probably athletes, she guessed, like her, going for an early-morning workout. Maybe she even knew them. Instinctively, forgetting about his warning, she yelled for help, and two men came running.

"He raped me!" she screamed, pointing in the direction her attacker had fled.

The two men gave chase through the bushes. It was lighter now, and in the distance they caught just a glimpse of him. He was about six feet tall, with blond hair shaved high on the sides, and he was wearing a dark windbreaker and gloves. He was running at a good clip, but so were the two men. They were both rowers in peak condition, so unless the attacker was also in training, he wasn't going to outrun them.

There were only so many options for the blond-haired man. If he stayed in the bushes he would be trapped, and they would almost certainly catch him. On the other side of the bushes was an open field leading to Main Street. Anybody fleeing in that direction would be easily spotted. He had only one effective escape route, to the west of the bushes where an enclave of homes bordered Richardson's Creek. The houses were on winding streets and most had fenced-in back yards that would make great hiding spots.

His pursuers weren't far behind. They were angry, and determined. But the predator seemed to be in good shape too. All too quickly the two men lost sight of him. When they reached the open field he had vanished, disappeared into the dawn shadows.

Neither of his pursuers had heard a car leaving, so they thought he had probably run toward the nearby subdivision. They searched that way, but he was nowhere to be seen.

It was as if he knew where to run. Later, one of the pursuers told a police officer from the Niagara Region force that the rapist probably lived in Port Dalhousie. The speed of his disappearance suggested the blond-haired man knew his way around that part of the community. Residents of the subdivision were canvassed, but no one had seen or heard anything.

Later, in hospital, the victim was questioned by detectives. Did she get a look a the attacker? Yes, she told them. He was blond, about six feet tall, good looking, with smooth features, something like the composite sketch of the Scarborough Rapist the police in Toronto had released 11 months earlier.

The investigators with the Niagara Region police in St. Catharines made some enquiries of their counterparts in Toronto. No arrests had been made in the Scarborough Rapist case, they were told, although a number of suspects were being actively investigated. As far as the police in Scarborough knew, their predator had never struck anywhere outside the city. A possible connection between the attack in Dalhousie and the Scarborough rapes, if there was one, was not pursued by investigators from either police force.

Karla Homolka was seated in the middle of the small group of women, laughing louder than any of them at the joke that had just been made about her upcoming marriage. For the first time since Tammy's death four months earlier, Homolka was really enjoying herself with her friends in the basement rec room where her wedding shower was being held. Several noticed the difference in her eyes, which were sparkling with true joy that evening. Gone were the forced smiles and the fake laughs that had been so typical lately.

Homolka was seated on the floor surrounded by mounds of torn wrapping paper, ribbons, bows, empty boxes, and gifts. All around her were cooking utensils, pots, pans, an assortment of knives, household knick-knacks. Out of all the presents, there was one in particular that interested Homolka. It was a metal can compressor, a manual hydraulic device in which a pop can was pressed flat by pushing down on a lever. Homolka had been trying it out, flattening several cans, when one of the women had some advice for the bride-to-be.

"If he ever gets out of line," the woman said, "just put his balls in there instead of a can."

"Yeah," volunteered another woman, "the only way to keep a man in check is to squeeze what he values the most."

Many of the women at the shower thought Homolka and Bernardo's huge June wedding a bit inappropriate so soon after Tammy's funeral. But none of them said anything about it that night. They were having too good a time, laughing, drinking, smoking, and teasing Homolka. Bernardo had remained firm on the wedding plans, including the arrangements for them to ride from the church to the reception hall in a horse-drawn carriage "just like Chuck and Di." Bernardo wanted pheasant at a huge reception for 200 guests at the exclusive Queen's Landing Hotel. It still annoyed Bernardo that the Homolkas didn't want to spend as much on a wedding as they had on Tammy's funeral. It was time, he told them — and his own parents — to put an end to the grieving.

Bernardo arrived at the shower later that evening with big smiles for each of the women there. He sat on a couch and, as if on cue, Homolka got up off the floor and sat dutifully beside him. She kept smiling, but never spoke much after his arrival, listening attentively as he talked about his accounting practice and his plans to go into business and become a millionaire.

"What sort of business?" one of the women asked.

Bernardo shrugged. "Just ... business," he responded

vaguely. And then he wanted Homolka to show each of the women her engagement ring, even though they had already seen it.

"It cost $4,500," Bernardo boasted while Homolka walked around the room. Several of the women rolled their eyes. Homolka's fiancé could be a showoff. But he was young, in love, and had a great body to make up for what might be a lousy personality.

When they got home, Bernardo went to his music room on the second floor to listen to some tapes. That was his private domain, and she was allowed in there only when he invited her. But she had once sneaked into the room and looked through his desk. In it she found maybe hundreds of lingerie ads cut from catalogues. Some of the cutouts showed girls as young as 12 posing in their underwear. He had talked about bringing young girls home, but she had never believed him. Now, after looking at the drawerful of ads of semi-naked little girls, she was beginning to believe anything might be possible.

She had to go to the bathroom and was on the toilet when the door burst open, startling her.

"I told you," he yelled, "to leave the door open when you pee!"

He had started watching her go to the bathroom. Watching her urinate apparently aroused him, and she let him do it. Anything to keep him from beating her. She knew she was becoming his sex slave. Someone who washed his clothes, made his meals, and was there whenever he wanted sex.

"I'm sorry. I forgot."

He watched her as she finished and wiped herself. "Because you're so stupid," he said, "be ready for the nightly terrorist attack."

She knew what that meant. He would either start beating her in the middle of the night or he would wake her up and demand sex. She made her bed on the floor, but it was a long time before she fell asleep. She kept staring at the door at the end of the hall, watching and listening as he played his rap music, singing along to the tunes.

When she awoke in the morning, he was sleeping on top of the covers, his clothes still on. For some reason, he had changed his mind about beating her. She kissed him on the forehead before she left, but he was sound asleep and didn't stir. So she dashed him off a short note and left it on the dresser by the bed:

Paul,
I'm so sorry about last night. I love you so much. Please forgive me.
Kar.

He needed to keep hearing how much she loved him. He had been complaining that she had stopped writing him notes. Since apologies pacified him, she resumed the practice. Appeasing him had become her most important function in their relationship.

Bernardo was waiting for her in his car after work. They were planning on staying home that evening and watching videos. He seemed excited when she got into the car.

"Did you get them?"

At first, she didn't know what he was talking about. And then she remembered. She had promised to get more Halcion sedatives from the pharmacist to keep around the house, "just in case I bring someone home and I need them." But she had forgotten all about it.

"That's earned you another five," he said.

She knew it was useless to argue. She trembled all the way home, and he swore at her most of the drive. Once home, he started punching her in the arms and the side of the head.

"Take off your clothes," he demanded.

She disrobed. He ordered her down on her knees. He took off his belt and wrapped it around his fist.

"I'm going to have to punish you," he said, walking behind her. When she looked back, he yelled at her to keep looking forward. "You're such a stupid bitch."

And then he started whipping her with the belt. She pleaded with him to stop, and he did. But then he took off his pants and shoved her head to the floor.

"Arch your back," he ordered, as he entered her anally. "Arch it!"

He started hitting her on the back until she did as told. Then, when he was finished, he got dressed and went up to his music room, closing the door behind him.

She had welts all over her body and didn't go to work for several days until the bruises healed. It was a simple lesson in arithmetic for Bernardo. If Homolka didn't work, then she brought home no money from her $8.25 an hour job. His unemployment insurance had almost run out, and the money he made from smuggling he spent almost as fast on liquor, gifts for the two young girls he wanted to seduce, and going out for dinner almost every night of the week.

At times, however, he could still be nice to her. She had always wanted a dog, and he had refused because he was allergic. But finally he consented. She was thrilled when they brought home a rottweiler, whom they named Buddy.

Bernardo joined the local chapter of the Masonic Lodge and got a Mason's ring. He didn't say much at meetings, but he wanted to show that he was an active member of the community. When the other members asked him what he did for a living, he told them he was a freelance accountant who worked out of his house. He never mentioned that he was collecting pogey. Homolka had called him the king so often that he was beginning to believe that he was the best.

"I want people to know we're successful," said the man who had recently declared bankruptcy with outstanding debts of $20,000. "In this world, appearances are important if you want to get somewhere."

He liked to quote her his sayings: "There are winners and there are whiners"; "Money never sleeps"; "I don't meet the competition, I crush it." "We're the winners," he was fond of saying. "We're the best team around."

She wanted desperately to believe their relationship could improve, and it seemed to be happening. It was an exciting time too. Arrangements had to be finalized at the church, the hotel, the travel agency for their honeymoon in Hawaii. They also threw a birthday party for Lori, who had warmed toward Bernardo after they moved out and had visited 57 Bayview Drive several times. They had a white bulletin board in the kitchen, and Bernardo got his guests to sign it.

"Oh Paul, I mass love you," Lori wrote in one scrawled note. "Paul Kenneth Bernardo is such a dude. I love you," she said in a second.

Homolka was beaming as she finalized arrangements for the day she had dreamed about since she was a child.

It was a fool's dream, however. Bernardo had met a woman while he was in Florida in March, a nurse whom he had driven back to her home in South Carolina. There was a tape he had made of the two of them in a passionate embrace. Two short months before his marriage, Bernardo chose to brag about his infidelity and showed Homolka the tape. "She was really hot," he said. He was the master, the center of the universe, and he did what pleased him, which was to take care of Number One first. Homolka's reaction to the videotape was perhaps predictable: she watched it in silence, pretending that it was nothing unusual.

"Maybe if you were a better girlfriend," Bernardo told her, the line he had also used after the death of Tammy Lyn, "this could have been you on the tape."

Suddenly Homolka began thinking that perhaps she had a chance to escape after all. Maybe if Bernardo found another woman, an American, he might run off and leave her alone. It was that hope, she later said, that allowed her to keep her sanity.

They held a party shortly afterwards, and one of the female guests was flirting with Bernardo. Tired, Homolka went to bed early. Immediately afterwards Bernardo took the blonde into the spare bedroom on the main floor. They emerged a short time later, the blonde adjusting the buttons on her blouse. Van Smirnis went up to his old friend and challenged him about his behavior.

"You've got a beautiful fiancée there," he said. "Why are you doing this?"

The King was not used to being questioned. "I can do whatever I want," he replied.

19
The Miracle Baby

Frank Martens had a lot to celebrate that Tuesday in June 1991. He had just got his driver's license, although the test results were less than sparkling. The examiner had told him he almost failed because he drove too slowly. But he had passed, and that night his parents said it was okay to take the family car, a brand-new Buick Regal, out for a spin around Burlington. The 16-year-old took the keys, and off he went, taking along five of his friends as he headed for Roller Coaster Road.

Roller Coaster wasn't its official name, but that's what the teenagers called Number One Sideroad. It was a dirt road at the top end of Burlington, a city on Lake Ontario between Toronto and Niagara Falls. Bushes lined one end of the road; farms and some homes the other. The road was mostly flat, but a hilly stretch at the western end gave Roller Coaster its name. Here the small risers gradually became large dips, and a car could get airborne if it was going fast enough on some of the crests. That was the thrill, to "catch air," to lift all the tires off the ground, to fly. And when Frank Martens turned onto Number One Sideroad, he intended to find out just how much power the big Buick really had.

Number One was deserted that night. Frank Martens glanced over his shoulder at his five teenage passengers, John Blais sitting beside him in the front seat and three boys and one girl in the back. Martens cranked up the volume on the radio: Rod Stewart's "Forever Young." Then he jammed his foot down hard on the accelerator, powering the Buick along the dirt road, the squealing tires kicking up stones. Soon the new driver, who had almost failed his test for going too slow, was doing nearly 60 miles an hour. The car was flying as it hit the big hills on the Roller Coaster.

Robert Julian was watching the news that evening when he heard the screech of tires, the loud thunk, and the grinding of metal. Like most of his neighbors, Julian feared that one day there was going to be a horrific crash on Number One Sideroad because of the reckless way the teenagers drove along it. He ran from his house just as a bright orange fireball lit up the night sky.

A car had flipped over into the ditch, the impact flattening the roof. The front end was on fire, and the flames were spreading fast to the rest of the vehicle. There were two teenaged boys by the wreck. One was staggering about, his face covered in blood. The other was screaming as he frantically tried to open the rear doors. Julian ran over to help him.

The boy had burned his palms pulling at the back doors, but the doors had jammed shut in the crash. The boy started shrieking at Julian, but neither could do much until the fire department arrived. When Julian tried to get close to the car, the heat and the flames drove him back. And so Julian, the boy with the bloody face, and the other one with burnt hands, stood watching helplessly as the fire engulfed the rest of the vehicle, its roar drowning out the screams coming from the back seat. One of the survivors was Frank Martens. Through the smoke and flames, Julian saw four figures inside the burning wreck.

They had partied that night with friends, and as he was going to bed, Bernardo told Homolka to clean up the mess before she went to sleep. She started but, tired from staying up late most of that week, went to bed before finishing.

Bernardo was furious when he awakened to find the house still cluttered with beer bottles and food trays. He started screaming at her. Knowing better than to argue, she started to clean off the kitchen counter. But that didn't pacify him. Bernardo grabbed a knife and threw it at her head.

The knife just missed her, striking the door behind her and taking a chunk out of the wood. She cowered as he kept up a torrent of curses that morning, just days before the wedding. He had been keeping his anger in check, but now it all flooded out. He spat at her, and the spittle landed on her cheek. There was a plate of partially eaten food on the counter, and he dumped it on the floor.

"Clean up that mess!" he yelled. Thinking he was going to hit her, she ran up the stairs into the bathroom, locking the door behind her.

Bernardo ran up after her and pounded on the door. "Open up right now!" he screamed. "Or you're only going to get it worse!"

Though terrified of another beating, Homolka knew he wouldn't kill her because it would be too difficult to explain. So close to the wedding, she hoped that he would take it easy on her because everyone would see the bruises. Reluctantly, she opened the door.

He burst into the bathroom, grabbed her by the hair, pulling up handfuls, and smashed her head into the cupboard. When she fell on the floor, he started kicking and punching her. "I could kill you if I want," he said. "If you were better, I wouldn't have to do this."

"I'm sorry," she apologized as the blows rained down.

Another time he made her write out lines as punishment, as if she were a misbehaving schoolgirl, because she had forgotten to tape the TV show *The Simpsons*.

"I promise I will always tape *The Simpsons*," she wrote some hundred times before he was satisfied.

Leslie Mahaffy was fussing with her hair on the short drive to school, tossing blond shoulder-length bangs from her eyes as she looked at the passenger-side mirror. Her mother, Deborah, was taking their usual route toward M.M. Robinson High School in Burlington. Deborah reminded her daughter about her dental appointment after classes. Leslie wore braces and was looking forward to them coming off. At times it felt like she had a pair of pliers in her mouth. She wanted to go by herself to the dentist's office, but her mother insisted on picking her up and driving her.

That drew a sigh from Leslie. It seemed they could never agree on anything anymore, and here was another flashpoint. But, although she had been constantly squabbling with her mother, Leslie didn't feel like another fight so early in the morning. So she agreed, but only after several loud sighs.

Arguing with Leslie was upsetting for Deborah as well. Her daughter was 14, rebellious and railing against parental authority. Her friends kept assuring her most parents battled with their teenage daughters, but everyone else having the same problem didn't make it any easier. Deborah tried her best to be as tolerant as possible of her daughter's outbursts, but their home life was suffering.

It still seemed unimaginable. Leslie, after all, had been their miracle baby, the child she and her husband, Dan, were never supposed to be able to have. At least that's what the doctors had told her when she was undergoing radiation treatments for her ovarian cancer. But she had proved the doctors wrong. And when they warned the elementary school teacher that her baby might be born with a deformity because of the radiation, even going so far as to suggest an abortion, Deborah had ignored their advice and gone ahead with the pregnancy.

On July 1, 1976, a day when Canadians were celebrating the birth of their nation, the Mahaffys had their own reason to cheer when Leslie Erin came into the world. There would be nothing else more important, the Mahaffys vowed, than protecting their daughter from the evils of the world.

Perhaps fearful of spoiling Leslie, Deborah and Dan had been firm in their discipline. There were certain rules they wanted followed. Doing her homework, for one; abiding by her nightly curfew, for another. The curfew had been a real sore point with Leslie. Her friends stayed out late, so why couldn't she? There was nothing to worry about. Nothing ever happened in boring old Burlington.

Fourteen-year-olds, thought Deborah, liked to think they knew everything there was to know about the world, but they could be naive about danger, especially at night. The fights over her curfew were one of the reasons Leslie had left home earlier that year. It wasn't as if she had run away. She had stayed with friends and called home every day; Deborah liked to think of it as a sleep-over. But it had still been a distressing time, those 10 days when Leslie was out of the house and beyond their protection. They knew where she was and could have brought her back at any time, but that would just have made matters worse. Far better to let her come back when she was ready. And they knew she missed her baby brother, Ryan. The two had always been close. Deborah remembered how excited Leslie had been, holding her newborn brother in her arms at the hospital, and knew Leslie couldn't bear to stay away from Ryan for long.

When Leslie returned, they noticed a change in her attitude. She showed renewed interest in her schoolwork and was talking again about going to university, studying to be perhaps a marine biologist or a fashion designer. Their relationship with her, while still strained, was improving. Perhaps it was time, thought Deborah, as she drove her daughter to school that day, to let Leslie have her own house key again.

Giving their daughter a key to their home had been symbolic to the Mahaffys, a sign of responsibility. Leslie used to have a key, but when she left home for those 10 days the Mahaffys had changed the locks on the doors, thinking what if someone took the key away from their daughter and tried to break into their home? But Leslie seemed more mature now; it was time she had a key again. There was only one problem: when they changed the locks, they hadn't asked for any extra keys. Cutting keys was like writing letters; it would get done, but at some later date. For the moment it didn't seem that pressing: Leslie had been following her curfew, getting home on time, so one of them was always up to let her in.

When Leslie reached school that morning, she realized something was wrong as soon as she got out of the car. Her classmates were milling around one of the doors, many of them crying.

"What's going on?" she asked a friend.

He told her about the car accident on Roller Coaster Road the night before and the four teenagers who had burned to death in the wreck. "Chris was one of them," he said.

Leslie threw her hand up to her mouth. "Oh no," she cried. "Not Chris." One of her best friends.

Friday was a night of mourning for the four teenagers killed in the car crash. The funerals were to be on Saturday, and the night before was a time for friends of the four teens to pay their respects at two chapels in Burlington. Deborah Mahaffy drove Leslie to the Smith Funeral Home, which was handling the arrangements for two of the victims, one of them Leslie's friend, Chris Evans.

Leslie had never been to a funeral parlor before, and her choice of outfit that evening stemmed from inexperience rather than any lack of respect for the dead. She wore a pair of beige shorts and a white silk blouse just sheer enough to expose her lacy bra. It was warm and sunny that day and she didn't take a jacket, although she knew she would be out late. After the visitations, a second, more informal, service was planned for the Rock, a spot in some bushes near Leslie's high school where the teenagers gathered to drink beer.

As she pulled up at the funeral home, Deborah Mahaffy reminded her daughter about her curfew, 11 p.m. But Deborah and Dan were willing to make an exception and let her be late just for that evening, as long as she called home so they knew where she was. Leslie gave her mother a hug.

"Goodbye," Leslie said. And then, as she was getting out of the car, perhaps as a sign that their bickering was over: "I love you, Mom."

"I love you too, dear."

She wasn't sure why, but Deborah Mahaffy stayed parked at the curb, staring at the entrance of the funeral parlor, long after her daughter had disappeared inside.

Inside the chapel, Leslie was quickly overcome by grief. Tears streamed down her cheeks as she walked up to Joe and Helen Evans, Chris's parents. She gave Helen a hug, and was quite distraught as she told the parents how sorry she was.

That Friday night around 11, Bernardo was rummaging in the kitchen cupboard where they kept the dog food. Finally he found what he was looking for: a ball of twine.

"I'm going out," he said to Homolka as he walked past her to the garage, "to meet some friends."

She noticed what he was carrying — the twine, a pair of her black pantyhose, and his green-handled knife in the camouflaged sheath. It was his rape kit. Often Bernardo took the kit with him when he went driving, just in case he got lucky and spotted someone he could kidnap and rape. He had told Homolka this several times. She knew he was serious, but she somehow never believed he would actually carry out what he had talked about so much — the abduction of a young girl.

She looked through the living-room blinds as he drove off that night, just two weeks before their wedding.

Leslie and a group of her friends stopped at the beer store in the Super Centre shopping mall after leaving the funeral home. They got an acquaintance in his early twenties to buy them a case of beer, then carried it to their meeting place, about a 10-minute walk away.

There were more than 50 people at the Rock when Leslie and her friends got there, and later the crowd swelled to twice that when other teens returned from Roller Coaster Road, where they had fashioned a makeshift memorial to the victims of the crash. One of Leslie's friends told her what had been written on the plaque: "Four Burlington teens died in an accident here. Let this be a marker to our four friends who are no longer here with us. We've learned to love, laugh and cry, yet we will never learn to forget."

Although most of the teens were upset after the visit to the funeral home, there was a party atmosphere at the Rock. Someone had brought a ghetto-blaster, and "Forever Young" was played over and over. Around midnight the gathering broke up, and Leslie headed for home with her friend Martin McSweeney. They got a ride partway, then walked on to her home on Keller Court, a quiet cul-de-sac in an upper-middle-class area.

But instead of going home right away, Leslie and her friend sat on a grassy knoll near her house and smoked cigarettes. She was late already, so an extra few minutes didn't matter. For over half an hour she and McSweeney talked, mostly about the imminent funeral. McSweeney was upset, he told Leslie, because he had been asked to be a pallbearer, and the thought frightened him.

Eventually McSweeney walked Leslie home, the pair cutting through a neighbor's back yard to get there. Her house was dark, and Leslie was hoping she would be able to sneak in through a side door and into bed without waking her mother. She told McSweeney she didn't feel like listening to a lecture for being so late and not calling. He was worried she was going to get into trouble.

"Yeah, I will," she agreed, but she didn't seem upset. "They'll just yell at me, and I'll still go to the funeral. Call me in the morning."

McSweeney watched as Leslie tried the side door. It was locked. She then headed toward the front of the house. McSweeney started to follow, but she stopped him.

"No, no, no," she said, putting up her hands. "Don't worry, it'll be open."

He was reluctant to leave until she was in the house, but she assured him she would be okay.

"Goodnight," she said, waving as he walked away toward his house, cutting through her back yard. "I'll see you at the funeral."

"See ya," he replied, and then was gone.

Leslie knew the front door was probably locked as well, but McSweeney later surmised in an interview with the police that she didn't want him to know that. Since she didn't

have a key, the only way into her house was to ring the doorbell, wake up her parents, and get the speech on why she
should have been home two hours earlier. She had spent the
night mourning the death of a close friend, and she didn't feel
like listening to her parents nag.

McSweeney had left believing his friend would
either get in through the front door or ring the bell. But Leslie
had something else in mind, which she didn't want to tell
McSweeney about because he would have waited until she
did ring the bell. Leslie had made up her mind to call her
friend Amanda Carpino, with whom she had stayed when she
left home before, to ask if she could spend the night at her
house.

There was a pay phone at an all-night grocery store
near her home, and Leslie headed that way. Carpino was
sleeping when Leslie called. She too had been at the Rock that
night, but had left hours earlier, well before her own curfew.
She was surprised to hear her friend was still out at 2 a.m.

"I've been locked out," Leslie explained. "The lights
are off and I don't want to ring the doorbell. Can I stay at your
place for the night?"

Carpino wanted to know how she would get to her
house, nearly an hour's walk away. Leslie asked if Carpino's
mother could come and fetch her.

"I can't ask my mom," Carpino said, reminding
Leslie that the last time she stayed over there had been trouble between the two families. "Your mother called my mother and gave her hell."

But Carpino felt sorry for her friend. Leslie was
speaking quickly and sounded anxious and confused about
her predicament, saying that if she couldn't stay at Carpino's
house, she didn't know what else to do. She hadn't taken her
wallet and didn't have any money with her. One other time

when Leslie had left home, she and some friends had stayed at a nearby motel for several nights.

Carpino was sympathetic, but her advice was to go home anyway. "You have to," she said. "Wake up your parents. Face the music. Your mom will still let you go to the funeral."

Leslie agreed, but wasn't quite ready to go home yet. They gossiped for more than 20 minutes about who had been at the Rock that night and who was seeing who at school. Finally, Leslie said she was ready.

"Goodnight, woman," Carpino said.

"See you tomorrow," Leslie replied, then hung up and headed back to her house.

Instead of ringing the doorbell, Leslie went into the back yard and sat down at the picnic bench. She had been there for a few minutes when a man wearing a hooded jacket suddenly emerged from the shadows and walked toward her. She was startled at first.

"What are you doing here?" she asked.

Paul Bernardo had been out that night stealing license plates from the quiet Burlington neighborhood. He used the stolen plates to cover his own whenever he went cigarette smuggling. It had become such a huge, clandestine business that the authorities were using special customs agents who routinely hid near the American outlets that sold the cheap cigarettes. They recorded the plate numbers of Canadian cars stopping to buy the cigarettes, and if the drivers didn't declare anything at the border, they were ordered over for a secondary search. Another trick was to spray customers' headlights with a special paint that could be seen only under the special lights at the customs booth. Bernardo was well aware of both tricks. He always left Homolka in the car to make sure no one painted over his headlights. And he always put stolen plates on after he crossed the border, taking them off before returning to Canada.

But he was a cautious man, always on the lookout for new plates to put on his car. That night he had chosen Burlington. He couldn't explain all of that to the pretty young girl he had stumbled on. So out came a lie. He explained that he was casing homes in the neighborhood, and planned to burglarize one.

"Cool," Leslie told him, according to Bernardo. At least this is how he later described the abduction to Homolka.

And then he asked her why she was out so late.

"I've been locked out of my house and I'm scared to wake up my parents."

She asked him for a cigarette, and he said he had a package in his car, parked on the next street over. She followed him there, and he motioned for her to get in on the passenger side. The man seemed friendly enough, but she was reluctant.

"Okay," she said, "but I won't shut the door."

She got into the Nissan, keeping her legs out on the road. The interior of the car was dark; the dome light wasn't working. He passed her a cigarette, then lit it for her. She inhaled deeply, then turned her head to blow the smoke out the door, taking her eyes off him for just a moment. Before she turned back, there was a knife at her throat.

"Get your legs into the car!" Paul Bernardo ordered.

She did as she was told. He reached across her, slammed the door shut, then hit the lever on her seat so that it fell backwards until she was lying almost flat.

"Do as I say or I'll kill you," he threatened, reaching into the back for a polo shirt while still holding the knife at her throat.

He tied the shirt around her eyes like a blindfold, then got a blanket from the back seat and covered her. Leslie was starting to cry as he drove off, heading for the expressway and the 32-mile drive to Port Dalhousie.

There were only a few cars on the Queen Elizabeth Way, and Bernardo kept just under the speed limit, not wanting to be pulled over by the police. Every so often he cast an admiring glance at his captive, the young teenager trembling with fear underneath the blanket. He amused himself on the 30-minute drive by running his hands up her bare legs and over her smallish breasts.

"Just do what I tell you," he warned her, "and you won't get hurt."

20
Cries of a Child

Disoriented by the blindfold, and paralyzed with fear, Leslie never struggled or fought back, just whimpered most of the way. The roads in Dalhousie were empty, and the garage door was open. Bernardo drove inside and got out of the car.

"If you try to run," he said to his prisoner, "I'll kill you."

He went to the back of the car, glancing up and down the deserted street before closing the garage door. His choice of the corner house in the quiet community had been a good one. His neighbors were not the nosy type. The old lady who lived behind him was nearly deaf and seldom left her house. The men beside him and across the street were both retired. Their homes were dark. They had long since gone to bed.

Bernardo opened the passenger door and helped his hostage out. Then he took her into the living room and told her to kneel, warning her that if her blindfold ever came off he would have to kill her. He raised his video camera to his face. "Here's what I want you to do," he said. "Unbutton your blouse and lift up your bra. Do as I tell you and you won't get hurt, okay?"

"Okay."

"Now I've got a camera here and I'm going to turn it on and I want you to do everything I tell you. If you don't, I'm going to have to punish you. Okay?"

"Yes."

"Okay, I'm turning the camera on. Now do as I told you."

Leslie undid the buttons on her white blouse and then shoved up her brassiere.

Bernardo trained the camera on her body. "Tell me your name."

"Leslie Mahaffy."

"Okay, good girl. Now, come here," he instructed, and she moved toward the sound of his voice as he backed up into the hallway. "Turn around and go straight."

She walked down the hallway, bumping into him as she went past, apologizing for hitting him.

"Don't worry about it," he told her.

"Okay."

He directed her into the washroom and over to the toilet. She pulled down her pants and sat on the toilet while he continued taping her. He got down on his knees and put the camera close to her groin.

"You can hear it, okay?" he said, referring to the humming of the camera.

"Oh my God," Leslie said, realizing that he was taping her going to the bathroom.

"Yeah, you knew," he said, getting the camera even closer to her vagina. She had tried backing away on the toilet seat, but he reached out and stopped her. "Come closer. Be good for me, okay?"

"Okay."

When she started urinating, he said: "Ooh, good girl. Good girl. Beautiful job. Fucking perfect. Just perfect. Very, very good. Good girl, yeah." He was getting aroused, and he rubbed his penis until she finished. Then he turned off the camera and directed her into the spare bedroom at the end of the hall. He closed the blinds and told her to lie on the bed.

Then he tied her hands to the bedpost with the twine he had taken with him that night. After she was secured, he hurried upstairs into the master bedroom, where his future wife was sleeping on the floor.

"Kar, wake up," he said, shaking her.

She opened her eyes slowly to see his face flushed and his eyes dancing with excitement.

"I did it," he said, sounding like a schoolboy who had passed an exam. "I got a girl. She's in the house, downstairs."

Homolka thought, at first, that he had picked up a woman in a bar. She didn't want to believe he had done as promised and kidnapped a woman.

"Stay up here," he told her, "until I call for you. Go back to sleep. We'll talk later." Then he rushed back down to the guest room. Homolka rolled over and soon was asleep.

Although it was after 3 a.m., Bernardo was acting as if it was midafternoon. This was his time of the day, when he was most aroused. Though Leslie was sobbing, asking him to let her go, it wasn't going to do her any good. He had waited a long time to get his very own sex slave, and he had no intention of depriving himself of the pleasure. He was also going to take his time with her.

He told her to stop crying, and when she didn't he punched her in the face, cutting her lip, which later appeared bruised on the videotape. Then he untied her, took off her clothes, and fondled her body, pinching her nipples so hard she screamed out in pain. Then he raped her, vaginally and anally. He wanted fellatio afterwards, and he directed her head toward his penis. It was a long time before he climaxed. There was no need for him to rush. And nobody knew she was there.

He got dressed and left her in the bedroom while he fetched some champagne from the kitchen. He took down two glasses, then got the sleeping pills out of the bathroom. He put one in her glass, went back into the bedroom, and filled the two glasses.

Bernardo told her he was happy with her performance and gave her the glass, making sure she drank every drop. He drained his own, poured them each another, then picked up the camera. He told her what he wanted her to do, warning that she would be punished if she didn't do exactly as he had instructed when the camera was on. "Okay," he said, positioning the camera close to her vagina, "you've got to give me something. You've got to touch yourself and tell me what you feel."

Leslie rubbed her hand over her vagina, attempting to masturbate.

"Tell me something," Bernardo ordered, his voice soft but insistent. "Tell me something."

Leslie's voice trembled. "I don't know what to say."

"I think you know, Leslie," he said, moving the lens even closer. "I think you know what to say. Tell me something."

"I ... don't."

"Yes, you do." Bernardo was becoming irritated with her for not giving the right response, but he was busy for the moment with his close-up shots of her vagina and anus. "You're touching yourself really, really well," he said. "I think you know what to say."

"I don't."

"Why don't you keep playing with yourself a little longer down there. That's perfect. Keep doing that." She moved a finger in and out of her vagina. "I like that sound. Now, who's your favorite guy right now?"

"I don't know," she told him, sobbing.

Bernardo's manner up to that point had been calm,

his voice soft. But as he turned off the camera, his mood changed dramatically. Enraged, he punched her several times in the chest, the arms, the side of the head. "You're supposed to say it's me!" he yelled as she cowered on the bed.

"I'm sorry," she said, and when the tape resumed she made the correct response.

"Now, who's your favorite guy? I think you know who I want you to say," he said.

"I want you," she replied, giving him the correct answer.

"Do you?"

"Yeah!"

"Okay, keep playing with yourself. You look fucking gorgeous. I want you too, Leslie."

He started to take off her blindfold. "You're a good girl," he said. "Now keep your eyes shut tight. Really, really tight." He put the blindfold down and trained the camera on her as she masturbated. She squeezed her eyes shut, terrified by her predicament, humiliated by his demands, trembling for her life. The sun was just coming up, and its rays poked through the blinds. A group of joggers passed by the corner house.

Homolka awakened around 8 that morning. Dutifully she waited in the master bedroom for Bernardo to summon her, reading one of his crime novels, *American Psycho*, by Bret Easton Ellis, to pass the time. Bernardo had bought the book some weeks earlier and had been raving about it. The novel was set in Manhattan, and its parallels to Bernardo were disturbing. The central character, Patrick Bateman, was a handsome, blond, 26-year-old businessman, seemingly well adjusted and successful, but in fact a boiling cauldron of hatred, arrogant and moody, with an explosive temper. Bateman was obsessed with his image, and his girlfriend was blonde and beautiful. He liked pornography, read up on serial killers, and had begun his own career as a serial killer by drugging his female victims with the sedative Halcion. Like Bernardo, he videotaped his crimes. Later he cut up the bodies for disposal, and in the end, he eluded capture by the police.

Another book Bernardo had bought was *The Perfect Victim*, the true story of how an American, Cameron Hooker, kidnapped a hitchhiker, then trained her to be his sex slave, putting a box over her head so she would have to rely on him for directions. Hooker kept the woman as his prisoner for seven years before the authorities finally arrested him. She became so conditioned that he even let her leave his house to get a job, knowing she would always return to his home at the end of the day, where he would often physically and sexually abuse her.

Later in the day, Homolka went downstairs to shower, stopping to look at the closed door to the spare bedroom. She crept up to it and listened for a moment, but it was quiet inside. She know better than to knock. Inside, Bernardo and his young prisoner were asleep, she from the Halcion sedatives, he from exhaustion.

Homolka glanced toward the dining-room table, and what she saw made her furious. It was two weeks before her wedding and her husband was in the guest bedroom with another woman whom he had likely kidnapped and raped, and whom they might have to kill. Yet what bothered her most on that cheery June morning was that he had used her finest crystal goblets to serve champagne to his guest. In her mind, that was definitely wrong: those goblets were supposed to be used only on very special occasions they both celebrated.

Homolka showered, and as she was dressing she heard Buddy, who was in his cage in the basement, barking to be let out. If Bernardo got mad at her for disobeying his instructions by not waiting upstairs, she was going to tell him she was afraid someone might hear Buddy barking and, thinking something was wrong, call the police.

Homolka went outside quietly, taking Buddy for his morning constitutional. It was a beautiful spring day, and there were joggers out everywhere. When she returned, the guest-room door was still closed. She took the dog upstairs, lay down on the bed, and awaited Bernardo's instructions.

Leslie awoke later that morning. Bernardo took her into the bathroom and told her to clean up. He taped her while she was showering. The blindfold became soggy and kept sliding down. She continually pushed it up over her eyes, desperately hoping that if she never saw her captor, he might let her go.

"Scrub your bum really well," Bernardo ordered, aiming the camera at her backside.

"Pardon?"

"Your bum," he said, "scrub it really well."

She did as she was told, toweled off, and dressed. Then he led her back into the bedroom and, despite her protestations, raped her once more.

Later, Homolka went downstairs for something to eat, trying to be as quiet as possible. She ate on the living room couch. Bernardo joined her. He was too pleased with himself to be mad about anything. He bragged about how he had tricked the girl into his car.

"Do you think anyone saw you?"

"No," he said smugly. "There was no one around."

He told Homolka to wait in the living room because he was going to take the girl upstairs to the master bedroom. When he was ready for her, he said he would call.

"I want you to take your clothes off," he told his blindfolded prisoner when they were upstairs. He turned on the camera while she slowly unbuttoned her blouse and took off the rest of her clothes. Bernardo ordered her onto her hands and knees, put down the camera, took off his pants, and started to penetrate her vagina from behind. It was painful for her, and she begged him to stop, telling him that she wasn't lubricated.

"Arch your back," he ordered, ignoring her cries.

When she didn't do it right away, he started punching her on the shoulders until she did. Then he wanted fellatio. He led her to the bed, told her to get on her knees while he lay on his back in his favorite position, his legs around her shoulders.

"Don't bite it with those braces," he warned, "or I'll kill you. Just do what I want and you won't get hurt."

Sobbing, she gave him oral sex until he climaxed. He forced her to swallow his ejaculate. Then he bound her legs with the twine, took handcuffs from the night table, and cuffed her hands behind her back. He left her on the floor while he lay down to get some rest.

Afterwards, he unbound her, took off the cuffs, and made her put her clothes back on, except her blouse. He went downstairs and told Homolka to follow him upstairs, but not to speak. Leslie was sitting on the floor by the hope chest, blindfolded. Bernardo and Homolka sat down beside her.

"Have you ever done it with three people?" he asked her.

"No," she replied, and started to cry.

"There's somebody else here," Bernardo said, "that I want you to have sex with."

She kept sobbing fearfully, pleading with Bernardo to let her go, promising that she wouldn't tell anybody. He let her talk for a few moments before revealing that the other person was a woman. Leslie seemed almost relieved that she wasn't going to be raped by another man.

"Okay," Bernardo said. "Now get up and take off your clothes."

She did as she was told, but had trouble taking off her shorts because her hands were trembling so much. Bernardo was staring at her.

"You know, you've got a pretty good body," he told her. "Except for the stomach. It's a little large."

He turned to Homolka. "What do you think?" She knew she wasn't supposed to talk, so she nodded her approval.

Bernardo turned back to Leslie. "Tell me if that blindfold slips," he advised. "I'll have to kill you if you see my face."

Then he directed Leslie to climb onto the bed and wait while they took off their clothes. "By the way," he asked, "do you have a favorite radio station?"

She told him CFNY, and he tuned in to that station. Pink Floyd was singing one of their hits, "Money." Then Bernardo ordered Homolka and Leslie to start kissing each other while he taped them.

"Good ... good," he told them. "Because you're doing such a good job, I want you girls to continue. Especially you, Leslie, because your freedom depends on it."

Then Bernardo lay down on the bed and ordered both of them to give him oral sex while he continued to work the camera. "Yeah, you're doing a great job," he said, moaning with pleasure. "Now what I want you both to do is to lick up the shaft and kiss the top of my dick." He positioned Leslie's head where he wanted it. "Here, start here," he said. "Put your tongue on this side, and lick up."

Blindfolded, Mahaffy wasn't sure what to do.

"Lick right up the side," he said. "I want you to do it about three or four times. Okay, now kiss it. Now again. Lick the whole dick, the whole dick."

"Yes," she said.

"Okay, now find your way up. Ooh, you're doing a good job. You're in my good books now, Leslie. Good girl. Good girl."

Explaining that next he wanted anilingus, he gave the camera to Homolka while he got down on his hands and knees. Homolka helped Leslie into position.

"Okay, put your tongue inside," Bernardo told her. "Right in. Right in. Okay, yeah, yeah. Good girl. Kiss my hole, Leslie. Kiss it. Make me feel good, Leslie."

She raised her head from his backside just long enough to say, "Yes."

"I'm judging you right now," Bernardo went on. "The next two hours are going to determine what I do to you. Okay? Right now you are scoring perfect. You're supposed to tell me something, Leslie. I want to hear something now and then. Don't forget."

"Okay."

"Put your tongue right in the hole, Leslie. C'mon, get it right in my asshole. Put it in deep. Lower. Dig it in. Yes. Yes." And then he began to moan. "Good girl, Leslie. Good job. Perfect, Leslie. Perfect."

Happy, Bernardo told Homolka to make them a round of drinks, motioning for her to spike Leslie's. She offered the first one to Bernardo. Leslie drank some of hers, which had a sleeping pill dissolved in it.

"It's great," Bernardo said, hoisting his glass, "being the king. You girls did really good. I'm really happy."

Bernardo now wanted Leslie to have sex with his friend, as he called Homolka. When he turned the camera back on, Leslie was to ask if she could suck on Homolka's breasts. "Ask her now," Bernardo said, hitting the record button.

"Can I suck your breasts?"

Homolka nodded.

"I think she says yes," Bernardo answered for her.

"Where is it?" Leslie asked, not able to see with the blindfold.

Homolka moved around and put her breasts right in front of Leslie's face, positioning a nipple so that it was almost in her mouth.

"Ask her now," Bernardo instructed.

"Can I suck your breasts?" Leslie asked, and Homolka shoved the nipple into her mouth.

"Good girl, Leslie. Good girl," Bernardo said, holding the camera close. "I think you should say thank you to her for letting you do that."

"Thank you," Leslie said.

"And for what?"

"For letting me suck on your breasts."

"Okay, now I want you to practice on yourself because you're going to be doing this to my friend," Bernardo said, moving Leslie's hand to her vagina. She had stopped trying to resist his orders. Her responses had become automatic, distant, even wooden. It was as if, Homolka would later recall, her body was there but her mind was elsewhere, in a safe place, away from the horror.

"Put your finger right inside." Bernardo held the camera close to her vagina. "Good girl. Okay, now tell me your full name."

"Leslie Mahaffy."

"Say it again."

"Leslie Erin Mahaffy."

"When were you born?"

"In July 1976."

"And what's your favorite pastime, Leslie?"

"I like spending time with my friends."

"You're a good girl. Do you like what you're doing now?"

"Yes."

"And why is that, Leslie?"

"Because it feels nice."

"Good girl. When you have to go to the bathroom, just tell me, okay?"

Bernardo motioned for Homolka to perform cunnilingus on their prisoner. She did so. "Just to let you know, Leslie, that's not me down there," said Bernardo, who was still operating the camera. "Touch your breasts, Leslie. Touch your breasts."

Bernardo directed Homolka to spread her legs. "Okay, Leslie, now I want you to do it," he said, putting the girl's head into position. "Put your tongue right in there, Leslie. You're doing good, Leslie. Keep it up. She's going to judge you on how good you do it. C'mon, let me see that head bob, Leslie."

Afterwards, Bernardo led Mahaffy into the washroom and filmed her while she urinated. Then he had another request for the frightened girl.

"Give me a big fart out of there," he said. "I want something really good, you see, because otherwise I'll kill you and dig it out myself."

Leslie started weeping when he said that, and couldn't stop.

"All right," Bernardo said. "I won't do that if you can't do it for me. But I want you to keep trying. Are you scared?"

"Yes."

"Is that why it's not coming out?"

"Yes."

"Is it coming out at all?"

"I can feel it," she answered, "but I can't quite make it."

"Even though you didn't do it," Bernardo told her as she got off the toilet, "you notice that I didn't fuck you up the ass. You noticed that?"

"Thank you," replied Leslie as Bernardo directed her back to the master bedroom for another round of sex.

Deborah Mahaffy awoke early, put on her nightrobe, and went straight to Leslie's bedroom. She was hoping her daughter would be in there sleeping. But as she walked toward Leslie's room she remembered they had forgotten to cut her the extra key. There was no way her daughter could have entered the house without waking them up.

When she reached the bedroom, Deborah took a breath. Then she slowly opened the door and peered inside. It was just as she had feared. The room was empty; the bed hadn't been slept in. Deborah didn't know why, but she just felt that something awful had happened to her daughter, and suddenly she felt sick to her stomach. Years later, she would remember exactly how she felt that Saturday morning. Indeed, from that moment on, her life would never be the same.

Deborah checked inside the closet. There, hanging up, was the green dress her daughter wanted to wear that day to Chris Evans's funeral. Deborah went into the kitchen and made some coffee. If Leslie had stayed over with friends, she would likely call later that morning. She could be contrite, apologize for not calling the night before, promise never to do it again. Deborah took her coffee to the chesterfield in the front room. The sun poured in. All she could do was wait.

By noon Deborah still hadn't heard from her daughter. She and her husband were worried, but did their best to hide their fears from Ryan. Deborah remained on the couch, hoping that Leslie would come bouncing up the front steps looking for forgiveness. But by early afternoon, when they still hadn't heard from her, Deborah started calling around to some of her daughter's friends.

21
Act of Atonement

Leslie hadn't performed well in the bathroom and Bernardo was going to punish her. He handcuffed her arms behind her back and bound her legs with some electrical cord. He positioned her on her knees in front of the hope chest in the master bedroom, head to the floor and buttocks in the air.

He held his knife close enough to her neck that she could feel the edge of the blade. He wanted her to know he had the power of life and death over her. Then he took off his pants, motioned for Homolka to turn on the camera, and mounted Leslie from her backside. "See, it's good and hard," he said, rubbing his penis across her buttocks. "Oh, yeah, you want it right now."

Her face was pressed flat against the floor, turned to one side. She was crying in pain. "I just want to do what you want," she sobbed.

"Good girl. Yeah," he said, as he started to penetrate her rectum.

She screamed in agony, but Bernardo didn't much care.

"Yeah, oh, yeah," he said, thrusting his pelvis against her. "You wouldn't shit for me. So you're going to get it up the ass, okay?"

Anal rape was the best way Bernardo knew to humiliate his victims. It was painful, and he liked to hear them cry. Leslie pleaded with him: "It hurts, it hurts. Please stop. Please. I'll try again, okay?"

"No," he said.

"Why?"

"You're going to shit after this." He was laughing as he kept pushing into her. "Trust me."

"I want —" she started to say, but couldn't finish because she was grimacing in pain.

"I'm pushing everything deep inside you now."

Leslie was screaming in agony with each forceful plunge into her rectum.

"Just take it, you cunt."

"Let me go, please," she cried. "I won't ever say anything about you."

But Bernardo wasn't listening. "Is this teaching you a lesson?" he asked, the thrusts coming quicker, harder, his grunting louder.

"Yes, this is. Yes. This is teaching me. I ... learned ..."

"What's it teaching you?"

"I'll never tell. I'll never double-cross you."

"Are you sure?"

"I will never even go to the police. I want to see my family again. I want to see my brother. I want to see Ryan. I want to see my friends. Please. Please."

Between grunts, Bernardo replied: "I'm gonna fuck you. Let me finish fucking you first. Keep telling me you're scared."

"Oh, please ... help me! Someone, help me!"

Homolka winced as she listened to the girl's screams, but kept taping the rape and did nothing to interfere. She had gone this far with Bernardo, and there was no stopping him anymore; he would just threaten to show her parents the Tammy tape. There was nothing she could do about his blackmail. Although Homolka later described how sick she felt, she just kept watching, taping the dirty picture she knew Bernardo would watch over and over again, and doing nothing to stop what was unfolding in front of her.

"Get your ass up in the air!" Bernardo screamed at Leslie. "I want your ass up there!"

And when she didn't respond immediately, he started pounding on her back, punching her on the shoulders until she complied.

"Keep arching it!" he shouted.

The blindfold was starting to come off as her face was shoved forward.

"My mask," Leslie pleaded. "Please fix it."

"Your mask is falling off?"

"No, it didn't. But it will."

"Okay," Bernardo said.

But he was close to reaching a climax, his breathing getting louder with every lunge. And then a final shove, and he was done. He moaned as he flopped down over her back, staying there until he caught his breath. Then he looked over at Homolka, who was still filming. He jerked his thumb across his neck. She dutifully turned off the camera and awaited his next instruction.

It was after midnight, and Bernardo was finally satiated. He and Homolka went downstairs to the kitchen and talked about what they were going to do with Leslie. They left her in the master bedroom, bound and handcuffed, still groggy from the sleeping pills they had given her during the day. Later, Homolka recalled what was said.

"We have to kill her," said Bernardo.

Homolka didn't disagree, but wondered if there was any chance they could let her go. But she readily agreed that if they freed their prisoner, she would go right to the police and they would probably end up in jail, and the thought terrified her.

But with her parents coming over later for Father's Day, she knew they had to do something. Bernardo said he wanted to question Leslie, just to find out how much she really knew.

Leslie was curled up in a fetal position on the floor in front of the hope chest. She was bleeding from her rectum and vagina. There were welts on her chest, her back, and arms. Bernardo peppered her with questions.

"If I let you go, would you remember what I looked like?"

"No. No, I wouldn't," Leslie promised, sitting up, shaking her head, crying.

"What do you remember about my car?" He asked her to describe the interior. But she recalled nothing, she told him, because it was dark.

"Not even the cell phone?"

"No."

"Would you go to the police?" he pressed.

"I promise I won't tell," Leslie pleaded frantically. "I'll just say I was out with a friend."

"Do you know where you are? Did you see where I took you?"

"I don't know where I am. I didn't see. Because of the blindfold."

"You're such a lying cunt," Bernardo said, stepping forward and punching her on the back and the shoulders. He turned to Homolka. "We let her go and she'll go right to the police."

Leslie was hysterical with fear. She wouldn't tell anybody, she said. She had run away from home before. She would just tell her mother she had been sleeping over with a friend. No one had to know the truth. But Bernardo had already made up his mind. He motioned for Homolka to follow him downstairs.

"She can identify me," he said in the kitchen. He reminded her that the police had questioned him about the composite sketch of the Scarborough Rapist. "They've got my forensics on file. If they put out another picture, I'll be identified. She has to be killed."

Homolka knew about his earlier interview with the Toronto force. She would later tell police that on this night he said to her that he was indeed the man police were searching for in connection with the rapes.

"She's really scared," Homolka noted, in a weak bid to save the girl's life. "She might not go to the police."

"Do you want to take that chance?" Bernardo snapped back. "Would you rather I go to jail for 25 years? Do you want to go to jail?"

"No."

"Then that's it. I'm going to kill her. There's no other choice." His voice had the finality of a judge handing down a death sentence.

Leslie Mahaffy's only offense was staying out too late. But she was going to pay for it with her life.

The doomed girl's pleas for mercy aroused feelings of shame in Homolka, she later testified. But though she felt terrible guilt, it wasn't enough to make her risk her own life and defy Bernardo. About all the room she had in her heart that night was for the wish that Leslie die as painlessly as possible. When she was eventually judged, Homolka wanted the record to show that, although she didn't try to stop the murder, she did her best to make sure the victim suffered as little as possible. She made a suggestion to Bernardo.

"Can we give her some sleeping pills so she won't have to be awake? That way she won't feel any pain." He agreed, and told her to drug their prisoner while he went into the basement.

Leslie, still naked, was curled up on the floor. Homolka took off the handcuffs and covered her with a blanket. They spoke for a few minutes. Leslie couldn't stop crying as she begged her female captor to free her.

"I won't tell anybody what happened," she promised. "I don't know where I am. If they ask me, I'll just say I didn't really see who did it."

Homolka gave Leslie her teddy bear, Bunky, to hold. The toy was the first Christmas present Bernardo had given Homolka.

"I shouldn't even be here," Leslie sobbed. "This never would have happened if I had gone home on time. I was supposed to go to my friend's funeral," she continued, telling Homolka about the car crash. There had been something in the papers about the accident, said Homolka, and asked to know more. When Leslie described what happened, Homolka commiserated with her, noting how awful it was to lose someone so close.

"My sister just died," she told Leslie. "It was also an accident. She had too much to drink and passed out. Then she choked on her vomit."

Leslie seemed buoyed that her jailer was so friendly. She reached out and gripped Homolka by the arm. "I can't take it anymore. I'm really sore. You must help me to get away from him."

"I can't do anything," Homolka replied.

"Untie me and let me escape."

"He'll beat me if I do that."

"We could both go to the police. I'll say that he forced you to do it."

But Homolka didn't reply.

"Please, you've got to help me," Leslie begged, clutching the teddy bear to her chest. "You must. I have to see

Ryan. I want to see my baby brother again. Please … please, let me see Ryan. I promise I won't tell anyone. Just let me go."

Homolka got a glass of water from the bathroom, took Leslie's hand, and put two sleeping pills in her palm. "Here, take these. It will make you feel better." Homolka watched as Leslie slowly fell asleep, rather like one of the dogs at the clinic.

Leslie had passed out when Bernardo returned from the basement, a section of black electrical cord in his hands. He took off the comforter, stood behind the unconscious Leslie, and put the cord around her neck. Then he started yanking on the ends, the veins in his neck bulging as he tugged. Homolka couldn't bear to look and turned away.

Bernardo grunted with exertion. The ligature bit deeply into the girl's flesh, lacerating the skin just above her Adam's apple and cutting off the oxygen to her lungs. The veins on Bernardo's arms and the backs of his hands were gorged with blood as he choked the life from the girl. His teeth were clenched, his eyes fixed on his victim. A growl came from his throat as he pulled, sweat dripping from his forehead. One minute, two minutes, he kept straining on the cord.

Blood started flowing from Leslie's nose and ears. A pool of urine gathered around her legs. Bernardo finally released the cord, allowing the top part of the body to flop down onto the floor. He stepped back, sweat glistening on his body. Then he turned to his future bride.

Her face was ashen. She had just witnessed an execution carried out by her fiancé just two weeks before their wedding and she felt ill. From the sight of the body. The stench of death. The mess on the floor. And the ghastly deed by her Prince Charming. She began to lose control.

"What are we going to do?" she shrieked. "What are we going to do?"

But far from being upset, Bernardo seemed exhilarated. He rubbed the soreness from his fingers, curling and uncurling them as he poked at the body with his foot, nudging it around as if he had just hit an animal with his car and was checking to see it was indeed dead. "I had to do it," he said. "She could have identified me, and it would have ruined all our plans."

For several minutes, they just stared at the corpse near the bed, when suddenly the body made a noise, like something being sucked up a vacuum hose. Homolka screamed and Bernardo jumped back.

"Oh God, oh God, oh God," Homolka cried. "You didn't kill her! You didn't kill her!"

Bernardo wasted little time. He put the cord back around Leslie's neck. This time, to get better leverage, he planted his foot in the small of her back, and started pulling ferociously on the ends of the cord, determined to squeeze every last remaining breath of life out of her. Satisfied after a time that she was truly dead, he once again stepped back to survey his handiwork.

"Even if she'd lived," he noted about her sudden revival, "she'd have had brain damage from a lack of oxygen."

"My parents are coming over for supper," said Homolka. "What are we going to do … with *that?*"

He threw the comforter on the body and they carted it down to the cold cellar in the basement. When they cleaned up later, Bernardo wanted to burn the comforter because there was blood on it. Homolka pleaded with him to let her keep it: her parents had given it to her as a Christmas present, and it was her favorite. By now Bernardo didn't have the energy left to argue.

"Okay," he said finally. "But just make sure you wash it. Wash everything. Sheets. Pillowcases. All of it. You know about DNA, don't you? I don't want any trace of her left in the house. Just in case."

Bernardo plopped down on the bed, and Homolka sat beside him, massaging his shoulders. He welcomed her touch, craning his neck as she rubbed his muscles. He gave her a kiss when she finished. And then they went to sleep.

Homolka stayed on the bed that night instead of the floor.

The Homolkas arrived shortly after noon on Sunday to celebrate Father's Day. Dorothy Homolka had been at the house before, but it was Karel's first visit. His daughter gave him a big hug, then the couple gave him a tour of the house, starting with the master bedroom. It was Homolka's mother who noticed the spot on the carpet near the hope chest that looked like blood. She bent down for a closer look.

"It's nothing, Mom," Homolka said while Bernardo directed Karel down the hall to the spare room. "I spilled some tomato juice."

On the main floor Bernardo boasted that he was going to set up a sound studio in the house. "I plan to be a rap singer."

He opened the door to the basement, but then stood blocking the doorway. There was no way he could let them go down there. "There's really nothing to see downstairs," he said. "It's unfinished." And then he closed the door and asked his future in-laws what they wanted to drink.

Conversation focused mainly on the wedding. Homolka was thankful her parents didn't argue about the plans for the horse-drawn carriage, and discussion then shifted to what the guests would be served. Bernardo again insisted on pheasant. Homolka's parents were opposed, and talk about the wedding continued as mother and daughter prepared the chicken for dinner. Dorothy noticed that her daughter had forgotten the potatoes.

"We have some in the basement," Homolka said, without thinking.

"I'll go and get them," her mother said, and headed that way. "In the cold cellar?" Having been to the house before, she knew the couple kept foodstuffs there.

"Oh, no, Mother," Homolka blurted out, elbowing around her to reach the stairs first. "I'll get them."

"I can do it," her mother said, giving her daughter a curious look.

But Homolka didn't respond, hurrying instead down to the cold cellar. From the living room, Bernardo watched anxiously as his future mother-in-law hesitated at the top of the basement steps.

"Mrs. H.," he called out, "can I make you another drink?"

It worked. She shook her head no, then went back into the kitchen.

A horrible thought flashed through Homolka's mind as she scurried to get the potatoes. If her mom found the dead body in the cellar, would Paul try to kill her parents to protect their secret? She had witnessed two deaths and done nothing. But she couldn't stand by and let him do that. He'd have to kill all of them. And then he'd have a houseful of bodies to get rid of.

She reached for the cold cellar's doorknob, paused, took a deep breath, then went inside and flicked on the overhead light. The only way to reach the shelf with the potatoes was to pass by the body stretched out on the floor and taking up most of the room. She could barely get by without stepping on it. Homolka avoided looking down or brushing against the corpse as she moved skittishly around it. Potatoes in hand, she turned to go. But she couldn't stop herself glancing down.

She nearly screamed out in horror; it was all she could do to keep herself from gagging. Her comforter covered most of the body, but the face was exposed, and it stared back up at her grotesquely, just like something out of a horror movie.

The laughter from upstairs drifted down into the basement. If only they knew ... But she could hardly cancel the wedding. What would she tell the guests? "I can't get married to Paul because we killed two people, and that's not the best way to start off one's married life?"

Homolka took several deep breaths as she closed the door to the cellar. Upstairs, she didn't say anything at first. Her mother noticed that something seemed wrong.

"Are you all right?"

Homolka smiled. "I'm fine. I'm just coming down with bronchitis."

During dinner, Homolka talked about her job, about how much she enjoyed working with the animals at the clinic. Paul, she bragged, was just getting going with his private accounting business. He had even set up his own company, Growth, Inc. Finally, Homolka and Bernardo stood on their front porch, watching as their dinner guests headed for their car.

"We have to get rid of that body," she said. "We can't leave it in the basement. How are we going to do it?"

Bernardo was waving goodbye to her parents when he replied: "I've been thinking of a way." He explained what he had in mind. "And don't worry. No one will ever find her. But you'll have to help me."

"I can't," Homolka replied, totally repulsed.

"Yes, you can. If I say you will, you will!"

It had been a long time since she had refused to do something for him. But she was opposing him now, even though she knew it probably meant a beating. "I can't do it," she said. "It would just make me sick."

Bernardo didn't push it, although he was not used to having her say no. He was the master, and she was the slave, and slaves did not rebel. But he didn't beat her that night.

What Homolka learned was that she could say no to his demands. It was the first time that she had showed strength and resolve in their relationship. For a brief moment, she found her missing backbone and the courage that went with it. If she had shown such fortitude earlier, it could have saved the life of her sister. But Homolka was far from traveling on the road to valor.

Bernardo and Homolka later gave differing versions of what happened next, and since they were the only two people there, it is likely that the truth lay somewhere in the middle between their stories. Bernardo likely said that if she wasn't going to help him, the least she could do was to assist him in preparing the basement for his task.

He probably explained that their first job was to tape over all the basement windows to ensure that no one would see inside. Then they would have to place newspapers around the drain to soak up the blood. Finally, they would have to do something to catch the splatters of blood that might cake the basement walls. Bernardo came up with the novel idea of fashioning a tent in the laundry room. Along with the tools his grandfather had bequeathed him had come a plastic tarpaulin. He spread it over the floor, taped down the ends, and set up a pole as the centerpiece. Late that Sunday night, he was ready.

A brief smile crossed Deborah Mahaffy's lips as she gazed at the picture of her daughter on the beach in Florida. There were so many good memories, and she just couldn't bear to think that's all she might have left. Even when Leslie had left home, and although the two had been squabbling, she had called every night. And finally there was that one phone call. "Hi, Mom," her daughter had said. "I'm coming home." Her heart ached to hear something like that again.

It was different this time, though. There had been no phone calls from her daughter. Nearly two days, and not a word. The police had been notified, but, since Leslie had left home before, she was considered, in their language, a runner. That meant the troops were not going to be mobilized to hunt for a wayward teen who had more than likely left home of her own accord. They didn't say it to Deborah's face, but she knew they didn't want to waste time chasing a runaway.

How could she make them understand that this time Leslie had not run away? There had been no argument, she hadn't taken a change of clothes, and Leslie would never have missed the Saturday funeral service. It was all she had talked about since the accident. She had gone to the viewing the night before. It didn't make sense that she wouldn't show up for the burial the following day.

Deborah had checked with Leslie's friends. None of them had seen her on Saturday. But try getting the police to listen. It was pretty clear that Deborah and Dan Mahaffy were on their own, at least for the time being, in trying to find their 14-year-old daughter.

Ryan came into the living room and over to his mother. She gave him a hug.

"When is Leslie coming home, Mommy?"

"Soon, I hope," she replied. "Very soon."

22

Boxed Human Remains

Karla Homolka got up at dawn that Monday morning, but couldn't coax herself out of bed. Beside her, Bernardo stirred slightly, then fell back asleep. It amazed her that he slept so soundly. She couldn't remember the last time she had a decent night's sleep, certainly not in the past six months, since her sister's death. People at work had started to comment on the tired lines under her eyes, and she couldn't keep blaming everything on the upcoming wedding. She would have to come up with a new excuse because in two weeks' time she was going to be married.

When she finally got out of bed, Homolka put on a nightgown and headed downstairs to make some coffee. She didn't want to go to work that day, but she knew that if she stayed home Paul would want her to help him get rid of the body, and she balked at that. Although she dealt with sick and dying animals every day at the veterinary clinic, she didn't have the stomach to touch a human corpse.

She dreaded the thought of making small talk with her co-workers. "How was your weekend?" "Not bad. I watched my fiancé strangle a young girl to death, but other than that, it was quiet." Homolka averted her eyes from the casual glances of passersby as she walked the short distance from her house to the bus stop on Main Street. Local residents would later recall a quiet, almost withdrawn, woman passing by. Sometimes she had noticeable marks on her arm. On this day she was petrified that if anybody gazed into her eyes they would see the guilt. She avoided the pleasant morning smile of the bus driver and walked with her head down past the other passengers, quickly taking her regular seat at the back of the bus, staring vacuously out the window as the bus traveled to the animal clinic.

She continued the charade with her co-workers, commenting blandly about the "quiet weekend" she and Paul had spent at home. Finally she could take it no more: she ran into the washroom, locked the door, sat down on the toilet lid, and started to cry.

Bernardo got up early that Monday morning, according to the prosecutor's version of what happened. He dragged the body out of the cold cellar and positioned it in the middle of the homemade tent he was about to turn into an abbatoir.

When Bernardo had been in high school, a Toronto homicide detective had once lectured there on the law and society. The officer had described a murder that the press had labelled "the Torso Case," in which a woman had been killed by her lover, who had then cut up the body to try to cover up the crime. But the body parts had been found and the lover eventually arrested and convicted. Several students had later asked the detective questions about his job. One was Bernardo. But his query was quite odd, and the detective would later recall it.

"Is anal intercourse a crime?" he had wanted to know. Only if the sex is with a minor, or not consensual, he had been told.

Years later, Bernardo, out drinking in a bar with friends, had inexplicably started to talk about committing the perfect crime. The way to do it, he told his pals, was to cut up a body, encase the pieces in cement, then toss them into a lake. On that Monday morning, just two weeks before his wedding, Bernardo was about to test his theory. He stripped to his shorts, put on a pair of welder's glasses, then went to the work bench and grabbed the power saw, the one with the seven-inch blade that his grandfather had given him.

He plugged the saw into an extension cord and pressed the trigger switch. The motor kicked in and the blade whirred. Five thousand revolutions a minute. More than enough power to slice through most anything, including a dead body. He glanced over at the corpse, sizing it up.

The blade wouldn't be deep enough, he estimated, to get through her torso. He unplugged the saw, found a wrench, and unloosened the wing nut that held the blade. He dropped the blade down as far as it would go, to the maximum cutting depth, and tightened the nut. Finally he was ready. He plugged in the saw and tried to figure out where to start the amputation. Dr. Bernardo was making a house call, and he was about to perform some radical surgery.

Later, in court, he would casually say: "It was the legs first, then the arms, then the head."

He knelt down by her knees, got a firm grip on her shinbone to keep it from moving around, switched on the saw, and started to cut.

The carbide-tipped blade sliced easily through the skin, but even at 5,000 revolutions a minute the machine whined when the blade hit the tibia. Blood, skin, and bits of bone shot out from the exhaust chamber of the saw. The blood splattered on the walls of the tent to a height of about three feet.

But Bernardo wasn't looking at the mess he was making. His attention was riveted on the leg, his hands pushing down on the saw handle as it sliced through the tibia. And then he was through. He released the trigger switch, but not before the blade left a shallow groove in the concrete floor. He had only just started, but already he was coated in blood. Bernardo drained as much blood as he could from the severed limb, then threw the leg down and started on the other.

He moved up to the thighs next, and bodily fluids from the torso spilled out onto the floor as each thigh was severed. Then he moved to the arms.

The right one gave him some trouble. The blade kept stalling on the skin. He couldn't find the best angle to sever it from the shoulder, and he had to make several passes at it, each time leaving little grooves in the skin from the blade of the saw, before he finally succeeded. At last, all that was left was the torso and the head.

The head was remarkably easy: he was through the neck in no time. He put down the saw and picked up Leslie's head by the hair. A clump of clotted blood seeped out of the neck and plopped onto the floor. He flung the head onto the pile of severed body parts.

For the first time, Bernardo felt exhausted as he stared at the heap of dissected flesh. The job had taken nearly an hour. But there was no time to rest. He cleaned himself up and went out to buy the cement.

Amanda Carpino couldn't remember, but Deborah Mahaffy kept pressing her anyway, hoping Leslie's friend might recall something — *anything!* — that would give them a clue to her daughter's disappearance. Carpino said Leslie had called the night she disappeared and asked to stay over because her parents had locked her out. But there wasn't much more Carpino could recollect about the late-night call, even though the conversation had been just two days earlier.

"She called from the grocery store near your place," Carpino said, adding that Leslie claimed she was heading home to "face the music."

At least Deborah had a fairly rough idea of her daughter's movements that night. She *had* gone home, but, finding the door locked, she had gone to the store on Upper Middle Road. She had finished the call to Carpino on a positive note, agreeing that she had to go home, so whatever happened took place on the walk home. Here was something that Deborah and her husband could do. They could start checking at the grocery store, and the bar beside it. They could canvass residents on the walk home. If the police weren't going to do their job, then it was up to her and Dan to try to find their daughter themselves.

"I'm building a deck," Bernardo said to the clerk at the Beaver Lumber store that Monday, "and I need some bags of quick-dry cement."

The clerk wanted to know the size of the deck, and Bernardo made up something off the top of his head.

"Uh, I'm dropping in about four posts, each three foot square." The lying came easily to him. "I want a firm footing."

The clerk tried some mental mathematics, but couldn't come up with an answer. He called his boss, who squinted as if in pain when the clerk asked him how many bags of cement the customer would need. They were joined by another clerk, then a third. Soon a small crowd of Beaver Lumber employees had gathered around Bernardo, each trying to figure out the answer. Bernardo described the back of his house and the size of the deck he was planning. Finally, one of the clerks ventured, "I think you'll need about 20 bags."

The purchase, with tax, came to $99. Bernardo reached into his pocket, pulled out a wad of bills, and peeled off one — a hundred-dollar bill. A clerk helped him load the bags of cement, 66 pounds each.

"Maybe you should make a second trip," he suggested, checking the sag on the rear axle of the Nissan. "You're carrying a lot of weight there already."

At home Bernardo unloaded the first batch of bags and took each bag down into the basement. Even though he was in good shape from working out with weights in his basement, it was heavy work. Not wanting to leave the body lying around in case someone came over, he drove right back to the lumber store and loaded up the remaining bags of cement.

"Good luck on your project," the clerk said, giving him a wave.

Maybe the idea was good, but it was turning out to be a long, hard day.

Back at home, Bernardo mixed the quick-drying cement in a plastic pail, then poured some into the bottom of each of the boxes he had picked up on his way home from the lumber store. He then placed the body parts in the eight boxes. The one holding the torso took the most concrete and was the heaviest, about 200 pounds. Later he would laugh as he described to Homolka how the head kept bobbing up in the cement until finally he had to hold it down with one hand as he poured in the rest of the concrete. Then he cleaned up again.

There were about a dozen bags of cement left, and since he didn't have any use for them, he decided to take them back to Beaver Lumber for a refund. He loaded up the car and headed for the lumber store, where the employee who had helped him load the heavy bags recognized Bernardo from earlier in the day.

"Didn't need as much as I thought," Bernardo told him.

The woman behind the customer service counter reached for a merchandise return form. She needed to know why he was returning the cement.

"The clerks," Bernardo replied, "overestimated how much I needed."

That satisfied her. But before Bernardo could get his money back, there was something else she needed for the form. "Can I have your name, please?" she asked. "And your address."

Bernardo hesitated for just a moment. If he gave his name, there would be a record of the purchase, a paper trail. He didn't think anyone would ever find the body parts, but if they did, they might be able to track him through the purchase. What had he been thinking of, going back for a $50 refund? It was a stupid mistake, and he wanted to kick himself for making it. But he just smiled at the woman, then gave her his name and address.

That's right, he told her. Bayview Drive was in Port Dalhousie. Yes, it was a beautiful community. He knew he had blundered by going back to the store, but if he had run out of the store, it would certainly have attracted attention.

On the drive back home, Bernardo thought about where he could get rid of the concrete caskets — a spot where no one would ever find them. He chose Lake Gibson. There was a remote spot where he and Homolka had gone to make love.

Bernardo picked up Homolka after work. He was quiet for most of the drive, but as he turned onto Bayview Drive he said, "Wait till you see the basement. It looks like an abattoir."

They went straight downstairs, and he pointed out the eight concrete caskets neatly stacked up along a wall. When he showed her the laundry room where he had done the dissection, she shrieked. She worked for a vet, and had experienced the stench of sick and dying animals, but nothing could have prepared her for what she saw. His makeshift tent was covered in blood. She opened a bottle of lemon-scented Lysol and kept pouring the contents into the pail, thankful that the cleaner's powerful smell partially masked the putrid stench.

The saw was covered with blood, on the blade, in the motor, all over the handle. There were bits of skin stuck in the exhaust vent. Bernardo held the saw under the tap, trying to rinse it clean. But the only way to do that thoroughly was to take it apart. And what if he missed a tiny speck of blood? That's all it would take to get a DNA match. There was only one choice: he would have to chuck it into the lake. He took a hammer and tried to smash the saw to pieces, but succeeded only in knocking off a piece of the handle and leaving several large dents in the frame. He wiped down the saw to obliterate his fingerprints, then he busied himself picking up the torn pieces of the cardboard boxes. He got a blaze going upstairs in the fireplace and burned the cardboard, along with the emptied cement bags.

When he returned to Homolka, she was on her knees, gagging, reaching down into the drain, which was plugged with hair, pieces of skin, bits of cardboard. Bernardo just watched her. He had already done his share. Finally, she got it unclogged.

Later, upstairs, they sat down at the dining table and he told her about his day.

"I don't ever want to eat meat again," he said emotionally. But he spoke in a flat, almost dead, tone, Homolka later recalled, as he described how he cut the body into 10 pieces. His voice grew animated again only when he laughed about the lightness of Leslie's head. He told her that some of Leslie's hair had been sticking through the concrete, so he had to spray-paint the casket black to disguise it.

The following evening, when he again picked her up after work, he told her there were two concrete blocks in the back of the car. They drove to Lake Gibson. Along the way he told her he had already dumped five of the caskets into the water.

The place he had chosen was near a bridge. When he got there, he backed the car in close to the water's edge, so that it was partially hidden by bushes from passing traffic on Beaverdams Road, then killed the engine and told Homolka to act as a lookout. He took the two caskets out of the hatchback one at a time and threw them into their watery grave near the inlet where he had thrown the other five. Then they returned home for the largest piece, weighing 200 pounds, that held Leslie's torso.

They struggled with it up the stairs, dropping it once. It was about the size of a large suitcase and it landed with a thud, as each would later testify. Some fluid spilled out from cracks in the concrete, so Bernardo wrapped a garbage bag around the casket before they carted it into the car.

Since the block was too heavy to throw, they chose a new spot, a lonely bridge off Faywell Road, at the western end of Lake Gibson. Bernardo pulled the car over to the shoulder. He put on his rubber gloves before he opened the trunk. When Homolka joined him, he glanced down at her hands.

"Put on your fucking gloves, you stupid cow," he shrieked. "Can't you do anything right?"

She took the plastic gloves from the car, but accidentally slammed the door. The noise startled Bernardo and brought on another torrent of verbal abuse. She knew that meant another beating. He eased the casket out, holding up one end, waiting for her to put her gloves on, yelling at her to hurry up. Homolka grabbed the other end and together they carted it to the bridge, groaning under the heavy load as they lifted it onto the wooden railing. Homolka ripped off the garbage bags, then Bernardo shoved it over into the rapids.

There was a huge splash and the spray kicked them in the face as they peered over. The concrete box struck the pilings of the bridge, and the impact knocked the top part off the casket, exposing the torso and loosening it from its container. But the water was so murky that it was impossible for them to see that this had happened.

Bernardo flung the housing from the smashed saw as far as he could, and it landed in the water about 20 feet away. He then threw the rest of the broken tool elsewhere in the lake. As they drove home, Bernardo said, mistakenly as it turned out, "Don't worry. No one will ever find anything. If we ever get caught, though," he said, "we'll go to jail for the rest of our lives."

23

Lonely Rivers Flow

When Donna saw her old friend from high school she was shocked. The Karla Homolka she had known back then always dressed in black, with six shades of color in her hair, several of them black. But there was her old friend, sitting at the counter in the coffee shop, looking as normal as any of her other customers. She was all decked out in white, in the clinic's uniform. Her hair was back to its natural blond. The two hadn't seen each other for almost two years, and Homolka smiled when she spotted Donna behind the counter waiting to take her order. But it was a weak, sad smile, Donna thought.

Homolka explained that she was working at the veterinary clinic in the mall not far from the donut shop. They talked about the old days for a few moments, but there was no mention of suicide and how unhappy they had both been back then. And then Homolka announced that she was getting married next week. She did her best to sound excited.

Donna congratulated her and asked if it was to the fellow she had been dating in high school, the handsome accountant from Toronto.

Yes, Homolka replied, then went on to describe how her life had been so wonderful after high school. "Paul is just the greatest." She beamed. "We're really in love. I'm just so excited about getting married."

It seemed to Wilson that Homolka was belaboring the point, almost trying to convince herself what a great husband he would make. Donna noticed the bruises on Homolka's arms and asked about them.

"It's the dogs at the clinic," Homolka explained, and started to look around, seeming uncomfortable with the line of questioning. "They can get really rough sometimes." Homolka gulped down her coffee and got up to go just as a gold Nissan sportscar pulled up to the donut shop.

"It's Paul," she said, waving goodbye.

Donna had seen the car before, and she recognized the man behind the wheel. She had seen him before, alone, cruising around the lot, maybe looking for someone. Donna recalled that one of her friends who worked at the donut shop had complained about a good-looking guy in a sportscar who had been driving around the donut shop late at night, as if he was prowling for women. Could it be, she wondered, the same man?

Her friend had described the car, but she couldn't remember the make. Was it a Nissan? Or a Toyota? No, it was more like a Nissan because it had the same style of rear lights as a Camaro, running the width of the car.

Donna was disappointed that Homolka hadn't asked for her home address. She assumed she wasn't going to get invited to the wedding. Could Bernardo really be, Donna wondered, so wonderful? How could any man be Mr. Perfect? But she was busy that day and quickly forgot about Homolka and her fiancé as she went off to serve the customers.

Homolka was out that day with some of her bridesmaids trying on her wedding gown at a shop on the American side of Niagara Falls. They were all in the changing room when Homolka started to undress, first taking off her blouse. It was then that one of her friends, Cathy Ford, noticed the bruises on her back, several grayish-colored welts on either side of her spinal column. Ford glanced at another of the women there, Lisa Stanton, who was also staring at the marks. It looked, the two women later said, as if someone had been hitting Homolka with their fists. But despite their concern, nobody said anything to her that day.

A week later some friends had a Jack and Jill party for Bernardo and Homolka. Though everyone had had a lot to drink, they were not too drunk to ignore the crude way Bernardo was treating his bride-to-be, constantly referring to her as "the bitch," as in "I hope the bitch and I will be happy together."

As was his custom Bernardo walked around that night with his camcorder, videotaping his friends. But not all of them had nice things to say to him.

"What I want to know," said Doug Ford, staring at the camera, "was how Karla met a mongoloid such as you?"

His wife Cathy again noticed some bruises on her friend, four welts on each forearm. This time she wasn't going to hold her tongue.

"How did you get those marks?" Ford asked when the two were alone.

"I was doing some gardening," Homolka replied. "I bruise easily."

Ford found that explanation hard to believe, but she didn't push it. Homolka seemed happy, although her eyes, the window into the soul, said otherwise. It was just a week before Homolka's wedding. Although she was smiling a lot, it all seemed forced, and many of her friends later talked about the lack of any joy in her blue eyes.

Dan Mahaffy had gone to Spencer Smith Park in Burlington that afternoon strictly on a hunch. He and his wife, Deborah, were running out of places to look for their missing daughter.

Leslie had now been gone for a week. The Mahaffys had checked the mall, Leslie's hangouts around Burlington, and the homes of friends where she might have been secretly staying. There had been one sighting, in Banff. But the police, who had finally got involved in the hunt, had looked into that one and written it off.

Leslie had never turned up at school on the Monday to write her mathematics exam. She had written two exams just before she disappeared, neither of which she expected to pass. But she had done well in math all year, and it was one of the few courses she had been counting on passing. Not turning up to write the exam just didn't make sense. None of her friends understood it, either. One of them had suggested the Mahaffys try Spencer Smith. Someone thought they had seen Leslie at the park by the lake.

It was one of Leslie's favorite places. When his daughter was younger, they used to take her there all the time. She loved playing in the sand and chasing the seagulls across the beach. The park was jammed that day for the annual music festival. Dan had been wandering through the crowds for nearly an hour and was just about to go home when he saw a girl in the crowd who looked like his daughter.

"Oh God, please," he said to himself as he started to weave through the crowd. For a moment, he lost sight of her. He called out her name, but the girl was too far ahead to hear.

Near a children's area, some swings, monkey bars, a sandbox, he began to run. But the girl had moved on.

"Leslie! Leslie!" he yelled out, desperately looking around the park.

He was attracting attention. People had stopped to stare. Many of them were parents who understood his consternation. Then he saw her again. In the distance, near the water. And now he was almost certain it was Leslie.

His heart was thumping with excitement as he ran closer. Same hair, build, everything. Thank you, God, Dan said to himself as he got closer, pushing people out of the way. He reached out and put an arm on her shoulder. "Leslie," he said. "We've been worried sick. We —"

The blonde turned to him and gave him a nasty look. Nearby, two teenaged boys started walking her way, coming to her aid because she was being accosted by a strange man.

"Oh, I'm sorry," Dan blurted out, "I'm sorry. I thought you were my daughter."

Homolka wore a sleeveless white blouse to the dress rehearsal at the church the night before the wedding. Ford noticed fresh marks on Homolka's elbows. So did another bridesmaid, Debbie Dalgleish. The bruises where easy to spot as Homolka put her arms around Bernardo's neck to give him a kiss. Although she was smiling, and he laughing, others in the wedding party felt uneasy about what was really going on.

While she was looking at the bruises, Dalgleish remembered a time she and Homolka had been walking to school in 1988, about a year after she had met Bernardo. Homolka had a bruise on her cheek, and when Dalgleish kept staring at it, Homolka had self-consciously put her hand to her face, then tried to cover the mark with her hair. But when Dalgleish had kept staring at it, Homolka had volunteered an explanation. "I must have done it in my sleep. I think I hit myself in a dream. I just woke up, and there it was."

Dalgleish had forgotten about the incident until now. But neither she nor any of the others said anything to Homolka that night. It was an awkward topic to bring up with a friend the day before she was going to get married. Homolka could easily have hidden the bruises by wearing a long-sleeved blouse that evening, but she had done just the opposite. It was as if she was sending out a signal to her friends that she was in trouble. And while they got the message, nobody knew what to do. And none of them was brave enough to step in and call a halt to the proceedings.

Deborah was sitting at the dining-room table when her husband returned. She had commandeered it as her command post, and it was covered with scraps of paper with phone numbers, notebooks of possible locations to check, posters seeking information about her missing daughter.

The newspapers had finally shown some interest in the case, but the stories usually contained quotes from the police saying that Leslie had left home before, implying, inaccurately, that she was a runaway.

There had been several sightings of Leslie, from British Columbia to New York, but Deborah knew they were all wrong. She had no proof, but she was almost certain that something terrible had happened to her daughter.

The pews were packed with family and friends on that warm, sunny Saturday afternoon, June 29, 1991. They rose when the bride entered St. Mark's Anglican church in Niagara-on-the-Lake and began her slow walk up the aisle. Karla Homolka was in traditional white, her veil adorned with garlands of delicate baby's breath. Paul Bernardo turned and smiled at her as she joined him before the altar of God.

Although it was supposed to be a joyous occasion, Cathy Ford and others in the wedding party were edgy. Homolka had supposedly been planning for the past year, but she and Bernardo hadn't even had a reservation that night at the hotel until her bridesmaids made frantic last-minute calls. Homolka's parents weren't very happy either. She had ignored their requests to postpone the wedding or at least cut down on some of the costs. And Bernardo was barely on speaking terms with his family. Nothing about the day seemed right, except for the lovely weather. But everyone tried their best to appear happy.

"Dear friends," the minister began, "we have come together in this place of God to witness the marriage . . ."

It was just after noon on that same Saturday afternoon when Michael Doucette and his son, Michael Jr., decided to go fishing. Doucette, a technician at a paper mill in Thorold, just outside St. Catharines, hadn't taken his rod and reel out once yet that year. Father and son packed up their gear and drove the short distance from his St. Catharines home to Lake Gibson, just south of the city.

People often fished and swam in Lake Gibson. But the lake served another purpose that Bernardo and Homolka never realized when they pitched the concrete caskets into its murky waters. It was a reservoir for one of Ontario Hydro's power-generating stations. The levels in the lake often fluctuated as the water flowed over the hydro dam at the western end — sometimes by as much as two or three feet. That Saturday afternoon the water in the lake had dropped nearly two feet.

Doucette and his son headed to a popular fishing hole at the eastern end of the lake, a small inlet just off of Beaverdams Road where the water was calm and shallower than usual. The ground was littered with pop and beer cans. Aside from the fishing, the area also served as a Lovers' Lane. If one parked far enough back, there were just enough bushes to hide a car from the road.

Doucette and his son walked to the edge of the bay with their fishing gear. The muddy banks were covered in footprints; several other fishermen had been there before them that day. A couple were just pushing their canoe into the bay, and the man pointed out to Doucette and his son something odd in the water. It was some 20 feet from the shore, and was square in shape. It wasn't a box, Doucette could tell that much, and there was something unusual about it. He was staring at the object so intently that he never heard the father and his two sons walk up behind him.

"We noticed it too," said the man. "Something strange there."

"What do you think it is?"

"No idea," the man replied, shrugging as he walked away.

Doucette couldn't take his eyes off the mysterious object. As he was scanning the water surrounding it, he spotted a second one, also square, but flatter and wider than the first. It appeared to be embedded in the muddy bottom of the cove, as if it had been thrown there from the shore. That was enough for Doucette. He kicked off his shoes, took off his socks, rolled up his pant legs, and waded into the water to have a look.

It was the part of the wedding ceremony in which Paul Bernardo got most animated, as if he had been waiting for just these particular words.

"If anyone present knows any reason why these two should not be joined together —"

Bernardo dropped his head slightly, a motion picked up on the video camera recording the wedding, then moved just his eyes, glancing furtively to left and right.

"— they must come forward now, or forever hold their peace."

Silence. Bernardo, still looking down at the floor, clenched his fists, then relaxed as the service resumed with the exchange of rings and vows.

"God bless you in this undertaking, and give you the strength to succeed," the minister continued. "You've set yourself a pretty substantial agenda. Let the strength of your love enrich our lives. May your marriage home be one of truth, security, and love."

And he pronounced them husband and wife. After they had signed the register, and as they walked down the aisle together, everyone rose for Mr. and Mrs. Bernardo. It was a perfect day for the union of the perfect couple, and they acknowledged the well-wishers with smiles and nods. Homolka scanned the crowd. Finally she spotted her old friend Renya Hill.

Renya smiled back, then mouthed "Congratulations, Barbie" to her friend, who acknowledged their little secret with her eyes. But then Homolka's expression changed, and for a long moment their eyes remained locked. Then the couple was past her and out of the church.

It was only much later that Renya Hill reinterpreted the strange look in her friend's eyes as one of grief. At the time she had believed it was just nerves. How could anyone feel anguish on their wedding day? But her thoughts kept returning to that changed look; the smile was still there, but joy had shifted to despair.

The water in the bay was barely knee high as Doucette waded out to take a closer look. As he got closer, he realized he had been staring at five concrete blocks of varying shapes, ranging from one the size of a hatbox to one the size of a two-four of beer. It looked to Doucette that the tops on several of them were coming off. He moved over to one and lifted the lid. It took a few seconds, but then the wave of nausea swept over him. He jerked upright and backed away toward the shore, calling out to his son.

Of all the people who gave speeches that afternoon, it was Karel Homolka, the father of the bride, who received the loudest applause. He remained in deep mourning for the loss of his daughter, as did his wife, but still neither suspected how she had died. Two years would pass before their daughter finally told them the truth.

"It's nice to have all our friends here," he began, "to celebrate the wedding of my daughter and son-in-law. I would like to take this chance to thank our friends and family for their love and support in the past six months. Please join me in a special toast to our little angel, Tammy Lyn. God bless you, darling. We miss you."

The guests were still applauding as he returned to his table and embraced Dorothy. At the head table, Bernardo turned to Homolka. He was smiling; she was not.

A speech by one of Bernardo's friends, Ed Douglas, drew plenty of snickers. "There are a lot of things I could say about Paul," he began, "but it wouldn't be appropriate at a wedding. Paul's one heck of an animal. I've never seen a guy with such animal characteristics. It's a good thing that Karla works at a vet's and loves animals, because that's what she's marrying."

Chrissie Mann worked at the pet shop where Homolka had got her first job, and had traveled to Toronto with Homolka in 1987 on the weekend when she first met Bernardo. "It was supposed to be a growth experience," she said about the trip, "but instead Karla picked up some guy from Toronto, some *slummy* Toronto guy. And you know the rest."

Finally it was the turn of the bride and groom. Bernardo spoke first, starting by thanking his parents, his grandparents, and his friends. Earlier in the night, however, he had been yelling at his mother when she started griping about the quality of the dinner. He had also been practically shouting at people in the wedding party, complaining that they weren't around for the dances, or weren't seeing to the needs of his guests. Although everyone was superficially having a good time, there seemed to be an undercurrent of anger, much of it stemming from the groom. It was as if the evening was a reflection of Bernardo's true character: glitz on the outside, turmoil within. Even his speech reflected that—though no one could have guessed, he was practically confessing to double persona when he said, "I have people here from all my different lives. And I have a lot of different lives."

He went on to talk about his and Karla's first meeting in Scarborough, and how difficult it had been to keep a romance going when they lived in separate cities. "We paid a pretty big price," he said, referring to all the commuting. "The Homolkas welcomed me into their family right from the beginning. If it weren't for the Homolkas, and their support, the relationship would never have survived." And then he smiled and waved to the gathering.

"I don't have a lot to say," Homolka began, and thanked her friends for helping her through what had been a very difficult time, the death of her sister. She thanked her parents for the wedding, and gave a special acknowledgment to her father "for doing the speech he didn't want to do" about Tammy Lyn.

"Most of all, I'd like to thank my new husband," she said, pausing to give him a sideways glance, "for making this" — one more pause, one more glance — "the happiest day of my life."

The guests started clinking glasses, and the newlyweds rose to their feet and embraced. But it was just a brief kiss, and the guests wanted something with more emotion. They kept tinkling their glasses louder and louder until Bernardo grabbed his bride tightly and gave her a deep, passionate embrace, at the same time raising a fist in the air, as if in triumph, while the guests cheered in approval.

Their wedding song was "Unchained Melody" by the Righteous Brothers. For the first part of the haunting love ballad, the two just stared into each other's eyes as they waltzed slowly around the dance floor: "Lonely rivers flow to the sea … I'll be coming home, wait for me."

Few people had helped Deborah and Dan Mahaffy in their search for Leslie. Her disappearance was of no interest to the press. "We need a fresh angle to the story" was the flippant remark of one reporter when Deborah called a paper for some coverage of the case.

The police had been doing what they could, but they hadn't turned up anything. They had released a composite sketch of a man they wanted to question about Leslie Mahaffy's disappearance, a good-looking man in his mid-twenties. He was clean-shaven with short, neatly trimmed blond hair and a muscular build and he had been seen in the area around the time Leslie made the telephone call that Friday night.

Neither Doucette nor his son could persuade any of the passing motorists to believe what they were telling them. The look from one passerby said it all: two fishermen with one whopper of a tale. Finally, Doucette noticed a fire truck that had stopped on the other side of the bridge on Beaverdams Road. His son went running and brought back a fireman, there with his crew to check on brush fires supposedly started by kids. The fireman waded out into the lake. He was gone only a few moments.

"It's human body parts, all right," fireman Gary Honsberger said. Doucette said that, judging by the shape of the severed leg he had seen, he believed it was a young woman. Honsberger hurried back to his truck and radioed in the call.

Within minutes police cruisers were on the scene and the area was roped off. Police chatter over two-way radios was picked up by local reporters, several of whom hurried to the barricades to find out more.

"We've got a homicide on the go," a sergeant told them. "Body parts in cement. I've never seen anything quite so gross."

Messages of goodwill were taped toward the end of the reception, with guests lining up in the hallway in front of the videographer and congratulating the newlyweds.

"Take it easy on all the women," Bernardo's brother, David, said to the camera.

From Lori Homolka: "Paul is the best thing that ever happened to you, Karla."

24
The Evil in Our Midst

The newlywed couple left their guests around 3 o'clock that morning and headed to their suite in the hotel overlooking the bay at Niagara-on-the-Lake. They planned to sleep in the next day, then head to the airport on Monday for their honeymoon in Hawaii. Three bottles of champagne were waiting for them. Karla Homolka kissed her new husband and headed for the washroom.

"I won't be long," she said.

Bernardo sat on the bed and began opening some of the cards from the wedding guests. There was money in many of them, and he made a neat pile of the cash before he counted it.

Homolka changed into her sheer silk negligee, freshened up her lipstick, and put on a dab of Chanel Number 5. She fussed with her hair in the mirror, adjusted her evening wear, and finally she was ready to crown their marriage. She opened the bathroom door — and was dismayed by what she saw.

Bernardo was sitting in front of the TV set, watching a movie. He was sipping on a glass of champagne and scarcely acknowledged her presence. She deliberately walked between him and the TV, lingering just long enough for him to have a chance to admire her naked body as the light from the set shone through the sheer nightgown. He barely looked at her.

"We've got about nine grand to spend in Hawaii," he said.

Homolka walked over to the bed and poured herself a glass of champagne.

"Paul," she said finally.

"Huh?" He glanced her way.

"This is our wedding night."

"Okay."

He flicked off the set and went over to sit beside her on the bed. She put down her glass and started undoing the buttons on his shirt, then his pants. When he was naked, she started kissing him.

"I love you," she said, taking off her nightgown and letting it fall to the floor. She was just about to pull back the bedsheets when he put his hands on her shoulders and pushed her down between his legs. He got into his familiar pose at the edge of the bed, legs wide apart, a pillow under his head so that he could watch her.

"But it's our wedding night," she protested. "Aren't we going to make love?"

He didn't care what she wanted. What he wanted was fellatio. Homolka knew what would happen if she didn't comply. So she assumed his favorite position, on her knees between his legs.

"And who's your favorite guy?" he asked, needing the dialogue to become aroused.

"You are."

"And what else?"

"I love your Snuffles," she said.

"And?"

"I'm your little cocksucker," she said, stroking his penis. "Your little slut. Your cunt."

She repeated the line again because she knew that's

what he wanted to hear. Suddenly he grabbed her by the hair, jerked her head up.

"What?"

"Can't you get anything fucking right?" he yelled. "You know how I like to hear it. Cocksucker. Cunt. Slut. In that order. Understand? How many fucking times do I have to correct you? You are so fucking stupid. Now don't make me hit you again, not tonight."

"I'm sorry," she said, and went back to stroking his penis.

He leaned back on his pillow. "Tell me who's the best."

"You are. And I love when you fuck me up the ass."

"And what are you?"

"I'm your little cocksucker."

"And what else?"

"Your little cunt."

"And?"

"Your slut."

"And who's your favorite guy?"

"You are, master. I'm your little sex slave. Your cocksucker, your cunt, your slut."

"And what else?"

"Your asslicker."

"That's perfect," he said. She kept repeating the lines. "Good girl. Good. Oh, that's so good. And what are you going to do when I come?"

"I'm going to swallow every last drop."

"Why?"

"Because I love you," she replied.

After the marriage had been consummated, Paul Bernardo–style, he crawled under the sheets and soon was snoring. It was a long time before she fell asleep, angry that even on her wedding night it was only his sexual desires that counted. But at least he let her sleep on the bed with him.

They had brunch with friends on Sunday, then went to see her parents. Everybody kept complimenting them on the wedding, said what a great time they had had. Homolka maintained the facade of how happy she was with "the catch of a lifetime," as one of her friends described Paul. Eventually they headed home, packed, and went to bed early, not listening to the evening news. The following morning her parents drove the couple to Buffalo for their flight to Hawaii, and their honeymoon.

That Sunday, Randy Zdrobov, his sister, Karen, and their friend Randy Corman went fishing at Lake Gibson. Like many anglers, they headed for the quiet inlet off Beaverdams Road where the bass, walleye, or perch were usually biting. But when they arrived, the road was blocked by a police cruiser.

"What's going on?" Zdrobov asked.

It was a crime-scene investigation, he was told. And that's all the officer was allowed to say. Judging by the number of police cars, Zdrobov figured it had to be something serious.

The area had been closed off while divers waded through the shallow bay and swam through the deeper waters beside it. So far, seven concrete caskets had been spotted, five in the inlet and another two near the rapids that passed under a bridge. The caskets contained all of a young woman's body parts except the torso. Until the divers found the last body part, the area would have to stay closed.

"You'll have to try somewhere else," the trio was told. As they were about to leave, the officer had a suggestion. "Turn left at Decew Road and go to the Faywell bridge. They're biting over there, from what I hear."

So they drove west to the other end of the lake and the bridge not far from the water filtration plant. Zdrobov pulled the car over and they unloaded their gear. Corman, who was ready first, walked onto the short bridge and began to cast. He immediately saw a lumpy object wedged in the rocks near the foot of the pilings. The water was fast moving, and soon the current had pushed it off the rocks so that it drifted under the bridge.

"Holy shit!" Corman screamed when he got a better look. Instinctively, he reached over and hooked it with the end of his fishing pole. Standing on his toes and reaching over as far as he could, he would just be tall enough to hold it there, his fishing pole bowed nearly in half under the strain, until his friends went for the police.

Corman yelled at Zdrobov and his sister to hurry over. They ran onto the bridge, peered over the edge, and were just as shocked as Corman: their fisherman friend had snagged the severed torso of a young woman.

Deborah Mahaffy heard about the discovery of the body on the news that Sunday evening. She had been following the news closely. The female body — the police didn't give an age — had been cut up into several pieces and then encased in concrete. No name yet. No indication how long the body had been in the lake. But St. Catharines was only about a half-hour drive from Burlington on the Queen Elizabeth Highway, and Deborah was troubled. She called the local police, and a detective promised to call her back as soon as he found out anything.

By June 1991, most of the bodily-fluid samples taken from possible suspects in the Scarborough Rapist case had been sitting at the crime lab for seven months, waiting for analysis.

Although it took less than half that time to run a DNA test, analysis of the samples had hardly started. Investigators with the Sexual Assault Squad were told it would probably be the fall of 1991 before the initial testing was complete — nine months after the lab had been given the samples and three times longer than it should have taken. Det. Steve Irwin had been checking regularly. He was told the lab technicians were doing the best they could.

The two newlyweds were walking arm in arm along the beach near their hotel in Maui when Bernardo saw a scenic backdrop he liked — several palm trees — and wanted his new bride to take a picture of him leaning against one. He handed her his 35-mm camera.

He beamed his smile as she fiddled with the camera, but she wasn't very good at taking pictures. He got impatient, she grew flustered, and she dropped the camera, cracking the lens. Bernardo's smile instantly vanished. He rushed over, picked up the camera, swore at her, loud enough for several passersby to look over, grabbed her arm, and marched her back to the hotel. She knew what was coming and started trembling on the elevator. In their hotel room Bernardo pushed her to the floor and kicked and cursed her. She tried to ward off his attack with her hands. He grabbed some large headphones that he had brought with him and started hitting her on the head. One blow cut her forehead, and the blood streamed down her face. Fetching her a towel, he told her to clean up.

"Why do I have to keep teaching you these lessons? You're so stupid, Kar. You ruined my camera."

He fixed himself a drink, went out onto their balcony, and stared at the ocean, calming down. Later, she came out and started videotaping the sunset. She had covered the bruise on her forehead with makeup.

"Kar," he said, "I shouldn't have to keep punishing you."

"I'm so sorry, Paul."

He looked at her, sadly shaking his head. "You're forgiven."

They went out for dinner, and when they returned he noticed that their bed had been freshened up by the maid, who had left two small seashells on the pillows, along with a form note hoping they were enjoying their stay.

"Isn't that nice, Kar?" he said, picking up the shells. He thought of the notes she used to write that had stopped after the death of Tammy Lyn. "When we get back, I think I'd like a note on my pillow every night. Just like all those love notes you used to write."

The eight blocks that held the 10 body parts were taken to the pathology section of the Hamilton General Hospital and kept in cold storage for two days while detectives searched around Lake Gibson for clues. Insp. Vince Bevan, with the Niagara Regional police department, was put in charge of the case.

The soft-spoken veteran detective was renowned for putting in long days. He wanted the key areas around the bay thoroughly searched. Although it seemed an obvious case of murder, investigators couldn't even assume that. It could have been a sick prank involving a corpse from a morgue. Though it was an improbable lark, one of the investigators' first jobs was to check all the morgues, hospitals, and funeral homes in the area to see if a body had gone missing.

The task of removing the body parts, except for the torso, from the concrete blocks was handled by Terry Smith, a civilian employee with the Niagara police department who worked in the identification section. Assisted by Dr. David King from the hospital's pathology section, he measured and weighed the tombs, then put them onto a steel gurney and chipped away at them with a hammer and chisel.

There were no distinguishable marks or tattoos on the body that might help identify the victim. Her ears were pierced, which was of some value. Her hair was blond, but it had been dyed from its natural brown. Probably their best chance for an identification came from the braces on the girl's upper and lower teeth. A vaginal washing was done to see if any traces of semen could be found. But since the torso had broken free and been floating in the water, it was likely that the vagina had been washed clean of any seminal fluid — possibly a fortunate break for the killer.

Since the torso had been exposed to air, some maggots were found on it. These were bottled and sent to the Royal Ontario Museum in Toronto to see if scientists could determine how long the torso had been lying in the open under the Faywell Road bridge. Certain types of flies are attracted to a corpse at various stages of its decomposition, and entomologists would be able to determine how long the torso had been in the water by the kind and age of maggot that was on it.

For some reason, the block containing the victim's head had been spray-painted black. Scrapings were sent to the Centre of Forensic Sciences in Toronto to determine the brand of paint. Bevan and his investigators also hoped the scientists would be able to determine the type of cement used. They might then be able to find out where it was purchased and — more important — by whom.

The detectives theorized that the person who dumped the body parts had backed up his car close to the water's edge so as to be hidden from the road by the bushes. Plaster casts of tire treads were taken, but the investigators weren't optimistic. It was a popular fishing hole, and it was likely that dozens of vehicles had subsequently driven over the same terrain. The same odds held true for footprints.

Had the person they were hunting got rid of the blocks a few hundred yards to the west, detectives speculated, in one of the deepest parts of the lake at the Beaverdams Road bridge, they might never have been discovered. That led detectives to believe the person was familiar enough with the lake to know about the Lovers' Lane hideaway but didn't know it well enough to know that the water levels fluctuated depending on the flow over the hydro dam. That might mean that he lived nearby but was new to the area. Maybe he had just moved into Garden City or one of the nearby municipalities. The act of cutting up a body and encasing the parts in concrete blocks also suggested that the killer either lived in a house or had access to a barn or factory building. Such a monstrous task would be extremely messy and would have to be done in the privacy of a basement or other remote building that could be washed down afterwards.

So how did that educated speculation help the case? Not much. About 130,000 people lived in St. Catharines, likely half of them male. Then they would have to add in all the men who lived in nearby cities, towns, and farmhouses. Obviously they had to hope for something better, such as a set of fingerprints off the concrete blocks.

But for the moment their main concern was identifying the victim. Where was she last seen? What was she doing? Who were her friends, her enemies?

Deborah Mahaffy regularly called detectives. Were there any updates on the body in Lake Gibson? She was told that lab tests were being done, missing persons files pored over, but there was still no identification. But Mahaffy was working with a mother's intuition and fears. Leslie wore braces, and so did the girl found in Lake Gibson. Leslie's ears were pierced, and so were the victim's. Deborah wasn't comforted by hearing that the eye color was wrong — Leslie had blue eyes, while the victim's eyes were said to be brown. There had to be an explanation for that, she thought.

It had been a difficult time for the Mahaffys. The media and even the police had barely acknowledged that Leslie was missing. Now the police didn't want to believe that her body had been found. Hers, she would later say, was the forgotten family.

Nearly a week after the discovery, Mahaffy got a call from investigators. Although they didn't believe the victim was her daughter, they wanted permission to check Leslie's dental records just to be sure. The testing would take another four or five days. By now Mahaffy knew in her heart her miracle baby was dead.

In July 1991, Canada played host to the summer's biggest North American sporting event: major league baseball's annual All-Star game. U.S. president George Bush was at the ballpark in Toronto, along with Canadian prime minister Brian Mulroney. In the week before the game, the American media had been filing glowing reports about the country's largest city. Toronto was like Canada, they said, a clean, safe place where you could walk the streets at night and not worry about being mugged.

Deborah and Dan Mahaffy had also turned on the game that night. It had been five days since detectives had asked to see Leslie's dental charts, 26 since she had vanished without a trace. There had been reported sightings of Leslie all over the country, and as far away as New York City, but Deborah didn't believe any of them. Deborah had stopped working as a supply teacher while she searched Burlington for her daughter. Her husband had also missed some time from his job in the federal civil service. But just sitting around the house waiting for news was depressing. They had to get away for a weekend, and so they and Ryan had traveled to Minden, a small town north of Toronto, to visit some relatives. Before they left, Deborah had called detectives to tell them where they were going.

Arriving late, they decided to spend the night in a motel room. After supper, they were watching the game when someone knocked on the door. Two detectives were standing in the doorway, with somber expressions. One was Det. Sgt. Bob Waller, with the Halton police. Waller was a husky six-footer with a policeman's hard edge about him, but on that night he told the couple in his most compassionate tone that their daughter was dead.

The police had been wrong all along in thinking Leslie might have run away from home; wrong in believing it was somebody else in Lake Gibson. And they had been dead wrong, as well, in determining the victim's eye color. The lime in the cement had probably acted like an acid, changing the color of her eyes from blue to brown. A check of the dental records had proved conclusive.

Waller promised the Mahaffys that everything would be done to catch the killer. A reward was going to be posted. Someone would come forward.

The television set was still on, and the stadium was erupting in joy: 52,000 people were cheering for Joe Carter, the right fielder with the hometown Blue Jays, who had just scored another run for the American Leaguers.

Deborah felt her knees buckle as the dreadful news sank in. Irrationally, she wondered how they were going to get the concrete out of her daughter's beautiful hair.

The front-page headlines in all the newspapers the following day were about the victory of the American League

and the impressive performances of Joe Carter and the Blue
Jays. The identification of the body in Lake Gibson received
far less coverage, being mostly buried in the back pages. The
police had no suspects, the papers said, but detectives were
making good progress.

Eight months had passed since the last of the fluid samples in
the Scarborough Rapist case had been given to the crime lab
for DNA analysis. In that batch were the samples from the
smiling junior accountant, Paul Bernardo. The scientists were
doing the best they could, detectives were told, but it would
probably be several more months yet.

The mourners packed the Knox Presbyterian church in
Burlington for the funeral of Leslie Erin Mahaffy. For many
teens who knew the four who had died on Roller Coaster
Road, it was their second funeral in less than a month.

"The family needs your support for they have lost
their darling daughter," the Reverend James Weir told the
mourners. "We ask, 'Why Leslie? Why anyone?' We know
that evil dwells in our midst in this sinful world."

25
Concrete Leads

Dorothy and Karel Homolka greeted the newlyweds when they few back from Hawaii. The couple was tanned and, to the Homolkas that day, they looked quite happy. The bruise on Karla's forehead was nearly healed, and she never told her mother about it, nor about the other bruises from a second beating Bernardo had administered in the car while they were touring the island. She just blocked out the bad parts, as if they had never happened. To her, the "honeymoon from hell" — a phrase she used at the trial — was a secret she would share with no one.

As they drove home, Karla told her parents about the wonderful time they had had, and particularly about climbing to the summit of a volcano. Bernardo was anxious to show the Homolkas the videos he had taken. During the drive, Dorothy filled them in on all the news. Although she knew neither followed baseball, she told them about the All-Star game and the excitement there had been about the visit by Bush and Mulroney.

"Oh yeah," she said, almost as an afterthought. "The police identified the girl they found in the lake."

From the back seat, Bernardo turned to Homolka with a fleeting look of shock and horror.

"What girl? What lake?" Karla asked.

Dorothy explained how the fishermen had stumbled across the concrete blocks and the torso. The lake, she explained, had dropped a few feet, leaving the blocks almost completely out of the water.

"Turns out it was some girl from Burlington named Leslie Mahaffy. She disappeared one Friday night after going to a funeral." Dorothy said the blocks had been found on the same day as their wedding. "That's probably why you didn't hear about it. You had other things on your mind."

When they got home, Bernardo started in on Homolka: "Why didn't you tell me about the dam and the water levels? You've lived here all your life."

"I didn't know."

Bernardo quickly regained his composure. "I had gloves on the whole time," he said. "We've got nothing to worry about. They're never going to catch me."

The hunt for Leslie's killer was moving ahead, but slowly. The Niagara Region police department was in charge of the case, even though her disappearance had first been handled by Halton Region. Halton patrolled the city of Burlington, where Leslie had last been seen alive, and it was Halton detectives who had done the initial investigation and checked out supposed sightings.

But the missing person case had turned into a murder manhunt, and where a body is found — not where the victim may have lived — determines which force will be in charge. Detectives from another jurisdiction could always help out, of course, as long as they understood that their force wasn't the one in charge of the investigation.

In Ontario resources are often pooled on big cases, such as drug investigations. There are clear advantages: more manpower, more expertise, and so forth. But murder investigations are different. Each force has its own way of handling a homicide. Some simply follow a suspect for months in the hopes that he will incriminate himself. Other forces believe in talking to the suspect as soon as possible, if only to make him nervous and prone to mistakes.

Although some joint-force investigations were seen as productive, there is another saying, not for the public's ears, among senior police officers in the province: The best way to screw up a case is to get two different forces involved. These officers feel that the best strategy for a killer who wants to get away with murder is to dump the body in another force's jurisdiction. The resulting confusion would frequently enable the culprit to make his escape. Police forces, by the nature of their work, are secretive. There are times when detectives on the same police force never share information with each other, let alone with officers from another force. The lack of communication often doesn't matter, but homicides are different. One clue buried in another force's files can be enough to solve a case. Sometimes the other force doesn't even realize it has the vital information.

Law authorities in the United States are way ahead of their Canadian counterparts when it comes to overcoming this lack of communication, at least in the area of homicide investigations. The Federal Bureau of Investigation has developed a computerized database, known as VICAP, which is a dossier of all the unsolved murder cases in the U.S.A. It breaks each slaying down to a hundred or so characteristics, such as the murder weapon, types of wounds, date of offense, characteristics of the victim, apparent characteristics of the killer, and so forth. A police department's check with the FBI's computer might reveal a similar crime in another part of the country, and the two forces could at least compare notes. In the summer of 1991 there was no equivalent to the FBI's database in Canada. The Royal Canadian Mounted Police are studying the FBI's system, but a similar undertaking in

Canada was still in the discussion stage.

Communication, of course, can always be improved. Egos are another matter. Officers who make it to the homicide squad are usually the best and the brightest. The public treats them with the utmost respect and tends to identify with them. The homicide squad is a calling, and the reputation of a force often rests on the percentage of killers it catches. The pressure to solve a case can be enormous, not only from within the force but from politicians, the public, and the media. Homicide cops often make it to the news. Sometimes there are books and movies of the week. With publicity comes stature, notoriety. Each force likes to think it has the best investigators. Encouraging homicide detectives from different forces, with their own distinctive styles and strategies, to work together is asking for trouble.

Then there is the prickly question of how to deal with the media. Some Ontario forces believe the best way to handle reporters is to tell them nothing at all. The public will be informed, eventually, in a press release; saying anything more might compromise the case. To these forces, the media are like a pesky fly that you swat away when it gets too close and hope it will vanish.

The Niagara Region police department, the province's fifth-largest force, had the reputation of tolerating the media, but not much more. There was no press office, no daily release of the traditional police blotter. Information was given to reporters, but it was dispensed judiciously, cautiously, often grudgingly, with the details meager. In the summer of 1991, the Niagara force also had problems of its own to focus on: it was the subject of a massive inquiry probing allegations of corruption. Morale was low as the honesty and integrity of Niagara police officers was under public scrutiny by provincial investigators.

The Mahaffy case was the second murder investigation for the officer in charge, Insp. Vince Bevan. Bevan was seen as a rising star within the Niagara force. A competent officer who did his job well, he had dark good looks and a neatly trimmed mustache. He often wore cowboy boots. His supporters in the rank and file predicted that he might make chief one day. Soft-spoken, almost shy, he was liked and respected by his fellow officers. He was friendly toward reporters, but didn't tell them anything.

Since Leslie was from Burlington, Bevan sought out the assistance of Halton Region. Det. Sgt. Bob Waller was assigned to help out. His force was considered by many a pioneer among police agencies in Canada for the way it treated the media. Under Chief James Harding, its policy was to tell the media as much a possible, except for certain key details that were vital to an investigation. The attitude was that the public had a right to know how its officers were doing their job. Relations with reporters were often cordial, as opposed to the more adversarial nature of interactions between the media and the Niagara police department.

However, the detectives didn't have to worry about the media in this case. Few reporters had followed Mahaffy's disappearance, and that ambivalence carried over to the murder investigation. "Good girl" murders tended to get all the press coverage. Leslie was still seen as a runaway teenager who never should have been out that late.

There weren't a lot of solid leads in her case. No fingerprints had been found on the concrete blocks. Barns, abandoned buildings, and old factories had been searched without luck. A woman had called Crime Stoppers shortly after the body had been found and talked vaguely about a car she had seen in the area near the fishing hole. The woman thought she saw concrete blocks in the trunk of the vehicle, but she never saw the license plate and couldn't recall the make. The Halton police had issued a $25,000 reward for information. "Fink money" traditionally generates a batch of leads from the public, but in this case there had been nothing.

The crime lab was still working on the concrete. If the lab could pinpoint the type of cement used, then investigators might be able to determine where it had been sold. That was assuming it was one of the many commercial varieties on the market and not taken from a construction site. If it had been bought in a hardware store, the killer might have used a credit card, which could be followed up. Even if he paid in cash, a teller might remember him. A lot of ifs, but tracing the cement was probably the best lead they had.

In most murder cases, lack of media scrutiny is seen as a blessing. Reporters get in the way, talk to potential witnesses, and pollute the evidence pool by making public information detectives are saving for court. But the Mahaffy case was different. It appeared to be an abduction by a stranger, as opposed to someone she may have known, so the investigators could use all the help they could get from the public by way of tips or sightings. The only way to get to the public was through the media. But the media didn't seem overly interested. Privately, reporters told investigators the problem was that Leslie was seen as a runaway, not the "good girl" type that generated the most public sympathy. But the investigators were sure she had not run away from home. The erroneous perception that lingered in the media could be corrected with a press release based on statements from her mother and her friends. But Niagara was in charge of the murder. That kind of information wasn't the type their force believed in sharing with the press.

Then there was the composite sketch of a man who had been seen in the area at the time of Mahaffy's disappearance. He was good looking, with neat, light brown hair parted on the left. Witnesses couldn't recall anything else about him, except that he spoke in a deep voice. At a press conference, a reporter commented that the drawing looked a lot like the composite sketch of the man being sought for the Scarborough rapes; had the Niagara police checked with the Sexual Assault Squad in Toronto? Was it possible, Bevan was asked, that the two forces were looking for the same man?

"We'll look into it," he promised reporters.

But on the day of that press conference, another young woman went missing from the same area. News reports focused on the disappearance of Nina de Villiers, who had last been spotted jogging near her tennis club in the south end of Burlington.

Unlike the Mahaffy case, de Villiers' disappearance caught the public's attention. She hadn't been wandering the streets after midnight, and so the public was dismayed when she vanished. Plans were quickly under way for a massive search. The Mahaffy case was mentioned only in passing; some television newscasts never even showed the composite sketch. Within a day newspapers carried stories of Nina's disappearance with huge headlines on the front pages. There was shocked outrage from local residents. The composite sketch in the Mahaffy case was buried deeper in the papers. Yet again the Mahaffys had become the forgotten family.

Bernardo narrated as he and his new bride showed her parents the video from their honeymoon. One segment showed them driving along a mountainside road. "This is from Hookipin Park," he said. Then came his voice on the tape: "Here we are going up the winding, touristy road. The CAA says this is a very scenic route, but not so far." The road was shrouded in mist, and when they cleared it, they passed a waterfall. "Look at that waterfall," Bernardo said on the tape. "Pretty waterfall, pretty trees, pretty boring."

They passed by a second waterfall, and Bernardo was heard directing Homolka to swing the camera around to photograph it.

"Fucking get something," Bernardo snapped. "Guy ... you're so stupid!" The camera jerked around, the picture went bumpy, then there was a blank sequence on the tape, a segment in which she later testified that he hit her. But her parents never commented on the gap in the tape, and she never told them what was missing. The banter on the tape between the two honeymooners continued as they reached the top of the mountain and looked down into the dormant volcano. Laughing, she taped him while he took a still picture of her.

Another sequence they showed was taken from the balcony of their hotel room. Bernardo panned over several women sunbathing below, then turned the camera out toward the ocean.

"How far inland do you think sharks would come?" Homolka asked.

"Beautiful sunset here," Bernardo said on the tape, ignoring the question. "Maui, the most gorgeous place we've been yet. We're totally relaxed, totally happy. One moment in time, now and forever."

Homolka taped a later sequence from the hotel room.

"Paul, I'm doing this while you're in the shower. I just want to tell you that the beauty of this ocean, of this beach, of everything here, doesn't even come close to equaling the love that I feel for you. I love you, sweetheart."

Bernardo's unemployment cheques had run out by the time they returned from their honeymoon and, since he had no interest in getting a regular job, he turned to cigarette smuggling as his primary source of income. He liked the instant cash. For him, cigarette smuggling was easier, and more profitable, then a regular job. Bernardo had a routine all worked out. At first he crossed the border just on Thursdays, Fridays, and Saturdays, loading up his car with cigarettes, hiding the packages in the door panels, returning home after closing time with the Canadian crowds who had gone to the American bars for the cheaper beer. Later he took Homolka, and they went every day right after she got off work. It was less suspicious for St. Catharines or other border residents to make regular crossings than for a couple from, say, Toronto. The locals did it all the time, buying cheaper groceries, gas, and liquor.

The door panels of the Nissan held up to 300 packages of cigarettes, a profit of $250 a trip. Five trips a week earned him over $1,000. He had a contact in Mount Albert, a community north of Toronto, who took as much as he could deliver. Only once was he ever seriously questioned by a border guard. After that he hired a friend to make some of the runs, paying him a portion of the profits.

Since he didn't have to get up early in the morning, Bernardo always wanted to stay up late, sitting around and drinking after they had unloaded their contraband. And he insisted Homolka stay up with him. Once, when he passed out on the living-room floor, she covered him with a blanket and went to bed. That infuriated him.

"Why did you leave me alone on the floor?" he demanded, then hit her on the shoulders. After that, whenever he fell asleep on the floor, she always lay down beside him, either waiting until he woke or sleeping there the night. But the lack of sleep, and the constant hangovers, were starting to wear her out. She was usually able to persuade him to sleep in his bed, but she decided she had to trick him about the drinking. She started making their drinks, pouring herself mostly pop. But after a while, when he noticed she wasn't getting as drunk as he was, he started tasting her drinks. As her next strategy she put pop in first and poured a little liquor on top, but didn't stir it, so that he tasted only the liquor. For a time this worked. But gradually he got suspicious. He beat her when he realized what she was doing, and when she tried it again, he ordered her to take off her clothes and get down on her knees.

"Why do I have to keep punishing you?" he said, taking off his belt. Before whipping her, he told her what she had to say, scripted dialogue that he also liked in his home-made videos.

"Please whip me, sir," she said. "Please, sir, I deserve to be whipped." When she didn't fight back, or even protest, the beatings became more frequent. It was as if Bernardo had no restrictions on what he could do to her. She couldn't risk a complaint to the police, and even though she certainly could have left him, she would need to explain why.

In her own strange way she still loved him. She kept remembering the way he was when they first met: charming, considerate, mysterious, electric in bed. She still hoped he might change back to the man she had first known. It was only when she made her mistakes that he got angry, for instance when she got nervous during their border crossing or when she forgot to buy him some favorite item. Once she had forgotten to leave him a pillow note and had been punched in the head. The point was, those mistakes were her fault, and correctable. If she did what he wanted, she could avoid his wrath. So when he told her about his latest plan, she agreed to help out.

The couple who lived in a new subdivision near Hamilton were surprised one evening when two detectives, one local, the other from the Niagara police department, knocked on their door. The two officers asked what the couple thought was an odd question: had they recently bought some cement from a hardware store? The particular brand was Kwik-Mix.

Yes, the couple replied, they had — at a nearby store and paying for the purchase with a charge card. It was then that the schoolteacher and the nurse realized they were suspects in the Leslie Mahaffy murder case. The police had held a press conference to announce they now knew the brand of the cement the killer had used and were checking to see who had bought the product. It was one of two developments in the case, but the only one the police shared with the public.

"Would you mind," one of the detectives asked earnestly, "telling us why you bought the cement?"

The couple pointed to the fenceposts in their yard that had been cemented in with Kwik-Mix. The two officers glanced at the fence, thanked the couple, and left. They still had hundreds of purchasers to interview.

Kwik-Mix, sold in 66-pound bags, is popular with homeowners, used in everything from small patch jobs to sealing in fenceposts. The investigators couldn't possibly check out every business in the province that sold the product, so they were focusing on the 75 building and lumber stores in the Golden Horseshoe area, between St. Catharines and Hamilton. Then they narrowed it to purchases made in June. Those two assumptions seemed reasonable, but it was a third limitation that worried detectives: they could check only people who bought with charge cards, because only those purchases were recorded by the stores. There was no way to track people who paid in cash. And since it was an inexpensive product — $3.99 a bag — there were no guarantees the killer had used plastic. The detectives were well aware they could be wasting their time.

Bernardo had been mad at himself for returning the cement to the lumber store and signing a voucher. He was convinced, he told Homolka, that the police would soon find the paper trail.

"Why did I do it?" he said over and over in the weeks after Mahaffy's murder. "It was the only mistake I made."

If the police ever came to their house, they would say they had bought the cement to repair a sidewalk but then changed their minds since they were only renting the property. Bernardo now read with interest that the police were looking for people who had charged the purchase. The man who had earlier declared bankruptcy laughed. All his charge cards had been taken away after the bankruptcy, so he had bought the cement with cash. "They're never going to get me," he bragged.

While the hunt for the buyer of the cement received extensive coverage, the other development in the Mahaffy case deliberately received none. The police had been culling lists of known sex offenders, ex-convicts, and men with a history of violence toward women. Detectives were intrigued to learn that several employees at the plant that packaged the Kwik-Mix cement had criminal records, and they also joined the burgeoning list of suspects. But one person in particular had generated great interest among the detectives. He was a married man with a penchant for young girls. He liked water and lived near the lake where Mahaffy's body parts had been found. One other police force in the province had him under active investigation for rape, and possibly murder, and he loved to drive around the countryside, trolling for young women.

In time, he would become the main suspect in the murder of Leslie Mahaffy. His name was Peter John Stark.

Not long after he killed Mahaffy, Bernardo pressed Homolka to set him up with her acquaintance, Jane.

"I'm just not pleased with you anymore," Bernardo

told Homolka one day. He commented that Jane had matured into a lovely young woman. "If you want to make me happy again, help me to fuck her."

Bernardo suggested they could maybe use the same technique as with Tammy, knocking Jane out with sleeping pills. Homolka decided that if her husband wanted the girl for his sexual fantasies, she was going to do her best to ensure it happened. Homolka's own survival had now become her sole concern. Her own well-being was tied to compliance with her husband's wishes: keep him happy and save herself a lot of grief. And, in the process, she could avoid jail and maybe even resurrect their love.

Homolka called Jane, inviting her over to see their new house.

26

The Perfect Hosts

Bernardo was acting like a giggly schoolboy when Jane first visited their home on Bayview Drive. He had bought her several expensive gifts he couldn't afford: a watch, jewelry, stuffed animals. Jane, not much older than the girl Bernardo had recently raped and murdered, was flattered by the attention from a man twice her age. She complimented the couple, who were acting the perfect hosts, as they gave her a tour. Bernardo was proudest of his music room on the second floor.

"I'm working on a rap album," he told her, a line meant to impress. "It's called *Deadly Innocence*."

Bernardo picked up his microcassette player and continued to flirt with the girl. "This is Jane in my room to say that she hates Paul," he said into the recorder, holding out the cassette for her reply.

"Not," she said.

"This is Jane to say she loves Paul with all her heart."

To which she answered, "Not."

Bernardo said he had been working on several songs off the album. One was called "Waste Some Time." "Darling, can you feel it?" he sang to Jane in his whiny, nasal, off-key voice. "And you know it's true. All I want to do is waste some time with you. Doooo-du-du-doooo."

Jane clapped, and Bernardo seemed pleased with himself. He had her autograph a white chalkboard on the wall.

"Howdy, I love you guys," she wrote. And then: "I love Paul." She drew a heart around the word *love*.

The tour continued through the master bedroom. Then downstairs Bernardo made drinks while Homolka taped Jane as she played with Buddy.

"Hi, Jane," Homolka said. "Tell us about yourself."

Jane was stuck for an answer. She was a high-school teenager, alone with two adults who were paying her an unnatural amount of attention.

"Well, I guess I'm going to see *Ghost*," she said. "And I'm playing with Buddy."

"Jane and Buddy," Homolka said. "Buddy and Jane." She moved the camera in close and used one of Bernardo's favorite lines: "Extreme close-up, whoooooaaaaa." Later Homolka added: "I just love videotaping."

Bernardo flirted with Jane most of that evening, but though she was warm and affectionate toward him, and Homolka, she gave no indication she wanted — or understood — that it should go further. She talked about her friends and her teachers, and Bernardo soon grew frustrated that she didn't seem to understand the three of them were supposed to end up drunk and in bed. He started talking about Margaret, a friend of theirs the same age as Jane. He was trying to make Jane jealous, but she missed that subtlety as well. Homolka quickly picked up his cue.

"We had so much fun with Margaret when she came over for a visit," she said.

Jane said Margaret sounded like a nice person, then went back to talking about school. Bernardo was getting increasingly impatient. He believed women couldn't resist his charms and wanted to have sex with him almost immediately. Homolka had. So had the woman he had met in Florida just before his wedding. Alone with Homolka, he told her she would have to take their thick-headed guest aside and explain some facts of life. Homolka knew a beating probably awaited her if her husband got any angrier, so she said to Jane when they were alone, "Paul is just the greatest guy. You know, I wouldn't even mind if you two had a relationship."

But Jane still didn't grasp it, and soon after said she had to leave. The couple drove her home. Bernardo was upset with Jane, but angrier at Homolka.

"You're not saying the right things," he told her on the drive home. "You have to get her to like me."

Homolka promised that she would call Jane the next day and arrange another evening with the three of them. Preoccupied with how badly the evening had gone for him, he forgot about punishing his wife.

The police task force investigating Peter Stark was code-named Hitchhiker and included officers from nearly every force around the Golden Horseshoe. Its head, Steve Reesor, a veteran homicide detective from Toronto, didn't want any publicity or leaks to the media, believing the press could screw up an investigation by talking to and confusing poten-tial witnesses. The team based themselves in a warehouse north of Toronto and were primarily interested in the unsolved murder of Julie Stanton, a 14-year-old who had disappeared from her home in Pickering, near Toronto, in April 1990. But detectives suspected Stark might also have killed up to five other young women, including Leslie Mahaffy. They believed Stark might have been active since the early 1970s, when he was arrested for stabbing a hitchhiker he had picked up. Stark had always been a suspect in the Stanton murder, but the local force had found no solid evidence to link him to the crime.

A police task force now decided to mount an all-out investigation of Stark after Stanton's family kept pressuring the police, through the media, to find her killer. The operation involved detectives from every community where Stark had lived during the previous 20 years. Vince Bevan was one of the officers consulted. Despite talking to hundreds of people who had purchased Kwik-Mix cement in June, Bevan and his investigators had failed to turn up any useful leads in the Mahaffy case. "What if the guy paid cash?" was a question several officers were asking. Stark now appeared to be the best suspect Bevan had. He was known to have a penchant for schoolgirls.

Bevan took his Mahaffy files to the Hitchhiker task-force officers in the hope that fresh eyes might help him crack the case. The task force put together a surveillance team, which included officers who had been working on the Mahaffy case. One member of the team was Eddie Grogan. They followed Stark as he drove around the Golden Horseshoe area, often between Hamilton and St. Catharines, presumably in search of young victims.

The streets were deserted as Ruth Wilson drove home through the northeast end of St. Catharines just after 2 a.m. When the sportscar passed her on Welland Avenue, going the other way, Wilson noticed that the driver seemed to be staring at her. She couldn't explain it, she later told the police, but something about the blond-haired motorist frightened her. She glanced in her rearview mirror just as the driver made a U-turn, ran a red light, and started following her. Wilson lived alone and, if he really was following her, didn't want to lead him back to her house. So she went past her street and kept driving, constantly checking the mirror and scanning the road ahead for a police car. There were none in sight.

The driver kept far enough back that she couldn't see his license plate. After a while, sure she had lost him on a sidestreet, she turned and headed back to her own street. There was no one about as she wheeled into her driveway. As she got out, a car pulled up. It was the blond-haired man in the sportscar, and he was leaning over into the passenger seat, staring at her.

Wilson thought about screaming, but instead ran to her front door, fumbling in her purse for her key as she glanced back. The motorist had stayed in his vehicle, just watching her. She hurried inside, slamming the door shut behind her. She checked out the front window, but the vehicle was gone and the street deserted. Wilson thought about calling the police, but she didn't have a license number and wasn't even sure of the make of car. Though disturbed by the incident, Wilson tried to put it out of her mind.

But a week later, she saw the man again.

Wilson was driving to the video store that evening when she saw the sportscar again in her rearview mirror, the same blond-haired man behind the wheel. He followed her, parked across the street, and watched her as she browsed at the store. When she left, the car was gone.

Wilson was too frightened to go home alone, and she drove instead to the house of a male friend. He wasn't home, so Wilson stayed in her car in the driveway, waiting for him. Farther up the street she saw the sportscar, parked, the man watching her. She was in tears when her friend finally got home. He went home with her, following in his car. They never saw the sportscar on the drive home, but as Wilson got out of her car, she noticed a blond-haired man hiding in some bushes down the street. He appeared to be a Peeping Tom.

"Look!" she shouted to her friend. "It's him! It's that guy!"

They ran after the man, but he fled, cutting through

a yard, hopping a fence, and disappearing into the night. As they walked back to her house, Wilson saw his empty car.

"That's a Nissan 240SX," her friend said about the gold sportscar. They waited a while in case he returned, each taking note of the license number: 660 HFH. But when he didn't show up, they returned to Wilson's house and called the police. By the time the cruiser arrived, the sportscar was gone.

An officer with the Niagara police took a statement, but Wilson could tell they weren't going to do much with her complaint. She had not got a good look at the man, other than to notice he had blond hair and was of average height and build. And although he was obviously following her around, she had never been accosted by him, and he wasn't breaking any law. (It would be three more years before Canada passed a law that made stalking a crime.)

The officers who dealt with the complaint radioed a dispatcher, asking for a check on the Nissan. Within a few minutes they learned that the car was leased by a resident of Port Dalhousie, Paul Bernardo. A further check showed that he didn't have a criminal record, the lack of which frequently led to a corresponding lack of interest from the authorities. The police, used to dealing with repeat offenders, are less inclined to believe someone with no record might be the neighborhood prowler. A report was written out on the incident, then filed away.

Several weeks passed before Wilson thought about checking with the police. She assumed they had taken some action because the prowler had never been back. Even so, for months afterwards she felt uncomfortable and always checked over her shoulder whenever she went out.

When Homolka got home, Bernardo was waiting for her. He was furious.

"Where in the fuck is my lemonade?" No amount of apologies for forgetting to buy it could placate him. "The reason I'm not in love with you anymore is that you're such a lousy wife," he told her, shoving her against the wall. "You've just earned yourself another five. Get ready for the terrorist attack."

The only way she might escape her punishment, Bernardo said, was to try harder to persuade Jane to go to bed with him. Jane had been over at the house several times, and had gone out on social evenings with them, but had never showed any inclination toward a sexual threesome. Bernardo now wanted Homolka to invite Jane over for the weekend. If she wouldn't go to bed with him willingly, they would have to repeat what they had done to Tammy. "Wouldn't it be nice if Jane got to know Snuggles," he said.

Homolka invited Jane over. Though Homolka was tired, Paul wanted her to go out with him later. There was yet another woman he had been following home, a waitress who worked in a restaurant they frequented. He told Homolka he had been hiding in the bushes, watching her undress, and tonight he wanted to videotape her. When Homolka complained she was tired, Bernardo swung out and punched her on the head. "You're going to do as I tell you!"

The beatings had been getting worse since the death of her sister, and people at work were beginning to notice the bruises. Several times she had been questioned about it and had blamed the family dog for her injuries. "I was wrestling with Buddy and he pushed me against a cabinet" was one excuse. "Buddy was chewing on my arm" was another.

But although she was now miserable in her relationship, she continued to help Bernardo carry out his videotaped sex crimes. Psychiatrists would later delve into her mind, trying to understand her reasons. Those who maintained that

Homolka suffered from the battered-wife syndrome cited research which showed that women who remain in abusive relationships often develop a feeling of hopelessness and helplessness about their situation, even to the point of blaming themselves for their troubles. Studies of thousands of battered women have shown that abuse can start slowly, perhaps with a slap or harsh words, and escalate into regular beatings; often the women believe there is nothing they can do to stop the abuse and they stay with their partners, perhaps believing that marriage is marriage, for better or worse. Some even join in as the men abuse their children, even though they hate themselves for doing it. It is not just the poor and uneducated who show signs of the syndrome. Intelligent women from middle- or upper-class families can also be victims.

Homolka was certainly in the top two percent of the population with her I.Q. of 130, and she was smart enough to know what fate awaited her if the police learned the truth about the crimes she and her husband had committed. Her reasons for staying with Bernardo had more to do with her fear of getting caught than any deep psychological problem. Homolka simply didn't want to spend the best years of her life in a jail cell not much larger than the walk-in closet of her sumptuous home. She was in so deep as an accomplice that she had become Bernardo's partner in crime, whether she liked it or not, and even if it meant becoming as despicable as him and letting her troubled conscience keep her awake at nights.

The smash on the side of the head that night merely reinforced her thinking. So she joined him as he went out prowling with his video camera for the red-headed waitress. Bernardo went so close to the woman's window with his camcorder that he was afraid she would notice him. But she never even looked outside as she got undressed. He held the camera in one hand and masturbated with the other.

After ejaculating, Bernardo hurried back to the car, describing to Homolka what he had done. When they got to a stop light, he asked her, "How come I haven't been getting my pillow notes?" His voice had just enough edge to it to make her nervous. There was a note on his pillow the next night. "I just wanted to tell you how much I love you," it said. "Please tell me about the love you have for me. I know it's hidden in your great big heart somewhere."

In another of the nightly notes she wrote: "Paul, you're the sweetest, nicest, bestest, cuddliest, most caring, lovingly gorgeous man in the whole, wide universe. I love you more every day. More than you'll ever know. You're my magical, fantasy guy. Sweet dreams. I love you. Karly Curls."

One day Homolka met Renya Hill at a drugstore when she was replenishing her supply of cards.

"Still lovey-dovey, eh?" her old friend remarked when Homolka explained.

"Marriage is just great," Homolka lied. She had lied to everyone for so long that it may have seemed impossible for her to tell the truth anymore about anything. "I've never been happier." She told Renya that her husband was on the verge of a music career and promised to let her know when he signed his record contract so they could go out and celebrate.

Hill noticed a bruise on Homolka's neck, just under the ear. Homolka turned her head away.

"That's Buddy," she fibbed. "He can get rough sometimes."

Homolka took her cards home and set about her task of writing witty, original messages to her husband. She would later claim she now hated him, and wanted to please him only for her own sake. At the animal clinic, while she was known for doing her duties promptly and without complaint, whether cleaning out cages or feeding the animals, she also showed a total lack of initiative on the job, doing just what she had to and nothing more. She never volunteered to stay late if there was an emergency, or to help a co-worker with some task, unless ordered to do so. They were paying her $8.25 an hour, and they were getting exactly $8.25 worth an hour of effort out of her. She had the intelligence to do better, but it was felt that she lacked the ambition to try. Perhaps it was so. But the other reason she kept secret from everyone.

Bernardo never let her out of his sight if possible, ever fearful that she might crack one day and go to the police. That summer Homolka kept him happy with a flurry of bed-time notes. "To the most wonderful man in the world," she wrote on one. "My fantasy man, just like the unicorn on this card. Fantasy and love is what our relationship is made of. Honey, I'll follow you faithfully wherever you lead me. I love you. Karly Curls."

Bernardo liked her to say how much she loved him. On one card she wrote "I love you, Paul" 10 times.

"Dear Paul," began another note. "You are the most wonderful, perfect man in the world. I love you more than you can imagine. Honey, through all our ups and downs and side-ways, we've always been best friends. Love, Kar."

One night she forgot to cover him up with a blanket after he had fallen asleep on the living-room floor after a night of sex during which Homolka had pretended to be Leslie Mahaffy. Bernardo had wanted some variety, tiring of his wife always playing Tammy. He had put one of the tapes of Mahaffy being raped into the VCR and watched it while Homolka performed fellatio on him. The next day she got a beating for not remembering to cover him with the blanket. She quickly wrote him a note of apology.

"I wuv you," she wrote, drawing a picture of a sad face. "I'm so sorry. I know what's happened to us is all my fault, and believe me, I'm changing. Please honey, let's try and have the fairytale romance we were meant to have. I love you. I will always love you. Once we were an unbeatable team, you and me against the world. I want it to be like that again. Love, Kar."

Another night Homolka awakened with stomach pains. Besides turning into an alcoholic, she feared she was developing an ulcer. A doctor had prescribed some antacid, but it wasn't helping. She went downstairs to get a glass of milk, and discovered she was alone. As so often, Bernardo had gone out late and would not return until early in the morning. Since she couldn't get back to sleep, she called him on the cellular phone in his car.

"I'm just cruising," he told her, "looking for another one."

One of his favorite trolling places was a 24-hour donut shop not far from his house. He had his portable camera with him, but there was no one there that night that he liked, so he headed for the home of the red-headed waitress. He was making plans to break in one night and rape her.

In the fall of 1991 investigators with the Sexual Assault Squad were told the lab results were finally finished on the 224 fluid samples in the Scarborough Rapist case. Some 16 months had passed since the lab had received the first samples. There was both good and bad news from the white coats: the list of suspects had been pared down, but only to 39. The crime lab now wanted the detectives to narrow down the 39 suspects to a workable half dozen or so. The lab was too swamped to do a full DNA test on all 39 samples. The detectives, busy with other cases, promised to do their best. Investigators pored over the 39 names, at that point all candidates to be the Scarborough Rapist. One of the names still on the list was Paul Bernardo.

27
The Final Five

Bernardo had been spending most of the evening flirting with Jane, telling her how much he liked her, but she still didn't understand what he meant and, as the evening wore on, he grew increasingly frustrated. When he was alone with Homolka in the kitchen, he told her to get the sleeping pills and spike Jane's drink. They were upstairs in the master bedroom when Jane passed out.

Bernardo brought his camcorder while Homolka fetched the bottle of halothane she had stolen from the animal clinic. They undressed the unconscious girl, then they both disrobed. As she had done with her sister, Homolka poured some of the ether-like substance onto a rag and held it to Jane's face. Then she stood back and watched as Bernardo anally and vaginally raped the girl.

"Look at that," Bernardo exclaimed at the sight of the vaginal blood. "I've fucked a virgin."

Homolka smiled at her husband, then performed oral sex on the helpless girl. He taped the assault, kept the camera on his wife as she inserted her fingers into the girl's vagina, widening the opening for him while he took a close-up.

"Take her hand," he told Homolka next, "and shove it up your cunt."

She did so, moaning with pleasure while he hovered nearby, taping. It was then that the girl started gagging.

Barely eight months had passed since the death of Homolka's sister under similar circumstances. Once again it appeared a girl had stopped breathing. Bernardo started mouth-to-mouth resuscitation, while Homolka hurried to dial 911. The operator assured her help would be sent immediately. But Homolka was barely off the phone when Bernardo called out that Jane was fine: "She's breathing. Cancel that call. Hurry, before they get here."

In larger cities, a distress call for a person not breathing brings a three-tiered response: police, firefighters, and an ambulance crew. As a rule, emergency crews cannot be canceled until they have checked out the call. Fire departments, for instance, have a policy of going to all calls, even if advised by the police that they are proceeding to a false alarm. Distress calls in St. Catharines were generally handled the same way. But that night, for some reason, the emergency crews never went to the pink house on Bayview Drive after Homolka called to cancel the alert.

The couple dressed Jane and put her into their bed. Bernardo went downstairs to make himself a drink and watch the tape he had just made. Homolka stayed up most of the night, checking to make sure the girl kept breathing. They kidded her in the morning about drinking too much and passing out, and later drove her home.

Not long afterwards, Bernardo was back cruising the streets, starting at the donut shop near his house and roaming past homes in the north end of the city. He made several more trips to the house of the red-headed waitress, still formulating his plan to break in and rape her. In the meantime, he kept an eye open for other victims. He had started to go out earlier in the afternoon, around the time students at a nearby high school finished their classes. He found the girls at Holy Cross particularly attractive in their uniforms of green leggings and

short skirts. He often parked near the school and watched
them as they left for home. It would be impossible to abduct
anyone from or near the schoolgrounds, but he noticed that
several girls walked home alone along secluded sidestreets. It
was information, he later told Homolka, worth filing away.

Kristen French took the same route home from school every
day, starting through the parking lot and wending her way to
Geneva Street and her family's modest bungalow. The trip
took about 15 minutes. The first half of the walk was through
a quiet upper-middle-class subdivision, but Linwell Road was
always busy with traffic, especially around 2:45 p.m., the time
she usually left Holy Cross. She arrived home around 3 p.m.
to let the family dog, Sasha, out of his pen. It was a little routine she followed religiously. Just like clockwork.

    Kristie, as her family and friends called her, was an
attractive 15-year-old, slightly taller than average at 5' 5", and
slender at 110 pounds. She had long brown wavy hair that
fluttered around her back as she kept up a brisk pace on the
daily walk. She was always in her school uniform: green plaid
skirt, green tights, usually with a green V-neck sweater over a
crisp, white blouse and, over that, a black jacket. She carried
her gym clothes in a green canvas bag, the words Kettle Creek
on the side.

    She was the youngest of the five children of Doug
and Donna French and she was the most athletic. In the win-
tertime, it was skating. She belonged to a team of precision
skaters who trained at the Merritton Arena in southeast St.
Catharines. The club was like a mini Ice Capades in which
girls skated in unison, performing dances and intricate rou-
tines, both for recreation and in competition against clubs
throughout southern Ontario. In the summer, she rowed for
her school at a club in Port Dalhousie. Kristen was also a top

Grade 10 student who maintained a straight-A average.

Like her classmates, she was disturbed by the unsolved murder of Leslie Mahaffy and the baffling disappearance of teenager Terri Anderson. Like many, she feared the murderer might live in Garden City.

Anderson had left her parents' house late one night in 1991, presumably to meet some friends, and never returned. A search near her home, not far from Holy Cross school, had failed to turn up any clues, and the police were assuming foul play. The two cases were often discussed by students at Holy Cross.

"If someone caught Terri and killed her," Kristen told some friends one day early in April, "then I really don't want to know the details of what happened to her. I'm just not interested in reading about it."

Her 15-minute trip at the end of classes was really the only time in her day when Kristen French was alone, unaccompanied by her family, friends or boyfriend. Donna drove her to school in the morning. She ate her lunch in the school cafeteria. And when she went out at night, it was always with friends, or her boyfriend, Elton Wade. Although she walked home by herself, she believed hers was a safe route, either along busy streets or through a quiet subdivision where nothing ever happened.

Lori Lazaruk had been out that night with her sister, Tanya, and on their way home the two women stopped for a coffee at the donut shop near Port Dalhousie. A sign near the front door warned customers that a man in a sportscar had been driving around the premises videotaping women. Several had seen the man, but nobody had caught his license plate. Lazaruk and her sister were just finishing their coffees when they noticed that a gold sportscar had gone by three times, always in the same direction. It went past a fourth time, then stopped near the store.

"Isn't that a camera?" Lori said, pointing to the passenger window and the man with blondish hair. When the driver noticed their stares, he drove off hurriedly. Neither woman was able to make out the license number: the plate had mud on it, blocking out some of the letters.

Later, when the two women were driving home, Lori spotted the vehicle again in her rearview mirror. The driver was clearly following them, because his headlights weren't on.

"There he is," Lori said, pulling over for a better look at the man. But the motorist saw what they were doing, and sped by.

"I think I got the license plate," Lori said to her sister. "It's 660 something," she said. "Six, six, zero, NF something, or MF something."

When they got home, they called the Niagara police department. The officer was polite as he noted down the details. The two women believed the car was driven by a man with light-colored hair. But they were fairly certain of his license plate, even though he seemed to have covered it over with mud. And just why, the police officer wanted to know, did they think that? Because otherwise the car was spotless.

The officer punched the number they gave him into the police computer. But the plate came back belonging to a four-door Mercedes-Benz. The women weren't sure of the make, but believed the car might be a Mazda. The officer tried a variety of letters, but none came back belonging to a sportscar. Were they sure they had got the right license plate? It was dark, they told him, and they couldn't be sure.

There wasn't much the police could do. Before hanging up, the officer advised them to call if they saw the car again.

It wasn't long after the incident at the donut shop when a Niagara police officer noted a gold sportscar, with its lights out, cruising through a neighborhood in St. Catharines. The officer radioed in for a check of the plate number, 660 HFH, as he pulled it over. It was a leased vehicle, owned by a man who lived in St. Catharines.

The motorist was polite and apologized for forgetting to turn on his headlights. Even though the driver seemed sincere and had done nothing terribly wrong, the officer checked that the man didn't have a criminal record, perhaps for burglary. But there was no record on Paul Bernardo in the police computer system, and the officer sent him on his way.

On the night he planned to rape the red-headed waitress, Bernardo assembled his kit — the knife, the twine, the gloves, and a pair of his wife's black pantyhose to use as a mask. He told Karla of his plans, but just as he was getting ready to go, someone rang the front doorbell. They hadn't been expecting visitors, and Bernardo hid his kit in a kitchen cupboard.

Several friends had dropped by and were inviting themselves in. Bernardo, ever the gracious host, mixed a round of drinks. One of the visitors was a man with whom Bernardo smuggled cigarettes over the border, and they spent the evening talking about finding new buyers. Although Bernardo kept smiling, Homolka knew he was annoyed because his plans had been ruined. By the time their visitors left, Bernardo decided it was too late to go out.

It was several weeks before Bernardo went back to the house where the red-headed waitress lived. He parked his car a few streets over, cut through several back yards, and hid in some bushes waiting for her to come home. It was around 1 a.m., the usual time he spied on her while she undressed. But the house remained dark. Bernardo made several more trips before he realized the house was empty. The red-headed waitress had moved.

The task force investigating Peter Stark had found a witness who had seen Julie Stanton climbing into his car just before she disappeared. Since her body had not been found, and in the absence of a confession, the circumstantial evidence of the sighting was a major part of their case. For months, investigators had tailed Stark, but, although they had built a case against him for the murder of Stanton, they had failed to find any solid evidence linking him to four other killings, including that of Leslie Mahaffy. The officers had watched Stark play the "hitchhiker game" with his wife, getting her to dress up in a schoolgirl uniform, dropping her off on a desolate road, driving off, then coming back, picking her up as if she were a stranger, and raping her. But there was no evidence that he had picked up Mahaffy.

Early in 1992 investigators with Project Hitchhiker were ready to arrest Stark — but only for the murder of Stanton. Vince Bevan, told of the coming pinch, drove over to ask them to delay the arrest, telling them he needed more time to link Stark to Mahaffy. But Bevan was told the task force had completed its primary job. Even if the courts convicted Stark of murdering both girls, under Canadian law he could receive only one life sentence. There wasn't much point in prolonging a costly investigation just to see if they could arrest Stark for a series of murders when the justice system was prepared to hand out only concurrent sentences. In Canada, unlike in the United States, convicted killers did not have to worry about the death penalty, or about being thrown into jail for 645 years.

The Stark investigation had been costly, running up a tab of some $4 million. The detectives wanted a suspected

killer off the streets, but they didn't want to bankrupt the
provincial treasury doing it. The Hitchhiker officers were
sympathetic to Bevan, but it was beginning to appear that
Mahaffy's killer had committed the perfect crime — no one
had seen him abduct her, likely rape her, or dispose of her
body parts. That meant he was either very good or just plain
lucky. Bevan was told Stark's arrest would go ahead. He was
later convicted of Stanton's murder, but is appealing.

At the start of April 1992, investigators with the Sexual
Assault Squad finally believed they had a handful of good
suspects in the Scarborough Rapist case. The original list of
224 possible rapists had been pared down by the detectives,
using blood analysis tests, to just five.

Twenty-one months — nearly two years — had
passed since the investigators had given the last fluid samples
to the crime lab. For most of that time the samples had sat on
a shelf, awaiting analysis. The crime lab now promised a full
DNA analysis on all five suspects, one of whom was the
junior accountant from Scarborough.

That was the good news. The bad news was that the
lab would not be able to start the tests until the fall. There was
still a backlog of cases to clear. And then the staff were on
summer holidays. The earliest detectives could expect some
results would be January of the following year, 26 months
after the last samples had been handed over.

Unless one of the five suspects suddenly confessed,
the hunt would have to be put on hold until the beginning of
1993.

Homolka got off work early on Thursday, April 16, 1992,
because the following day was Good Friday and the clinic had
closed for the Easter weekend. But instead of going home she

took a bus downtown and browsed in the library for some books to read during the holiday. With Bernardo fascinated by rap music, she borrowed a book about the street idiom of black people. Perhaps if she understood the phrases he used, he wouldn't get so angry. When she got home around 2 p.m., Bernardo was waiting. And he was furious.

"Where the hell were you?" he screamed.

She half expected another beating, but he was preoccupied with his plans. She had accompanied him on his nightly excursions looking for girls, but recently he had changed his thinking, coming to believe he might have more luck trolling for virgins during the day. Fourteen- and 15-year-olds were less likely to be out late by themselves. And if they were, they weren't the kind of girl he wanted. His next victim had to be chaste. It was all he ever talked about.

There were several schools nearby, and he had been scouting them. The best time to find a virgin was right after school, he had told her. He wanted her with him because a young couple didn't seem as suspicious as a lone male in a car. But normally she never got home from work until long after school was out. And that was why this particular Thursday was so special; he had been primed and ready to go all day.

"Put your hair in a ponytail," he ordered.

He believed it made her look preppy, less like a criminal out to snatch a young girl off the street, and also made it more difficult for a witness to judge the length of her hair.

He loaded his rape kit into the car and unlocked the garage door so that when they returned they would be able to open it from the outside. At 2:34 p.m. they headed for Lake Street. There was a secondary school Bernardo had been watching, Holy Cross, about a five-minute drive away, and from what he had seen it held dozens and dozens of good candidates.

Kristen French got her jacket and bag from her locker and headed for the exit. Browner, as her friends called her, was looking forward to the long weekend. She passed one of her friends on the way out.

"Goodbye," she said to Tara Wilson. "Have a good weekend." Wilson wished her the same, and then Kristen was outside.

It was a brooding afternoon, drizzling, but not so much that Kristen needed an umbrella. Although she was dressed in the Catholic school's required uniform, she stood out from the others as she hurried through the parking lot: her slim build and long, bouncy, athletic stride set her apart. The light rain dampened her chestnut hair as she walked. Her mood was cheerful that day, but then it always was. When she got home she was going to call her boyfriend, Elton, to discuss what they would do that weekend, aside from attending church services for the most holy of Catholic holidays. But before that, she would let Sasha out of his pen as usual. Kristen loved animals; she had thoughts of one day becoming a veterinarian, but often wondered if she had it within her to put a sick or aging animal to sleep.

Kristen wasn't paying any particular attention to the motorists on Linwell that gray, misty, brooding afternoon, but two drivers noticed her. One was an acquaintance from school, Mark Lobsinger, a Grade 12 student. He didn't wave because she wasn't looking his way. The last time he saw her was a brief glimpse in his rearview mirror. The other motorist who gave Kristen a second look was Paul Bernardo.

In case they spotted someone he liked, Bernardo had his strategy all worked out. They would park and Homolka would ask the girl for directions, acting dumb, giving him enough time to move behind their victim. Homolka was to open her door, get out holding a map, and put it on the roof, standing far enough back that their victim would be between Homolka and the car while pointing out directions and not easily able to escape. Homolka repeated the plan several times at Bernardo's insistence to ensure she knew what to do.

"You can be so fucking stupid sometimes, Kar," he said. "I just don't want you to screw things up."

Bernardo was driving along Linwell Road, scanning the faces of students they passed, when he noticed one girl walking alone. She had a trim build and brown hair to her shoulders. Bernardo got excited the moment he saw her.

"I like her," he said, turning the car around and driving past her again to double-check that she met his requirements: good looking and likely a virgin. "Yes. Yes. That's the one. She's perfect, just perfect."

He turned around, drove past her again, and pulled into the empty parking lot of Grace Lutheran church, parking about two car lengths back from the sidewalk, far enough in that passing motorists would be less likely to notice what was about to happen, but close enough to the road that his victim would probably still feel safe walking over to the car.

As Kristen approached Grace Lutheran, she noticed the gold sportscar parked just back from the sidewalk, its engine idling.

"Excuse me," Homolka called from the car, "can you help me with some directions?"

Although she had warned her friends to be careful about talking to strangers, Kristen walked right up to the car without hesitation. They were such a handsome couple.

"Where are you going?" Kristen asked.

"The Pen Centre," Homolka replied.

Kristen started to describe the route to the city's biggest mall.

"Wait," Homolka said. "I'm so bad with directions.

Maybe you could show me on a map?"

Homolka was supposed to have the map ready, but she had forgotten and had to fumble through the glove compartment. She knew that would make Bernardo angry, but Kristen waited patiently as Homolka stepped out and began to unfold the map. In her haste, Homolka had grabbed a map of Toronto, but Kristen never noticed. She was just about to look at the map spread out on the roof when Bernardo got out of the car and walked quickly around the front, holding the knife tight against his side.

"You're coming with us," he said once he was behind her. He held the knife to Kristen's neck as he shoved her toward the front seat. Homolka knew that was her signal to step into the car; Bernardo had said he wanted her in the back seat because he felt it would be easier for him to control their victim if she sat beside him. Kristen fought with Bernardo, trying to punch him as he pushed her forwards. She hit her shoulder on the edge of the door frame and cried out in pain. Homolka barely had a chance to retrieve the map in the struggle.

"You bastard!" Kristen screamed as Bernardo grabbed her by the hair and shoved her roughly onto the passenger seat. He hit the side lever and pushed the seat down so that it was almost horizontal. Again French screamed, "You bastard!"

Barbara Packham was driving past Grace Lutheran when she noticed a man standing by the passenger side of a car in the lot. She couldn't be sure, but he seemed to be struggling to get something into the vehicle. At the time, she would later tell the police, she thought he was putting a package into the rear seat. All she saw of him was his backside, and she couldn't tell if there was anybody else in the car. She was intrigued enough to give the scene more than a passing glance, but what she saw wasn't suspicious enough to make her stop and investigate.

"Hold her there," Bernardo told Homolka, who grabbed their captive's hair, yanking hard from the rear seat.

Bernardo slammed the passenger door and glanced at the passing traffic as he hurried to get into the car. Several cars had gone by, but none had stopped. In his haste he never noticed the Bass loafer that had fallen off Kristen's left foot in the struggle, or the piece of torn map on the ground.

He power-locked the passenger door, then headed away.

"I've got a knife," he said, holding it closer to his victim's face. "Be quiet, or I'll use it."

Kristen was being held down hard against the seat by Homolka, who had a firm grip on her hair, and she had stopped struggling. Bernardo drove slowly, going right past Kristen's school and the stragglers who were just leaving for the weekend. He kept to the speed limit. He had often told Homolka: "When you're doing something illegal, follow all the traffic rules. It would be stupid to get caught for something small when you're doing something big."

They were at a stop sign, just about to turn onto the main road through Dalhousie, when Homolka looked up to her right and saw the man in the delivery truck close by. From his high vantage point, he could easily see down into their car. Bernardo had seen him too, but said nothing. Homolka knew he was mad at her for not following his instructions. She was supposed to have covered up their captive with a blanket Bernardo kept in the back seat. But she had forgotten, and she knew that meant another beating. For what seemed like an eternity, they sat beside the van before they could make the turn. But the man never looked down, and they drove the rest of the way home without any trouble.

28
Words of Love

Homolka jumped out to open the garage door, then pulled it closed as soon as the car was inside. Bernardo made their prisoner exit from his side of the vehicle, forcing her to climb over his legs and becoming even more aroused as her body brushed against his.

Homolka went straight into the house, closed all the blinds, and unplugged the phones, putting them in a closet in the master bedroom. She moved the answering machine out of the living room into the spare bedroom on the main floor. She handed Bernardo one of his polo shirts as he brought their hostage into the house, and he tied it over Kristen's eyes, not because he didn't want her to see the house, but to disorient her and force her to listen to him even more. Take away a person's sight, and you take away some of their aggression. It was just as he had read in *The Perfect Victim.* He wanted a compliant, frightened victim.

"You wait down here till I call you," Bernardo told Homolka, and he grabbed the frightened girl's arm. Upstairs in the master bedroom he led her over to the hope chest and told her to get down on her knees. "You do what I say and I won't hurt you."

The next sound she heard was the zipper on his pants.

"Oh my God," she said, and started crying.

He stepped behind her, shoved her head to the floor, then flipped up her skirt and pulled her panties down.

"Arch your back," he ordered. When she didn't do it right away, he punched her on the shoulders.

She was crying as he vaginally raped her. Before ejaculating, he penetrated her anally. Finally, he wanted fellatio. When she refused, he punched her on the arms and hit her in the mouth. "Do what I fucking say," he threatened, "or I'm really going to have to hurt you."

In the privacy of his own bedroom, with his accomplice downstairs watching for any signs of trouble, and waiting to be beckoned, Bernardo was once again the master. He was patient as he told Kristen how best to perform oral sex. It was clear she had never done it before, and it pleased him even more to know that he had his virgin. He wanted to know her name, and she gave him a fake one. When he finally climaxed, he held the back of her head tightly against his penis, forcing her to swallow it all.

Afterwards he let her put her underwear back on and then he called downstairs for Homolka to make drinks. She brought up alcoholic refreshments on a silver platter, saying nothing to their prisoner, still blindfolded and huddled in a corner. Bernardo noticed that his captive was missing a shoe, and he told Homolka to check the house and the car for it. Bernardo left the bedroom to check on his wife's progress. He was furious when she told him the shoe must have come off at the church during the struggle.

"Everything would have been perfect if you hadn't fucked it up," he said, and punched her on the arm.

He was also mad at her for not having the map ready and for not covering their hostage with the blanket when they drove back. "You're just so fucking stupid, Kar."

"I'm sorry."

"Fine," he said, but her punishment would have to come later.

When he returned to the bedroom, his captive asked if she could use the washroom. Bernardo got his video camera and led her there. "Just hold on to me," he said, directing her to the toilet.

"Here?"

"Pull your pants right down," he said, getting on his knees and aiming the camera at her vagina. "Right down."

"I know."

"Show me something nice, huh?"

"There's not much nice to see."

But Bernardo was getting aroused. Aside from the sexual stimulation, he wanted her to know he was in total control of her life, everything she did.

"Spread it open," he ordered, putting a hand on a knee and pushing it to one side so he had a better view with his camcorder.

Embarrassed by having someone watch her perform a private bodily function, Kristen held back at first. But then she urinated.

"You're right," Bernardo said. "You did have to go a lot." Watching her urinate had aroused him again, and he directed her back to the bedroom.

"Is it past 6 o'clock?" asked Kristen.

"Yeah," Bernardo replied.

"My mom's going to be worried."

Donna French was thinking of her daughter as she pulled into the driveway just before 5 p.m. Kristie's boyfriend, Elton Wade, had been calling the house but getting no answer. Donna's daughter was supposed to be home just after 3 p.m. to let Sasha out. Wade had been worried enough to call

Kristen's father, Doug, at work to ask why she wasn't at home. With Leslie Mahaffy's killer not yet caught and Terri Anderson still missing, most of the residents of Garden City were on the alert for trouble.

Donna had a sudden, terrible feeling something was wrong when she saw Sasha still in the pen in the back yard. After letting the dog out, she searched the house.

"Kristie?" she called repeatedly. But there was no answer. She phoned her husband. Although it had been only two hours, they were both worried. There was no reason for the unexpected change in Kristen's routine. Donna sent her son, Darren, to look for her, to walk the route she usually took from school. Darren thought she might have been hit by a car, but there were no emergency vehicles anywhere. And by the time he got to her school, it was deserted, locked up for the long weekend. Darren hurried home.

In the meantime, Donna had been busy calling her daughter's friends. As far as they knew, Kristie had gone right home after school. When her son returned home with no news, there was only one thing to do: she called the police.

"We can't use the same ones," Homolka told Bernardo when he said he was going to drug their captive with Halcion. "The police will be able to link the two cases."

Neither had said it, but it was clear that they would eventually have to kill the young girl they had just kidnapped. Unlike their first victim, she had seen their faces. Bernardo, though, was for the moment consumed with sexual fire and not thinking that far ahead. Homolka was just being practical: she didn't want to leave behind any forensic evidence that might link the two murders when the police found the body.

Bernardo agreed, and they spiked their prisoner's drink with other sleeping pills that Homolka had got from a doctor. Knowing she couldn't stop her husband, she had made up her mind to be as coldly efficient as possible at not getting caught. She went downstairs while Bernardo went back to have more fun with his latest sex slave.

Kristen was sitting on the floor beside the hope chest, clothed and still blindfolded. She took the spiked drink from Bernardo, and began to cry when he told her that he wanted her to perform more fellatio, only this time he was going to tape it. She begged him to free her, promising that she would never tell anyone. But he wasn't listening as he set up his camera and took off his pants. He told her to put down the drink, then shoved his penis toward her mouth.

"Put it inside your mouth, really deep," he ordered. "Tell my dick you love him."

"I love you," she said, on her knees, sobbing.

"You make me feel good, and I'll make you feel good. Now suck it. Keep sucking it. Put it in, tighter. You've got to pull over the head, okay?"

He told her to fondle his scrotum, and she complied.

"Yeah," he said, beginning to moan. "That's good. Keep going. You're getting really good at this."

"Do you want me to keep . . . going?"

"Put it in your mouth all the way. Yeah. Good girl. Now tell it you love it."

"I love it."

Bernardo threw his head back in pleasure. "Yeah, keep going over the head with your mouth. Suck it. Tell me how you like sucking dick."

"I like sucking dick."

"Again, once more."

"I like sucking dick." She stopped. "Is it okay?"

"Keep going," he said, pushing her head back. "You're doing good. I'm happy right now, and that's what you want, right?"

"Uh-huh."

"Tell me you want me to be happy."

"I want you to be happy."

"So maybe you can go home later," he offered, knowing it was a lie.

"Okay," she said, with slight optimism in her voice.

He didn't climax; he was saving that. Now he wanted to videotape her in a different position.

"You suck good cock," he said, getting his camcorder from the chair. "You sure you've never done this before? Okay, here's what I want you to do now. There's a chest there to lean on. I want you to lean back and pull off your leotards and lift up your skirt and show me your cunt, okay? Now, make me happy and don't make me mad."

"I won't." Hesitantly, she reached back for the chest.

"Okay, be good to me," he said, aiming the camera up her skirt as she climbed onto the chest. "No matter what."

"Sure," she replied in a trembling voice.

And when she hesitated, he urged her on: "Make me happy. Do it. Take them off."

"Please," she begged, then reluctantly pulled down her tights and underwear.

"Put your knees up," he ordered, down on the floor and holding the camera close to her vagina. "Spread your cunt for me. C'mon, spread the lips for me."

"What?"

"Spread your cunt lips for me."

"I can't," she protested.

"Do it with your fingers."

"No," she said defiantly.

Bernardo turned off the camera and hit her on the side of the head several times. He told her he would keep hitting her until she complied. When he turned the camera back on, she did as she was told.

"Okay, okay. That's good," he said, holding the camera close to her vagina. "With your fingers. Yeah."

Then he inserted his forefinger into her vagina as he held the camera just inches away. Satisfied with the angle, he told her to turn over and lie across the chest, then he flipped up her skirt and put the camera close to her anus. A while later she asked to use the washroom. As before, he took her there, along with his camcorder.

"Okay, spread your legs," he said as she sat down on the toilet, pushing on her knee and almost tipping her over.

"I'm going to pee all over you."

"You're not peeing on nothing."

"My stomach's upset," she said.

"You're going to get something to eat in a second."

Police forces don't usually respond to reports of people missing for only three hours. But there was just enough urgency in Donna French's voice to convince the police, especially since the missing girl lived close to Terri Anderson.

Later that night, a command post was set up at Holy Cross school. Insp. Vince Bevan, still looking for Leslie Mahaffy's killer, was handed this second case. As the evening wore on, it became pretty clear that foul play was involved. A schoolfriend had seen Kristen walking along Linwell Road, yet she had never reached home. The police desperately needed an eyewitness, so a news release was put out to the media.

The Niagara police department was a model of efficiency during the first 24 hours of the investigation. The force had moved quickly: a command post was in place, a team of detectives had been assigned, and a preliminary search started on both sides of Linwell Road. The Niagara police had even gone to the media for help, something they seldom did. Their fast start would later lead to the first real break — but also to the first of several blunders in the case. Unfortunately for the Niagara police, there would be few successes to match the achievements of Day One.

Homolka had spent most of Thursday waiting in the living room, watching TV for news reports on the abduction, peeking out the blinds to check for the police. So far she was just a supporting actress in her husband's murderous drama. Several hours passed before he summoned her to center stage. First he wanted her to do some taping. Their prisoner, he explained, had been told what to say once the film was rolling. Bernardo then ordered French to take off her clothes, along with the blindfold. He told her to get on the bed, where he joined her after he too was naked. He grabbed her shoulders and pulled her head toward his penis.

"Okay," Homolka said, as she turned on the video camera.

"I'm 15 years old," Kristen said, repeating the line Bernardo had told her to say, "and I love to suck dick."

Homolka stepped close to the edge of the bed. "That's good," she told their captive. "Now smile."

Kristen didn't, and Bernardo warned her, "Smile the next time she says to."

"I'm 15 years old, and I love to suck dick," Kristen said, making a weak effort at a smile.

Bernardo looked at Homolka. "Did she smile?"

"Yeah."

Bernardo soon wanted a change and, as he took over the camera, told Homolka to perform cunnilingus on Kristen. Eventually he gave the camera back to his wife, ordered their prisoner onto her hands and knees, and penetrated her vaginally from behind. It was painful to her, and she cried out, "No."

"Shut up!" he shouted. "Put your ass up. Arch your back, bitch!" And then he thrust his pelvis violently at her buttocks. "Do you like this?"

She screamed in pain.

Bernardo grabbed her by the hair as he raped her. "Turn your face to the side."

Homolka positioned herself so that she was pointing the lens at Kristen's face. Kristen looked up at Homolka, a look of terror and pain on her face. Homolka stared back, and kept taping.

"Smile," she told the girl.

"Tell me you love me," Bernardo ordered.

"I love you."

"Smile when you say it."

"I love you."

Bernardo was pushing harder and faster against her.

"Tell me . . . again. Keep telling me."

"I love you," she said, fear in her voice.

Bernardo was tugging on her hair as he kept pumping. He wanted to see her face, kept demanding that she turn sideways and tell him how much she loved him. When she didn't immediately respond, he punched her on the back.

"I love you," she said just once.

Bernardo hit her again.

"I love you, I love you, I love you," she now said over and over, a total of 26 times, until he ejaculated and withdrew. He jerked his thumb across his neck, a signal for Homolka to turn off the camera.

They ate some chicken Homolka had cooked, and French fell asleep on the bed soon after, exhausted from the repeated rapes and the sedatives. Not long afterwards, Bernardo also fell asleep as he lay beside her. Homolka lay down on her mattress on the floor, not wanting to sleep because she was afraid their prisoner might escape. But soon she too was sleeping.

29
Playing God

Kristen, still groggy from the sedatives and the liquor she had been forced to drink, was the last to awaken the next morning. She felt dirty after being raped repeatedly the previous day and wanted to clean up. Homolka was in the bedroom, watching as Kristen put on one of her T-shirts and asked if she could bathe.

"You'll have to ask him," Homolka replied, turning to look down the hall into the music room, where Bernardo was working on one of his rap songs.

He was still blindly optimistic about a record contract for his album. Previously, Homolka had been his only audience, but now he had a new listener. He sang some of the lyrics for her.

> A Deadly Innocent first, with a spell-bindin' curse,
> I am crazy swearin' not really carin'
> Total cop hatin' innocence fakin'
> 40-ounce slammin' never act dammin'
> Like lay low watchin' it flow
> Leave the fly girls waitin'

Bernardo asked Kristen what she thought. She had listened because there was nothing else she could do, but Homolka knew from her expression that she didn't think much of the song. Kristen never told him that, though, because she had learned that to make him angry meant a beating. They had already discovered that Kristen had lied about the first name she had given them, and Bernardo had punched her because of that. The couple had tuned in to the TV news that morning, and the newscasts had given out her name.

Bernardo kept singing, waiting for some praise, truly believing that the young woman he had repeatedly raped might actually like him and his music. He was convinced his raps would make him rich, famous, and loved by the masses. All he had to do was keep polishing the lyrics. "Young and Hype" was the title of one of the cuts.

> So remember young hype is a white boy
> A white boy rapper that's neither fool nor toy
> With tremendous outrage
> 'Cause I can't sit and wait for my day to arrive
> I've got to struggle and fight
> To keep my dream alive
> 'Cause I've got the right to recite and excite
> Lyrics that bite, delight and ignite
> Topics that ill and display my skill
> Watch me fulfil as I earn a couple mill
> I like to train with pain, I am just that type
> I am always coolin' on the mike
> 'Cause I am young and hype.

Kristen shrugged after listening to the song. She just wanted to clean up and look for a chance to escape. Bernardo let her use the bathroom, but told her he was going to watch. He followed her in, taking along his camcorder and closing the door behind them.

Kristen filled up the tub, took off her shirt and settled into the warm, soothing water. For a few moments, at least, she closed her eyes and drifted off, enveloped in the pleasures of a bath, washing away the filth. But then the lens of the camera was shoved close to her most intimate parts. There would be no privacy, and no point in trying to cover herself up. Bernardo was getting aroused as he watched her bathe.

"You know what I want you to do," he told her, sitting on the floor beside the tub, the camera aimed at her body. "I want you to do your ass again just like you were doing."

Kristen did as instructed, lathering her buttocks while Bernardo taped.

"Smile," he told her. "Is that nice?"

"Pardon me?"

"Do you like the Jacuzzi?"

"It's nice," she acknowledged, with little feeling.

"C'mon, smile. Smile," he urged, directing her to wash her vagina as he moved in for a close-up.

After she dried off, Bernardo told his prisoner she was going to take part in a little competition with his wife. He told Kristen to put her school uniform back on and directed his wife to put on a similar-type outfit. Then he summoned them both back into the bathroom. It was time, he said, to play the Perfume Game.

Barbara Packham was relaxing at home that Good Friday, watching TV, when a newsflash during a break caught her attention. A St. Catharines teenager named Kristen French had been abducted on her way home the previous day, around 3 p.m. Although no one had witnessed the kidnapping, the police believed from passing motorists that the missing teen had been taken from the parking lot of Grace Lutheran Church. A left shoe, a Bass loafer, had been found in the lot, with an arch support similar to the type that the missing teen used because of a bad back. The shoe had likely fallen off in a struggle.

Packham got a chill and sat bolt upright in her chair. She got right on the phone to the police.

Sgt. Brian Nesbitt of the Niagara police department took her statement. She told him she had seen the back of a man leaning into a car parked just a few feet in from the sidewalk. It appeared that he was struggling with something, perhaps a package. She said she didn't get a clear look at the man's face or anybody else who might have been in the car. Then came the key question: Did she notice the type of car? Packham replied that it was a sporty two-door type, similar to one driven by an acquaintance, a Camaro. Packham was quick to add: "I'm not saying it was a Camaro, and I don't know if it was. It just looked like a Camaro."

Whereas everything else in the investigation had been going well, the make of car used in the abduction was troubling the detectives. They wanted to describe the vehicle in their next press release, but none of their witnesses were that positive about the model. They were fairly sure about their site of the abduction, however. Besides the shoe, a lock of hair had been found there, and forensic testing with a sample taken from the missing girl's hairbrush would confirm if the two matched. What the police weren't telling the public was that a section of a map, showing several streets from Scarborough, had also been found in the lot. The detectives had surmised that Kristen was lured toward the car on the pretext of giving directions. Did the torn section of the fold-out map mean she had been abducted by someone living in Scarborough? From talking to other motorists, the police surmised two people had abducted the teenager. But none of the eyewitnesses had managed to get a decent look at the faces of the abductors. As the detectives made plans for a huge search of the area, the one detail that bothered them was the car.

Packham and several other eyewitnesses believed the

vehicle might be a Camaro, but none would say positively that it was. From their brief glimpses they had noticed a sloped back and rear taillights similar in design to those of the popular General Motors car. The fact that one of these eyewitnesses happened to work at a GM plant finally clinched it for the detectives, who were about to make the first of several blunders. "This is a GM town," reasoned one investigator as the team mulled over how to describe the car in a press release, "and people here know their GM products." One witness had told detectives the rear lights had a checkerboard pattern, a design on Camaros in the early 1980s, so an approximately 10-year-old Camaro seemed a reasonable conjecture.

The bulletin that went out from the Niagara police to all law enforcement agencies in North America proclaimed that the vehicle wanted in the kidnapping of Kristen Dawn French was a Camaro, about 1982 or newer. It was a two-door coupé, beige in color. The body was in good shape. There was no chrome or stripping on the vehicle, and no spoiler at the back, as on some Camaros. The license number was unknown. The police asked for the public's help.

Within hours of the bulletin's release, police stations on both sides of the border were flooded with calls. Everywhere on the continent, it seemed, people had spotted the Camaro that might have been used in the kidnapping. A Canadian driving a Camaro through Arkansas on his holiday was pulled over at gunpoint by a vigilant state trooper. A man in Niagara Falls was waved down four times by different police cruisers as he drove his Camaro home from work. A waiter in Toronto found himself surrounded by a group of suspicious, and hostile, bystanders as he got into his Camaro. They refused to let him leave until he opened his trunk. In the days after the press release, it became too much for some motorists, who pulled their Camaros off the road, tired of the scrutinizing stares.

The huge public response was just what the Niagara police had been hoping for. Kristen's disappearance had captured the nation's attention, and its sympathy. Although it was a slim chance, Insp. Vince Bevan and his team hoped that someone who spotted the right Camaro might give the police an opportunity to save the girl's life.

And so a small band of dedicated officers from the province's fifth-largest police force proceeded for the next 10 months, their well-intentioned efforts hopelessly doomed from the start by their erroneous premise that they were looking for a Camaro. Later, the team would swell to 30 detectives and a bevy of support staff. Unfortunately, they would compound that original gaffe during an ineffectual investigation that rang up a staggering tab of probably around $10 million of taxpayers' money. That figure is just an approximation. The exact figure may never be released, even though it was the public who footed the bill. Repeated requests for both the overall cost and specific costs of the task force under the Freedom of Information Act were turned down by government officials.

As Homolka and Kristen stood in front of the mirror in the second-floor bathroom, Bernardo explained to them the rules of his little contest. He wanted them to put on makeup and perfume. "The one who smells the best is the winner," he declared, "and won't get fucked by me up the ass."

He stood behind them and switched on his camcorder. Homolka gathered up various brands of perfume, spreading them out on the counter for their prisoner to sample.

"So what kind of perfume do you like?" Homolka asked.

"Eternity," Kristen replied. "Or Giorgio."

"Yeah," replied Homolka, "I like Giorgio as well. I

have some of that new perfume, Halston. I haven't worn it yet, but maybe I will today."

Bernardo, who had so far been standing quietly behind them, now had some instructions. "Okay, girls, you know what I want you to do. Each one of you pull up your skirts at the same time."

"Okay," said Homolka.

Kristen, who had already been beaten several times for not performing well on the tapes, knew what a refusal meant. Perhaps, until she had a good chance to flee, she had made up her mind to comply with his wishes, distasteful as she found them. As per his instructions, neither was wearing underwear.

"Okay, now bend over," Bernardo ordered, down on his knees and moving in for a close-up. "Give me a nice ass shot."

Each bent over, and at the same time flipped up their skirts. Bernardo's breathing grew labored as he panned from one to the other and back.

"Good girls," he said. And a few moments later: "Okay, go back to work."

"Let's see what we have here," Homolka said, rummaging through the bottles.

"Eternity," Kristen said, reaching for the bottle.

"Oh, Eternity," Homolka replied. "I like it." She pointed at another bottle. "That's Escape. I hate that one."

Kristen reached for the bottle of Escape.

"Really? Can I smell it?"

"It's gross," said Homolka.

"I've never used it," Kristen said, dragging out the conversation as long as she could, knowing that she was likely to be raped again, and perhaps hoping to delay the inevitable.

"I was at work one day," Homolka continued, chatting as if talking to a girlfriend as they got ready for an evening out, "and I bought one of those magazines, like Mademoiselle, and then the whole place stunk because of that perfume in a page. I've got others here to try, like Alfred Sung."

"Can I try this one?" Kristen said, reaching for an amber bottle.

"Sure," Homolka replied.

"Tell the camera," Bernardo said, and they turned to face him.

"Mmm, gorgeous, gorgeous," he said, putting the camera down and sniffing Kristen's neck. The he turned to his wife. "No way, lady." He crunched up his nose. "This is not a nice smell."

Homolka sniffed at Kristen's neck. "That is a nice smell," she said.

Bernardo ushered them into the master bedroom.

"Even though you smell the best," he told Kristen, as he unzipped his fly, "I'm still going to fuck you up the ass anyways. She's my wife, after all. And she's got brownie points on her side."

Kristen began to cry, looking on helplessly as Bernardo took off his clothes, then forced her down on her hands and knees. He flipped up her skirt and penetrated her anally for the first time that day. Homolka stood by, watching, making no effort to stop the rape.

Later, Bernardo wanted to know if Kristen had a boyfriend.

"His name is Elton Wade."

Bernardo repeated the name several times while he shoved his penis toward her mouth. "Tell me that you hate him," he demanded. She refused. Impatient, he nonetheless gave her a second chance. "Say you hate him!" Kristen still refused, and for that insubordination he punched her in the face. When she still wouldn't denounce her boyfriend, he kept hitting her on the side of the head. Finally, when she could take no more punishment, she told him that she hated her boyfriend. Satisfied, he focused his attention on the way she was performing fellatio. "You're not opening your mouth wide enough!" he yelled and hit her on the side of the head, and kept hitting her until she did as he ordered.

Homolka stood nearby, still watching, still doing nothing, all the while waiting patiently to begin the threesome. After Bernardo had ejaculated into his prisoner's mouth, he wiped himself off, dressed, and went for his knife. He put it on the floor in front of Kristen, then stepped back a few paces.

"Go for it," said Bernardo.

Kristen stared at the knife for a long time. Although she was an athletic young woman, he was at least seven inches taller and 70 pounds heavier. If she grabbed at the knife, he would probably take it away from her quite easily and punish her for trying. She hoped her opportunity to escape would come, but she didn't like this particular wager with her life.

"Go on," Bernado said, taunting her. "Grab it and stab me. If you do it, you can get away."

But Kristen refused to pick up the knife.

"Then you're mine," Bernardo said, grabbing her by the hair and twisting her head back. "I want you to do everything I tell you from now on. If you're good, maybe I'll let you go."

He told her the next time they made a video she would have to say what he wanted to hear: he was the king, the master, and she was the cocksucker, the cunt, the slut, the Holy Cross sex slave. If she said those words, he wouldn't punish her. Kristen knew that she had to maintain her strength and seize any chance to escape. If that meant complying with all his disgusting sexual desires, she was ready to dissociate her mind from her body in order to survive.

Bernardo then wanted a massage. He sat on the edge of the bed, snapped his fingers, and ordered his captive to give him one. Kristen complied, doing such a good job that he kept complimenting her. Bernardo told Homolka he was hungry, but first he wanted a drink, one for him and Kristen. Homolka made the drinks, then went downstairs to cook chicken. When she came back, Kristen saw her opportunity. She turned up her nose at what Homolka had prepared.

"I don't want to eat that."

Bernardo, realizing that his sex slave had to eat if she was to satisfy his sexual demands, asked what she wanted.

"I want pizza," Kristen said, probably realizing that they would never take the chance of home delivery, with someone coming to the house. "McDonald's pizza."

Kristen, born and raised in St. Catharines, knew the city well. She knew there were two McDonald's and to each the round trip was at least half an hour. If Bernardo went out for the food, she would be alone with her female captor. And it was with another woman that Kristen probably saw her best chance to escape. With no way of knowing about the other deeds in which her captor had participated, Kristen may well have assumed Homolka had been more an unwilling accomplice in the abduction than an equal partner in the crime.

Bernardo agreed to bring them some food. Before he left, he led his prisoner into a closet off the master bedroom, where he bound her legs and handcuffed her. Then he went downstairs for the rubber mallet his late grandfather had bequeathed to him. He handed it to Homolka, saying, "Stay in the room and guard her. If she tries to escape, or if she starts screaming, hit her with it."

He drove off, listening to a news report on the missing girl and the hunt for a 10-year-old beige Camaro. Along the way, he passed a police cruiser, but the officer was probably too busy scanning for Camaros to notice a blond-haired man driving a Japanese import.

Once more, Bernardo would later brag to Homolka, the rebel hype, as he liked to call himself, had fooled the police. It was just like the lyrics he wrote:

> Stop foolin' yourself, give up the chase
> You got no confession, you got no case
> You ever get caught? You ever get caught?
> No. Why?
> 'Cause I'm a deadly innocent guy.

No one suspected the truth about Tammy, the Leslie Mahaffy investigation had dropped right out of the news, and now the police were looking for the wrong car. Let them search all they wanted, Bernardo would later say over and over to Homolka, it wasn't going to help them. No one was ever going to catch Paul Bernardo. He was just too smart.

Homolka stood guard by the closet. Kristen had started to work on her the moment Bernardo had left. "I know you don't want to do this," she said, a conversation Homolka later recalled. "I can tell you're not really a part of this. Help me escape. We can get away together."

"You don't understand," Homolka replied. "I can't. I'm afraid of him."

"Does he hit you?"

"Yes."

"I'll tell the police that you didn't want to do any of this. I'll say that he forced you." There was an urgency in Kristen's voice. She knew that she didn't have much time and might not get a second opportunity. "You can take your dog," she continued. "Bring him. We can go to my house. I have a dog as well. Please, please help me."

With Bernardo gone, Homolka was in control. It was in her power that Good Friday to play God and save the teenager's life. One quick phone call would do it. But if she let her go, the police would probably learn the truth about Tammy and Leslie Mahaffy. She might not want to participate in a second murder, but she didn't want to go to jail either.

"I can't do it," Homolka said. "I'm afraid. He's threatened to kill my family."

But Kristen kept up the conversation. She began talking about her family and her boyfriend. "He's a really great guy," she said about Elton Wade. "I really love him." And then: "I want to see him again. Please, you must help me. You know he's going to kill me. Is that what you want?"

With two killings already on her conscience, a third was not going to make a critical difference to Homolka. Her own freedom was of more concern to her now. She walked over to the dormer window and looked out at the street below for his car. She hoped he would hurry home so that she wouldn't have to listen to any more pleading.

The gray-haired gentleman, a long-time resident of Port Dalhousie, was out for a walk when he passed by the pretty pink house with green shutters on Bayview Drive. He knew almost everybody in Dalhousie, but he didn't know much about the young couple who had rented the old Borland house. They had lived there for nearly a year, but few in the neighborhood knew much about them. The woman was friendly enough. She always smiled, said hello whenever she took the couple's dog out for a walk. She was usually out by herself, which seemed strange since the couple had just recently married. Her husband was more aloof, and seldom around. But he had to be doing well to be able to rent such a pricey house. Neighbors said he was from Toronto, a freelance accountant.

As the gray-haired gentleman walked by the house, he noticed the garage door was open, the car gone. He couldn't be sure, but he thought someone was staring down at him from an upstairs window. He looked up, but no one was there.

30
A Wrong Turn

Bernardo picked up two movies when he went for the pizza, *Angel Heart* and *Criminal Law*, a Canadian flick about a serial killer. When he returned, his prisoner was still in the closet handcuffed and with her legs trussed. Homolka said nothing about Kristen's pleas for freedom. He took off the cuffs, untied her, and led her into the bedroom. They watched television while they ate.

Kristen now realized Homolka would never risk her own life to save that of another. While they ate, it is possible that she was already formulating a different strategy. Perhaps Kristen was thinking what she might do the next time she was alone with Homolka — if there was a next time — beyond another fruitless appeal to the woman's compassion or altruism. Kristen was at least four inches taller than her female guard, and heavier by a dozen pounds. Could she overpower her if she had another half-hour window of opportunity to save her life? Meanwhile, by succumbing totally to Bernardo's wishes, could she avoid further beatings, and thus conserve her precious energy?

Kristen's disappearance was now the biggest news item in the country, and television stations were carrying updates on the case nearly every hour. Although the French family wasn't saying much to the media, Austin Delaney, with CFTO-TV, secured an interview with the missing girl's father, Doug, which was carried live late that afternoon from the family home. Choking back tears, French made an impassioned plea for his daughter's life. Looking weary, the grieving father stared straight into the camera and spoke directly to his daughter.

"If you can see this, Kristie," he began, "I want you to know we're thinking of you. Everything that can be done is being done to get you back."

He had no way of knowing that his daughter was watching the live broadcast from a house not more than a five-minute drive away.

"Oh, Dad," Kristen cried out when she saw him. "I want to see my father."

"We love you, Kristie," Doug continued. "You are constantly in our thoughts and our prayers. We'll get you home real fast. If you can get to a phone, Kristie, call home or the Niagara police."

Bernardo didn't want his prisoner too upset because it might affect her performance, so he flicked off the set. Kristen kept crying for a long time afterwards. Whatever plan she may have had, the sight of her father on television had made her feisty. She wasn't afraid of Bernardo any longer, and told him as much. It was more gumption than he had seen from a woman in the past five years with Homolka.

"Someone saw what you did," Kristen said, her eyes brimming with tears of defiance. "You're not going to get away with this."

"The police would have been here a long time ago if anybody saw anything," Bernardo retorted.

But Kristen was in a pugnacious mood, even though she probably realized it might hasten her death. "The police are going to come here. You'll see."

Bernardo had to calm her down. She would never perform duties as his sex slave if she remained so recalcitrant.

He put on *Criminal Law*, and the three watched it in silence. He didn't share her confidence in the ability of the police force. In fact, he looked upon the authorities as a bunch of bumbling fools. He had said as much in the rap album that was going to make him an international star. Didn't she realize she was dealing with the Rebel Hype? Didn't she know she was messing with the one Deadly Innocent Guy in the world?

Vince Bevan and his team of investigators were in dire need of another break. The parking lot had failed to reveal any clue as to the identity of the kidnappers, save for the corner of the map of Scarborough. There had been hundreds of Camaro sightings, but none had turned into a promising lead. Investigators were still trying to determine in which direction the Camaro had gone. Although the eyewitness reports were sketchy, a car, possibly the wanted Camaro, had been sighted driving erratically around the church at the time of the abduction. And from several accounts there appeared to be some struggling going on inside the back seat of the vehicle. Developing a theory from these accounts, the detectives surmised the Camaro had turned left out of the parking lot and headed east along Linwell Road for a short distance, traveling away from Port Dalhousie. The driver had then turned south, onto Geneva Street, ironically roaring right past Kristen French's house. He was driving erratically, several witnesses had said, speeding through one red light and almost getting into an accident with an oncoming car at Scott Street. According to one witness, there were three or four people in the car, two in the back seat. If the abductors had taken the service road to the expressway, they could have fled to any of the hundreds of communities between Niagara Falls and Toronto.

The media was summoned for the latest update. The police were anxious to talk to anybody traveling along Geneva or who had witnessed the near-collision at Scott Street. The girl's life could be saved, the police said, if everybody worked together.

At that point the 60 or more journalists covering the case on both sides of the border were very supportive of the work done by the police, and reporters hurried to file this latest bit of news. No one questioned it; no one could know it was yet another faux pas by the team of diligent and hard-working detectives, one that shifted attention away from Port Dalhousie and the house where Kristen was being held little more than a stone's throw from the police command post at the school.

After the movie, Bernardo was ready for more sex. He ordered Kristen and Homolka onto the bed, and he got out his video camera. Like a director of a pornographic movie, he told them what to do.

"I like you, Christian," Homolka said, mispronouncing their prisoner's name.

"I like you too," responded French, once again choosing to comply.

"Do you want to have some fun?" Homolka asked, moving closer to her.

"Sure," Kristen replied warily. "Okay." And then: "How come your teeth are so straight?"

"I don't know," Homolka replied, somewhat taken aback. "How about yours?"

"You're so silly," said Kristen, giggling, apprehensive over what was coming.

"Don't be so nervous," said Homolka, undressing Kristen before removing her own clothes. "It's okay."

"Am I shaking?"

"No," assured Homolka. "Just try to feel at home." She ran a hand over Kristen's thigh. "You have nice legs."

"This one's kind of short," she said, touching her left leg.

"That's okay."

"Can I ask you a favor?" Kristen enquired. "Before I leave, can I see your dog . . . without it attacking me?"

Homolka looked at Bernardo, who was panning over their bodies with his camcorder. "It's up to him."

"Yeah, sure. Before you leave," Bernardo promised.

"I like dogs," Kristen continued as Homolka began stroking her breasts.

"Me too," said Bernardo.

Homolka ran her hands through Kristen's hair as she sucked on a breast.

"I have a knot there," Kristen said, touching her hair. "I used to have straight hair."

Homolka instructed Kristen to move her legs apart so she could perform cunnilingus. "Comfy?"

Kristen nodded.

"Close your eyes," Homolka encouraged. "Just get comfy, okay?"

"If I close my eyes, I'll fall asleep."

"No, you won't," Homolka said. "Trust me, you won't."

"I like your breasts," Homolka said, sucking on one, then the other.

"Thank you."

"You're a pretty girl," continued Homolka, her breathing heavy with passion.

"You're pretty, too," responded Kristen. "When I first saw you at the car, I thought, 'Holy cow, is she pretty.' It's definitely frightening."

"Good girl," said Homolka, burying her face between Kristen's legs. Then pausing, looking up: "You've got a sexy body."

"Thank you." Kristen gazed down at the back of Homolka's head. "It seems like you're experienced at this."

"Trust me, I'm not," Homolka lied.

"I guess there's a first time for everything."

"Uh-huh," Homolka acknowledged, moaning with evident passion.

"You know what?" Kristen said.

"What?"

"When I go home," she said, but didn't finish, possibly because, in spite of herself, she was aroused by the deft tongue movements of her more experienced captor.

Homolka paused to look up at Bernardo, who had the camera lens just a few inches away. "She's getting hooked on this," she proclaimed, sounding somewhat proud of her efforts.

Bernardo turned off the camera long enough to tell them to reverse their positions.

"Yeah," Homolka moaned as Kristen performed oral sex on her. Although she would later tell the authorities how much she hated having sex with another woman, Homolka's sighs of pleasure told a different story on the videotapes.

"Use your fingers," Bernardo ordered. "Put two right up inside of her. She likes that."

Kristen did so, and Homolka leaned back, her eyes shut as her body went limp.

"That . . . really . . . feels . . . nice," said the woman who supposedly hated lesbian sex.

"Just like that?" Kristen asked, glad enough that Bernardo wasn't hitting her.

"Yeah," Homolka moaned. "That's so nice."

"Put your fingers deep inside her," Bernardo ordered, maneuvering the camera even closer to Homolka's vagina.

"Like this?" Kristen asked.

Homolka was writhing on the bed in bliss. "Yeah, that's nice."

"Okay," Bernardo instructed, "now move your fingers in and out, like you're fucking her."

"Are my nails hurting you?"

Homolka barely managed to shake her head. "No," she said euphorically, "that feels really good."

"Tell her what she needs to do, Karla," said Bernardo, "to make you feel good."

But Homolka could find no fault. "She's doing good. That's just perfect."

"Christian," Bernardo said, also mispronouncing her name, "give me a smile. Tell me you love me."

"I love you," she obediently replied.

"Tell me that you love Karla."

"I love Karla," she said. "Is that your name?"

Homolka was too aroused to reply.

"Tell her you love her cunt."

"I love her cunt," she quickly responded.

"Good girl," said Bernardo, rubbing his penis. It was soon going to be his turn. But first he wanted them to kiss again. "You guys can finger each other while you kiss," he said, moving himself into position with the camera.

And when Kristen was awkward with her hand movements, Homolka guided the girl's fingers into her vagina.

"Feel good?" asked Kristen.

"Yeah, that's so good. You're great."

"Okay for the first time," Kristen responded.

"Very good," said Homolka. "I like little girls."

"Thank you."

"Are you having a good time?" Homolka enquired.

"Uh-huh."

"Good."

"Way better than yesterday," noted Kristen.

"Good girl," said Homolka. "I love you, Christian."

"I love you too, Karla."

Bernardo then told Kristen to perform anilingus on Homolka, who got on her hands and knees. Kristen gently parted her buttocks and began.

"Is that too hard?" she asked.

"No," said Homolka, her face exuding bliss, "that's really, really good. A little deeper please," she said, and then moaned.

"Too bad my tongue's so short."

"She's shoving it in there, is she?" asked Bernardo. Homolka nodded. "Shove it inside her asshole. Deep inside. Good girl."

Wanting even more stimulation, Homolka took Kristen's hand and directed it toward her vagina. "Just do that every so often," she said.

Bernardo was more blunt. "Caress her cunt with your hands."

"That's so good," said Homolka. She glanced at Bernardo. "She knows what she's doing."

Homolka then performed anilingus on Kristen.

"You taste really good," she said.

"Thank you," replied Kristen.

"That looks beautiful," Homolka said. "I really enjoy doing this to you."

Bernardo, anxious for his turn, passed the camera to Homolka and assumed his familiar position on his back at the edge of the bed. Kristen, on her knees at the side of the bed, began performing fellatio while massaging his penis. Homolka kept the camera trained on his crotch.

"Tell me if I'm pulling on you too hard."

"You'll know," Bernardo told her.

But French was having trouble, twice letting his penis slip out of her hands. "I'm sorry."

"Don't drop it again," he warned. "Three times and you're out. You know that?"

Kristen apologized, but his penis slipped again from her fingers.

Bernardo scowled at her. "Uh-oh. That's three times. Give me the knife," he said to Homolka. "I'm going to kill her right now."

"It's slippery," Kristen said, desperately anxious.

"You're forgiven," said Bernardo, leaning back on the bed.

"Thank you."

"That's because you make me feel good."

Kristen kept masturbating Bernardo until he climaxed, gagging as he forced her to swallow his semen.

Afterwards, he put on the other rented movie, and the three watched it together — Friday night at the movies — as if nothing was wrong.

Later that evening, Bernardo led his prisoner back into the closet off the master bedroom, where he bound her legs and cuffed her hands. Several of his friends had been phoning over the past two days, and if he didn't return their calls they might wonder what had happened and drop by the house for a visit.

"Just staying home, watching movies with the wife," he said to one friend.

Upstairs sat his prisoner, bound hand and foot, helplessly waiting to fulfill his next carnal whim. Homolka stood guard outside the closet to ensure she didn't try to escape. But after two days of forced sex, booze, and drugs, Kristen was feeling too sick to try anything. She vomited, splattering both the floor and herself. Homolka opened the door to see what was wrong, but made no more effort to help her prisoner until she had first checked with Bernardo.

Bernardo had had enough sex for the day. Before turning in, they forced Kristen to drink more liquor and take another sedative, waiting until she passed out before going to sleep themselves.

She would have to die, and all three of them knew it. The question was when. She had seen their faces, their car, their house. She even knew they had a dog. None of the precautions Bernardo had taken with Leslie Mahaffy, such as the blindfold, had been used with Kristen French. But on the third day of her captivity, Bernardo wasn't thinking about murder. He was pleased with her, and he wanted to keep his sexual fantasy going as long as possible.

Homolka was more realistic. "We can't keep her here forever," she told him. They had avoided their friends since Thursday, and it was only a matter of time before somebody would start to wonder what was wrong, she told him. And they were supposed to go to her parents' house on Sunday for Easter dinner.

"Why don't we just cancel?" Bernardo asked. "Tell them you're not feeling well."

But Homolka, who had read crime novels all her life, knew about the importance of alibis. "Spending Sunday with my parents would be a perfect alibi if we ever need one."

Bernardo acknowledged it was a good idea, but still wanted to keep his prisoner alive. "We'll just tie her up," he suggested. "And keep her in the closet."

Homolka told him it was far too dangerous for both

of them to leave her alone in the house. Everybody in the Niagara Peninsula, she pointed out, was looking for the missing teenager. It wasn't at all like the disappearance of Mahaffy, where no one had seemed to care. From the newscasts, they knew that even though the police were looking for the wrong car traveling in the wrong direction, a huge search of the area was being planned for that Monday. The entire top end of the city, including Port Dalhousie, was going to be canvassed by volunteers hunting for clues. Anything suspicious, such as a house with all the windows shuttered tight like theirs, would surely catch someone's attention.

While Bernardo agreed with his wife's reasoning, he wasn't ready to carry out the execution just yet. Happy over the way Kristen had tried so hard to please the two of them during sex, he had plans for a porno movie.

Bernardo wasn't a morning person when it came to sex; his time was late at night. That Saturday he felt like working on his rap music. He told Kristen to go into his music room. He wanted to know what she thought of a song he had written. He sang it in his high-pitched, off-key voice. Kristen complimented him just enough to avoid another beating. Probably she would have liked to tell Bernardo what she really thought of his performance: that he was a goofy man-child with a lousy voice who wasn't as handsome as he liked to think. But soon they might ask her what she wanted to eat, and Kristen likely had already thought about her next food order.

Although Vince Bevan's team refused to speculate on the matter, the media were already theorizing that the unsolved murder of Leslie Mahaffy and the disappearance of Kristen French were linked. Both cases had the obvious ties to Garden City. Bevan was soon besieged with questions from reporters that put him in a difficult situation.

He couldn't even acknowledge the likelihood of a link in the two cases. For that would mean he would have to discount the earlier theory that a man called Peter Stark might have been involved in Mahaffy's death. Stark had been arrested for Julie Stanton's murder and was already in jail when French was abducted. Alibis didn't come any tighter than that. For months, right up to Stark's arrest, Bevan and his team had searched for evidence linking Stark, who lived near St. Catharines and liked young schoolgirls, to Mahaffy. Although investigators hadn't found any proof, it was an option they had to leave open nonetheless. If Stark was eventually charged in Mahaffy's murder, it wouldn't help prosecutors if that death was linked to another disappearance while he was in jail. A good defense lawyer would use that to put some doubt into the minds of the jurors. So until he was ready to rule out Stark as a suspect, Bevan couldn't say much to reporters about their theories.

Bevan's reluctance to comment on a connection between the French and Mahaffy cases just fueled the speculation. His reticence was taken as proof by some journalists that the cases were linked, even if the police wouldn't confirm it. Bevan needed the help of a public relations officer, but his force didn't even have a media liaison officer. Bevan was on his own. The initial goodwill between the Niagara force and the media started to evaporate.

Late that Saturday afternoon, Bernardo asked his prisoner what she wanted for supper. He wanted her fed and energetic for the evening.

"Swiss Chalet chicken," she replied. She knew it would take Bernardo at least half an hour, if not longer, to fetch the order from the restaurant, which was near the center of the city.

Once again, Bernardo tied her, putting on the handcuffs and binding her legs with electrical cable. He gave his wife the rubber mallet and left her with the same instructions as before. This time Kristen knew her female guard was either too scared, or in too deep, to help her.

Homolka's version of what happened was later criticized in court for being too self-serving. Downplaying her part in the deaths was certainly in her best interest.

"I know you don't want to be part of this," Kristen said, according to Homolka. "You can come with me, and I'll tell the police you weren't a part of it."

"I can't," Homolka replied. "I just can't."

Then, according to Homolka, the two just talked about "girl things," like makeup and Kristen's boyfriend, almost as if they were having a pleasant Saturday afternoon chat.

It is possible to envisage a different scenario. Kristen might have asked to use the washroom. She had already made one mess in the closet when she vomited, and if she made a second it was likely Bernardo would punish her. For Kristen to go to the bathroom she would need her legs untied, and Homolka would have to put down the mallet. With her legs freed, even though her hands were cuffed behind her back, Kristen might have been able to kick out and knock her guard to the floor, stun her just long enough to make it to the stairs. Surprised by the sudden attack, but petrified that if her prisoner escaped she herself would be spending the rest of her life behind bars, Homolka would have dashed after the weakened captive. There would have been a struggle, two desperate women both, it could be said, fighting to save their lives.

Maybe it never happened. But unless we believe everything Karla Homolka told the authorities, we shall never know. Later, in court, Homolka could not explain deep bruising in two places under the skin below Kristen's eyes, marks that could have been made by a rubber mallet. If Kristen tried to escape, the most effective way the smaller Homolka could have stopped her would have been to pound her on the face with the rubber mallet, hoping to knock her unconscious.

Lori Lazaruk was driving home that afternoon after visiting friends in Port Dalhousie when she noticed the car that passed her, going the other way over the Martindale bridge. She recognized the driver immediately: he was the same man who had been taping her and her sister at the donut shop. He had escaped before, but she was determined it wouldn't happen again. Lazaruk did a U-turn and followed him into the lakefront community.

As well as buying the chicken for his sex slave, Bernardo had rented the movie *Shattered*, possibly smirking to himself over the title. Ruining people's lives didn't bother him. As he said in his songs:

> I'm the solo creep, I make the girls weep
> Committing my crimes while the others sleep.

He didn't care about the pain of others. He had his own set of rules to live by. His music said it all:

> The world is yours for the takin'
> Stop what you're doin' 'cause hype ain't fakin'
> I'll drain your brain and steal your gold chain
> 'Cause I've got no remorse
> And I've got no shame.

Remorse was for losers. You had to take what you wanted from the world, because the world would screw you every chance it got. That's what he had told Homolka over and over.

It frustrated him that she never fully grasped his concepts. There were occasions when she seemed to agree with everything he said and did, but then other times she became depressed and talked of suicide. He was just a short distance from his home, heading east along Main Street, when he noticed that a female motorist seemed to be following him.

Lazaruk was determined to nail the son-of-a-bitch who had taped her and her sister with his camcorder and followed her home several weeks earlier. The last time it had been too dark for a good look at the license plate. But this Saturday it was different. It was daylight, and Lazaruk had seen the license number clearly and written it down as she drove: 660 HFH. She even recognized the car, a two-door Nissan sports coupé, gold in color. The man behind the wheel had a distinctive look, blond, with a buzzcut about the ears. It was a face she wouldn't forget.

Bernardo, extra-cautious because the news of the abduction was dominating the airwaves, and presumably convinced that he was being tailed, hit the accelerator, quickly overtaking several cars. When he had put some distance between him and the woman in the car, he turned sharply onto a sidestreet and drove home and into the garage, quickly shutting the door.

Lazaruk was mad with herself. She had lost sight of the creep, probably because he had noticed her. For a little while she drove up and down the streets bordering Lake Ontario, searching for the gold Nissan and the blond pervert. Finally, she gave up and headed home. It didn't really matter that she had lost him. She had his license number. He wouldn't get away a second time. As soon as she reached home, she was going to call the police.

31
Worth Dying For

Lazaruk's phone complaint was taken by an officer at the downtown headquarters of the Niagara Region police department. She went through the whole story again, starting with the surreptitious videotaping at the donut shop. Lazaruk explained that although she got the license number wrong the first time because mud obscured it, she was positive she had just seen the man again driving in Dalhousie, and this time she had the correct plate number.

He punched it into the computer and within seconds the driver's name, type of vehicle, and registration number appeared on the screen. The officer asked Lazaruk to describe the car again, and her description matched what was on the screen: 1989 Nissan 240SX, gold. The officer checked the screen for the man's name. The car was leased out to a resident of Port Dalhousie — Paul Bernardo.

Bernardo hopped out of the car and went quickly into the house, peering out through the closed venetian blinds for the car that had been following him. He checked the street for several minutes, but didn't tell Homolka about the incident, not wanting to spook her more.

He was angry with his prisoner after he returned from Swiss Chalet, one of the videotapes showed, a mood change that might have been occasioned by an attempted escape or by his having been followed. Not long after return-

ing home, Bernardo ordered Kristen into the bathroom, then
told her to take off her clothes and climb into the empty tub.

The officer taking Lazaruk's call noted Bernardo's date of
birth, typing it and his name into the computer, curious to see
if he had a criminal record, such as arrests for being a Peeping
Tom. The search through the databank took several moments.
It was against the law for the officer to reveal the man's name
and address to Lazaruk, but he did tell her what he was doing.

   In the meantime, he asked if either Lazaruk or her
sister had been accosted by the man. She knew by the tone of
his questioning that, although he appeared sympathetic, he
wasn't taking her complaint very seriously. There wasn't
much the police could do, he explained. Driving around with
a camcorder wasn't against the law. Tourists did it all the time.
And she had been in a public place, after all. It would have
been different had the man hidden in some bushes, secretly
videotaping her in her home.

   The officer studied the screen as he spoke. There was
no criminal record for a man named Paul Bernardo. The officer punched in the particulars again, just to be sure. The result
was the same. About the best the police could do, the officer
said, was perhaps have a talk with the man and warn him
about his conduct. Her complaint would be treated seriously,
he told her. But it was a holiday weekend, the force was short-
staffed, and almost every available officer was busy in the
search for Kristen French.

After pushing Kristen into the bathtub, Bernardo put his camcorder down on the counter, aimed it toward the Jacuzzi, turned
it on, then took off his pants. "Stay there, okay," he warned her.

   "Okay," she said, cowering against the far side of the
tub.

Bernardo was partially aroused as he leaned into the bathtub, aiming his penis at her face.

"I need a better angle here," he said, trying to aim his nearly erect penis down at her face. "You know what I'm going to do to you."

"Uh-huh," she replied.

"I'm going to piss on you. Then I'm going to shit on you. Okay?" And when she didn't immediately reply, "Do you know that?"

"Uh-huh," she answered, her voice trembling.

"Tell me why."

"Because I deserve it."

"Keep your eyes closed," Bernardo cautioned. But he was having difficulty urinating with an erect penis.

"I'm getting hard," he complained. "I can't piss. And you look so good."

"Thank you."

"You're welcome."

"Can I itch my nose?"

"You can do nothing — nothing! You understand? Nothing!"

"Uh-huh."

"Don't make me mad."

"Okay."

"Don't make me hurt you."

"Okay."

"I'll hurt you bad." Bernardo climbed onto the edge of the tub, pushing down on his rigid penis. "You make me so hard. How can I piss on you when I have a hard-on?" Kristen cringed in the tub. "Why'd you call me a bastard?" he asked, referring to the abduction.

"I was scared."

"So why'd you do it?"

"I don't know. I'm sorry."

"Who the fuck do you think you are?" he asked, leaning into the tub and hitting her across the face with his penis.

"Pardon?"

"Who the fuck do you think you are?"

"I couldn't help myself."

"Yeah, but you called me a bastard."

She was crying. "I'm sorry."

"You know what I'm going to do to you?"

"You're going to piss on me."

"Are you scared?"

"A little."

"Close your eyes," he told her.

"Thank you."

"Are you ready? Keep your mouth shut. If you don't, you're in big trouble," he said, then began urinating on her head.

"Why am I pissing on you?"

"Because I deserve it," she answered, knowing the answer he wanted.

"Ask for more," he said.

"More, please."

"Ask!"

"More please," she repeated, louder.

"Tell me you love me," he demanded.

"I love you."

"Do you love me?"

"I love you!"

After he had finished urinating, he climbed onto the sides of the tub, positioning himself so that his buttocks were over her.

"Keep your eyes shut," he warned.

"Okay."

He tried defecating on her, but succeeded only in urinating again.

"I'm going to fart all over you. Understand?"

"Okay."

"Tell me you want it."

"I want it."

"What do you want?" he asked, grunting.

"I want you to fart on me."

"What else?"

"I want your shit."

"Why?"

"Because I love it," she answered, her voice breaking.

"You're a fucking piece of shit. Did you know that?"

"Yeah."

"But I like you."

"Thank you."

Unable to defecate, Bernardo climbed off the tub and directed his penis toward her face. "Okay, I'm going to piss on your head," he said, then urinated on her once more.

"Thank you."

"Tell me you love me — cunt!"

"I love you."

"You're lucky I didn't take a shit on you. But you look good covered in piss." He picked up the camcorder. "Pretend like you're in Hollywood. Okay. Now give me the classic Hollywood smile."

She did her best, summoning up a fleeting smile.

Then he let her bathe, keeping the camcorder on while she washed her vagina and anus. Homolka was showering in the other washroom, freshening up for her next performance. When Kristen got out of the tub, he wanted more fellatio, but she refused, and he started to punch the side of her head.

"You won't do it, huh?" he said. "You won't do it? Well, I'll show you something." He dragged her by the hair into the bedroom, put a tape into the VCR, and forced her to watch it. Kristen gasped when she saw who was on the tape, a young girl on her knees, blindfolded, giving her name — Leslie Mahaffy.

"You know who that is, don't you? What happened to her will happen to you if you don't do what I tell you."

But though drugged and beaten, raped and sodomized, forced into lesbian sex, mentally tortured, and humiliated for the previous three days, Kristen still had courage to stand up to her tormentor.

"There are some things," she told Bernardo, "that are worth dying for."

And Bernardo beat her for her defiance, punching her on the side of the head and about her body so hard that Homolka, out of the shower, couldn't stand to look and turned away. When he got tired of punching her, Bernardo started kicking her, and kept it up until she begged him to stop.

He told Kristen she had a chance to redeem herself if she helped him make a good videotape. When the camera was rolling, he told her, he wanted to hear from her all the words that he loved: he was the king and master, and she was his compliant sex slave. Then he ordered her to dress while he got his camcorder ready, positioned it on a chair beside the bed, and pressed the Record button. He told Kristen to climb onto the bed in the master bedroom, and he joined her.

"So where do you want me?" Homolka asked, standing beside the bed in her housecoat.

"Wherever you want, Karla. I love you," he replied.

"I love you too."

She took off her housecoat, climbed onto the bed, and began licking the sole of his foot. Bernardo turned to Kristen. It was her cue for dialogue.

Still sore and shaking, she said to him: "I love you too."

"Kar," Bernardo said.

"Yeah?"

"I want you to guide her through this."

"Okay," she replied cheerily.

"Just take your time, Kar," he said, as she began fellatio on him. Kristen, unsure what to do, began to kiss Bernardo on his chest. "Include Christian."

Homolka began to lick Bernardo's penis, while Kristen continued to kiss his chest. Bernardo leaned back in obvious pleasure.

"You girls are wonderful."

"You're the best, master," Kristen said.

"You're the king," chimed in Homolka.

"Start licking at the bottom," Bernardo directed Homolka, "and work your way up to the top."

"Christian," Homolka said, "come down here." She pointed to one side of Bernardo's penis. "Start licking right there."

"Do both sides," Bernardo said. "Christian, start first."

Bernardo wanted the camera, and told Homolka to fetch it off the chair. He held the camera while they rubbed and kissed his penis. "Kiss it near the top," he told Kristen. "Do it slow. Put it deep in your mouth. C'mon, Christian, you're not home yet."

Next he wanted the two women to touch each other. "Christian, touch her breasts," he said. "C'mon, let's hear some love stuff."

"I love you, Christian," Homolka said as she kissed their prisoner.

"I love you too," Kristen replied.

"You're a good sex slave," Homolka told her.

"Thank you."

"Now suck his dick, Christian," Homolka ordered.

"Tell me something, Christian," Bernardo said.

"I like sucking your dick," she said.

"Say master." Bernardo had an edge to his voice, irritated that he had to keep prompting her.

"I like sucking your dick . . . master."

"Good girl," said Homolka, who directed Kristen to use her hands as well. "Good girl. Keep on talking."

"You like this, master?" Kristen asked, stopping to look up.

"Don't fucking look at me, you fucking idiot," he snapped. "Look at my dick, and talk to it."

"I like sucking your dick, master."

"Give it a nickname."

"Can I call it master?"

"Yes."

Then Homolka interjected: "Tell him what you are, Christian."

"I'm a 15-year-old Holy Cross sex slave."

"Don't you wish I had all the girls there doing this to me?"

"I wish you had all the girls doing this to you," Kristen responded. "You deserve it."

Homolka kept up the coaching of their prisoner. "Move your hands away from his penis," she said, "and just suck. Good girl." And a few moments later: "Now go back to the way you were doing it before."

Bernardo turned off the camera, just long enough to slug Kristen because she wasn't doing enough talking.

"I like sucking dick, master," she said, when he turned the camera back on.

"And what's your favorite dick in the whole world?"

"My favorite dick in the whole world is yours. I love

sucking your dick." And then: "I hate Elton. You are my boyfriend, master. I wish you could fuck all the girls at Holy Cross to make you happy."

But Bernardo was growing more annoyed with her efforts at fellatio, and his penis was going flaccid. "Christian, you fuck," he said angrily.

Sensing a beating, she tried to appease him. "You're the king, master," she said. "I'm your 15-year-old Holy Cross sex slave."

"C'mon," he snapped, "pull more at the top."

Homolka, also realizing their prisoner was about to be punished, tried to spur Kristen on: "You're a good cocksucker."

"Thank you."

"C'mon, Christian," she encouraged. "I want to see you suck until that mouth is full."

Annoyed at losing his erection, Bernardo gave Homolka the camera and punched Kristen again. "You fuck. Talk! I'm losing it, you fuck. That's the last fucking time I'm gonna tell you. You still don't speak, even after you get hit."

"I love you, master. You're the best."

"Well then, you better do better, you fuck."

"You're the best, master. I'm your 15-year-old Holy Cross sex slave."

"Okay . . . just don't fuck me around." And, to show his anger, he punched her on the back and the shoulders. Teeth clenched, he hit her several more times, and she cringed under his blows. Homolka did nothing except operate the camera.

"You deserve all the girls in the world," Kristen told him. "You should be able to have all the Holy Cross girls you want. I came here to make you happy."

But Bernardo had the look of someone who wasn't getting his own way. "You just don't suck good enough," he complained.

"You're the king, master."

"Then suck better, you slut. I'm horny. You can't get me off, you fuck. You're never going home if you can't. C'mon, suck, you fuck."

"You're the king," Kristen said.

"Tell me I'm the most powerful man in the world."

"You're the most powerful man in the world. You deserve to rule the world."

"Who do you hate, Christian?" Homolka prompted.

"I hate Elton, and I love my master."

But Bernardo was still getting angrier, and kept hitting her on the back with his fists. "Suck, you fuckhead."

"You're the best, master."

"Move your hair, Christian," Homolka said, realizing that if Bernardo saw her face, he might be stimulated. "Keep your hair out of your face."

But it was too late to revive his erection. He turned to his wife, jerking a thumb across his neck. "Cut, Kar," he said, and she turned off the camera.

Kristen lay trembling on the bed as Bernardo started to punch her hard. Homolka stepped away and didn't look as Bernardo beat his prisoner until his frustrations were gone. When he paused to catch his breath, he told her he was giving her another chance. He leaned back on the bed and told his wife to switch on the camera.

"You're the most powerful man in the world," Kristen said, resuming the fellatio. "All the girls at Holy Cross love you. I hate Elton, and I love you."

Bernardo still wasn't happy. "Suck it better, you fuck. C'mon, suck me, you cunt. Suck for your life, bitch."

Kristen was in tears. "I hate Elton," she said unconvincingly. "I love you."

"Suck faster, you fuckhead. You piss me off."

"You're the most powerful man in the world, master. All the girls at Holy Cross went you."

"Pull on the fucking thing. C'mon, pull it up."

"I hate Elton," she told him, desperate at not being able to please him. "And I love you."

But it wasn't enough, and Bernardo punched her, five quick blows as Homolka turned off the camera. He told her she would have to do better, then had Homolka switch on the camera again.

"Put it deeper in your mouth, fuckhead," he told her.

"The Holy Cross girls want you, and they want to have sex with you. Thousands of women want you."

"Squeeze it tighter!" he yelled. "Open your mouth wider. Pull up on it. Pull up! C'mon, talk to me, you fucking cunt."

"You're the most powerful man in the world. All the Holy Cross —"

"Keep doing that. Keep doing that," Bernardo said, and suddenly the edge was gone from his voice.

"We're running out of tape," Homolka warned.

"Suck, you fuckhead, suck. Yes. Yes. Yes." His moans grew louder. "Pull up, pull up." And then he turned to the camera and smiled as he forced her head down while he climaxed. "Keep it inside your mouth," he told her, and leaned back, breathing heavily, as the red warning light started flashing, signifying there was no more film in the camera.

Bernardo knew he had to kill her, and soon, but first he wanted something to drink. Homolka brought up a bottle of wine, and they each had a glass while sitting on the floor. Then Bernardo told Kristen to stand up and take off her clothes. Crying, she stripped. Bernardo wanted more sex before the execution. He picked up the camera and told Kristen to perform cunnilingus on his wife.

"Do you want her finger in you?" he asked Homolka.

"No. It's really sensitive there."

"Did you like the way she tastes?" Bernardo asked Kristen.

"Uh-huh."

"What are you right now?"

"What do you mean?"

"What kind of person are you sexually?"

"I'm a lesbian. Is that what you're looking for?"

Bernardo laughed. "What are you?"

"A lesbian."

Then Bernardo gave the camera to Homolka and he climbed onto the bed, getting down on his hands and knees. He told his prisoner to perform anilingus on him.

"Do you like my finger in there, or just my tongue?" Kristen asked.

"Your tongue."

"There," she said, doing her best to follow his orders. He told her to massage his penis at the same time. "Is that okay?"

"Good girl."

It was getting late, and both Bernardo and Homolka knew the death sentence would soon have to be carried out. Bernardo fetched the electrical cord and bound Kristen's ankles. He cuffed her hands behind her back and positioned her on her hands and knees in front of the hope chest. Then he got the empty wine bottle and gave it to his wife.

"Put it in there, Kar," he said, pointing to their captive's anus. "Hard."

"What?"

"Put it in her really hard. Ram her hard. She called me a bastard. Shove it in hard. It's okay if it hurts."

Homolka did as Bernardo ordered, inserting the tip

of the bottle into their prisoner's anus. But she did it slower than he wanted, hesitating when Kristen cried out in pain.

"It hurts," Kristen pleaded.

"What do you say?" Bernardo asked as he pushed on the end of the bottle, causing her to cry out.

"I'm sorry."

"Sorry for what?" he asked, shoving the wine bottle in still deeper. She screamed.

"Sorry for being an asshole."

"For saying what?" Another shove of the bottle. Another scream.

"For saying that you were an asshole and a bastard."

"That wasn't me, was it?"

"No, I shouldn't have said it."

"Say it to the camera," he ordered. It was positioned nearby on a chair.

Kristen turned her head toward the lens. "I'm sorry," she said. "I didn't mean to hurt you, or insult you."

Bernardo took out the wine bottle and pushed his penis into her. Again she cried in pain.

"You're a nasty bitch," he said.

"I didn't mean to be. I'm sorry."

"Say it loud," he said, as he pushed against her buttocks.

"I'm sorry!"

"Who am I?" Bernardo asked, grunting as his body pounded against hers.

"My master. You're my master. I'm very sorry. I didn't mean to call you those things. I had no right, and I should be punished for doing that."

Bernardo reached for an electrical cord and put it around her neck, tugging on it as he continued pumping.

"Who wants me?" he asked.

"Pardon?"

"Who wants me?"

"Oh. All the girls at Holy Cross want you."

"Would you like me to fuck everyone at your school?"

Perhaps realizing that he was shortly going to kill her, there was an appalling desperation in Kristen's voice, as if she hoped she might still appease him and gain another chance to escape.

"Yes, I'd like you to fuck every girl at my school you think is pretty. As long as it makes you feel good. I'm glad you punished me. I deserved it. You deserve all the girls at my school." And then, as he kept on anally raping her: "I think I'm going to shit."

"Don't you shit on me."

But it was too late, a reflex action. "Ohhh, I'm sorry."

"Look at the camera and say you're sorry."

She turned to it, her face pressed against the floor as he held her buttocks in the air and vaginally penetrated her.

"I'm sorry," she said.

"Say you're sorry."

"I'm sorry. I'm sorry. I'm sorry, sorry, sorry. I'm really, really sorry."

Bernardo was grinning as he shoved deep inside her. "One more time," he demanded.

"I'm sorry," she obliged. "You're my master, and my boyfriend. And you're the king."

"Most powerful?"

"You're the most powerful man in the world."

"Are you sure?" he asked.

"Yes, positive."

"Really?" Bernardo was beginning to enjoy himself.

"Yes, really."

Some feces was dribbling down Kristen's leg. "Can I go to the bathroom?" she asked.

"Fuck you."

"Master, I'm really sorry. You deserve all the girls at my school you want to make you happy."

Bernardo was enjoying himself immensely, raping his compliant sex slave with his compliant wife dutifully taping. He turned to her. "Lick my ass, bitch," he said, and she positioned the camera on the chair and did as he ordered.

"You're the most powerful man in the world," Kristen told him. "You deserve anything you want. I shouldn't have said what I said. It really hurt you, and I didn't mean to. I'm glad you punished me. I deserve it. You deserve a lot better than me. You have a very beautiful wife, and you two really stick together.

"All the girls at my school want to fuck you because you're the most powerful man in the world, and the most sexy, and they'd never say anything to bother you because they're just bitches, like I am. I'm glad you punished me for what I did. I'm really sorry, master. It's good you're getting me back. If you went to my school, all the girls would line up to have you."

"You're a fucking bitch," Bernardo said between moans.

"You're so nice, powerful, sexy. So much in control of everything. Nobody can overpower you. Nobody. I'm really sorry for what I said. I had no right, because you're the king. The master. The king of all kings. The best man in the whole world. It's good that I'm getting punished."

Bernardo let her talk, and she kept it up, perhaps hoping he might put off killing her.

"I'm surprised there's not ten thousands of girls waiting in line for you. It's good I'm before them. I don't deserve it, but it really feels good. You're my master, my supreme master. I have no other boyfriend but you. You make me feel the best. That make you feel good, master?"

Bernardo kept thrusting his penis deep into her. "Yes," he said.

"That's good," she continued, "because you deserve the best."

"Tell me how you're going to line up all the girls' cunts when you get back to school."

"I want to line up all the girls' cunts when I get back. All the ones you've had and the ones who want you. Which is all of them. You're going to get them all to make you happy."

"And make who else happy?"

"Make your wife happy."

"And who else?"

"And me. I'm glad you're doing this to me. All the girls at Holy Cross, they want to say that to you. They're not like me. I'm a bitch."

With several loud groans, Bernardo ejaculated. He withdrew, turned to his wife. "Get me a Kleenex."

She got him one.

"Get me a couple, Kar," he said, annoyed. "Get me a whole fucking lot. What are you, a fucking idiot? Get me the whole fucking box."

Kristen collapsed on the floor, her legs still trussed and her arms behind her back. She had just enough energy to look back at Bernardo. Probably realizing she would soon be dead, and there was nothing she could do to stop him, she said, in her final act of defiance, "I don't know how your wife can stand being around you."

"Just shut up, okay," he told her. "Just shut up."

At this point the camera was turned off. Soon after, Bernardo put the electrical cord around her neck. Just before he pulled on the ends, he bent over and whispered into her ear.

Homolka later told police she heard one line: "What do you know about dying?" he said.

Then he jerked hard on the ends of the cord, glancing at the digital clock on the dresser, timing himself, not easing up until seven minutes had passed. There would be no second breaths, as with Leslie Mahaffy.

PART FOUR:

"DEAL WITH THE DEVIL"

32
Murder, They Wrote

The clean-up started on Easter Sunday morning. On Day Four of Kristen's disappearance the story continued to receive prominent play in the media. Bernardo, following the reports, knew of the huge search that was planned for the next day. They had to get rid of the body that night, he told Homolka, right after Sunday dinner at her parents' house. He didn't want any evidence around when the searchers blitzed the community.

Bernardo told Homolka to cut off Kristen's hair, fearing that traceable carpet fibers might have attached to her scalp. At first, Homolka didn't want to even touch the body.

"I killed her," Bernardo complained. "The least you can do is help me get rid of the evidence."

He was right, and she knew it. They each put on a pair of rubber gloves and went to work. Rigor mortis had set in by the time Bernardo lifted the corpse by the shoulders to make it easier for his wife to cut Kristen's shoulder-length hair. Homolka used a pair of scissors to hack off huge chunks at a time, giving the head a crude brushcut, before collecting the hair in a bag.

Then they carried the corpse into the bathroom, filled the tub with water, and scrubbed the body down to remove any fingerprints. Bernardo knew crime lab specialists had developed a technique to take fingerprints off skin. He told Homolka to douche the vagina and anus to get rid of his semen. Although 17 months had passed, Bernardo was worried that his forensic samples were still on file. They let the body soak while he burned all of Kristen's clothes in the fireplace, along with her hair, the sports bag she had been carrying, and the map they had used to lure her. In his slavish attention to detail, Bernardo even wiped clean the crystal face of Kristen's Mickey Mouse watch, then smashed the glass, telling Homolka they would pitch it later. He burned the watch straps.

Next they carted the body into the master bedroom, where Homolka wiped down the counter, the perfume bottles, and anything else their prisoner might have touched. After covering the corpse with a blanket, they went downstairs to clean themselves up.

Homolka had just finished blow-drying her hair as he stepped from the shower. She had kept herself in check after Tammy's death and the murder of Mahaffy. But now she began to lose control and challenge Bernardo.

"I can't live like this anymore!" she screamed at him, holding a vial of sleeping pills in her hand. He was unusually sympathetic, reassuring her they weren't going to get caught as he took the pills away from her. He spoke like a master criminal who has just committed the perfect crime. Everything, he said, would be fine. In a rare moment of compassion, he gave her a hug.

"You're just the best wife in the whole world."

She came around. She had always wanted to be the perfect bride, and even after two murders and the death of her sister, she still loved Bernardo. Maybe she didn't like seeing young girls murdered, but she was apparently able to live with that on her conscience. Going to the police was hardly a viable option, she would later say.

The main topic of conversation around the Homolka dinner table that evening was, of course, the disappearance of

Kristen French. Aside from the recession and the factory closings, the kidnapping was the biggest news in the city.

"Imagine something like this in Garden City," remarked Bernardo. "I thought that sort of stuff only took place in Toronto." He was fond of telling the Homolkas he had left Toronto for the smaller city to get away from the crime and all the immigrants. "I hope I didn't make the wrong choice," he said, trying to make light of a serious conversation.

Dorothy Homolka told how her brother, Calvin, was having a difficult time because he drove an old Camaro and also wondered, given that they used to live near Grace Lutheran, whether her daughter remembered watching her friend Renya play road hockey in the church parking lot. But Homolka changed the subject. Her mother's favorite television show, *Murder, She Wrote*, was on that night, so she watched a fictional homicide case being solved on TV while the country's biggest true-life murder mystery was unfolding right in her home. Bernardo had promised his wife that if they were ever caught, he would take all the blame and then write a book about their crimes, turning the profits over to her.

Driving home that evening, Bernardo told Homolka of his plans to dump the body in Burlington. If French's body was found in the same city where Mahaffy had lived, the police might think the killer was from Burlington. As soon as they got home, the couple loaded the corpse into the car, covered it with a blanket, and headed for Burlington. Amazingly, given that this would link the two murders, they toyed with the idea of draping the body on top of Mahaffy's grave, and headed for the cemetery. But after driving around and not finding the gravesite, Bernardo drove north, turning onto Number One Sideroad — Roller Coaster Road.

Bernardo turned the car onto a dirt path that led to an illegal dumpsite littered with everything from worn-out tires to broken-down washing machines. They carted the body out and let it roll off the blanket, watching as the naked form slid down the bank of a creek. As an afterthought, Bernardo covered the remains with leaves. But he wanted the body found, hoping the police would shift their attention to Burlington and away from Dalhousie.

Homolka barely spoke on the drive home. Later she would tell the police that French's death had left her numb. This murder, apparently, was not so easily pushed from her mind as Mahaffy's. She had helped in the abduction, and passed up two chances to save the teenager's life, perhaps even foiled a bid to escape. This time, although she hadn't done the killing, there was no question she was just as much to blame as Bernardo.

He was careful to keep to the speed limit on the trip back, well aware that the blanket in the back seat probably contained trace evidence from a murder victim. He knew his wife was having a difficult time getting over the murder, and he tried to soften the enormity of what they had done by explaining that it didn't really hurt to be strangled. He recalled his training in karate and a time he was almost choked unconscious by another student.

"It's a euphoric feeling, Kar," he told her. To his way of thinking, it was a nice way to die. "Really. It can be almost pleasant."

When they got home, they continued their clean-up. Bernardo burned the blanket and told Homolka to strip the bed, take the sheets into the basement and look for any of Kristen's hairs, which he would burn. Then he wanted her to wash the bedding, the tub, and the walls in the master bedroom, and finally vacuum the carpets in the bedroom and on the floor of the car.

Bernardo was at the fireplace, sifting through the smoldering embers, when she finished. She was still worried about being caught, and he told her they had nothing to fear: if the police had solid leads and were on to the two of them, they wouldn't be organizing such a huge search.

All the newscasts had been predicting a huge turnout of volunteers for Monday's search, which would focus on the north end of the city. Although the police still believed the car had traveled south, they also had misgivings about the eyewitness accounts. The abduction had happened so fast that nobody had really got a good look. Several investigators were privately asking if they weren't putting too much stock in the supposed Camaro sighting.

On Monday morning well over 2,000 volunteers were divided into search teams. Hundreds of others had to be turned away when the police ran out of officers to head the teams; the Niagara force had clearly underestimated the enormous distress and anger in the community. Several teams were sent to Port Dalhousie. A young woman had been raped there a year earlier, and Terri Anderson had disappeared from somewhere around the lake. The searchers started at the eastern edge and worked their way west, street by street, almost house by house, looking through back yards, picking through garbage cans, searching the boulevards for anything suspicious. One of the teams passed by the pink house on Bayview Drive. But the windows were shuttered tight and neither of the occupants was at home. Homolka had gone to work, and Bernardo had climbed into his car in the morning and driven off.

Scrapmen like Roger Boyer had their own little territories that they always checked for choice bits of refuse. Though he lived in the east end of Toronto, he often scavenged for metal in areas west of the city. On a gloomy, overcast day, the last one in April, he set off early, heading for an illegal dumpsite in Burlington. The place was tucked away in some dense brush right next to the Halton Hills Cemetery. The locals had known for years that if you had something bulky to pitch, this was where you took it.

Boyer was cruising by the dumpsite when he noticed what looked like an old conveyor belt sticking out of the bushes. He pulled onto the dirt path, parked his truck, and got out to look, thinking maybe he might get a motor or perhaps some metal from the discarded machinery.

There was a gully next to the dumpsite, with a small creek at the bottom. Boyer was walking over to the conveyor belt when he noticed something unusual partway down the embankment; it looked like a pink blanket, partially covered over with brush. Guessing that it contained something salvageable, he slid down the bank to take a closer look.

Nearly two weeks had passed, and Bernardo couldn't believe no one had found the body. He had been happy with Kristen, and wished he could have kept her around for longer. What he now realized was that he needed his own specially designed house, one with a dungeon in the basement for his sex slaves. He dreamed of the day when he could afford to build it in the countryside. Perhaps when he became a famous rap musician.

There was a song he was putting together referring to one of the characters in the movie *Criminal Law*. He liked the character's nice short, catchy name, Thiel, but not the spelling. Teale, spelt more like the color, was better. For years he had wanted to change his surname; hip rap singers weren't named Bernardo. That handle was far too ethnic, he had told his wife. But before he applied to the government to make the change, he wanted to do some research at the library, to make sure Teale wasn't some commoner's name. He also wanted to add the name Jason—the deranged maniac from *Friday the Thirteenth*.

He was convinced that when he got his album deal he would become an overnight sensation and would have to move to the United States. In the meantime, he was happy with his work on the still-unfinished Teale Song. He had an ending:

> I am crazy swearin', not really carin'
> Born to steal the show, my blood burns nitro
> Ya wanna size me up, well let's kick it
> A new kid on the block, and I am wit' it
> Come on, everybody, gotta scream and shout
> Rock with the hook while I hype it out
> The work is yours, the illusion has become real
> How does it feel?
> Got it at a steal
> You're the big wheel
> Paul Jason Teale

Bernardo was pleased with himself. His music was going well, the cigarette smuggling business was booming, and it would soon be time to hunt for another young virgin. Getting up around noon, as he often did, he had switched on the radio to check for updates. Not much had changed. Kristen French was still missing, though the police were optimistic she might be found alive.

"I'll never get caught," he shouted, punching a fist in the air. It was a line Homolka had heard quite often.

Boyer crawled closer to see what the blanket might be wrapped around. He brushed away some leaves. Then he started to scream — he had just touched skin. He ran for help.

Const. Kenneth DeBoer of the Halton Region police was on a routine patrol that morning when a call came over

the radio that a body had been found off Number One
Sideroad. DeBoer found Boyer, pale and shaking, standing
with Greg Hughes, whose nearby home Boyer had gone to for
help. Within the hour, the road had been closed off and more
than a dozen investigators were on the scene. What struck
many of them was the pinkish color of the skin. The body was
also very clean, as if it had been washed down. The weather
had been cold, and since the body was in such good shape
several officers speculated that the victim had only recently
been killed before being dumped.

The Halton detectives were quite aware that Kristen
French was still missing. One of the detectives on the scene,
Sgt. Bob Waller, had even been working with Vince Bevan on
the Leslie Mahaffy murder. Niagara was called, and not long
afterwards Bevan and several other investigators arrived.

The body was lying on its side, and with the face dis-
torted in death, it was impossible to recognize Kristen immediately. But the Niagara investigators knew French was missing the top part of the smallest finger of her left hand. She had
been born with that slight deformity. Det. Leonard Shaw, a
Halton forensic officer, crawled down the embankment to
check. He reached for the left hand, held it up, then turned to
Bevan and the other investigators. He nodded. The missing St.
Catharines teenager had been found.

Much later that day, Bevan made the journey to the
French home on Geneva Street. As he walked up to the front
door of the modest bungalow he glanced over at the scrum of
reporters gathered on the street for what they called a "death
watch." He would give them official confirmation in due
course. First he had to perform the worst part of any police
officer's job, and break the news to the family.

Afterwards, Bevan held an impromptu press conference on the driveway of the French house. An autopsy was

being done to determine the cause of death; other than that, there wasn't much more he could say. It was a tradition among police forces in Canada that once a missing persons case turned into a murder manhunt the information tap was turned off.

The detectives found the "hold-back" information they couldn't share with the media very disturbing. Already they had a gruesome picture of what had happened to the unfortunate teenager. Bruising showed she had probably been beaten and raped. Her hair had also been crudely shorn off. A sexual fantasy by her abductors? And then there was the rather pristine condition of the remains.

Determining the exact time of death is always a controversial area in forensic pathology. Although it is usually not possible to pin a death down to a specific hour, or even a day, detectives often turn to the blowfly for help. Entomologists have determined that the blowfly, a metallic-colored insect slightly larger than the common housefly, is attracted to carrion at an early stage, usually within 24 hours, and lays its eggs on the body soon after. The larvae go through several identifiable cycles before departing the remains. By checking the stage of larvae development, it is possible for scientists to establish approximately how long a body has been in the open. Pictures of Kristen's body had been taken showing larvae development in the nose, ears, and mouth. The samples had been bagged and shipped off to the American scientist Dr. Neal Haskell, one of North America's leading experts in the field. But it would take several months before the police had an answer.

If Kristen had been alive for some of the two weeks she had been missing, could the Niagara force have done more to find her? Detectives were confident they had done everything they could. Besides moving quickly, locating key witnesses, organizing huge searches, and having everybody on the lookout for the elusive Camaro, the Niagara force had also been consulting with the FBI on a criminal profile of the type of person who would have abducted Kristen French.

Since her body had been found so close to where Leslie Mahaffy was buried, detectives were now leaning to the theory that the two murders were connected. They knew two people had abducted Kristen, but the eyewitness descriptions were not good enough for composite sketches. The FBI crime analysts described the duo as a dominant and submissive pair, probably with criminal records for sexual offenses, and one, or both, had a blue-collar job, such as a tradesman or a car mechanic.

"We're looking for a pair with dirty fingernails," one of the investigators told Const. Eddie Grogan one day when he was in the area on another case. Grogan wanted to know how the investigators were so positive that the wanted car was a Camaro. He received the standard answer: "This is a GM town, and we know our GM products."

The Niagara detectives planned to start with the standard procedure of rounding up the usual suspects. Known sexual offenders who either lived in the area or had just been released from jail were identified. Each would be questioned later about alibis. But before the detectives got rolling they felt they needed to form a task force and secure extra government funding to cover what could be a very expensive manhunt. It might take millions of taxpayers' dollars. Office space would have to be located, cars and cellular phones, fax machines, and copiers rented for the detectives, computers set up to handle the flood of tips that poured in daily.

Kristen's schoolmates had been wearing green ribbons as a tribute to her during the two weeks she had been missing, so on the suggestion of one of the investigators, they named the task force Project Green Ribbon. They all agreed it was a wonderful idea. One of the team was put in charge of acquiring letterhead bearing the name. Lapel pins were purchased and they were handed out to team members. The pins quickly became collector's items among police officers. Reporters bold enough to enquire about the cost of the task force were told curtly by government bureaucrats that divulging expenses might hamper the investigation. "I'd hate to think the killer got away because I wrote a story about how much coffee Green Ribbon drank," quipped one journalist.

The task force set up its base in Beamsville, a small community west of St. Catharines. Movie-poster-sized prints of Mahaffy and French were placed near the front door and, since Terri Anderson was still missing, her case was also handed over to the team and her picture added to the wall.

The task force was barely under way when the first news leak hit the papers. The *Toronto Star* carried a front-page banner headline saying that Kristen had been held hostage, and sexually assaulted, for part of the two weeks she had been missing. Green Ribbon was immediately deluged with calls from other media wanting to know if there was a sadistic killer on the loose.

An officer branded the *Star* story a lie at a press conference, but only after checking with the Green Ribbon task force. Much to his chagrin, the officer later learned that Kristen had indeed been held captive and raped before being murdered. Green Ribbon investigators had withheld information from one of their own, and the officer soon quit as spokesman for the already-beleaguered task force.

Kristen was likely abducted by two people, said another *Star* story. Other papers followed with their own scoops: her hair had been cut off; a motorist had been sighted near Holy Cross school in the days before the abduction, apparently on the prowl for young women. Smarting from criticism that they weren't giving worried citizens enough information, Chief John Shoveller gave the task force permission to make an infomercial on the case for one of the local TV stations. But in the meantime, a wall of silence descended on what was quickly becoming the costliest, and by far the most controversial, murder manhunt in Canadian history.

Insp. Bill Bowie stepped into the fray as a fresh spokesman for the task force and defused some of the media's anger with his genial personality. Soon, the portly career officer was giving out regular running totals on the number of Camaros that had been checked. Each week the figure went up by several thousand. To speed up the inspections, special depots were set up where Camaro owners were asked to drop by to be checked out and receive an orange sticker signifying they had been cleared by Green Ribbon.

All across the province, the Camaro blitz was on. Scores of billboards, thousands of pamphlets all asked: "Have You Seen This Car?" But Camaro owners were puzzled. Green Ribbon had originally said they were looking for a 1982 Camaro, but their literature and posters showed a 1981 model. The car changed drastically in design over that one-year period, Camaro owners tried to tell police, the rounded curves of the 1981 model being dropped in 1982 as the sports-car took on a European look with angular styling; the police had to be wrong either about the year or about the type of vehicle. A growing number of owners of old Camaros believed the police were looking for the wrong car, but their complaints fell on deaf ears. So in typical Canadian fashion, they dutifully took their vehicles to the depots, lining up for hours to prove they were not suspected murderers.

Eddie Grogan dropped by one of the depots one day and watched while a friend from Green Ribbon quickly cleared half a dozen vehicles.

"So tell me," Grogan finally asked, "what's the hold-back on these Camaros?" He wanted to know what would pinpoint the car as the one used in the abduction. Was it a scratch on a certain part of the hood? A stain on the upholstery? There had to be something that only the police knew.

His friend was puzzled by the question. "There's nothing that we know of."

"So then how can you tell if the car was used in the abduction?"

His friend just shrugged. "We'll know . . . somehow."

"Do you plan to eliminate every single Camaro in the country till you find the right one?"

"If we have to."

"How do you know the car hasn't already been stripped down, or pressed into a cube by now?"

Again, his friend shrugged. It was not a question he wanted to contemplate. Indeed, no one at Green Ribbon seemed to be asking what killer with any brains would still be driving around in a beige 10-year-old Camaro.

The business executive had known Paul Bernardo socially for several years after a mutual friend had introduced them. One day over supper he confided to his friend that he thought Bernardo was weird, especially the way he always bragged about becoming a millionaire but never explained how he planned to accomplish that feat. Then there was Bernardo's eerie resemblance to the composite sketch of the Scarborough Rapist. The executive also wondered if it was more than just coincidence that two St. Catharines girls had been murdered, while a third one had vanished, soon after Bernardo moved into St. Catharines. There was also the unsolved rape near the rowing club, not far from Bernardo's house. "There's just something odd about Paul," the executive said. "Like something's not right with him."

His friend only confirmed the executive's fears when he told him Bernardo had once bragged about raping a former girlfriend because she had angered him.

"Why don't you call Green Ribbon?" another member of the dinner party asked.

"You know," said the executive, "I probably would, but Paul doesn't drive a Camaro. And the police seem so sure about this Camaro business."

One of Bernardo's friends had gone to the police, however, in May 1992. His neighbor from Scarborough, Van Smirnis, knew an officer with the Ontario Provincial Police and had talked to him about his suspicions. Like many others, Smirnis had been disturbed by Bernardo's remarkable resemblance to the composite sketch. Smirnis said it was interesting that the rapes in Scarborough had stopped in 1990, around the time Bernardo had moved to St. Catharines, and that there had been a subsequent murder with links to St. Catharines. Smirnis also knew how often Bernardo talked about raping women and the way he had behaved in Florida.

It took some time for the Smirnis tip to be processed. The OPP constable had to fill out a report, which was passed in turn to his senior officers. From there the tip went to the criminal investigation branch of the force, and then through inter-force liaison channels to the Metro police. Next it was passed to the offices of the Sexual Assault Squad, whose officers had already interviewed Bernardo and taken his fluid samples. Finally, it was given to the Green Ribbon team. Twelve days after Kristen French's body had been found, two Green Ribbon detectives knocked on the door of Bernardo's home.

33
King of Cool

Even though it was 2:00 p.m. Bernardo was sleeping when he heard the sharp raps at the front door. He looked out the window at the porch below. Whoever was there knocked a second time, and Bernardo waited at the window until they started to leave. The unexpected visitors were two men in suits with short hair and erect postures.

"Cops," he said to himself, now on full alert.

He guessed they were there to question him about Kristen French. Either that, or the cigarette smuggling. If he didn't talk to them now, he knew they would be back. And maybe the next time he might be more nervous. Best to get it over with, he thought.

"Hey, guys, can I help you?" he called after hurrying down and opening the front door.

The pair identified themselves as Detectives Scott Kenney and Brian Nesbitt with the Green Ribbon task force. Could they have a word with him? Bernardo invited them in.

"So what can I do for you?"

Nesbitt did the talking while Kenney glanced around and was struck by how neat the house looked. He noticed the wedding pictures of Bernardo and his attractive wife that adorned the fireplace mantel. Both detectives later noted in their books that he was a well-spoken man with bright, blue eyes, and preppy good looks. Nesbitt said they were working on the murder of Kristen French and were checking out some leads. But first they wanted to know if Bernardo had ever been involved with the police. They already knew he was a suspect in the Scarborough Rapist case and had earlier provided hair and fluid samples, which had still not been analyzed. They were just testing Bernardo's honesty. Bernardo acknowledged that he had been questioned about the Scarborough Rapist case because he looked so much like the composite sketch. Then the police turned the questioning to the abduction of French.

"Can you tell us where you were on Thursday, April 16, about 3 in the afternoon?"

It was less than two weeks after French's body had been found, and two officers were in the house where the murder had taken place, face to face with the schoolgirl killer. Their information about him included the Smirnis tip — suspicion from a friend who knew him well — and the knowledge that Bernardo was still on the Sexual Assault Squad's shortlist.

But there were many factors working in Bernardo's favor that day. Police miscommunication, for one. Neither Kenney nor Nesbitt knew about the complaint filed against Bernardo by Lori Lazaruk; there had been hundreds of suspects in the Scarborough Rapist case; and Bernardo didn't fit the FBI profile at all. He was an accountant with no criminal record, and he was married. Most important, though, Bernardo didn't drive a Camaro. He owned a Nissan.

"I was probably at home," Bernardo lied, giving the officers his winning smile. "I'm working on a rap album."

Though he was extremely nervous, Bernardo looked the two officers right in the eye. He had learned that from his many border crossings. Feeling his hands start to tremble, he touched the tips of his fingers together. He had nothing to fear, though. He was cool and hype.

> A professional liar, with time to waste
> Stop fooling yourself, give up the chase
> Ya got no confession, ya got no case.

Bernardo offered to give the officers a tour of the house, but they had already seen more than enough. They talked for a while about his wedding, and where his wife worked. Then, 15 minutes later, they thanked Bernardo for his patience and left quickly, satisfied he wasn't the man they were looking for. Later, in their books, the two officers noted that while Bernardo had seemed nervous at their presence, he seemed willing to co-operate.

Bernardo couldn't wait for Homolka to get home that evening. He called her on the phone to brag. She was fearful when she heard the news, but he was exhilarated by the encounter.

"I was just so cool, Kar," he told her. "The king was like a cucumber. They never suspected a thing."

Eddie Grogan was checking out complaints about a prowler along a row of businesses on Kingston Road in Scarborough when the call came over the radio that the vehicle used in the abduction of Kristen French had been sighted on Highway 401 in Toronto. The vehicle was being chased by an officer with the Royal Canadian Mounted Police, who had spotted it near Pearson International Airport. He was requesting backup.

Grogan slapped his emergency light on and jammed his foot on the accelerator, heading for the expressway about two miles away. All other police radio communication was stopped as the chase took priority. It was believed the car was taking one of the off ramps in Scarborough, not far from Grogan. He reached over to the glove compartment and took out his service revolver, placing it on the seat beside him. Like every other law enforcement officer in the province, he badly wanted to arrest the killers of Kristen French.

Scout cars from at least two other forces had joined in the chase. More than a dozen Metro cruisers had radioed that they were going to the cut-off ramp. Grogan ran three red lights and narrowly missed a delivery truck, but when he got to the intersection where the car had been sighted, all he saw was flashing lights. Several police officers were redirecting traffic. A police plane circled overhead; near it, newsrooms having picked up the general alert, was a plane from a local TV station. Scout cars prowled sidestreets. Officers on foot were checking laneways and garages for any sign of the beige sportscar. And everywhere there were television crews.

Grogan cruised a few sidestreets. Radio reports kept pouring in. A light-colored sportscar was seen near a donut shop. It turned out to be a Mercedes-Benz. A suspicious-looking man was spotted jumping into a car and speeding off. A cruiser pulled the vehicle over; the driver was a pizza delivery man. And on it went. Grogan headed for the parking lot of a mall that was being used as a temporary command post.

"Has anybody actually seen this Camaro?" he asked one of the senior officers.

Only the Mountie who had supposedly spotted it on the expressway, he was told.

Grogan smirked. "I didn't think they allowed the Mounties to take their horses on the highway," he said, getting guffaws from fellow officers, but a scowl from the senior man on the scene.

Cruisers continued to search the streets near the expressway until the next shift change. No one found the phantom Camaro.

A few days later Green Ribbon issued an update about the hunt for the Camaro. A total of 15,000 sightings had been phoned in to Beamsville. The task force had been increased to 28 officers and 10 civilians who were checking out each and every tip about the car. A spokesman for the Niagara police department went on television to stress that "the strongest lead we have right now is the Camaro."

Green Ribbon investigators also had to contend with the nutbar factor. One man who called them constantly said he was a numerologist and offered to put relevant dates of the case into a special machine he had concocted that would spit out the location where Kristen had been held. Another man who offered his services was a water diviner who assured them his trusty Y-shaped stick would lead them to the killer's lair.

Paul Bernardo made several trips to the genealogy section of a public library in downtown Toronto, checking through the family histories of some of the hundreds of thousands of names on record there. He wanted to be a Teale, and he liked what he read about his adopted surname and its roots in Great Britain. The Teales had had their own coat of arms: a greyhound for speed, and a dragon, perhaps a symbol of evil. He traced the name back several centuries to Thomas Pridgin Teale, a gentleman surgeon from Leeds and a fellow of the Royal College of Surgeons. Was Bernardo thinking that, in a bizarre way, he too had been a surgeon?

Bernardo and Homolka stayed at home the night Green Ribbon ran their infomercial on the murder of Kristen French. During the program investigators finally confirmed that two people were involved in the kidnapping, but went on to describe them as blue-collar types.

"Wrong!" Bernardo shouted.

They could be car mechanics, or tradesmen.

"Wrong again!"

Either one or both likely had criminal records for sex offenses, and they may have met in jail.

"Wrong!" Bernardo yelled.

The program went on to describe the hunt for the Camaro.

Bernardo taped the program and replayed it, bragging to Homolka that once again he had fooled the police.

"I want to do it again," he said in the flush of excitement. "I want to get another girl."

"Kar," Bernardo said one morning, "how come you're not leaving me anymore pillow notes?"

On her lunch break that day, she went to the drugstore near the animal clinic and bought a batch; she wanted to keep him happy. Their relationship seemed to have improved after the visit from the two Green Ribbon detectives. He was always boasting about how he had fooled them, right there in the room where the two girls had been. He wasn't as angry with her anymore, and she wanted to keep it that way. Maybe she might be able to save their marriage. Since she couldn't leave him, it was worth trying. If cards pleased him, then it was a little enough thing for her to do. One she bought had a drawing of a snake on the front. Inside she wrote: "Love from the girl who wiggled her way into your life." She put it on his pillow that night.

They role-played with her pretending to be Kristen French whenever they had sex. On these occasions she dressed up in the outfit that looked like French's school uniform, ready for some role playing.

"Hello, master," she said one night, knowing what he wanted to hear. "I'm your Holy Cross sex slave."

"Are you ready to get fucked up the ass?"

"Yes, master. All the girls at Holy Cross want to get fucked up the ass by you."

Another time during sex, Bernardo put on the tape in which he was raping her sister Tammy.

"I loved it when you took her virginity," Homolka told him. "I loved the way you shoved Snuffles inside of her."

Most nights after work she went across the border with him while he went to Smokin' Joes on his cigarette runs. She added another pet to their household, an iguana she named Spike. She talked about Spike and Buddy in a letter she wrote to her friend Debbie Purdie not long after the police had found French's body. She was happy with Buddy: "He's getting more mature," she wrote. She had taken Spike to the clinic because the animal had been listless, but, to her relief, the vet had told her Spike was fine. Then she wrote about her husband.

"Paul and I are changing our last names because of the way things are with his parents, and because he doesn't like having an Italian-sounding last name. It's going to be Teale. Do you like it? Also now I'll finally tell you what Paul is doing. He's making a rap record. His raps are amazing. He's very excited with it, and it won't be longer than a few months until he gets a contract.

"That's why we can't have kids . . . yet. It may hamper his chances at a contract. So as soon as he signs with the record company, I'm getting pregnant. I can't wait."

One day she saw an article in the *St. Catharines Standard* and brought it to Bernardo's attention at supper: it said the police had just exhumed the remains of Leslie Mahaffy to do another post-mortem. Bernardo snapped at her. She couldn't talk about the murders unless he brought them up. (Although the results were never released, the second autopsy showed two bruises on each side of the spinal column. There had been similar marks on French's body, perhaps another sign the two killings were linked.)

When they went that Saturday on another cigarette-smuggling run, they encountered a vigilant customs official who noted the many cross-border trips they had been taking. Bernardo put on a brave face for the suspicious guard. As usual, he looked him in the eye, answered his questions crisply and politely, and didn't volunteer anything. But Homolka, uneasy about the dozens of packages of cigarettes between the door panels, was jittery, and the guard sensed it. He made them open the trunk and checked around the car before he let them through.

Bernardo held his anger in check until they were well away. Then he pulled over to the side of the road and began hitting her on the head so hard that he broke his Masonic ring. That angered him even more. He told her she would have to get it fixed. "You're not to speak to me anymore," he said, "until I say you can."

That night she slept in the spare room instead of on the floor in the master bedroom. In the morning, he was still angry.

"You didn't leave me a pillow note last night," he said, and slugged her on the arm. They had planned to go to her parents' house for supper, and she asked him if he still wanted to go.

"What do you think?" he replied.

Assuming he didn't want to go, she later phoned her father, asking him to drive her over for supper. Bernardo, upstairs in his music room, called her up and told her to cut his hair. Who had she been talking with on the phone? When she told him, he was enraged, and he threw her against the wall.

"You called your dad? I can't fucking believe you called your dad."

He grabbed a handful of her clothes from the closet and threw them down the stairs. "Tell your dad to take you away and never come back!" he yelled at her.

She was sobbing when her father arrived and she told him they had had an argument.

"I'm leaving him," she vowed as they drove off.

Her mother seemed happy with the news. She had sensed her daughter was unhappy after the marriage; she always looked too pale, and her hair was losing much of its luster. Karla could have her old room back, her mother said, and they made plans to pick up her clothes.

The couple who lived in the farmhouse near Woodstock, in western Ontario, were surprised one evening when they got a visit from two Green Ribbon detectives. Like everyone else in the province, they had been following the murder investigation closely — as they had another unsolved murder, that of Lynda Shaw.

Two years earlier, on the Easter weekend, Shaw had been abducted by a passing motorist after she had pulled over to fix a flat tire on Highway 401, not far from where the couple lived. Shaw's mutilated and burned body was found shortly afterwards in a lovers' lane just off the expressway.

The two detectives said they were checking out a lead in the French case and wanted to know more about a license plate the couple had earlier reported stolen from their car. The plate had never been found, and the couple had forgotten about the incident. It was possible, they were now told, that their stolen plate was being used by a man who drove a Camaro, perhaps the same motorist who had recently eluded police in Toronto following a high-speed chase on Highway 401.

Could the couple tell them anything more about the theft of the plate? They couldn't, but asked if the police suspected a link between the French, Mahaffy and Shaw murders; both French and Shaw had disappeared on an Easter weekend, each abducted by someone driving a car. It was a possibility the police were exploring, the couple was told, but so far there was nothing to link the murders.

Bernardo had said he wouldn't be home the day Homolka came with her parents to pick up her belongings. But when they arrived, the doors were chainlocked from the inside and no one answered the doorbell. They went to a phone booth and called. Bernardo answered, drunk and slurring his words. He told them he would open the door.

"Yeah, get her the fuck out of here," he said to the Homolkas as Karla followed her parents in. He had a drink in his hand. "I don't want the bitch around here anymore."

He went upstairs, locking himself in his music room as Homolka helped her parents load up the van. Every so often he would leave the room to watch. "Good riddance," he shouted at his wife, who was crying. Finally, with all her possessions removed, they were ready to leave and were heading fo. the door when Bernardo appeared at the top of the stairs.

"Kar," he said in a much calmer tone, "can I have a word with you?"

Reluctantly, she walked up the stairs and into the bedroom. He was standing near the hope chest, where the two young girls had been murdered.

"Are you fucking crazy?" he said, speaking in a low tone so her parents couldn't hear. "Do you know what I could do to you right now? I could show your parents the Tammy tape. You can't leave me. You can *never* leave me."

Homolka thought about calling his bluff, she later recalled. He couldn't tell anyone about her involvement in Tammy's death without implicating himself and risking wider exposure. But she was afraid he was drunk enough to do it. And then her parents would be faced with the horrible choice of turning in their own daughter to the police or committing a crime with their silence.

"Karla, are you all right?" her mother called out.

"Everything's okay, Mom," Homolka replied from upstairs. "I'm going to stay."

Her parents were surprised by her sudden reversal, but helped her unload the van anyway. Bernardo stayed in the house and kept drinking. Homolka kept making drinks for him that evening, hoping he would pass out. She knew what was in store for her otherwise. "I'll be okay," she had lied to her mother as she had walked them to the door.

Homolka was lying on the bed in the main-floor spare room when Bernardo burst in.

"I can't fucking believe you tried to leave!" he screamed, grabbing a book and flinging it at her head, hitting her just below the eye. Then he started pounding her on the back, the side of her head, her arms. The beatings continued over the next several days, she later told police. After one, he complained that he had hurt his wrist.

"I don't know why I'm hurting myself when you're the one who has to be hurt," he told her, hitting her with a flashlight.

After that, most times he hit her it was with the flashlight, usually on the legs and the back. One day, though, she had a bruise on her face, and when she returned home after work he was furious because she hadn't put on enough make-up to hide it. He ordered her into the living room, then told her to take off her clothes.

"Down on your knees, bitch!" he yelled. He took off his belt and started whipping her across the back. Then he took off his pants.

"Okay, bitch," he said, "start sucking." After he climaxed and had forced her to swallow it, he led her by the arm into the basement, throwing her naked into the cold cellar. He turned off the light and shut the door.

"You know who's coming for you?" he shouted through the door, laughing. "Leslie Mahaffy."

On the nights when they weren't smuggling cigarettes, Bernardo took Homolka out with him while he trolled for his next victim. Sometimes they went to the Pen Center in St. Catharines, following women who were alone. One night, they tailed a woman to her home in nearby Fonthill.

"This bitch I'm going to rape," he bragged. But although she appeared to be at home by herself, there were no bushes for him to hide in. He toyed with the idea of just breaking in, but decided against it and drove off.

Another night, as he was cruising by a bus stop with Homolka, he spotted a blond-haired teenager. He pulled the car over and parked, gauging his chances of abducting her. As he stared at the blond, his breathing quickened. "Turn your head the other way," he ordered Homolka, then he undid his pants and masturbated while he watched the girl.

He often fantasized about attractive women on the street, imagining what they would look like taking off their clothes for him. At home, alone, he would often masturbate thinking about it. Other times he watched his videotapes of the women he had raped, reliving his fantasies, sometimes masturbating six or seven times in a row.

In constant need of new stimulation, one night he told Homolka, "Go out on the back porch and do a striptease for me." She refused, but a few belts on the arm changed her mind. After checking there was no one around, Homolka stepped outside and took off her clothes, while Bernardo masturbated in the kitchen.

He found it even more stimulating when he later ordered her to strip in front of the house. This was trickier, because they lived on a corner and cars were always passing. One evening a neighbor across the street was enjoying a quiet smoke in her back yard when she noticed someone on the front porch of the pink house. Although her eyes weren't as good as they used to be, she was certain the woman at 57 Bayview was taking off her clothes.

"Young people today," the woman said, shaking her head. Something odd about that couple, she also thought. But she was caring for a sick husband and didn't have time to worry about eccentric neighbors.

Although Bernardo didn't like Homolka to be out by herself, one night he let her go with some work friends to a wedding shower. Afterwards, everyone wanted to move on to a popular bar in Port Dalhousie, the Port Mansion.

"I don't know," said Homolka, knowing it was a bar Bernardo frequented. She didn't know how he'd react if he saw her there after she told him she was going to a shower. "Maybe not." But her friends persuaded her to go, and she had fun shooting pool and drinking screwdrivers. Later, however, she began staring over her shoulder at the front door.

"Kar, what's wrong?" one of her friends asked.

"Nothing," she said.

That August they went to Daytona Beach on Bernardo's annual pilgrimage to Florida. One night, as they were returning to the hotel from dinner, he saw a woman walking alone and followed her in the car, telling Homolka he planned to abduct her, using the same trick he did with Kristen French. He tailed the woman for several blocks and was just about to make a move when the woman turned in to a house.

"Damn!" Bernardo said.

On the return trip, he told Homolka he wanted a three-some with a prostitute, so they stopped in Atlantic City, staying at the Trump Plaza hotel. One evening Bernardo went out cruising on the boardwalk and, seeing a blonde who looked like his wife, pulled over and asked her if she wanted to do a threesome.

"Only if I get to see the third party," the prostitute, Shelly Banks, told him. Bernardo went back to the hotel to get Homolka. But before he left, he set up his camcorder, hiding it in a sportsbag with the lens aimed at the bed. The prostitute sat on Homolka's lap as Bernardo drove to the hotel. After negotiating a price of $300, the two women took off their clothes while Bernardo surreptitiously flicked on his camera.

The tape shows that they sat around on the bed for several minutes, talking about the type of sex they wanted. Bernardo was the last to take off his clothes, feigning shyness. Banks noticed bruises on Homolka's arms, which resulted from a beating Bernardo had given her in West Virginia because he thought she was flirting with a man at a rest stop.

"You're more bruised up than me," Banks told her. "I'm the working girl. You'd think I'd be the one with all the bruises."

Homolka gave her standard excuse. "I work at an animal clinic. I have to handle a lot of big dogs."

"She likes to come first," Bernardo told Banks. "Why don't you two caress each other and suck on each other's breasts?"

"If you guys do this all the time you should just hire a maid."

"We don't like to reveal our secrets to anyone," Bernardo said with a smile.

He offered the prostitute a drink, as he had before, but she shook her head. Banks felt he was being just a little pushy with the liquor, perhaps because he had spiked the drink.

"You guys can start fingering each other," Bernardo said, and as Banks turned to Homolka, he started kissing the hooker's buttocks.

"God didn't make that for dicks to go in there," she told him when he tried to enter her anally.

"It's the way I get off," he protested.

"It's not big enough, sweetie," she said, then began giving him oral sex.

For more than an hour, Banks tried a variety of techniques to bring Bernardo to orgasm. Finally she said, "My cunt's just not made for your dick."

"You're a bit more aggressive than what I'm used to," Bernardo said. He suggested Homolka and the whore get on their hands and knees on the bed and put their buttocks in the air. Bernardo then entered the prostitute vaginally while he stroked his wife's clitoris.

"You've got such a nice ass," he said to Banks. "I want to fuck you so bad."

When nothing happened for him, she told him to stop, but he wouldn't.

"Please, just two more minutes," he pleaded. "Say you love me."

Banks glanced back at Bernardo, then to the side where Homolka was staring straight ahead, saying nothing.

"Are you coming yet?" Banks asked, turning back to Bernardo. He didn't respond. Finally, Banks got up. "Okay," she said, "that's enough. You guys just expect too much for the money. Never thought I'd have to work for the whole hour and a half." Banks stared at her two customers and said, "I don't know what else I can do. I don't know what you guys like."

"You're really cool," said Bernardo. "It's really hard for me to come, that's all. I'm hard all the time."

"You're really a nice couple. Maybe you need to get help on this."

"It's not totally my fault," noted Bernardo. "I'm used to the submissive type."

"If you're ever in Atlantic City again," said Banks, "look me up." She turned to the washroom.

"Oh, can I watch you?" Bernardo said, standing by the door as she urinated.

"Fucking weirdos," Banks thought to herself as she rode down the elevator.

34
The Last Beating

Not long after the trip south, Homolka returned from work one evening to find Bernardo in the living room, his hunting knife on the floor beside him. He had been at home all day and had been drinking. These days he was angry at her most of the time. The pressures of his world were closing in on him. His unemployment insurance had long since run out, and her salary of about $350 a week barely covered the rent. Though he was making sometimes as much as $1,200 a week smuggling cigarettes, he was spending it even faster. He was also frustrated with the way Margaret, Jane's friend, had rejected his advances, even though he had been courting her with expensive gifts he couldn't afford. Though the police had never been back to the house, the Green Ribbon investigation was always in the news. Press releases suggested an arrest was imminent.

Bernardo picked up the knife and walked up behind his wife. He held the blade against her throat. "How would you like to die?" he asked in a chillingly calm tone.

"Please, Paul," Homolka begged, as he pressed the knife against her neck.

"You don't want to die?"

"No."

"If you don't want to die," he said, reaching for a shot glass full of vodka, "then drink this."

She took a sip.

"All of it!" he screamed. "Now!"

After she downed the glass, he shoved her toward the basement. He had been mad because she had told him she wouldn't go along with his plans for another sex slave. He wanted her to kill their next victim, and she had refused. At the top of the stairs Bernardo pushed her, and she tumbled down, landing hard on her side. She started crying in pain and clutched her left hand. Bernardo stared down at her, then he shut the door and turned out the lights.

"Leslie's coming for you!" he yelled once again. "She's down there in the basement. Right where I cut her up."

The door opened about 10 minutes later. Bernardo, carrying a pillow and a blanket along with a flashlight, dragged her into the cold cellar.

"You sleep in there tonight," he snarled. "I'm going out, and you better be there when I get back."

Then he slammed the door and walked away. A few minutes later she moved closer to the cold cellar door, listening. But there was no sound. Finally she opened it, looked out, and then screamed. Bernardo was standing right there in the dark, by the doorway.

"I told you to stay in there!" he yelled and shoved her back inside.

The next day she almost fell asleep at work because she hadn't slept much in the cold cellar. One of her colleagues asked her what was wrong. Homolka told her she didn't want to talk about it, then went into the washroom and cried.

Bernardo had a new surprise for her when she got home that night.

"Zap! Zap! Zap! I'm going to get you," he shrieked, coming at her with the stun gun he had bought in Daytona Beach and smuggled into Canada. The device was about the size of a hand and emitted an electric shock that could immobilize a person for nearly 20 minutes. Bernardo had bought it to use on his next victim. Homolka screamed and ran upstairs. He chased her, laughing, but didn't zap her because he needed her that night to go on another cigarette-smuggling run.

Bernardo kept drinking and demanding she renew her friendship with Jane's friend Margaret and help arrange for him to take Margaret to bed. Homolka began calling Margaret, whom she hadn't seen much since the death of Tammy. The three went on several social outings, including a trip into Toronto to the CN Tower. Bernardo joked about how it was the world's best phallic symbol. But although he kept telling Margaret how attracted he was to her, she didn't respond. She was a naive 15-year-old who simply enjoyed the company of two adults.

One weekend, they invited her over to their house. Bernardo had several presents for her, a gold ankle bracelet, a stuffed bear, and a necklace. The card with the gifts said: "I love you forever, pal. Love, Paul." Margaret was thrilled, but still didn't realize that Bernardo, who was nearly twice her age, was trying to seduce her into bed. When Homolka was alone with Margaret, she explained her relationship with Bernardo.

"We're not really husband and wife." Homolka showed her the mattress on the floor upstairs where she slept. "We're just friends."

Margaret sat down on the bed and began to cry, saying, "It's not supposed to be like this. That's not what marriage is about."

Homolka tried to comfort her and finally went downstairs to confront Bernardo. She was angry with him, an emotion she had rarely shown during their six years together. She told him she did not want to act as his pimp anymore. "It's over," she said, referring to Margaret. "That's it. It's not going to happen."

Bernardo brushed past her and went upstairs. He was gone a long time, and when he came back down he was smiling. "I don't know what you're talking about," he told Homolka. "Everything is fine."

Margaret didn't talk on the drive back to her house. After they dropped her off, Bernardo had a confession to make: "I fucked her," he said. "She kept saying no-no-no, but she was just teasing."

Margaret didn't return any of their calls for a time. When she did finally get in touch, it was after she had been in an argument with her mother.

"You can live with us," Homolka suggested.

Bernardo was ecstatic about his wife's offer. He could hardly wait for Margaret to come. But when she visited them, it was with her boyfriend. She wasn't as friendly as on previous visits, told them she wouldn't stay with them, and left soon afterwards. Bernardo went into a rage, took off his Masonic and wedding rings, opened a window, and pitched them outside.

But he refused to give up, still believing he might win Margaret's affections. He began to write to her. "I love you," he said in one note. "I took a major chance on you and maybe you took it for granted. I don't know. I do know that I'll love you until I die." In another he wrote: "I love you so much I'll fucking die for you." But she never returned his calls or replied to his notes. Finally, around Christmas, he gave up. He blamed Homolka and began beating her, tearing out clumps of her hair at a time. When they visited her parents for Christmas, her mother remarked on how pale she looked and how her hair seemed to have thinned out. Homolka assured her she was fine.

Two days after Christmas, Bernardo wanted Homolka to accompany him while he dropped off a load of cigarettes to his contact in the bike gang north of Toronto. On the drive back she fell asleep, and she awakened later to find herself alone in the car in a suburb that she guessed was Mississauga. Bernardo returned a few minutes later, his face flushed.

"I followed this girl," he said, describing how he had hidden in some bushes, masturbating while she undressed in her bedroom. Homolka didn't say anything as he drove off.

"How come you don't hug me anymore?" he asked a little later, and when she didn't have an answer he became angry. Homolka braced herself while he worked himself into a fever pitch of resentment as they drove along the expressway. Then he began hitting her, only this time he hit her in the face.

The next morning when Homolka looked in the mirror, she gasped. The side of her face was swollen and her cheeks had turned a deep blue from the punches. One eye was nearly swollen shut.

"You look like shit," Bernardo said when he got up. He was going out with some friends and told her to hide in the closet when they came so they wouldn't see her face. When he returned after a day of drinking, Bernardo gave her a hug.

"I know things have been pretty rough for us lately," he said. "But I promise everything will get better."

"Oh, Paul," she said, tears rolling down her cheeks.

But several days later he was punching her in the head again when he didn't like the way she had taken a phone message for him. He reminded her how stupid she was and of the time when he had had to beat her because she kept forgetting to videotape *The Simpsons* while he was gone.

"Things will never change between us, will they?" she asked.

"Things will never change," he said, "because you will never change."

Her face was still badly bruised when she went back to work in the New Year, 1993. Her friend Wendy Lutczyn cried when she saw her. Homolka told her co-workers she had been in a car accident, but they didn't believe her. Lutczyn got a friend to make an anonymous call to her parents early that evening.

"You better get help for your daughter," the woman said. "She's hurt really bad." And then she hung up.

Unsure what the woman meant, the Homolkas hurried over to Bayview Drive, but no one was home. Bernardo had taken Homolka on another cigarette-smuggling run.

"What do we do?" Dorothy asked her husband as they stood on the porch. The caller had seemed genuinely concerned, so they went to a phone booth and called 911. Two police cruisers and an ambulance soon pulled up in front of the house. The Homolkas described the anonymous call, but were told it was possible someone had played a sick practical joke on them.

Bernardo and Homolka returned well after midnight, the car loaded with smuggled cigarettes. He had been furious with her from the moment he had picked her up after work: "I thought I told you to hide these bruises with makeup!" After they crossed back into Canada, Bernardo started hitting her with the flashlight, several times in the head.

"When we get home," he told her, "you're gonna get fucked up the ass."

"Okay," she meekly replied.

He told her to put on his favorite black dress, a tight-fitting number cut just above the knees. He got out his handcuffs and the electrical cord he had used to strangle Kristen French in the spare bedroom, he cuffed her hands behind her back, pulled up her skirt, and penetrated her anally, at the same time tugging at the cable around her neck.

Once she nearly lost consciousness, and he eased up to let her get some air. But he drew the cord tight again, and she began gasping once more before he eased his grip. She was gagging, choking, her face turning blue, but he had to keep punishing her until she understood that he was the one in control, the one who had the power to snuff out her life at any moment, just as he had with the others. When, finally, he stepped away from her, there was anger and hatred in her eyes, but, more important, there was fear.

The next morning her face was worse than the previous day. Her mother was called again, only this time she was told to go right to the animal clinic. "If you want to save your daughter's life, you better hurry."

Homolka's mother began to shake when she saw her daughter's face. "My God, what happened?" Dorothy held her hand to her mouth and felt a sudden pain, as if she was about to have a heart attack. But her daughter was cheerful and tried to downplay the damage that had been inflicted: two black eyes, swollen cheeks, lumps on her forehead, bruising on her arms and legs. They went out to a nearby McDonald's for lunch, though Homolka was barely able to walk because of the bruising on her legs. Despite her mother's protestations, she said she still wanted to go back to work. And she refused to blame her husband.

Dorothy was mad at herself for not insisting that her daughter leave Bernardo. Later that day, she drove over to Port Dalhousie with her other daughter, Lori. Homolka was at home alone. She had difficulty walking to the front door.

"You're coming with me," Dorothy said, but Homolka refused to leave.

"I can't!" she screamed. "I can't! You don't understand."

But Dorothy was not going to leave without her. She

and Lori grabbed her arms and bodily dragged her from the house. Soon the three were on their way to the hospital.

Despite the freezing temperatures that morning in early January 1993, more than 200 people had gathered on the banks overlooking a recently drained spillway of the Welland Canal in St. Catharines, attracted by the television crews setting up to record what might be the long-awaited break in the Kristen French case. About twenty crews were training their cameras on the flattened wreck of an old Camaro lying in the channel below, being closely examined by police divers. A row of police cars was parked nearby, and two officers were filming the crowd with their own portable camera, perhaps believing the killer might be among them.

As the morning wore on, the crowd grew. Shortly after noon, a buzz went through the throng as a grim-faced Insp. Vince Bevan walked up the hill to brief reporters. Almost in unison a score of TV lights clicked on.

The previous nine months had not been kind to Bevan and Project Green Ribbon. Many would-be leads had turned into dead ends; several good suspects had turned out to have solid alibis. One man had been tailed for weeks after he had visited French's grave late at night to lay flowers. Brought in for questioning, the man had been flabbergasted by accusations that he might have murdered the teenager. He said he had gone to pay his respects at night because he didn't want to disturb family members who visited it most days. Several Camaro owners had also fallen under particular police scrutiny, as had several employees at the cement factory who had criminal records.

After nine months, detectives still didn't have a good suspect, and the cost of their investigation continued to escalate. About the only progress the police had made was in ruling out any link to the Terri Anderson case. Her body had been found lodged in a dam in Port Dalhousie harbor. When an autopsy failed to find any signs of foul play, the death was ruled accidental. It was believed she drowned after taking LSD and wandering into the Martindale Pond.

Despite all the false leads, the Green Ribbon team remained committed to the hunt for the Camaro. And that's why the media and the public had gathered above the spillway. The beige Camaro down below looked just like the wanted vehicle, and someone had obviously ditched it over a cliff.

Bevan scanned the crowd when he got to the top of the hill. The soft-spoken investigator had kept his composure throughout, never publicly attacking the many people who had been criticizing his handling of the case. He had given regular, and personal, updates on the investigation to the families of all three girls. Critics said he was acting more like a social worker than the lead detective on the country's biggest murder case. But that was his style, and he made no apologies for it. Colleagues said he was being unfairly singled out for the failure of the task force.

Several members of the Niagara police department had spoken quietly to reporters, asking them to lay off their personal attacks, saying they were hampering the investigation, hurting the morale of the detectives. Bevan, they said, was doing everything he could, often putting in 14-hour days. He was a good, honest cop. Real-life murders weren't solved in an hour like those on television. The media had to be patient.

Bevan waited until all the camera crews were ready. Then a TV reporter asked the obvious question. Was it the right car?

"It's not our vehicle," Bevan said, disappointment evident in his eyes. "One of these days our luck will change."

He explained that at least one witness had come forward who said the Camaro had been in the spillway for at least three years. In addition, said Bevan, the inside of the Camaro was loaded with zebra mussels, and a marine expert had estimated it would have taken four or five years for that many mussels to accumulate.

The doctor who called the police on the night of January 5, 1993, from the emergency room of St. Catharines General Hospital was reporting a case of wife assault. The victim was named Karla Homolka. One of the doctors said it was the worst case of wife abuse he had ever seen. She had been beaten with a flashlight, suffering two black eyes along with bruises on her arms, legs, and buttocks. She was being admitted for further care. It was obviously a police matter, and a cruiser was dispatched to the hospital.

Bernardo was arrested later that evening. He was taken to the downtown headquarters of the Niagara police, questioned, fingerprinted, photographed, and charged with assault. He appeared in court the following morning and was released after promising to appear later at a preliminary hearing.

When he got home, he was furious. He called the Homolka house, but no one there would talk to him. He persuaded friends to call, asking for her, but the response was the same. The hospital refused to tell him what room she was in. When he checked several days later, he was told she had been discharged. He called his in-laws again, saying he could clear up the trouble if only they gave him another chance.

"Please," he told Karel, breaking down and crying, "I have to speak to her."

But his father-in-law just hung up the phone.

Then he drove to the Shaver Hospital in St. Catharines, where Dorothy Homolka worked, stormed into her first-floor office without knocking, and demanded to know where his wife was hiding. Her mother refused to tell him.

"I warn you," Bernardo threatened, his voice rising loud enough that others stopped work to see what was happening. "There's going to be serious trouble if you don't tell me where she is. It will be bigger than you, or I, could ever imagine."

But Dorothy Homolka was adamant. "You hurt my baby," she said. "I don't want you near her. I don't want to see you ever again."

Soon after, Bernardo changed the locks on his house. Then he called his insurance company and canceled his wife's coverage on the Nissan.

"You've probably heard that I've been charged with assaulting my wife," he told the owners of the house when he dropped off a series of post-dated rent cheques. "There's nothing to it."

Then he staked out the store where Lori worked as a cashier, thinking Karla might go there. Finally, he went in and confronted Lori.

"Where is she?" he demanded. Lori wouldn't tell him. "You don't understand," he said with a desperate tone to his voice. "It's important that I talk to her."

Still she refused, and when he became insistent, the store manager threatened to call the police if Bernardo didn't leave. Bernardo waited outside the store until closing time, and followed Lori, hoping she might lead him to Karla. But Lori went straight to her home, and he knew his wife wasn't there: he had already secretly watched the house for days. He called his wife's friends, but if any of them knew where she was, they weren't saying. He went around to the bars where they had often gone, but she wasn't at any of them. And no one had seen her. She had vanished.

For weeks, the blond-haired woman with bruises on her face was treated as the mystery woman at the apartment building in the city west of Toronto. Some called her Raccoon Face because she had deep, half-moon marks under her eyes. Homolka spent much of her time in the hot tub in the recreation area. She walked along the corridors with her head lowered, trying to hide the marks on her face. Gradually, as the injuries healed, she stopped to chat with the other residents, mostly friendly banter about the weather. Her aunt, Patti Seger, didn't try to hide the truth about the injuries; she told the other tenants that her niece was going through a nasty divorce, and let them draw their own conclusions about the injuries. Calvin Seger was more emotional about what had happened. "I'll kill the bastard," he vowed when he first saw her, and had to be talked out of going after Bernardo with a baseball bat.

After several weeks of recuperation, the Segers finally persuaded their niece to go out for a drink. There was one local nightclub that was very popular, the Sugar Shack. It played music from the 1950s and 1960s, the sort one could dance to, and Karla was told it was just what she needed to take her mind off her troubles.

35
Less Than Zero

The sound of a car horn jolted Paul Bernardo awake from a fitful sleep. He had been lying on the bed reading *American Psycho* when he passed out earlier that day. He stumbled off the bed, checking the time on the clock radio: nearly midnight. Then he heard a sound.

"Kar, is that you?" he called out. "Karly Curls, are you home, Snuggle Bunny?"

He listened, but there was no answer. Homolka had been gone for over a week and Bernardo was desperate. He had been looking everywhere in St. Catharines. None of their friends had seen her since the beginning of January, and when anyone called, he told them they had had a spat and she had left for a few days until things cooled down.

In truth, of course he had been charged with assault, and that's why he was worried. She had talked to the police. Had she also told them about Tammy Lyn, Leslie Mahaffy, and Kristen French? Would she dare? If only he could talk to her, somehow persuade her to come back.

He went downstairs, calling, "Kar! Kar! Are you home, Kar?"

There was no answer, except the scratching of Buddy on the basement door. Bernardo opened it, and the dog bounded out, licking his hand. He got Buddy some food and watched him eat.

It was depressingly lonely, and he couldn't stand to be alone. He began to think about taking his life. In the living room he took Karla's wedding picture off the mantelpiece. He stared at the photo as he paced from empty room to empty room, becoming more and more depressed.

He went to the garage and took down his hunting knife from its hiding place in the rafters. He had used it many times on the women he had raped. Maybe it was time to use it on himself. He moved the blade close to his wrist and held it there for a few moments. If she had gone to the police, he would spend the rest of his life in jail and suicide would be his only escape.

He went up to his music room, grabbed the mini cassette recorder, and started to talk. Maybe if she somehow got the tape she would feel sorry for him and return.

"When you know you've lost it all, and there's no one to turn to," he began, "death's welcome mat is the only place you can go."

He switched the tape recorder off as he began crying. When he regained his composure, he hit the Record button again and started on a maudlin and interminable monologue.

"Kar, this one is for you, pal. I don't know what to say. You know I love you, man, I love you tons. Right now you know what I'm doing? I'm holding up your wedding picture and looking at you. You're so beautiful, and I let you down. I really let you down. I'm sorry, Kar. God, how I wish I could make it up to you.

"You know what I'm going to do, pal? I'm going to do like an honorable thing. I'm going to give you my soul, my entire life, Kar. I just want to touch you, to hold you. I want to make love to you, and look right at you. I want to stare at your eyes and caress your face.

"Okay, I fucked up this life, right? When I go to the

other side, okay, I'm going to make it better for you there. I'm going to set something up real nice. So when you come it'll be all right. You know what I'm saying? You don't know the remorse I'm feeling . . .

"You know, Kar, I don't have you with me right now. But I've got your pictures, and I've got our memories. These are my last thoughts, and with these I'm happy. I love you, Kar. Fuck, this is corny."

He paused for a moment. "Hey, Kar. You know this won't sound the best because of the type of recording it is, but I'm doing this one for you. I know I'm crying and stuff, but I still want you, okay, pal? . . . I loved you more than anything in my life . . . Don't listen to the crap I said before . . . You made me so happy, y'know? Like I really needed love in my life, and you gave that to me . . . I treated you like shit, man. I'm so sorry . . .

"I used to tell people in the morning that the sunlight would come through the windows upstairs and highlight your face, just illuminate it, and did you look beautiful. I don't know if I ever told you this, but I love you, Kar.

"You were my rock, you know. My security. My stability. I need you, Kar. I love you, my princess, my queen, my everything. I think about you every day now. Okay, check this out Kar. I wrote a letter to you. It goes:

"My dearest Karla, it has been over a week now. God, it seems like a lifetime. I realize now you're never coming back. Fucking kills me, pal. I wish I just could have been given a second chance to make things right . . . I know you had to leave, and I don't blame you. In fact, it was the best thing you could have done for me. It snapped me out of whatever state I was in. It made me realize how much I care for you . . . You are the most special person who ever touched my life. Yes, even more than Tammy.

"Guess what, pal? I cry a lot. We had some good times. I mean, at least some of the time. Here's the problem, Kar. I tried to be larger than life. I really did. I didn't try to be average like the average guy. I tried to be larger, the best thing that there ever was. Maybe because I needed love . . . I just really tried to be the best for everybody. I wanted to be the world. I wanted to get Tammy the forest-green Porsche. I wanted your parents to have the speedboat. I wanted to take care of you, and buy you this huge house and have four children. I wanted to be greater than anything there ever was, and when I didn't reach it, I got frustrated and angry. And I took it out on you. The person I loved the most. Don't hate me for that. This is not going to be the most emotionally correct thing, just please don't hate me for my mom's genetics."

There is more about how lonely he feels.

"We were the best team," he rambled on, "we were great, man. United we stand together. I'm going to fall for us, okay? You keep standing, pal. I gotta go. My time's up. I'm going to go see Tammy. I know you don't want me anymore. I'm not wanted here. My life's over. I've got nothing. I'm less than zero. I've got fucking nothing.

"Kar, when you think of us, please man, don't think of it as lost time. I don't know what fucking went wrong. We were the best, man. The envy of everybody. Please remember the good times. Don't remember the last piece of shit. Fucking, at times it wasn't me. I don't know what it was, but it wasn't me. Just not me, okay, babes?

"Karly Curls, Snuggle Bunny, my little rat. Remember those? You might as well tell your parents and Lori that I love them. I hear they don't feel the same, and won't talk to me. I won't blame them. Just tell them I tried, Kar. I'm only human and I tried to be bigger. I tried to set up a better life, and I didn't make it. I failed above all else, pal. I want you to remember this, okay? Some things are worth dying for, and the only thing worth dying for is you, Karla . . . I'm going to give you my soul, my energy . . . I'm going to try and make up for the pain and suffering I cause you. I love you so much, Kar. An undying love. I'm taking it with me to the grave."

He put the tape recorder down, picked up the knife and ran it across a wrist. But the blade barely grazed the skin, leaving no blood. He put the knife down.

"You're my best friend, Kar," he continued. "You always were. I was born a bastard and I'll die a bastard . . . I really wasn't that bad a guy. I just tried too hard. I tried to be too macho, too domineering. I thought those were the qualities that were important to be successful. But I forgot a lot of the qualities like the qualities you have. I forgot how to cherish and love.

"I guess I'm just hard to read, hard to understand. I'm just an asshole. I'm going to go, okay? You do what you want in the burial, okay? . . . You don't have to do anything special. I mean, throw me in a ditch if you want. I know you won't have much money, and I understand.

"You know, there's a lot of things I could have fucked you guys on, but I'm choosing this option instead because I have an undying love for you and a hatred towards myself. I'm gonna miss you, Kar, and if I can, I'm going to watch over you. I'm going to be your guardian angel."

He now started petting the dog, who licked his hands.

"I was just saying goodbye to Buddy. He's licking me now. He knows. He knows. When I do this now, you're going to know how much I felt for you. My last word is: 'Kar, I love you.' If you can ever forgive me for the terror, the hate, and the pain I've caused you, I will be eternally grateful . . . The only person in the world I've ever loved is you.

"I wish I had made love to you staring at your face. I wish I had done that a lot more. I wish we had a kid. I wish a lot of things. These are my tribulations," he finished pathetically, " my anguish, joy, and sorrow."

The tape recorder is switched off. When the recording resumes, Bernardo is shouting.

"Oh God, Kar! Oh God! Oh God, how it hurts! Kar! Kar! Kar! Oh God! Fuck me! Aaah, it hurts so fucking much!

"Kar, this is my only comment. I hope it gets to you. I smacked the flashlight against my head. It hurts a lot. I've just been running around the house. God, I wish you were here. You were my support system. I'm nothing without you. Why doesn't life ever give you a second chance? If I had a second chance, life would be so much better. You've got to have some fucking compassion. Give me a second chance! Nothing can be over that fast. Nothing can go from total submissiveness to 'That's it' until the end of the world . . . We were right for each other, better than any other couple in the world. Kar, we're the winners. We deserve to be together, not apart. Karla-Karla. Paul-Paul. The Teales. The best fucking couple in the world."

The maudlin rant continues in the same vein. At one point Bernardo says, "My number-one priority is getting you back with me. I'll do everything it takes. I'll go to jail for as long as I have to . . . You put me in jail and I'll still love you. Understand it, Kar. I love you a hundred percent . . . I don't care about other girls. I realize that now. I want you. Anything less and my life isn't complete . . . Kar, if you ever hear this after I'm dead, I want you to remember, okay? This is for you."

There is no evidence that Paul Bernardo tried to commit suicide that night.

The dance floor at the Sugar Shack was packed that early January evening. The nightclub happened to be near the headquarters of the Peel Region police department and was a popular spot with off-duty officers.

Karla Homolka and two friends arrived at the club shortly after 9 p.m. They had been coming to the club two or three times a week, and went to their regular table on the second floor overlooking the dance floor. Homolka was wearing a short black Spandex dress, cut low at the top. It was obvious to those nearby that she was wearing nothing under the tight dress, except for a G-string. It was also pretty clear that she was prowling. The waiter who took their orders noticed that the bruises around her eyes were healing.

Ever since leaving Bernardo, Homolka had started to feel better about herself. She kept a diary, and the first few entries reflected the change in her outlook.

"I was feeling free," she wrote several days after leaving Bernardo. "I finally escaped him. I was very afraid that he was going to come and find me and kill me like he threatened he would always do. But the fact that I was actually physically away from him and that my family knew that he had been abusing me, I felt very free. I hate lying, and I had lied to my family for so many years."

In another entry she admits, "I'm so confused about what to do with my life. I don't know where I should live, or what career I should choose. What I want is security. I want so badly to go back home and live with mom and dad and Lori, work at the animal clinic again.

"I want to live freely in St. Catharines, and not be terrified to go out alone. I need to live a normal life. I love being here, but I miss my old world — not Paul but everything else. I'm not afraid he'll tell any of my secrets. He has everything to lose on two things, and a lot to lose on a third."

As the evening wore on, Homolka left the table and went down to dance by herself. Although she was petite, in her black dress she appeared to have a lush, full figure. And that night she could have had her pick of any of the men in the club.

She knew they were watching her, and she played up for them, just as she had played up for Bernardo over the past two years. She enjoyed the admiring stares. For the first time in ages, she was having fun again. And there was one man in particular she liked.

He stood alone near the dance floor, about six feet tall, with a solid build. He had short blond hair, a square jaw, and deep blue eyes. She had seen him there before.

"Who do you think I should dance with?" she asked the waiter when he came to their table later with another round of drinks. "Him?" she asked, looking at a man with long, wavy hair.

"Too greasy," replied the waiter.

"How about him?" She was staring at a man whose muscular arms were bulging from his shirt.

"A meathead, likely a cop."

With all the secrets she was carrying, the last pick-up Homolka wanted that night was a police officer. The waiter, a sturdy six-footer with a rugged face and black hair, rather fancied her himself, but he was working. And even though he found her quite attractive, there was something about the woman that told him to stay away.

"There's the one I want," she said, pointing at the blond standing by himself, nursing a drink. The waiter went over to him.

"Blond lady over there," he said, pointing to Homolka, "wants to dance."

The man looked at her, apparently confused about what the waiter had just said. "You joking?" he asked.

"Better hurry before she changes her mind."

The man walked over and asked Homolka for a dance. Much to his surprise, she accepted, instantly making him the envy of most of the men in the club. They had several dances and then he joined her at her table.

"My name's Jim Hutton."

She smiled. "I'm Karla, Karla Homolka."

He stayed at her table that evening, talking, buying drinks, dancing. She was so mysterious, deflecting the conversation to another topic when he tried to find out more about her. He noticed the bruising around her eyes, but never asked what had happened.

Homolka's friends left, and they were alone. They liked each other, and although they had only just met, they were touching each other enough that both were aroused. Toward the end of the night, Hutton, who knew the waiter, asked him about the private room at one end of the club. Later they went there and made love.

Afterwards, they exchanged phone numbers and made plans to meet again at the club. Hutton was seeing two other women at the time. He had just found Number Three.

Bernardo broke open the bottle of champagne one night. As if expecting his wife to suddenly return home, he took two crystal glasses from the cupboard, put them and the bottle on the silver tray, and went into the living room. Buddy was sleeping by the fireplace as Bernardo filled the glasses. He picked up one glass, took a sip, then reached for the tape recorder.

"It's been over two weeks, Kar. I'm breaking. I'm breaking real fast. I try to hold on but you're not calling me. We went through so much . . . Don't worry about Tammy. Don't worry about nothing. Just fucking throw me somewhere. I used to be a powerful man — now I'm a destroyed man. I got nobody. I don't know what you said about anything, but I got no income and I'm going to lose.

"I just don't understand. I would rather have someone do something to me. I made a mistake. I'm larger than life most of the time, but I wasn't then but no one can understand . . . If you came back I would have treated you like a queen for the rest of your life, but I guess you just don't give second chances. I think I deserve one . . . I'll never fuck you, you know, in the sense of getting you in trouble. Maybe it's best I be gone . . .

"I know I was bad at the end, but I did some honorable things. Kar, how can you not call me? . . .

"Bad guys like me gotta go. Born a bastard, die a bastard. I tell you, when you're down, everybody gets their boots in on you. I'd rather die than be alone like this. I'm going to go, because that's what you want. It's what everyone wants."

He poured himself another drink, sipped it slowly, and started to cry.

"Kar, he's coming to get me now. The Grim Reaper's coming. No. No. No. I'm afraid, Kar. I'm so afraid. I love you, Kar. I'm too young to die. I'm too fucking young. You never called, Kar. You never did. Oh, Kar, Kar, Kar, He's outside my door. He's outside my car. He's coming for me, oh God, he's coming."

Jim Hutton wanted to know more about his mysterious new lover. They were at the Sugar Shack one evening in late January when he began asking her some questions.

"Are you married?"

"Kinda," she replied. "But I'm leaving him. We don't get along."

The look on her face showed it was a painful topic. He didn't push her for details, and she didn't volunteer any.

She told him that she had some legal problems, and he assumed it had something to do with the fact she was a heavy drinker, probably facing a drunk-driving charge. But again, she never elaborated, and he never pressed her.

"I've had a pretty awful time of it lately," she told him, "and I just want to have some fun." But she never told Hutton that night, or later, just what a troubled past she had. He would learn about that from the media.

Det. Steve Irwin of the Sexual Assault Squad was at his desk at Metro police headquarters in late January 1993 when he got the call from the crime lab. More than two years had passed since the lab had received all the fluid samples from the Scarborough Rapist suspects. The original list had been whittled down, from 224 to 39, to five candidates. Now scientist Pam Newall had done the DNA testing on the samples from those five men, and the results were back. The tests pointed to one man.

Six years had passed since the first attack. At least eight women had been raped over three years, and possibly many more. Then, in 1990, the predator had simply vanished. Detectives speculated that he had lived in Scarborough but moved after the composite sketch was released. It had generated hundreds of tips, and dozens of good suspects. Perhaps too many.

"Oh, hell," Irwin blurted out, when he heard the name.

It was a man he himself had talked to 26 months earlier in that very same office, the smiling accountant from Scarborough who had since moved to Port Dalhousie, Paul Bernardo.

Eddie Grogan was working the late shift in Scarborough when he got a call from an old friend who worked with a little-known section of the Metro police called Mobile Support. When you worked for Mobile, you did one job, and one job only: you followed people around without them knowing it.

The officers on the team never had to write out parking tickets or take statements from criminals, and they seldom testified in court. Often they had to go against their policing instincts and look the other way when a man they might be tailing for a murder, for instance, ran a red light. Making arrests was not their job. They were there to do "obs," then pass the information to the investigating officers.

The officers in Mobile practically lived in their cars. Eating, sleeping, and, at times, even urinating into plastic bottles they carried while on the job, they were there because they wanted to be.

With six people on a surveillance team, it was virtually impossible for a target to elude them. One driver kept the "eye" on the target while the other five "ringed" the suspect, following behind, driving parallel on sidestreets, or leading from the front. Each crew had a "pit boss" to co-ordinate surveillance, and they kept in touch on two-way radios.

Grogan had done some work for Mobile Support, and that was one of the reasons his friend was calling. The unit had a special project, and they wanted him on the team.

"Who are we following?"

"A suspect in the Scarborough Rapist case."

"Oh shit, not another one."

Grogan had followed around what seemed like dozens of suspects. Friendship or not, Grogan wasn't sure he wanted to spend his time on yet another "can't miss" project in the Scarborough Rapist case.

"This one's for real," he was told. "This time we've got the forensics."

36

A Sweet Deal

The meeting with the "boys across the pond," as the Niagara Region police department called their counterparts from the Metropolitan Toronto force, was held in Beamsville at the offices of Project Green Ribbon. There was a "major sexual deviant" living in St. Catharines, the Niagara officers had been told, an accountant by the name of Paul Bernardo. Metro's Sexual Assault Squad was working on the case, and they had a team of surveillance officers following the suspect.

If Bernardo was such a dangerous sexual predator, the officers from Niagara asked, might he not also be a good suspect in the sex killings of Mahaffy and French? It was a reasonable assumption.

Their counterparts from Toronto didn't quite see it that way, though. Bernardo didn't fit the description of the killers supplied to Green Ribbon by the FBI. He was an accountant, not a blue collar worker. And he drove a new Nissan, not an aging Camaro. If he was the killer, then who was his partner? His wife?

The murders of French and Mahaffy, the Toronto officers were told, were the most serious crimes on the table. Millions of dollars had been spent on the case. Thousands of Camaros had been inspected. Hundreds of suspects had been interviewed, men from all over the province. The public demanded the killers be caught, yet they were still free. Every possible lead had to be investigated.

The main concern of the Toronto force, though, was the rapes, not the murders. Those were Niagara's investigation. The Toronto detectives had been hunting the Scarborough Rapist for years and, now they had their culprit in sight, they were not about to hand their case over to another force.

What followed was a lively, and tense, discussion about how to proceed. It was finally agreed that both forces should work together. With the surveillance on Bernardo in place, the next task was to interview the suspect's estranged wife.

A detective from the Niagara force traced her through her parents and called her for an interview, and Homolka assumed the police wanted to ask her more questions about the beating she had suffered the previous month. A meeting was arranged for the following week, in February 1993. She was told detectives would meet with her at her aunt and uncle's apartment, where she had remained for the past month because she was still afraid that Bernardo would kill her if he ever found her.

She was expecting two detectives, and when four officers showed up on the evening of the interview, Homolka was apprehensive. Her fears that she would be arrested grew stronger when they identified themselves. Det. Ron Whitefield and two other officers were from the Metro Sexual Assault Squad. Then the fourth man stepped forward and gave his name.

"Det. Sgt. Robert Gillies," he said, "with the Niagara Region Police and Project Green Ribbon."

The police had been hoping for a reaction, and that's just what they got. Homolka flushed. She turned to her uncle, Calvin Seger, as if for support. Seger didn't know why his niece was upset, and he was puzzled why it took so many police officers to investigate a simple assault.

By now Homolka thought the police probably knew everything. And the detectives suspected Homolka knew the real reason they were there. But neither side was saying as much.

Homolka was still recuperating from the beating and she walked with a limp as everyone sat around the kitchen table. There was still some bruising on her face, and the four detectives commiserated with her before getting right down to business.

"Do you know why we're here?"

Homolka told them she thought it was about the assault by her husband. She wasn't going to tell them anything else.

The investigators wanted to know more about Bernardo. "How does he make his money?"

"He's an accountant. He works for himself."

"Has your husband been involved in any other criminal activity?"

"No."

"He seems to take a lot of trips to the United States. Were the trips for business or pleasure?"

"He's got friends down there," Homolka said, and told them about his friend who ran a business in Youngstown.

"Do you have haircutting equipment at your home?"

She was sure she knew why they asked, and hesitated.

"Who cuts the hair in your family, Karla? You or Paul?"

"Paul has a haircutter. He cuts his own hair. I help to trim it."

"Have you ever cut anybody else's hair, I mean, besides your husband's?"

"Uh. . .no."

"You don't sound sure."

"I only cut Paul's hair."

"Okay, Karla. We appreciate your co-operation with this. I can't say much at this point, but your husband is a suspect in some very serious crimes, and there are a few more questions we'd like to ask you. There's an investigation going on in Scarborough in connection with a series of rapes. Do you know anything about that, Karla?"

She told them she didn't know anything about the assaults in Scarborough.

"But Paul is from Scarborough, am I right?"

"Yes."

She was then asked some intimate questions about her sex life with Bernardo. Did he go in for rough sex? Anal intercourse?

Homolka was uncomfortable with the line of questioning, but not because she was prudish. She knew what the police were getting at. Then they switched direction again, this time asking her about locations in St. Catharines.

"Do you know where the Grace Lutheran church is, Karla?"

"It's in St. Catharines."

"Have you ever been there with Paul? Or maybe, helping Paul in the area there?"

She told the detectives neither she nor her husband were religious.

"Do you know why we're asking you these questions?"

She knew, but pretended not to.

"Are you sure you don't know why I'm asking you about that location?"

Again Homolka said no.

"Are you sure you don't know why?" she was asked a third time, and again she shook her head.

"We don't live around there," she said. "We live in Dalhousie."

And so it went for most of the night. Not long after the detectives had left, Homolka blurted out something that didn't make any sense to her aunt and uncle.

"Christ, they know everything!"

Her uncle was confused. "What are you talking about?"

But she wouldn't answer him. He was already mad at her for lying. Seger knew that Bernardo smuggled cigarettes for a living and felt Homolka should have told the police.

"You don't understand," Homolka told him.

"Don't understand what? What the hell are you talking about? Why are you protecting that asshole? He beat you up."

"You don't understand."

"What's there to understand? Guy's a wife beater and he's going to go to jail."

Homolka began to cry. "You don't understand," she kept repeating. It was a line Seger had heard far too many times since his niece had moved in. "I just can't tell you."

"You're the victim here," Seger said. "And the truth will come out soon enough. So why can't you talk about it?"

"I can't tell you. I just can't."

Seger threw his arms up in frustration as he headed for the bedroom. He worked in a lumber yard and had to be up before 6 in the morning, and it was already well after midnight. Homolka went to the bedroom her relatives had made for her in the sunroom. She was still crying when Aunt Patti went in to try to comfort her.

"Is there anything you want to talk about?"

"They know everything," Homolka sobbed. "They know everything."

"What do you mean, Karla? What do you mean, they know everything?"

"I can't tell you. I can't."

Her aunt pressed the issue. Why, she wanted to know, was a detective from Project Green Ribbon questioning her about a domestic assault? "Does this," her aunt asked, "have something to do with the murders of Kristen French and Leslie Mahaffy?"

For more than two years Homolka had kept the horrible secret from everybody. Bernardo had beaten her and threatened to kill her and her family if she ever told anybody. But he didn't know where she was, and she couldn't bear to keep the awful truth inside her any longer. Tears welled up as she looked at her aunt. She had never told anybody, not even her mother. And how could she? Bernardo was right. Her parents and her friends would hate her forever when they discovered the truth. But it was time for her to talk.

"Yes," Homolka replied, "it does. I'm in trouble, Aunt Patti. I'm in real trouble."

For the next two hours it came pouring out of her. From the abductions of the two schoolgirls to the videotaping, the forced sex, the murders, the dumping of the bodies. She told her aunt everything except what she and Bernardo had done to Tammy Lyn and to Jane. She couldn't tell the truth about Tammy, at least not yet. It was the middle of the night when Homolka finally went to sleep, exhausted.

Calvin Seger was shaving that morning when his wife walked into the bathroom. She told him about their niece's confession.

"Oh my God!" Seger said, nicking himself on the chin before slumping down onto the toilet seat, his face covered in shaving cream. "She's going to have to get a good lawyer."

Detective Whitefield called around suppertime that day to check on Homolka. Calvin Seger told him that he had advised his niece to talk to a lawyer.

"Everything will come out in time," he told the detective. "You'll just have to be patient for now." Homolka eventually arranged to meet a lawyer from Niagara Falls whom she had read about in the newspapers, a veteran criminal counselor named George Walker.

The woman walking alone near the shopping mall in the city of Oakville, west of Toronto, was in her mid-twenties, a brunette, quite attractive. But she was having trouble walking home in a straight line. She never saw the man in a gold Nissan slowly driving behind her.

Paul Bernardo had been watching the teetering woman as she stumbled along. Several times he had driven close up behind her and just stared, as if sizing her up. Each time he had checked his rearview mirror, glanced around in all directions, and then pulled back.

Now he moved close to her again. This time his Nissan was right beside her, and she saw him. But if she was frightened, she didn't show it, just kept staggering along. Bernardo drove alongside, still staring at her, then pulled up just ahead of her, as though he was going to stop. He checked the rearview mirror again but seemed to see something in the distance that he didn't like. The woman was almost alongside the car when he looked at the mirror once again, then jammed his foot down on the accelerator.

The tires on the Nissan squealed as he pulled away. He got to a corner, ran a stop sign, kept on speeding.

"Our boy's spinning," said the officer on point duty, the eye of the surveillance team that night. He meant Bernardo was trying to lose them.

Had he spotted the surveillance? They had been following standard procedure: every 20 minutes or so another member of the team, driving a different car, had taken over the eye position so that there was always a fresh car to prevent him from becoming suspicious. They didn't think he had burned them, yet he was so careful, always checking his mirror.

This tailing before they spoke to the suspect was always a sensitive stage of any investigation. They were hoping Bernardo might do something incriminating. They wanted to learn his routine and, if possible, gather fresh evidence that could be used against him in court.

But tonight he kept getting farther and farther ahead of the officer on point duty. If he sped up, Bernardo would know for sure that he was being tailed: there weren't many cars around to act as cover, or "pieces of shade." But if he let Bernardo get any farther ahead, he risked losing him. The others were following his dilemma as he relayed his position on his radio.

They were all nearby, on sidestreets, following at a discreet distance. But suddenly the time for subtlety was over. They raced to the area, each taking a different sidestreet. But nobody could find the gold Nissan.

There was no doubt in the minds of any of the officers that Bernardo was on the prowl that night, trolling for another victim. They knew that if he struck again when they were supposed to be watching him, there would be hell to pay, so they spent the next few hours patrolling the area. Yet the Nissan was nowhere to be seen.

There was only one thing to do. They drove to Dalhousie. They would see if he had gone home, and wait for him if he hadn't. Eddie Grogan had a knot in the pit of his stomach as he merged onto the expressway.

It was after 4 that morning when the Nissan pulled into the driveway of the corner house on Bayview Drive. Bernardo got out and went into the house. He had been alone in the car. As far as the team knew, there had been no sexual assaults that night.

"Thank God," Eddie Grogan muttered as he headed back home to Toronto.

George Walker couldn't believe what he was hearing. The woman who had made an appointment to see him at his office in Niagara Falls the second week of February 1993 was confessing to two of the most horrendous crimes in the country. But Karla Homolka was sincere, and she had plenty of horrific details to back up her story. Walker had no doubt that Homolka was telling him the truth, and even though he had been shocked by the crimes, he had to put those personal feelings aside. He had a job to do and a client to represent. His advice to her started off with a warning: "Don't talk about this to anybody."

She hadn't for more than two years. Aside from Walker, the only others who knew the truth were her aunt and uncle, Calvin and Patti Seger. Later that day, when her uncle asked her how the interview with Walker had gone, Homolka had a new-found optimism.

"Good," she replied. "He told me not to worry. He's going to try to get me total immunity."

The Segers had trouble understanding why their niece, whom they saw at that point as a victim of Bernardo, was even worried about going to jail. He was the criminal, not her. She had just been forced into it by an abusive husband. But the Segers didn't know the truth about the death of their other niece Tammy Lyn. And Homolka wasn't telling them.

Next, Walker contacted local Crown attorney Ray Houlahan, and negotiations about her fate began. Ordinarily,

Crown attorneys are allowed to strike their own deals involving criminals who confess to their crimes and are ready to accept their punishment. An admission of guilt is seen as the first step in the process of rehabilitation. Plea-bargaining between lawyers is a time-honored, accepted practice that ensures the court system doesn't get clogged. But the killings of French and Mahaffy were clearly no ordinary criminal case.

Not only Canadians but people around the world had been following the manhunt. And now that there were two suspects, any decision about how the courts would deal with them would have to be made at the highest level of judicial authority in the province, the Ministry of the Attorney General. Lawyer Murray Segal, a senior official in the ministry, was assigned to start preliminary discussions with Walker.

Walker advised Segal and his team of prosecutors that he was seeking the best possible deal for his client, perhaps even total immunity in exchange for her testimony. Since Homolka was the only witness, aside than Bernardo himself, her evidence was the key to the Crown's case against him. If Homolka was ready to plead guilty and help the authorities, then she would have to be shown some sort of consideration. That was how the system worked. Since spouses couldn't testify against each other in a court of law, the Crown was told that Homolka was ready to start divorce proceedings against Bernardo so that she could take the stand against him at his trial. Walker's initial request for immunity would have to be considered, he was told, and quite obviously, no quick decision could be made. Segal told Walker that the Crown would be in touch.

There is an old prosecutor's saying that applies to Homolka's case: When the crime is committed in hell, you need the devil as your witness. The authorities can't afford to be choosy about where their information about a crime comes from, so long as it is reliable. If Homolka was the only one who knew anything about the two schoolgirl slayings, then some sort of a plea-resolution deal would have to be arranged. The authorities didn't have much choice.

The massive police investigation, Project Green Ribbon, had found not a single scrap of evidence against Bernardo, prompting the later comment of Bernardo's defense lawyer John Rosen that: "The police investigation turned out to be a big fat zero until Karla Homolka came along, and then things started to fall into place."

Ten months had gone by since the murder of Kristen French, and the police had no solid leads. Indeed, right up until Homolka's confession to Walker, investigators had still been looking for a pair of scruffy-looking men who drove an old Camaro. Investigators were even about to take out a wiretap on a man in the city of Hamilton they believed could be one of their suspects.

Crown attorneys have the authority to exercise prosecutorial discretion in criminal cases: the guilty person can receive a reduced sentence in exchange for information that will help the authorities in later prosecutions.

Walker told Homolka it would take a few days for the Crown prosecutors to respond. He told her to go back to her aunt and uncle's and wait. She did as she was told, spending her time in the building's hot tub, or talking on the phone with her new boyfriend while awaiting news of her fate.

Walker called her several days later to say that the Crown had replied. Homolka wanted to know what they had said, but Walker wouldn't talk over the phone. Homolka's aunt and uncle drove her to his office the next day.

Homolka was nervous during the one-hour trip to Niagara Falls, fearful that she was going to end up in jail. The tone of her lawyer's voice had worried her, as if he was about to deliver bad news. When they got to Walker's office, Homolka went in alone.

It had been well over a month since Paul Bernardo had last seen his wife, and he was convinced that she had told the police everything. He was almost positive the police were following him around, he told an old friend who came to visit one day.

The friend wanted to talk about another run over the American border to smuggle cigarettes. They were in Bernardo's music room, and when the friend started to speak, Bernardo put his finger to his lips, led him into another room, and turned up the radio.

"We can talk now," he said. "The house is bugged. It's the police. They're watching me and listening to everything I do."

"You're paranoid," said his friend. "It's just an assault charge. A domestic dispute. The police have bigger things than that to worry about."

"You don't understand," replied Bernardo, peering out through a blind. "I know they're out there."

"Look, you and Karla should go for counseling. The judge will see that as a good sign. It might help."

"Marriage counseling?" Bernardo looked almost insulted by the suggestion. "That's for losers."

Tears were streaming down her cheeks when she left Walker's office. She was so distraught that she had to be helped into the car. At first she wouldn't talk about what had happened. But then it all came pouring out. "I'm getting burned," she wailed. "They're going to arrest me."

"But you're the victim," Calvin Seger protested. "The truth will come out and that will be that."

"You don't understand," Homolka replied between sobs.

"Don't understand what?"

But Homolka didn't explain. She just kept crying. "I'm going to be arrested," she wailed. It was more emotion than she would show later at her trial, or at his. "I'm going to end up in jail. What's going to happen to Buddy? What about my dog? Who's going to take care of him?"

"I think you have more to worry about than that," her uncle said.

Crown prosecutors had told Walker that Homolka would have to serve time in jail for her involvement. A sentence of 18 years was being considered, but Walker was confident there was room to negotiate. There was some good news, however, in how the authorities would handle her.

The Crown prosecutors would not be seeking a first-degree murder charge against her, Walker had been told, although the Criminal Code of Canada clearly called for such a charge when death followed a sexual assault. Instead, her deal called for two counts of manslaughter in the deaths of French and Mahaffy. (The text of the deal is reproduced in the Appendix.) And Homolka would receive what the police called "a friendly arrest."

This meant that, despite the seriousness of the charges against her, Homolka wouldn't be processed like regular criminals, who are handcuffed and led off to jail, then put into a holding pen, incarcerated until a judge determines if they should get bail. Homolka would be allowed to go home after being charged, and would be given bail. The police were even offering to chauffeur her and her family to and from the courthouse so she wouldn't have to fight her way past the public and the expected crush of reporters.

But none of this seemed to matter to Homolka, who kept crying well into the night.

Homolka seemed preoccupied when she met her new lover,

Jim Hutton, soon after for a drink. He wanted to know what was wrong, but she didn't tell him. The woman who had spent the previous three years lying to everybody about her personal life was not about to suddenly become open and truthful. Over the coming months, through her discussions with the authorities about her fate, she would continue to hold back information, and the full truth would not even come out at her trial.

"A lot of stuff is going to happen soon," was all she told Hutton that night. "I'm sure you'll hear all about it. I might even have to go to jail."

But she didn't elaborate, and he didn't press the issue.

Eddie Grogan had just finished his surveillance shift one evening in early February, and had stopped for a drink before the long drive back to Toronto when he spotted a friend who worked on the Green Ribbon task force.

"Tell me something," said Grogan. "For months you've been telling everyone that the killers are driving around in a Camaro, right? Then why is it that I'm tailing a guy who drives a Nissan?"

It was a touchy subject for the Green Ribbon team. Over the previous 10 months officers from their own force and from other departments had been asking the same pointed question.

"There is no Camaro," the detective with Green Ribbon acknowledged. "Never was."

"No Camaro? You mean you've turned the province upside down for months looking for a car that didn't exist? Everybody in the nation was hunting for that vehicle."

"We could only go by what the witnesses told us," his friend countered. "They said what they saw looked like a Camaro, and we had to take them at their word. St. Catharines is a General Motors town, and people know their GM products. If we hadn't gone looking for a Camaro, we'd have been criticized for that. I make no apologies for the vehicle."

"But you were wrong. C'mon, admit it."

"No. We just acted on what we were told."

"Then what about this FBI stuff and the two men with dirty fingernails, mechanics or something, who were the likely killers? Bernardo and his wife seem pretty clean-cut to me."

"Do me a favor, Eddie," his friend said. "Can we talk about something else? Maybe we'll take some heat, but what does it matter? We got the right guy, and he's going down. The public will forget soon enough about all the rest. That's all that counts in my books. Who cares what the media thinks?"

"And what about Karla Homolka?"

"He's the maniac here, not her."

"As long as she doesn't get a kiss," Grogan said. "Because people will get mighty upset."

Rumors that something was about to happen with the investigation had been floating around for days in newsrooms throughout southwestern Ontario. Detectives were closing in on a suspect, the stories went. Unlike the raft of other promising leads, this time the detectives seemed to have the real goods.

Every other lead was now being shelved: the phone tips, the composite sketch, the psychics and their wild hunches, the wackos who had confessed. Investigators were confident the endless controversy that had plagued the investigation was going to end. The police had done their job, perhaps slower than everyone would have liked, but good detective work took time, patience.

News of an imminent arrest was supposed to have been kept on a "need to know" basis, but it had leaked out.

Green Ribbon investigators guessed that the leak had come from the Toronto police department—the big-city police force warming up its publicity machine for the pinch. Several reporters had been staking out the Green Ribbon office in Beamsville. The media just didn't know where or when the arrest might be. One television station had even set up a mobile studio outside the Beamsville office. But when nothing happened for several days, the crew was told to pack up.

      "I wouldn't be taking that satellite dish down just yet if I were you," one Green Ribbon detective said to a technician as he started pulling out hookups. "It might be worth your while to hang around for a bit longer." Then he walked away with a big grin on his face.

37
Video Evidence

The take-down of Paul Bernardo was planned for Wednesday, February 17, 1993. Vince Bevan and the Green Ribbon detectives were hoping for a few more days before making the pinch, but Metro Toronto was calling the shots and they were ready to move. Although a surveillance team of some eight officers was following Bernardo around, there was always the danger he might elude them. Metro's case against him on the rapes was solid: his DNA sample matched samples from at least three of his victims. And with his wife rolling on him for the murders, it was felt — by Metro at least — that the police had more than enough to put him away for the rest of his life.

Michelle Andrews was driving home from work that day when she saw two men peeking through the backyard fence of the pretty pink house on the corner. Parked nearby was a Humane Society truck, and for a moment she guessed they were two animal-control officers. And then she noticed the guns they were holding tight at their sides.

Paul Bernardo was frying up some hamburgers that evening when the telephone rang. It was a man trying to sell him a subscription to some magazines. Bernardo said he wasn't interested, but the caller was persistent. He was still talking on the phone in the living room when someone knocked on the front door.

Bernardo glanced over and saw a man standing on the doorstep. He put the phone down, and as he opened the door he noticed a second man on the front porch. Bernardo was just about to ask what they wanted when one of the men showed him a badge, then barged into the house, shoving Bernardo face first against the wall. A gun was pointed at his head and his hands were clasped behind his back and then handcuffed. The other man walked over to the phone and picked up the receiver.

"He's ours now," he said, then put the receiver down. The subscription-seller had really been a police officer, serving to distract Bernardo while the police took up their positions. The house was surrounded.

"We have a warrant for your arrest," the officer who handcuffed Bernardo told him, "for a series of rapes in Scarborough."

Bernardo was read his rights, then quickly taken from the house, past a gauntlet of police officers. Had he been looking at their faces, Bernardo would have noticed many of them smiling. Bernardo started weeping when he was put into the back of a police car. And then he remembered something.

"My dog," he said. "Will someone be looking after Buddy?"

The officer behind the wheel nodded at the Humane Society truck parked nearby.

"It's all been taken care of."

Karla Homolka heard the news of her husband's arrest on the car radio as she was returning home to her aunt and uncle's apartment in Brampton. She rushed upstairs and turned on the television. A newsreader had interrupted the Geraldo Rivera show to announce that the police had taken into custody a man whom they believed was the Scarborough Rapist.

"My God! My God!" Homolka blurted. "They've arrested him. They've arrested Paul." And then she burst out crying. "I'm next," she wailed. "I'm next."

Deborah and Dan Mahaffy were just about to go out that evening when the telephone rang. It was a detective from Project Green Ribbon. Deborah listened intently, then turned to her husband and started yelling.

"They got him!" she exclaimed. "They got the bastard who killed Leslie!"

Doug and Donna French were at home when they were told of the arrest. They took the news calmly and asked for details. Paul Bernardo was the suspect's name, they were told, and he would be appearing in court the following morning in Scarborough for a series of rape charges.

Eddie Grogan had been hoping to hoist a few at the party that traditionally follows major take-downs of suspects. But there wasn't one that night; there was too much to do. Bernardo was driven to Halton Region police headquarters in Oakville for interrogation. There, he was led in by a side door and escorted into a room ordinarily used to conduct polygraph tests. But all the lie-detector equipment had been moved out that day. As he entered the small beige-painted room, Bernardo paused, looking up at the far wall.

On it hung two huge pictures, the size of movie posters: photos of the girls he had murdered. The investigators had put the pictures there on purpose — an old detectives' trick. At his arrest, no mention had been made of the two killings. But now that he was in custody, the police wanted him to know he had a lot more to answer for. The blow-ups were meant to unnerve him, maybe even rattle him into making a confession. But as he sat down in one of the three chairs, Bernardo just smiled. He wasn't going to tell them anything. He had said it all before in his rap songs, the ones that were going to make him famous.

> Get outta my face, stop fooling yourself.
> Give up the chase.
> You got no confession, you got no case.
> You think I'm nervous?
> You think I'll break down?
> Stop fooling yourself,
> 'Cause you got no confession, you got no case.

He was going to record his album when he finished with the police. For six years he had fooled the authorities, and everybody else. He was proud that no one suspected he was the Scarborough Rapist, despite his similarity to the composite sketch. But at the same time, it bothered him that most people thought of him as just a pretty face, a wimp, a goody-two-shoes. Most people couldn't even believe he was just over six feet tall, and nearly 190 pounds.

The only person who knew about his confession to the rapes was his wife Karla. And she wouldn't talk, she couldn't, because she would only implicate herself and go to jail along with him. He wasn't going to tell the detectives a thing. But if Karla talked, then he was — to use her expression — "fubbed." *Fucked up beyond belief.*

To the detectives who watched quietly as Bernardo sat down in the chair, he didn't appear worried. Nearby, in another office, his face flashed up on a video screen, beamed in by the camera that was going to record the interview. The investigators wanted to nail him, but they didn't really know who they were dealing with. They hadn't heard his theme song:

I'm young and hype. I get paid to rock the nation.
Sometimes I be cool,
Sometimes I be chilling.
Sometimes I'll be killing.
I'm one in a million.
I'll drain your brain,
And steal your chain.
I got no remorse. I got no shame.
Do or die.
Do you ever get caught?
Do you ever get caught?
Do you ever get caught?
No, why?
'Cause I'm a deadly innocent guy.

Bernardo kept smiling as one of his interrogators entered the room, Det. Steve Irwin of the Metro Police Sexual Assault Squad. Nearly three years earlier, Irwin had interviewed Bernardo about the rapes and then let him go. At the time Bernardo was just a face, one of 200 or more who resembled the culprit. It was different now. There was evidence. And there was Homolka.

Bernardo had to know he was in deep trouble, Irwin thought as he sat down opposite him, but he didn't seem worried. Well, thought Irwin, the night is young.

Bernardo didn't recognize Irwin right away. Irwin had to remind him of the previous time they had talked at Metro police headquarters, some 27 months earlier. Bernardo remembered, but still didn't appear perturbed. Just as he had said in his theme song:

Come at me, take your best shot.
You come at me, you think you're tough,

> But I'll fucking kill you,
> Then I'll kill your sister,
> And I'll fuck your wife.

For most of the next four hours, Bernardo just listened, nodding sometimes, smiling occasionally, as the police laid out what they had on him, starting with the rapes and moving on to the two murders. Most times he responded to questions with a simple: "I don't think I should comment on that without a lawyer." He gave them nothing, and it was more or less what they expected. Later that evening, he was taken back to Scarborough and booked for the rapes. Soon after he hired lawyer Ken Murray, a former prosecutor who was now running a thriving private practice in Newmarket, Ontario. Bernardo had heard of him through a friend.

Over 200 police and media packed the auditorium at Metro Police headquarters the following morning to hear the news that a suspect had been arrested and charged with some 50 counts of sexual assault. The same suspect, Paul Bernardo, was also going to be charged with the murders of Kristen French and Leslie Mahaffy.

"The arrest," the audience was told, "was another example of the fine co-operation and team work between the various forces in the province who worked on the case."

That message was beamed live across the nation on an all-news channel. A bank of some 30 television crews recorded the event, as did dozens of reporters from all over southwestern Ontario and upstate New York.

Police officer after police officer took the podium to extol the excellent detective work that went into the arrest and stress that it had been accomplished through joint police efforts. But what was not said by the roomful of mostly male officers was that it was actually the work of three women which had led to the arrest on the rape charges: the rape victim whose description led to the composite sketch; the Metro police artist Bette Clarke; and Pam Newall, at the Centre of Forensic Sciences, whose DNA work had pointed to Bernardo.

"There is another suspect in the case," Insp. Vince Bevan told the gathering, being careful not to identify even the person's sex. "We know where that person is 24 hours a day. That person poses no threat to the community."

Jim Hutton watched the press conference that evening on TV. Like most people, he wondered who the second suspect was. The next day he found out when he saw her picture on the front page of a tabloid newspaper: the woman he had been sleeping with was implicated in the most infamous murders in Canadian history.

Homolka had been calling Hutton, leaving messages on his answering machine. He had been ignoring them for the past several days. She wanted to resume their romance, but he wasn't sure what he should do. All his friends knew who she was after seeing her face in the papers. But his parents didn't know. Nor did the people at work. She might not be the second suspect. But in all probability his friends were right: she was the pick-up from hell.

She was depressed. Away from her family, avoiding her friends, scorned by her new lover, she had started drinking heavily in the weeks after her husband's arrest. Now the whole world knew her secret; what worried her most was what was going to happen to her.

She had resigned herself to going to jail, but for how long was still being worked out. There was something else she had to face up to soon...

Not long after Bernardo's arrest, Homolka checked herself into the psychiatric ward of Northwestern Hospital in Toronto. She was there for nearly two months, heavily sedated with valium most of the time. While in hospital she finally confronted her worst fear, and told her parents the truth about the death of her baby sister.

The confession came in a letter. Her parents, still numb over their daughter's involvement in the French and Mahaffy murders, were appalled—devastated. Soon afterwards, the authorities were informed. There was now an added edge to the plea bargaining.

Within days of the arrest, forensic specialists in "moon suits" had made their way into 57 Bayview Drive. They knew that the girls had been raped and murdered there and that Mahaffy's body had been cut up over the drain. They were looking for hair, skin, blood, anything that could forensically put the girls there. But they were also looking for something even more important, the videotapes.

A list had been prepared by Green Ribbon investigators of possible hiding places in the house. The list mentioned everything from hollow doors to fake walls to secret compartments. If the tapes were in the house, the investigators would find them. The crime scene was under their control, and they were going to squeeze every single bit of evidence out of that house.

By early afternoon on the last day in April 1993, a Friday, nearly two dozen reporters were milling around the front of 57 Bayview Drive, standing behind the yellow police tape that barricaded the property.

For the previous two months a team of forensic specialists, under the guidance of Insp. Vince Bevan and Project

Green Ribbon, had been probing through the house for evidence that could link Paul Bernardo to the murders. "The most intensive forensic search for evidence in the history of policing in this country" was the way one detective described it to reporters who had camped outside the house. "If there's anything incriminating in there, we'll find it."

They had dug up the basement floor around the drain and hauled out the trap, examining it for bits of flesh, hair, skin, or bone that might have been caught in the pipes. Part of a wall where specks of blood had been found had been taken from the house. Every room had been painstakingly searched, from floor to ceiling. Holes had been punched in walls. Doors had been cut open, part of the garage floor had been ripped up, all in the search for clues. More than a thousand potential pieces of evidence had been catalogued, from newspapers with stories about the murders that Bernardo had saved to staples from the boxes he had burned — the containers he had used in making the concrete caskets.

Although the police had Homolka's version of what happened in the house, they needed forensic evidence to back up her story. But what they wanted most of all was precisely what they hadn't found: the videotapes of the two schoolgirls being raped.

The police knew they existed. Investigators had found dozens of other videos in the house, everything from old Hollywood movies to homemade videos of Bernardo and Homolka entertaining friends at a backyard picnic and frolicking around the pool at her parents' house. Those tapes had been played every night in the mobile police trailer parked in front of the house. Homolka claimed she didn't know what her husband had done with the incriminating tapes. The crawl space off his music room on the second floor was one favorite hiding spot. That had been searched, and nothing found. As the investigators wound down their search, they were confident that Bernardo had not hidden the videos in the house. It was unlikely that he destroyed his prized tapes, but at that point the authorities believed it likely that he had hidden them elsewhere, possibly in a safety deposit box.

Finally, after more than two months, the police were ready to give the house back to the three couples who owned the property.

Around 4 p.m. a lone police officer rolled up the yellow tape.

On Monday, Bernardo's lawyers and the owners were in court to settle a dispute over the property. Although Bernardo was in arrears on the monthly rent of $1,200, in the eyes of the law he still had rights to the house because he had a year's lease on the property. After the media was ordered out of the courtroom, it was agreed that Bernardo's legal team would get "limited access" to the property to collect his personal possessions.

Later that same week, on May 5, 1993, Ken Murray and his associate Carolyn MacDonald, along with an assistant, arrived at the house. An investigator from Green Ribbon let them in. They were milling about on the first floor when Murray got a call on his cellular phone. What happened next would later become the focus of a police probe, an investigation that is still not completed. Ray Houlahan, the chief prosecutor in the case, gave the court his version of events during pre-trial arguments.

"The police were in the house for nearly three months and couldn't find the tapes," he told the court. But the incriminating tapes "had been hidden in the house, and the defense had to be told where to look."

Houlahan said that when Murray answered his cell phone that day, he said to the others that it was Bernardo calling. Around this time the police officer left the house, leaving the trio alone for an hour. They were later watched by police as they left the house, carrying out garbage bags, presumably containing some of Bernardo's possessions.

It was while the three were alone, Houlahan said, that the six 8-mm tapes were removed from a location that — incredibly — had been overlooked by the police during their three-month search for evidence. The hiding place, Bernardo himself would later say in court, was behind a pot light inside the drop ceiling in the second-floor bathroom. The light had first to be pulled down from the ceiling to get at the tapes hidden in the rafters. In court Bernardo said he had put the tapes about an arm's length up into the rafters, tucking them behind the insulation. Although detectives and forensic specialists had searched through the house for 72 days, the long arm of the law had failed to come up with the goods.

The six videos were taken away, Houlahan said. Then they were locked in a drawer while the plea-bargaining negotiations with Karla Homolka continued before a deal was finalized.

It was later revealed in court that Murray had the tapes in his possession for a full week before Homolka's final deal with the crown was signed on May 14, 1993. Another 15 months would pass before the authorities were given the damning evidence. Murray's decision not to hand over the videos immediately, while the authorities were still in plea-bargaining negotiations with Homolka, meant that she received a lighter sentence than she probably would have otherwise, it was said later in court. She was very lucky the authorities didn't have the tapes when they gave her the deal. Ironically, it was Murray who later lambasted the Crown for the plea bargain, calling it "the deal with the Devil."

While Homolka would later say in court that she never tried to deceive the authorities, the facts suggest otherwise. Through her lawyer, she had been asking for total immunity from all charges, or even to be put into the Witness Protection Program and given a new identity after testifying. While prosecutors suggested she might receive 18 years, an initial deal saw her getting 10 years for two counts of manslaughter.

One of the crown negotiators was lawyer Murray Segal of the Attorney-General's office. Musings in his note-book show the difficulties he was having in trying to reach an agreement with Homolka on her sentence.

"God only knows how much she was involved in," reads one passage. Elsewhere: "It's difficult to assess the (appropriate) sentence."

What Segal and his team of legal authorities needed, of course, was the videotapes. Without them, all they had was Homolka. There was some forensic evidence from the house that appeared to put both girls there, but the crown needed more to take to court. The authorities badly needed Homolka to testify against her husband, and she knew it. She had told police she had tried to find the tapes before fleeing the house, but didn't know where they were.

It would not be unitl May 1993, three months after her first interview with the police, that Homolka would finally reveal the truth about the death of her sister. The authorities then tacked on an extra two years. Homolka's deal—a dozen years for her involvement in the three killings—became legally binding on May 14, 1993, and cannot be overturned. However, it called on her to reveal all the crimes she and Bernardo had been involved in. If she did not disclose everything, she risked further charges. Despite that warning, she would proffer one more troubling revelation long after her trial.

Homolka was at her parents' house in Merritton getting a massage from one of the therapists who worked with her mother at the hospital. The telephone rang. Her mother answered, listened silently for a few moments, then suddenly went pale. The police had told her the charge of manslaughter was going to be laid that day. As part of the friendly arrest, the police wanted Homolka to drop by the station for the formal arraignment. Dorothy was crying when she put down the phone. But not her daughter. The shock of learning that she was going to jail had long since worn off.

"I guess I'll be going away for a little bit," she said to her mother, as if she were going off to college. And then, as an afterthought: "Maybe I could take some university courses to pass the time."

Homolka thanked the therapist, then headed for her room. Her mother followed her.

"What should I wear to the police station?" Homolka asked, perusing her wardrobe. "A pant suit? Or a dress?"

Then she stopped for a moment, deep in thought. When she turned to her mother, there was a look of consternation on her face.

"I hope they'll let me do my hair in jail," she said. "I would just die if my hair went all to hell."

Paul Bernardo was in his cell at the Metro East Detention Centre in Scarborough when one of the guards rapped on the door. A justice of the peace entered the cell and informed Bernardo that he was being formally charged with the sex slayings of Kristen French and Leslie Mahaffy. Nine charges in all, Bernardo was told: two counts of first-degree murder, two of kidnapping, two of forcible confinement, two counts of sexual assault, and one count of committing an indignity to a human body, namely the dismemberment of Leslie Mahaffy.

When the papers were delivered to his cell that day he learned that the police had charged Homolka with two counts of manslaughter, and that was all. This is when he punched the wall and screamed, "Bitch is sicker'n me and all she gets is manslaughter."

Ken Murray faced a decision that some would call a lawyer's ultimate nightmare. He had in his possession what were surely the most crucial pieces of evidence in the country's most sensational murder case. As an officer of the court, Murray had a duty to uphold the law. He had sworn an oath to that effect. But as a lawyer, he had sworn an oath to defend his client to the best of his ability. Turning over the tapes would guarantee Bernardo's conviction for murder. What was he to do? It was a gray area of jurisprudence, and the sort of ethical dilemma that lawyers dread.

The gray-haired man who walked with a limp recognized her immediately. She was in the next aisle, shopping for groceries as if nothing was wrong. And that infuriated him. He started toward her, unconsciously clenching his fists, his bad leg trailing slightly behind. It wasn't right that she was in a grocery store mingling with other shoppers. She didn't deserve to be out in the world with normal folks.

Others had noticed her as well. Some pointed, most just stared. She tried to pretend she wasn't aware of their gawking curiosity. But she knew the whole country had been following her case. Hers was the most recognizable face in St. Catharines, probably even the country: the full lips, painted a bright red like a scarlet beacon, the high cheekbones, prominent nose, those creepy eyes, the luxuriant blond locks well past her shoulders.

The man felt he had seen that face a thousand times on television and in the newspapers. He hobbled closer until he was directly behind her. She turned suddenly, as if she had just felt his cold stare on the nape of her neck.

"You have no right to be here," the man challenged, wagging his finger menacingly close to her face.

Homolka looked back at the angry old man with a vacuous gaze. She said nothing. It was late June 1993, and her trial was just a month away.

"Garbage like you should be locked up in jail," he said. "You're such ... such ... scum!"

He was really into it now. Nearly a year had passed since Kristen's murder, two years since they found Leslie, but the anger of many was still there. He wasn't finished.

Homolka saw it coming, jumped back barely in time, and the projectile that sputtered out from between the old man's lips fell well short of its target. A crowd started to gather at the spectacle beside the frozen-food section. The old man pursed his lips again. But he didn't get the chance to fire another volley. Homolka turned and ran from the store.

"Bitch," the old man shouted after her. "I hope you rot in hell."

38
Unspeakable Crimes

In Courtroom 10 of the courthouse in St. Catharines, Crown prosecutors were asking for a publication ban on the evidence that was going to be heard against Homolka. Since her husband and co-accused, Paul Bernardo, was going to court after her, the ban was needed to preserve his right to a fair trial, the prosecutors said. They reasoned that if the country heard all the grisly details before Bernardo's trial, there was no way he could get a fair hearing.

The Crown said they weren't asking for a secret trial, just a trial that couldn't be reported, for the moment, by the press. There was, however, one difficulty with this strategy, prosecutor Murray Segal told the judge, Francis Kovacs. And that was "the Buffalo Factor."

While the Canadian media had to comply with a court order, or risk going to jail, American journalists weren't bound by the same laws. There were at least half a dozen American journalists in the courtroom for the start of Homolka's trial, and their reports were being run by Canadian cable companies. The Crown suggested that if the Americans were allowed to stay in the courtroom and didn't comply with the ban, all the horrific facts would come out and bias any jury selected for Bernardo's trial.

There was, however, a solution outlined by the Crown prosecutors: close the courtroom to the public and foreigners and just let in Canadian journalists. The Canadians could take notes, which they could save and report on after Bernardo's trial. To the Crown's way of thinking, what they were proposing was just a temporary publication deferral, a delay in bringing the public the news. This approach was a "balance of freedom of expression with the administration of justice regarding a fair trial." The media had to realize, prosecutor Segal told the court, that "freedom of speech does not exist in a vacuum." Sometimes it clashed with other rights that were also protected by law.

Predictably, the media didn't quite see it Segal's way. "The public," *Toronto Star* lawyer Bert Bruser told the court, "has a legal right to know in a timely fashion how justice deals with cases like this one." The whole foundation of the system of justice, Bruser went on, is that trials are held in public. Two other newspapers, and the Canadian Broadcasting Corporation, also urged the court not to shut its doors to the public and the press.

The media were not alone in their bid to keep the trial as public as possible. Paul Bernardo's team also supported an open trial. Lawyer Timothy Breen had been hired by Bernardo's defense team to argue that a publication ban would, in fact, do the opposite of what the prosecutors were suggesting, and actually hurt Bernardo's chances for a fair trial.

"Shielding Karla Homolka from publicity," Breen told the court, "is perpetuating the myth that she is a victim."

Breen went on to describe how the police had talked confidently at press conferences about "getting their man," meaning Bernardo, as if he was the only suspect who counted. He noted that on the day Bernardo was arrested the police had acknowledged that there was a second suspect in the murder case, but they hadn't identified her, and by not arresting her were implying that she wasn't a danger to society.

Breen turned to the prisoner's dock behind him. Homolka, wearing a somber, dark blue business suit, was looking straight ahead, but she avoided Breen's scrutinizing gaze. Breen then cast an accusing finger at the woman who was shortly going to plead guilty to two counts of manslaughter.

"Is it fair to describe her," he asked rhetorically, his voice filling the huge courtroom, "as posing no danger to the community?"

On Day Three of Homolka's trial, the debate over whether the trial should be closed to the public was still going on. Some schoolmates of Kristen French decided it was their turn to speak, and they took their message to the streets.

"Ban the Media," said one sign. "Enough is enough," read a second. "I'm scared, I don't want to know any more," pleaded a third. Their protest march wound its way past a group of reporters standing at the front door of the courthouse. The journalists who had been fighting with the police for information were not amused.

"Idiots," cried out one reporter. "Did the cops put you up to this?" asked another. "You're being used, and you're too thick to see it."

Freedom of the press had to take a back seat to an accused's right to a fair trial, Judge Kovacs ruled later that day. Canadian reporters could sit in on Homolka's trial, but they wouldn't be allowed to report on the evidence until after Bernardo's trial. As for the foreign press, especially the Americans, they wouldn't be allowed into the courtroom. They weren't governed by Canadian laws, Kovacs noted, and could break the ban without retribution from the courts. And since American reporters might try to get in by posing as spectators, the judge went on, the public would also have to be excluded from the trial.

The defense team of Ken Murray and Carolyn MacDonald listened intently. Both shared a secret about the case that they chose not to reveal to the court on that July afternoon. Had Murray and MacDonald divulged their knowledge of the videotapes, they would have dramatically altered Homolka's fate, for the worse. If the authorities had found the tapes first, prosecutors would have had no choice but to be a lot tougher in their handling of Homolka's plea-bargaining.

Under the Criminal Code of Canada, causing a person's death during a sexual assault brings an automatic charge of first-degree murder. In jail time, that draws a life sentence. The sentence for manslaughter is far shorter. With the videotapes as evidence, Homolka would have been facing a charge of second-degree murder and not manslaughter. A conviction on second-degree murder called for a life sentence as well, but parole was possible after 15 years. For Homolka, manslaughter might mean getting out of jail on parole while still in her twenties, as opposed to getting her freedom back as a woman in her forties.

Murray was aware of the implications, and he knew that Homolka would soon be testifying against his client, so it was in his best interests to try to discredit her as much as possible. But by graphically implicating Homolka, Murray would of course be sinking his own client. He kept silent.

The courtroom was cleared, and then just the Canadian reporters were allowed back in, along with the police, lawyers, and court officials. The families of the two victims were allowed in for humanitarian reasons — they wanted to witness justice being handed out to one of the people accused of killing their daughters. As a special consideration for Homolka, her family was also allowed into the courtroom.

Crown prosecutor Murray Segal began by going through the litany of crimes. He started with the death of

Homolka's sister Tammy Lyn, then moved to the murders of French and Mahaffy. Homolka sat impassively as Segal gave the Canadian reporters a thumbnail sketch of the three deaths. The only time Homolka showed any emotion was when the mothers of the two girls, Donna French and Deborah Mahaffy, read a prepared text about what the loss had meant to their families. Like many others in the courtroom, Homolka wept softly as she heard of the grief the two families had suffered.

Then Segal said, "It was the position of the Crown that murder charges could have been laid [against Homolka], based on what this accused has presented to the authorities. Prosecutorial discretion was used in deciding on a sentence of manslaughter."

Seated just a few feet away from Segal was Ken Murray, the man whose silence meant that Homolka would be getting out of jail while she was still a young woman.

Perhaps anticipating there would be a public outcry over the perceived leniency of Homolka's sentence, Segal had a rhetorical question for the court. "Why not a greater penalty in light of the horrendous facts?" he asked, then answered his own question. "Without her, the true state of affairs might never be known. A guilty plea is the traditional hallmark of remorse. Her age, her lack of a criminal record, the abuse and the influence of her husband, and her somewhat secondary role were factors. She's unlikely to re-offend."

Homolka's lawyer, George Walker, addressed the same concern when it was his turn to speak. "Twelve years may appear to be a lenient sentence," he began, "but this is a lengthy period of time, and Karla Homolka has been trying to undo some of the harm she has caused."

The treatment she had received from Bernardo, he went on, was a "classic case of wife abuse." Through verbal and physical abuse, Bernardo had taken away her self-respect, isolated her from her friends, then forced her into his murderous schemes. "Once her sister died, there was no returning. In her mind, there was very little she could do."

Judge Kovacs continued with the theme that Homolka had been victimized by her husband. Homolka had known what was happening to her but she felt totally helpless, he said, quoting a psychiatrist's assessment: "She was paralyzed with fear and became obedient and self-serving. She is not a dangerous person, but someone that requires much assistance. Karla Homolka is a passive, non-violent person. She was unable to attack her husband, even to protect herself from what seemed like certain death at his hands. She requires lengthy psychiatric treatment for a number of years to allow her to recover from the emotional scars inflicted on her."

Judge Kovacs said that her guilty plea was the first step in the 24-year-old's rehabilitation. In handing down a sentence of 12 years — one that had been agreed to by the Crown and the defense — the judge said he took into account Homolka's "youth and previous unblemished character ... I have considered too that she was described by the experts as a battered wife, whose self-esteem was destroyed."

Outside the courtroom, Murray attacked the Crown's handling of the case and the special treatment they were according Homolka, who would be the star witness at his client's trial. The prosecutors insisted on portraying Homolka, he told a scrum of some 60 reporters, as the victim of her husband, when in fact she was a willing participant in the crimes.

It was a theory that met with much agreement from the journalists. What little sympathy there had been for Homolka had all but disappeared when they had learned in the closed courtroom that she had set up her own sister to be raped by Bernardo. The revelation had taken most of the reporters by surprise. Even those closely following the case had never expected it, believing they would hear only about the deaths of French and Mahaffy. Although the court had heard that Homolka was supposedly forced into the betrayal by an abusive Bernardo, few reporters believed that was the case.

At the press conference, Murray also complained that prosecutors were withholding evidence from the defense, making it difficult for them to prepare for Bernardo's court appearance. Some 15 months would pass before he started questioning his own lack of disclosure.

The man who called the newsroom of the *Toronto Star* that day was an editor with a tabloid based in Florida. He said he had a deal for one of the reporters who had covered the Homolka trial. The Americans had just discovered the case, he said, and were hungry for details. The offer was cash for banned details.

"I'll give you $5,000 for the exclusive rights."

"If I talk to you, I go to jail," the reporter told him.

"That's $5,000 U.S.," the editor emphasized, ignoring the reporter's concerns. "With the exchange rate, we're talking well over $6,000 Canadian."

"We've been warned about talking to the Americans," the reporter said. "Telling you anything means a lot of trouble for me."

"Look, we've got a big Canadian market down here. Retirees from the Great White North, mostly. Lot of people want to know what happened in that courtroom. A country shouldn't be holding secret trials. Okay, you're driving a hard bargain here. I'll bump up my offer a grand, but that's all the story is worth. Whaddaya say?"

The answer was the same.

"You guys sure got funny laws up there," he said.

"I'm glad I live in this country. If you don't mind, I'll keep shopping around." And he hung up.

The bar in the west end of Toronto was a favorite with police officers, not all of them off duty. That afternoon, a detective with a force in Ontario recognized a reporter he knew who had been in the courthouse at St. Catharines. The detective exchanged a few niceties, then got right to the point.

"Can you tell me what was said in the courtroom?"

It turned out that he had an unsolved homicide on the books and was wondering if there was anything from the Homolka trial that might be useful in his case.

"Why don't you call Green Ribbon?" the detective was asked. "You're all working on the same side, aren't you?"

"You gotta kiss their butts to get anything out of them," the detective moaned. "I don't feel like kissing another copper's ass."

"I do it all the time to get my information. Why shouldn't you?"

"You gonna help me or not?"

The reporter mentioned another case the detective's force was working on, still unsolved. "I hear you might have a suspect in that one. Can you tell me who it is?"

"You know I can't do that."

"Then I guess we can't do business."

The detective was silent for a moment. "Next time you need help on a story," he said, "call 911." Then he stormed off.

The lawyer who called a reporter he knew had some information for him on the Paul Bernardo case, but he wanted some cash in exchange. "I've got a client," the lawyer said, "who's got an exclusive scoop on Bernardo. Everything from his attitudes on sex to evidence that would incriminate him in a court of law. For 15 grand, you can have the scoop of the century."

"Shouldn't you be going to the police with this information?" the lawyer was asked. "Especially since you're an officer of the court yourself."

"I see no reason to," the lawyer replied. "My client will probably eventually go to the police, but right now he wants to cash in on the crime of the century."

Distraught that people seemed to be exploiting her daughter's death, Deborah Mahaffy began to press the Ontario government for legislation banning criminals from profiting from their crimes.

"My daughter didn't die for the profits of others," she told a parliamentary committee.

Mary Garofalo, a reporter with the American tabloid TV show *A Current Affair*, had been in Toronto for several days working on the Bernardo story when she got a call late one night from a man who wouldn't identify himself.

"Get your pen out," he said authoritatively, "and start writing. I don't agree with what's happening in the courtroom. I don't believe in all this secrecy."

And then he told her many of the banned details that had been read out in court. Garofalo's report, and the entire 30-minute show, was later blanked off Canadian screens. But all across Canada, in many of the half a million households with satellite dishes, people huddled around their sets, taking in the forbidden information, taping the show for their friends, and talking about the horrific details that the judicial system did not want them to hear.

The *Washington Post* later broke the ban as well, on November 23, 1993, with a detailed story by Anne Swardson that included the death of Homolka's sister Tammy Lyn. Canadian reporters could only watch in silence as details of the *Post* story flooded across the country, with the Canadian authorities in close pursuit.

Keeping the *Post* story away from Canadian eyes was an impossible task, but the authorities still tried. When copies were taken off Canadian shelves, along with other American newspapers that carried reprints of the story, some people crossed the border to buy the papers. For days after the *Post* story, Canadian border guards shifted their attention more to newspapers and less to contraband. People returning to Canada were asked if they had any newspapers in their vehicle. Those with copies of the offending issue had them taken away, although no charges were laid. Dozens of people were caught red-handed; some were even briefly detained.

In addition, the complete *Post* article was carried on the Internet, the worldwide computer network with thousands of subscribers in Canada, including universities, government institutions, and private citizens. By the time the authorities realized what was happening, and were threatening to shut down computer systems, untold numbers had read the story. Computer printouts taken off the Internet were headlined: "Unspeakable Crimes. This Story Can't Be Told In Canada. And So All Canada Is Talking About It." There was even a bulletin board set up for news in the case. The people who were putting out the stories on the Internet went under pseudonyms to avoid prosecution. Neal the Ban Breaker was one, Abdul was another. One of the more popular items for those surfing the net is FAQ — Frequently Asked Questions. FAQ tried to separate the truth from the rumors, and often succeeded.

Throughout it all, the mainstream Canadian media outlets remained silent. Many reporters believed what the courts were doing was wrong and some talked about defying the gag order and the wishes of their bosses. But none did — at least, not in print.

Word got out nonetheless. One reporter held a press conference for everyone in the newsroom, although Kovacs had warned journalists that they could discuss the information only with their immediate superiors. Other journalists had told spouses, partners, relatives, friends, and parents. One reporter recounted the banned information to his barber, who in turn passed it on to his customers. Rumors abounded, of course, and the inaccuracy of much of the information — tales of cannibalism listed on the Internet, for instance — was another reason many journalists felt that the public should hear the truth.

The plan by some of the country's biggest media outlets was to challenge the validity of the ban at a higher court. Journalists would maintain their silence for the time being. No one knew then that they would be muzzled for a whole year.

Early in 1994, some of Canada's biggest news media went to the highest court in Ontario in a bid to overturn the gag order. The 15 lawyers representing the *Toronto Star*, *Globe and Mail*, *Toronto Sun*, and the CBC met with a frosty reception from the five high court judges. The ruling from the judge in the Homolka trial was not a ban, the media lawyers were told, merely a publication deferral.

"The media was there, the events were recorded," said Chief Justice Charles Dubin. "In due time it will be exposed to public scrutiny." And later: "What's so important about immediacy?"

Several arguments were made for overturning the ban: it was an infringement on the freedom of the press; the ban was ineffectual, and had been broken many times; the rumors caused by the ban were far more prejudicial to Bernardo's chances of a fair trial than the truth.

Lawyer Casey Hill, arguing the Crown's position, told the judges that while "Mr. Bernardo has his own defense . . . and he doesn't have to tell us," Murray's strategy seemed clear: it was to attack Homolka, thus lessening her credibility when it came time for her to testify against her husband. Indeed, Murray had been doing that for months. Putting himself in Murray's mind, Hill then told the court: "I want the media to print things about her that will influence a jury to think things about her before he goes to trial."

The five judges reserved their judgment. There was still no ruling from the Ontario Court of Appeal when Bernardo's trial started several months later with pre-trial motions.

The St. Catharines courtroom was packed on the Monday in May, 1994, as the proceedings against Paul Bernardo began. Ken Murray stood beside his client as the nine charges were read out against Bernardo.

"I plead not guilty, sir," Bernardo said in a loud, clear voice to the trial judge, Associate Chief Justice Patrick LeSage, as each charge was read out.

In the hushed courtroom the only other sound was the squeaking of felt pens as seven court artists seated nearby drew sketches of Bernardo, who looked more like a businessman in his black suit, white shirt, and flowered print tie than the accused man in two gruesome murders.

As Murray sat down at the defense table, he knew what was coming next. Bernardo was about to be charged with manslaughter in the death of Homolka's sister Tammy Lyn. In her plea-bargain, Homolka had escaped prosecution in her sister's death.

Murray rose as the prosecutors tried to present to the court the new charges. The Crown wanted to lay the charges and then have the judge seal the documents. It was a ploy that incensed Murray.

"I have a great deal of difficulty having this presented here," Murray said, his normally soft voice booming in Bernardo's defense. The new charges, he said, had nothing to do with the murders of the two schoolgirls before the court that day. "This is trial by ambush. This completely prejudices my client's chances of a fair trial. Each and every time my client comes to court, the Crown has done something new to enhance its case."

Judge LeSage was not eager to seal the documents. By so doing, he would be imposing a gag order to prevent the media from publishing the new charges. "This will be a public trial," he said. "It may be that some things can't be published . . . but I am very much disinclined to get a document and then seal it. That does far more harm than good. It only serves to generate curiosity."

The start of the trial was adjourned shortly afterwards as the Crown regrouped to consider its strategy regarding the manslaughter charge.

About two months later, the prosecutors got their biggest break in the case, the one that they had been hoping for ever since Bernardo had been arrested. They had never believed that Bernardo had destroyed the tapes of Kristen French and Leslie Mahaffy. He might have put them in a safety deposit box or a public storage facility. That belief was backed up by FBI reports that suggested sexual sadists always kept souvenirs of their attacks and were loath to destroy anything that reminded them of their assaults. The authorities were convinced Bernardo would never destroy the tapes because he derived too much pleasure from viewing them over and over. The tapes were out there, somewhere.

Private conversations heard on wiretaps led police to believe that Bernardo's lawyer, Ken Murray, had the tapes but had kept their existence a secret. The revelation set in motion a chain of events that would delay the start of the trial for a year.

When he found himself in the difficult ethical situation of possessing incriminating evidence against his client, there were some avenues of help for Ken Murray. The Law Society of Upper Canada, which governs the legal profession in Ontario, has a mentor program in which he could have received some off-the-record and confidential advice from an experienced lawyer. The second option was more formal.

The Law Society has a professional standards conduct committee, a three-member board whose direction, while still confidential, is more authoritative than that of the informal mentor program.

When the police discovered, through their wiretaps, that Murray had the tapes they coveted, a number of discreet inquiries were made of him. Did he have any evidence in the case, they wondered, that he might want to hand over to the authorities?

The tapes had been in Murray's possession for more than a year. Toward the end of 1994 he revealed his dilemma to the professional conduct committee and then awaited their decision. Their advice to Murray was that he hand the tapes over to the court. But by turning them over, it was possible that Murray might end up being called as a witness at Bernardo's trial. The court would want to know the circumstances under which the tapes had come into his possession.

A lawyer cannot defend a client if he has to testify at his trial. If he turned over the tapes, Murray would have no choice but to resign from the case. In seeking new counsel for his client, Murray turned to a veteran lawyer who had been involved in well over a hundred murder trials, John Rosen.

Rosen was somewhat reluctant to take on the case because he already had a full schedule; as one of the top lawyers in the province, he had at least a half dozen cases on the go. Murray was insistent.

"I can't give my client the kind of advice that you can," Murray told Rosen at one meeting. "I just can't."

Later, Murray gave Rosen the incriminating tapes, and it was Rosen's advice as well that the videos be handed over to the authorities.

Bernardo, who was now in protective custody at the Thorold Detention Centre, near St. Catharines, was incensed by Murray's decision, believing it an act of betrayal. He had hired Murray to defend him, not help the Crown send him to jail for life. But there was nothing he could do to stop it from happening.

Murray's next step was to withdraw from the case. His departure was not opposed by the trial judge, who ordered that the case be handed over to Rosen. Murray's co-counsel, Carolyn MacDonald, later resigned as well.

Soon afterwards, the provincial Ministry of the Attorney-General ordered an Ontario Provincial Police investigation into the matter to determine if there was any case for criminal charges to be laid.

Rosen told the court he needed time to study the case; another seven months passed before jury selection began in Toronto, where the trial was moved because polls had shown there was too much animosity toward Bernardo in St. Catharines for him to get a fair trial.

On May 1, 1995, two years after Bernardo's arrest, nearly four years after the death of Leslie Mahaffy and eight years after the first of the rapes in Scarborough, jury selection began at a hotel in downtown Toronto.

Nearly a thousand people — one of the largest jury panels in Canadian history — crowded into the banquet hall of the Colony Hotel. About 350 names were then drawn out of a drum. Those people were told to report to the court, where they would be asked, one at a time, a series of questions to determine if they were suitable for jury duty in Canada's biggest murder case. If 12 people couldn't be culled from that group, the remainder of those on the panel would be brought to the court for questioning. Despite fears that the Crown would have trouble picking an unbiased jury because of the widespread publicity, it took just three days to select the eight men and four women.

The defense had wanted more women on the jury, reasoning that females would be less inclined to believe the Crown's version of events, that Homolka had been manipulated by her husband into helping him commit the murders. Crown prosecutors wanted just the opposite, more male jurors. Potential jurors were told they would have to watch disturbing videos, and many female candidates were excused after saying they didn't want to see what was on the tapes.

There wasn't much point in fighting the rape charges, Bernardo's lawyer, John Rosen, told the court during pre-trial arguments. The video evidence clearly showed him as the culprit. But Rosen and his co-counsel, Tony Bryant, had a strategy for the defense of their client. It had already been started by Ken Murray.

It was their belief that Homolka was just as guilty as Bernardo for the murders, and they planned to attack her as much as possible during the trial. There were no witnesses to the murders besides Homolka, and the woman who had set up her own younger sister to be raped was hardly the most credible witness. If Rosen and Bryant could introduce just the slightest bit of doubt into the minds of the jury that Bernardo was the perpetrator of the slayings, by suggesting that

Homolka might have done the two killings, then it was possible Bernardo could get something less than first-degree murder.

There was evidence to show that Homolka was more than just a victim in the crimes. In one segment of the videos, she was even heard to say that she would go with Bernardo to get young virgins — as many as 50 — if that would please him. The Crown claimed that bit of dialogue was scripted by Bernardo, but it wasn't a persuasive argument.

If the jury felt Bernardo and Homolka were equally guilty, and given that the crown had charged Homolka only with manslaughter, perhaps Bernardo could get second-degree murder and not first. It would mean 15 years before he could apply for parole rather than 25, and could possibly see him out of prison while he was still in his mid-forties. With damning video evidence, and with public sentiment against him, it would be the best possible deal Paul Bernardo could hope for. Anything less than a conviction for first-degree murder would be seen as a huge victory for the defense.

39
Exposed

Karla Homolka's mother, Dorothy, was one of the first prosecution witnesses to take the stand at the murder trial of Paul Bernardo. She was led through some gentle questioning by Greg Barnett, an amiable prosecutor whose even-tempered disposition and pleasant smile calmed the nervous mother while she testified before a packed courtroom, many of whom had lined up since 4 a.m. for one of the 120 seats available to the public.

Barnett wanted to know how Dorothy had been affected by the Christmas Eve death of her youngest child.

"Part of me went with her," she replied. "Nobody knows the feeling of losing a child. There are no words."

Barnett was focusing on Dorothy's grief for a reason. He wanted to elicit some sympathy for her from the jury, perhaps make them more amenable to a portrait of Bernardo as the manipulator, the schemer, and the one solely responsible for the killings of French and Mahaffy and the death of Tammy.

Barnett got her to talk about the dynamics of the relationship between her eldest daughter and Bernardo. He delved into Bernardo's affinity for video cameras. Bernardo was always making tapes of her family, she said, sticking a camera in front of their faces around the swimming pool, at barbecues, in the rec room. On the evening her youngest child died, Bernardo had been taping the family as they relaxed in the rec room before retiring for the night.

She told Barnett how Bernardo had tried to keep Karla away from her family after Tammy's death. This implied Bernardo was fearful Karla might reveal what had actually happened. It was part of the prosecution's strategy to show that Bernardo was the only person who was to blame. He alone controlled events before, during, and after, the three deaths, and not the woman who was now his ex-wife. (Homolka had initiated divorce proceedings soon after her arrest, and the dissolution had been finalized before the start of this trial.)

Dorothy testified that Bernardo always seemed to be hovering near Karla after Tammy's death, monitoring all her conversations. "I don't remember being alone with her for any length of time."

Bernardo was always there, listening, and butting into their conversations. Once, the two of them were alone in the kitchen, she recalled, while Bernardo was off watching television. But as soon as he noticed they were talking, he intervened and began ordering her daughter around. The insinuation was clear: Bernardo was worried that Homolka would break down and confess, and so he was always scrutinizing what she said. That control was extended two months after Tammy died, when the couple left the Homolka household for Port Dalhousie. It was a move, Dorothy recalled, that she and her husband had opposed.

But when John Rosen began his cross-examination, a slightly different picture of the relationship emerged.

"I know how difficult this is," a solicitous Rosen began, the politeness of his smile not a true reflection of what was to come. "I'll try to be brief, all right?"

"Okay," Dorothy replied uneasily.

Rosen asked her about the relationship that had been described by the prosecution as a classic case of wife abuse.

Under Rosen's cross-examination, Dorothy admitted that she had never noticed any signs of trouble between the two for about the first five years of their relationship.

"The couple looked bubbly and happy?" Rosen asked. "Karla had a glow she never had before?"

"Yes."

Wasn't it true that before her daughter met Bernardo, Rosen asked, she was rebellious and always dressed in black?

"Yes," Dorothy acknowledged.

"But when Paul came along she dressed more conservatively, like an adult? You and your husband were happy about the change in her, right?"

"Yes," she responded, admitting that Bernardo became their "weekend son," the male child she and her husband never had.

She also agreed that she still believed the couple was happy even though she noticed signs of possible trouble in the summer of 1992. One time her daughter had what appeared to be a broken finger, and a black eye on another occasion, injuries Karla had blamed on the couple's dog, Buddy.

"So it came as a total shock to you?" Rosen asked later, referring to the incident in early 1993 when Bernardo beat Karla with a flashlight.

"Yes."

"You never suspected any physical abuse until then, right?"

"Yes."

"You thought they were a happy, loving couple?"

Again she replied in the affirmative.

She admitted that after Tammy's death, Karla had had several good opportunities to talk to her alone about what had really happened. One such time was at the memorial service at Tammy's school when just the family attended.

"She had every chance to talk to you about Tammy there?" Rosen asked, and Dorothy agreed.

"Karla never once said to you or your husband, 'I don't want to see Paul' or 'I'm breaking off the relationship, and I never want to see him again.'"

She acknowledged this.

"In fact," Rosen said, referring to the days just before her daughter's wedding in June 1991, "she seemed happy, excited, busy, and just a little bit tired from all the preparations."

"Yes."

"You and your husband never thought for a moment that your daughter's wedding was anything but a happy occasion, right?"

"Yes."

"And when they came back from their honeymoon they were all lovey-dovey, right?"

Dorothy acknowledged this.

"And it didn't seem to you like they had just returned from the 'honeymoon from hell'?" Rosen asked, using an earlier comment made by Crown prosecutors.

She agreed, and Rosen ended his questioning. He had made his point. The bruised and battered Homolka had had plenty of chances to let her parents know what was really going on, but had chosen to remain silent. If she really was a victim of her husband, then why didn't she tell anyone, or seek help from the police?

Rosen's co-counsel, Tony Bryant, had already made a similar point to the jury in an earlier cross-examination. Even though Homolka had moved to Port Dalhousie, help was only a short bus ride away. Homolka could, for instance, have just stayed on the bus that took her to work every day and ridden it to the headquarters of the Niagara Region police in downtown St. Catharines. Or, with a "modest amount of effort," Homolka could have transferred from that bus and boarded a second that went past her parents' home in the south end of the city.

Rosen and Bryant were laying the groundwork for the coming cross-examination of Karla Homolka. Her credibility was the key to their defense. Rosen and Bryant hoped to discredit her version of events and convince the jury that she might have done the killings herself. Only in that way could Bernardo perhaps get second-degree murder and not first.

During the pre-trial negotiations, a deal had been discussed that would have seen Bernardo plead guilty to second-degree murder in the French and Mahaffy murders, with credit for the two years he had served in custody before his trial began, so that he could apply for parole after serving 17 years. Under Canadian law, even if he was convicted on the other charges against him — the Scarborough rapes and the death of Tammy Lyn — those sentences would be served concurrently with his murder conviction. But the deal had been nixed at the last minute by government officials, perhaps fearful that the public would be angered by yet another secret plea-bargain arrangement. So Bernardo had to take his chances in court, and Rosen and Bryant had to defend him the best way they could — by attacking his former wife, the Crown's star witness.

But long before Karla Homolka took the stand, the jury and the rest of the courtroom were given a different view of the woman whose testimony was so crucial to the Crown's case. And it was not what the public — or even the media — had been expecting.

For the first time, the public was finally going to see some of the homemade videos taken by Paul Bernardo. More than 200 people had crowded into the sixth-floor courtroom, curious about what would be shown during Day 10 of the murder trial. Associate Chief Justice Patrick LeSage had ruled that the public would not be allowed to watch the videotapes of French and Mahaffy being raped. Only the jury and court officials, along with Bernardo, would see them, along with the tapes showing the sexual assaults on Tammy Lyn Homolka and Jane Doe. But Bernardo had made many other tapes, and the judge put no restrictions on who could see those videos.

These tapes were to be played on two 30-inch video monitors at the front of the gallery, one on each side of the courtroom. The sets were on 6-foot-high platforms that were discreetly sheathed in a somber black cloth. There were also two huge television sets in front of the jurors, while Bernardo, the defense, and the prosecution lawyers, along with the judge, all had their own smaller screens.

Just before the tape was turned on that morning, Judge LeSage looked down at the gallery that was filled to capacity and issued a warning: "I want to caution the audience that what you are about to see next is explicit . . . if you wish to remain, you can."

Nobody moved.

"Play it, please," said Crown prosecutor Ray Houlahan.

The first scene had been taped in the basement recreation room of the Homolka house not long after Tammy Lyn's death. Karla Homolka was on her back, lying on a rug before the fireplace, naked, her legs spread wide apart while she masturbated for the camera, which was positioned a few feet away, at about knee level, and pointed directly at her vagina.

Gasps of surprise and disgust, perhaps even shock, along with plenty of embarrassed giggles, could be heard throughout the courtroom as the camera lingered on Homolka's exposed body for several minutes while she stimulated herself.

To many in the courtroom, showing that particular video seemed an amazing way for the Crown to treat the woman who was scheduled to be their chief witness. For the previous two years, ever since her arrest, Homolka's face had been almost as well known as the prime minister's. She had been seen on television in footage taken at her wedding, with her friends, and at her trial. There had been countless photographs of her in newspapers and magazines around the world. But few people in the courtroom that day were expecting to see a triple-X-rated tape, a close study of the country's most infamous woman in a variety of sexually explicit positions.

The prosecutors, though, had their reasons for showing the video. On it, she and Bernardo talked about the death of Tammy Lyn. Although Bernardo's trial for her death might well follow his trial for first-degree murder, the Crown wanted to present evidence on Tammy's death as part of its general picture of the relationship between the two. Homolka's dialogue on the tape, Houlahan had said in his opening address, had been scripted by Bernardo. That is, Bernardo had told her what to say when she was on camera, and if she didn't obey him, she was punished with a beating.

But what the court saw was a seemingly relaxed Homolka pulling down her husband's pants, fondling his penis, which she called Snuggles, and then performing fellatio during most of the tape, stopping every now and then to talk about what had happened to her dead sister.

"I loved it when you fucked my little sister," Homolka said to Bernardo, who was lying on his back beside the roaring hearth, moaning softly while she rubbed his penis.

"I loved it when you fucked Tammy. I loved it when you took her virginity. You're the king. I love licking your ass, Paul. I'll bet Tammy would have loved to lick your ass. I loved it when you put Snuggles up her ass."

Bernardo could be seen reaching for his drink while Homolka continued to fondle his penis. She did it for several minutes, but he never climaxed. He took a sip from his drink, glancing at the back of her head while she worked on him, and asked about her thoughts on the night Tammy died. "How did you feel?"

"I felt proud. I felt happy," she replied.

"What else?"

"I felt horny. It's my mission in life to make you feel good."

"This is why I'm gonna marry her," Bernardo said, looking at the camera and holding up his drink while Homolka continued performing fellatio. "Sköl to the king."

"I'm glad you made me lick her cunt," Homolka continued, after pausing to take a break from the oral sex.

"Are you a fully fledged dyke?" Bernardo asked, a reference to Homolka having sex with her sister.

"No, I'm not."

"You were having sex with your little sister."

"That was different. It was my little sister," she replied, stroking his penis.

"Love in the family," Bernardo said. "Do you believe in that concept?"

"You know I had fun doing it," Homolka said. "You know I liked it."

"What did it teach you?"

"Well . . . we like little girls. I like you to fuck them. If you're gonna fuck them, then I'm gonna lick them. All the little girls."

"What age should they be?"

"Thirteen."

"Why?"

"Because it will make you happy."

"But why 13?"

"That's a good age."

"Because why?" he persisted.

"Because they'll still be virgins."

"What are you saying?" Bernardo asked, looking down at Homolka's head. She stopped to look up at him.

"I'm saying I think you should fuck them and take their virginity. Break their hymens with Snuffles. They're all our children, and I think you should make them ours even more."

"You're right," Bernardo said. "You're absolutely right. That's a good idea. When did you come up with it?"

"Just now," she replied. She resumed the oral sex for a while longer, then stopped and told Bernardo she had a surprise for him. She walked past the camera to her bedroom, beside the rec room, came back with a paper bag a few minutes later, and sat down beside Bernardo. Inside the bag was a brassiere and a pair of panties.

"It's Tammy's," she said, handing him the bra. He smelled it while she began stroking his penis with the underwear, before resuming the fellatio. A few minutes later, when he still hadn't reached a climax, she stopped and continued talking about her dead sister.

"I want to rub Tammy's underwear all over your body," she said, and did so. "It will make you feel so good. I'm so glad you took her virginity, Paul. I wish we had four kids, Paul."

"Yes?"

"So you could fuck each one of them. How does the king like that?" she asked, stroking his penis rapidly with her sister's underwear.

"Yeah," he replied, in obvious pleasure. She continued for several minutes, but when he never climaxed, she said,

"I think the king should turn over." He did as he was instructed.

"Okay," he said.

"Because his little slave has some more things to say and do."

Bernardo rolled off his back and got down on his hands and knees while Homolka positioned herself behind him. Then she probed with one hand for his anus and began licking it while she stroked his penis with her other hand. She did this for several minutes, and he moaned in pleasure, at times calling her his "little asslicker." When he failed to reach a climax, they changed positions yet again.

Bernardo lay on his back again and rested his hands behind his head. Homolka took a long-stemmed rose from a nearby vase and dragged it slowly across his chest, and then up and down his erect penis.

"You know what we're gonna do with this?" she asked, holding up the rose. "We're gonna take this to Tammy's tomorrow, and put it on her grave."

"Why?"

"Because it will give you pleasure. You loved her. She loved you. You were her favorite, you know. The things that you did, you know I loved it. The way you fucked her in what, 60 seconds? She loved it. She loved it."

"Your titties are bigger than hers."

"I know."

"And they taste better," he said. "When Tammy was alive, what did you used to do?"

"You made me lick it," she replied, resuming the oral sex, "and suck it. And now I'm doing it on my own because I loved it, Paul. I loved everything you did with her. She was our little playtoy."

"And we both loved her so much."

"Yes," Homolka agreed, fondling his penis again. "Our little virgin. She loved us."

"What else?"

"I didn't give you my virginity, so I gave you Tammy's instead. I loved you enough to do that."

Homolka then talked about another time Bernardo had brought a young girl home and had sex with her in the basement of her parents' house while she watched. "You fucked her," Homolka said, "with this."

She gazed at his penis, tenderly stroking it. "You fucked her cunt," she said. "She sucked you. She sucked Snuffles. She put it in her mouth, like this." After more minutes of oral sex with no climax, she continued: "You put her on her knees. You fucked her. And I let you do that because I love you, because you're the king."

She rubbed his penis for several moments before saying, "I want you to do it again."

"When?"

"This summer, because the weather is too bad in the winter. If we can do that then it's good."

"Good," he agreed.

"If you want to do it 50 more times, we can do it 50 more times," she said, a reference to him bringing home more young girls. "If you want to do it every weekend, we can do it every weekend. Whenever we can. Because I love you. Because you're the king. Because you deserve it."

"Virgin cunts for me," Bernardo chimed in.

"Yeah."

"Virgins just for me. It'll make me happy . . . going from one cunt to another, from one ass to another. Will you help me get the virgins?"

"Yes, I'll go in the car with you if you want, if you think that's best. Or I'll stay here and clean up afterwards. I'll do everything I can because I want you to be happy. Because you're the king."

Bernardo still hadn't climaxed. Homolka shifted down toward his feet.

"Ooh, footsies," he said.

She started sucking on his toes, first one foot, then the other. "Got to treat the king like a king," she said.

"Good. And what else?"

"I'm your little cocksucker," she said. "My nipples are so hard. I'm your cunt. Your little slut. Your little asslicker. Your little virgin."

"It's good to be king," Bernardo said, looking at the camera and raising his glass again.

Homolka licked the soles of his feet. "I'm your cunt-licking slut," she said, "the keeper of your virgins. Your ass-licking bitch. And I love you. I want to marry you."

And there the tape ended, with Bernardo still unable to climax.

Crown prosecutor Ray Houlahan said the video would be played again, to enable the jurors to follow the dialogue on the second viewing with a transcript prepared by the police. But before the monitors were turned on, many in the public gallery got up and left. They had seen more than enough of the illustrious couple on the first playing of the tape.

40
The Secret of Tammy

Some were calling it the crime of the century, so it was perhaps fitting that Karla Homolka began her testimony against her husband on what turned out to be the hottest day in a hundred years: the thermometer was to rise to over 100 Fahrenheit. Spectators had been lining up overnight in the sweltering heat outside the courthouse hoping to grab one of the 120 seats available to the public. "I'm here to see the Canadian version of Bonnie and Clyde," said one man.

Every seat in the public gallery had been filled for more than an hour when Homolka was led into the courtroom. She was wearing a taupe business suit, conservative in style. Her blond hair, well past her shoulders, was limp and stringy. She had what is called "jailhouse pallor," the look of someone who has spent most of her time inside a cell. She wore no makeup. And as she walked into the witness stand, everyone waited to see if she would look over at the man she used to call "the king." Spectators at the back had to be told to sit down after they stood for a better look at the diminutive blonde who, at barely over five feet, was just tall enough to see over the top of the witness stand.

Homolka knew what awaited her, and she was ready. Crown prosecutors had spent hundreds of hours preparing her, trying to ensure she would do her best to put "the master" behind bars for the rest of his life.

"Are you Karla Homolka?" Ray Houlahan began, once she had been sworn in by the court registrar.

"Yes."

"The ex-wife of Paul Bernardo?"

"Yes."

"Where is he? Point him out!" Houlahan blurted out, as if he had forgotten where Bernardo was seated.

"That's him," she said, looking toward the prisoner's dock and casting an accusing finger at the man she had once so passionately loved.

Bernardo stared back at her, and for a moment their eyes locked. It was the first time they had seen each other in more than two years. Homolka quickly turned back to the prosecutor, awaiting his next question. Bernardo picked up his notepad and began scribbling.

Seated just two rows behind him were his former in-laws, Dorothy and Karel Homolka, and their other daughter, Lori. When he had been led into court, Bernardo had looked over at Karel, as if hoping to get his attention, maybe even share a nod. But Karel had never once returned the gaze of the man who had raped his youngest daughter. Bernardo's own parents never showed up for any of his court appearances.

Homolka told the court she had pleaded guilty to the manslaughter of French and Mahaffy.

"Did you kill them with someone else?" Houlahan wanted to know.

"Yes."

"Who else?"

"Paul Bernardo."

Houlahan asked her how French and Mahaffy had died.

"Paul strangled them with a black electrical cord in the master bedroom of our house."

"And where were you?"

"I was in the same room, watching."

Homolka then described how she had reached the plea-resolution agreement under which her penalty for taking part in three deaths, along with one rape, was 12 years in jail, with the hope of getting out in three. "Even though I'm guilty of murder, I was allowed to plead guilty to two counts of manslaughter."

There were those who said her sweet deal should be appealed and that she should be made accountable to the full extent of the law. If the public's trust in the court system was to be regained, the arguments went, then if Homolka could have been charged with first-degree murder, she should have been charged with first-degree murder. Yet others said that tossing out a plea-bargain deal would create chaos in the courts. What criminal would ever trust the Crown when a deal was put on the table for their co-operation? As distasteful as Homolka's deal was, it had to be respected.

Before Homolka had begun her testimony, Judge LeSage had warned the jury that there was a "natural inclination" for people convicted of a crime to downplay their own involvement and point the finger elsewhere. They should therefore look upon Homolka's testimony with some skepticism.

Houlahan explained that Homolka's testimony would be divided into three main areas: her life before, during, and after being with Paul Bernardo.

Homolka said that before she met Bernardo she had wanted to study criminology in university and become a police officer, a remark that drew a round of guffaws from the gallery. But the chance encounter with Bernardo in October 1987 had changed her life forever. Over time, she said, the confident, outgoing teenager who had always been somewhat of a rebel became a submissive sex slave whose sole job in life was to do anything to please the man she would eventually marry.

Their relationship had started off with such promise, she said. Bernardo had plied her with expensive gifts and blinded her better judgment with his animal charm and his magnetism. He was courteous, polite, attentive to her needs, she said. There were trips, and plenty of good times in those early days. "I was swept off my feet. He treated me like a princess, like I was the only girl in the world."

But gradually, the man she had thought of as her Prince Charming began to take charge of her life, telling her how to dress, who to see, and even how to comb her hair. She wasn't allowed to go to clubs anymore because someone might try to pick her up. Soon their relationship had evolved into one of total dominance by Bernardo.

There were his sexual fetishes, the bondage, his choking her while engaging in anal sex. And then there was the abuse, both physical and mental, that crippled her will to fight back, she said. "When he wanted something, I would do it. When he told me to get something, I would get it. If I didn't do it, he would verbally abuse me, or threaten me, or hit me."

Still, she never left him. Prosecutor Houlahan wanted to know why.

"Stupidly," she said, "I loved him . . . For the most part he was treating me nicely. I kept hoping things would improve."

She said she never wanted to help him rape Tammy Lyn, but went along with his idea, hoping that the "one-time thing" would end his obsession. But after her sister died, she said, she was trapped. "I felt like I had to do what he said because he had this major, horrible thing over my head. I didn't feel I had a choice, and he knew it." If she ever tried to get away from him, or go to the police, he threatened to kill her and her family, she told the court. "Paul had something he could hold over me for the rest of my life. I was terrified my family would hate me if they ever found out."

And so she kept the secret of her horrible life, Homolka said, and never told anyone the real truth — that she was Bernardo's sexual plaything, a hundred-pound woman he used as his personal punching bag. "I let them think we had a loving relationship. I wanted to maintain that illusion. The reason I stayed with him was the secret of Tammy. I couldn't tell people he beat me and treated me terribly without explaining why he did it."

So she hid the bruises on her face with makeup, blamed her dog, Buddy, for the marks on her arms. When Bernardo wanted other virgins, she complied. To refuse meant a beating, and the threat that he would tell her parents about Tammy, she said.

"That's what Paul wanted" became a familiar refrain during her testimony. Why did she go along with his sexual fetishes? "That's what Paul wanted." Why did she pose in such sexually explicit photos? "That's what Paul wanted." Why did she set up her own sister to be raped? "That's what Paul wanted."

And when he brought home Mahaffy and French to use as his sex slaves, later killing them, she took part because "that's what Paul wanted."

She was trapped in a nightmare world, she said, with only two ways out: jail or death. But although she blamed Bernardo for everything that went wrong in her life, at one point the finger of guilt was pointed squarely back at her by prosecutor Houlahan.

"Could he have committed the act [against Tammy Lyn] without your help?"

"No," she replied. "I don't think so."

Said a spectator afterwards outside the courthouse,

"You'd think the eldest sibling would fight to the death to protect her baby sister, not hand her over on a silver platter to get raped."

Homolka showed little emotion during her first four days on the stand. But that changed when she watched the taped segment of Leslie Mahaffy pleading with Bernardo to free her.

"Please," Mahaffy cried. "*Please*. I want to see my family and friends again. Please help me."

"She seems to be asking someone for help," Houlahan said to her. "To whom was she talking?"

A pause. "That would have to be me," Homolka replied.

"And why didn't you help her?"

And for the first time, Homolka lost her composure, her voice cracked. "I didn't feel like I was able to help her because I was too afraid of Paul."

She told Houlahan how she didn't want Mahaffy to feel any pain when she died, so she persuaded Bernardo to give the frightened girl some sleeping pills before she was strangled.

Deborah Mahaffy was seated in the first row of the public gallery. She had been coming to the trial every day, sobbing as the gruesome details of her daughter's death were described. But the self-serving comment from the woman who had witnessed her daughter's murder was just too much for her.

"How kind of you," she said sarcastically. And later, when Homolka said she felt ill the day after the death, Mahaffy blurted out: "Good."

Another time, Homolka told Houlahan that she never wanted to get married to Bernardo.

"Then why did you?"

"I didn't feel I had a choice because he had the secret of Tammy over me, and then there was Leslie. I didn't feel I could leave him."

That's when Judge LeSage intervened with a question.

"Miss Homolka," he said, "someone may eventually ask you this question, but wouldn't Mr. Bernardo put himself in an equally bad position if he told anybody?"

"He told me he would tell my parents," she replied. "And then they would be in a horrible position of what to do. I didn't want my parents to know about this. It's very difficult to explain, but that's how I felt, Your Honor."

Although Bernardo was on trial, it became clear after a few days on the stand that it was Homolka who was finally undergoing a public airing of her involvement. The public had been shut out from her private trial, but there was no ban on these proceedings.

"You're both murderers!" one man called out from the gallery when Homolka testified about her role in the rape of Jane Doe. "Make a deal with a lawyer, get one year. Have a spine, Canadians. Stand up for yourselves."

Homolka left many of the 70 or so journalists in the courtroom shaking their heads when she tried to explain how she had forgotten about her role in the rape of Jane Doe. Her memory got better, the court heard, after the police were given a videotape of that rape. Some of the details of her involvement, like having oral sex with the drugged woman, came back to her in a dream, she said.

"My mind won't let me remember," she testified. "I just can't believe I did it."

But she wanted the court to know who was really on trial. During Day Five of her testimony she glanced over at Bernardo, who had been staring at her.

"I think he's a monster," she said.

As the court was adjourning at the end of the day, their eyes locked briefly.

"Fuck you," Bernardo mouthed to her as he stood up in the prisoner's dock, putting his hands behind his back to be handcuffed.

She gave him the briefest of smirks as she was led out of the court by a jail guard and taken back to her prison cell.

Speaking in a clinical, detached voice, Homolka continued with her eyewitness account of the murder of Kristen French. She knew that French had to die on Sunday because earlier they had made plans to go to her parents house for Easter dinner, she testified. They couldn't safely leave French alone, so their only choice was to kill her. After Bernardo strangled her, Homolka said she went into the bathroom and blow-dried her hair.

"I felt very, very numb," she said, her flat voice cracking only slightly. "I felt guilty and ashamed. I hated Paul and I hated myself. I just wanted to die. I couldn't believe it was happening. I felt absolutely terrible. It's so difficult to put my feelings into words because that will just trivialize it."

The scripted tone of her testimony changed dramatically, however, when she began to describe the abuse she had suffered. Her voice grew louder, her eyes sparkling, as she rattled off incident after incident of the battering she had taken from Bernardo during the latter part of their life together. She didn't need coaching from prosecutors to describe how Bernardo used to whip her, pound her in the head with a flashlight, throw her down the stairs, or force her to eat his excrement. It was as if she was purging her soul of the torment she had suffered in silence for so long.

Among the reporters covering the trial, there was a slight shift in their perception. Homolka had been seen as the loser in a power relationship with a madman, and she had suffered greatly. When she talked of how Bernardo started using a flashlight to hit her because his hands were getting sore, even some of the more cynical journalists almost started to feel sorry for her. Almost, but not quite.

Just before she left him, Bernardo had told her that things would be better between them, and she admitted that she hoped it was true.

"I was incredibly stupid," she said, about her expectations for future happiness with Bernardo. "I half-wanted to believe him. I knew he wasn't going to let me go, so the only option I had was to make him love me so he wouldn't beat me."

So she kept writing him the love notes, she said, hoping they would appease him and stop the battering. But it didn't stop.

Homolka ended her nine days of examination from the prosecutors with a statement about her remorse and about how much better off she was in jail. "Prison is not really punishment for what I've done. The real punishment is living with my guilt and my shame for the rest of my life."

And then, one last dig at Bernardo: "I couldn't stand to live with him any more. I hated myself for staying with him. In prison, it's a lot better than living with Paul because I don't have to worry about being beaten and being threatened every day. In prison, I have a lot more freedom than I ever had with him."

Now it was the turn of the defense team of John Rosen and Tony Bryant to start their cross-examination, but a holiday weekend intervened. Anticipating that the crown would want to debrief their star witness before the tough questioning began, Rosen obtained from the judge a court order forbidding the prosecutors from talking to Homolka over the holiday.

As she was led out of court and back to her cell to brood about what lay ahead, Bernardo had a big grin on his face. Homolka had turned traitor, and he wanted to see her squirm under the defense grilling.

For Rosen, it was just a matter of doing his job. His task was clear: he had to destroy Homolka's credibility, knock down the Crown's depiction of her as an abused spouse forced to tag along while a domineering Bernardo kidnapped and killed the two schoolgirls. If he could show that she was the liar, then maybe the jury might question her testimony, which pointed the finger squarely at Bernardo. She was the only witness to the murders, and if the veracity of some of her testimony could be successfully challenged, then everything she said would be suspect.

Rosen had given few hints as to the strategy he would employ, and had even asked reporters what they would do. The genial lawyer was known for his charm in winning over jurors, but the veteran of more than a hundred murder trials had also shaken many witnesses with the ferocity of his questioning. And despite Rosen's playing coy with the media, he and Bryant had carefully mapped out their plan of attack. When court resumed after the weekend, Rosen started off with a dramatic flourish in what may possibly have been the most eagerly anticipated cross-examination in the history of Canadian jurisprudence.

41
Karla's Kill Count

Rosen held a series of photos in his hand as he strode across the courtroom, stopping right in front of the Crown's chief witness. Then, glancing at the jurors, he thrust one of the pictures right in front of Homolka's eyes. She winced.

"And who's this?" he demanded, as the hushed courtroom looked on. Spectators had lined up for the start of the cross-examination since noon the previous day.

"My sister Tammy," Homolka replied, averting her eyes from the high-school picture.

Rosen showed her a second photo. "Who's this?" he asked.

"My sister Tammy," she repeated.

"On a gurney," Rosen added. "You saw her on the floor of your bedroom where you drugged her before you sexually assaulted her. It's a picture you can't possibly forget."

"That's correct," said a shaken Homolka.

"You'd think that these pictures, that nightmare, would have bothered your conscience every living moment of your existence."

"It did."

"Oh, it did, did it?" Rosen asked, returning to the lectern for a fresh batch of photos. He took several from an album and marched right back.

"See that picture?" he asked, sticking another photo in front of Homolka's face. "That's Leslie Mahaffy alive, isn't it?"

"Yes."

"You saw her. You know what happened to her. Right? You took part in the disposal of her body. Right?"

"Yes."

He showed Homolka the next picture. "That's the torso of Leslie Mahaffy after it came out of the cement block in the lake. You participated in that, right?"

"Yes."

"You'd have thought that would have bothered your conscience and driven you to do something, right?"

"Yes, I did do something," Homolka protested.

"We'll get to that in a moment," responded Rosen, thrusting a fresh picture before Homolka. "Who's that?"

"Kristen French."

"Kristen French alive. Fifteen years old."

"Yes."

"You know who that is?" Rosen continued, showing her yet another color photo. "That's Kristen French dead at the scene. Dumped in a ditch. And that?"

Homolka glanced at the next one, then turned away.

"Look at the picture!" Rosen ordered. "That's Kristen French dead on a gurney. I would have thought that would drive your conscience to do something. Keep you awake at night. Just dreaming of the day when you would have the opportunity to speak with someone to relieve your conscience. You'd think a normal person would do that, right?"

Homolka was close to tears. "I did," she said.

Her skin was a pale white, her hair stringy, and it seemed she was shrinking on the witness stand under Rosen's verbal barrage as he cataloged her kill count. For the packed gallery — for the country, for that matter — this morning was the unofficial start of the public trial Homolka had never had. Finally, two years after her closed-door court appearance,

Homolka was being made to answer for her crimes in an open court of law. And the gallery loved it.

"Zing it to her, Johnny," one spectator said quietly to his neighbor, then later asked Rosen for his autograph at the break.

Rosen's voice crackled with righteous indignation as he dived into what many thought an impossible defense of his client, a man who had been captured on videotape raping four young women. But he and Bryant had carefully mapped out their opening salvo.

Rosen returned to the lectern and began a slower series of questions about the beatings Homolka suffered just before she left Bernardo. After the pedantic questioning of Homolka by the chief Crown prosecutor, Rosen's dramatic start had the eight men and four women on the jury leaning forward in their seats. He then focused on the days immediately after she left Bernardo.

"When your parents rescued you and took you to their home, did you say you wanted to speak to the police about Kristen French, Leslie Mahaffy, and Tammy?"

"No, I was too scared."

Rosen plowed ahead, pointing out that Homolka eventually went to her aunt and uncle's apartment because Bernardo didn't know where they lived. "You went there so you'd be safe, right?"

"Yes."

"And to give yourself time to heal, and think about what to do?"

"Yes."

"Well, did you pick up the phone and call Green Ribbon, or the police, and say you wanted to speak with them about Kristen French, Leslie Mahaffy, and Tammy?"

Homolka had been backed into a corner by this deft questioning. She clearly had been in a safe haven, far away from her husband, who had been frantically searching for her. She had only one answer.

"No," she said glumly.

"You went out and had a heck of a time," Rosen said, referring to her affair with Jim Hutton at the Sugar Shack.

"No!" she protested.

"You were happy."

"Part of me."

Rosen knew there was more to her state of mind at the time than that glib response indicated. He had the initial statement she gave to the police. " 'I felt like I was seventeen,'" Rosen said, reading her words. " 'As soon as I left him, I was so happy. I couldn't believe I was so happy. I locked everything with him away in a corner of my mind. I forgot about Tammy. I forgot about Kristen. I forgot about Leslie. I forgot about everything, and went out and had a great time.' "

"That doesn't explain everything," Homolka said, but her protestations sounded hollow. "I had nightmares. I tried to forget. When you live in a relationship like that, it affects you in ways you never thought it would."

Rosen then focused on Homolka's reasons for not going to the police and confessing her role in the murders. "He had everything to lose, and nothing to gain, right? You were abused, and bludgeoned, but he was the murderer, the rapist. He loses everything. He's not going to call the police."

"Yes," Homolka acknowledged. "I was obviously not thinking straight or none of this would have happened."

"But you were thinking straight enough to cancel your credit cards," Rosen shot back, referring to how Homolka had canceled the joint cards she held with Bernardo so he couldn't make any more purchases on her tab.

Rosen then asked her about the Toronto police wanting to question her on a weekend. Although Rosen never said so to the jury, the interview was presumably about Bernardo's DNA samples, which had shown a match with those taken from several rape victims. But Homolka canceled the scheduled interview.

"I remember I had a funeral," she recalled.

"Well, let's see what else you did that weekend," Rosen said, and opened a folder chronicling Homolka's activities at the Segers'. "You went to the Sugar Shack," Rosen began, "where you met a man on Friday, and then again on Saturday, when you had sex with him."

"Yes," Homolka acknowledged.

Rosen moved on to the first interview Homolka had with the police after leaving Bernardo. "You never said one word to them about Kristen French or Leslie Mahaffy, did you?"

"No, I was too scared, and didn't know what to do."

"And when the police asked you about your sister you looked them right in the eye and told them the same lies of how your sister had too much to drink that night?"

"Yes."

Rosen asked about her visits to George Walker and her attempts to not go to jail for her crimes.

"I didn't know anything about law, or blanket immunity," she said.

Rosen was sarcastic in his response, pointing out that she was a voracious reader of crime books and had an I.Q. that put her in the top 2 percent of the population. "And you didn't know about blanket immunity?"

"That's right."

"Let me suggest to you that you knew very well what it means."

She clarified that she knew what it meant, but didn't know how to go about getting it. But Rosen wasn't buying that answer either.

"You knew that if you got it, then it would be good for you," he said.

"Yes."

But Homolka never got her blanket immunity, and after a series of meetings with the authorities, it was decided that she would receive 10 years in jail, "five years for Leslie and five years for Kristen," Rosen pointed out. Later the police found out the truth about Tammy, "and the deal changed slightly, from 10 to 12 years," Rosen continued. "Kristen was worth five, Leslie was worth five, and Tammy worth two."

"I wouldn't put it quite that way, Mr. Rosen."

"A long sentence, isn't it?" Rosen commented, his voice oozing sarcasm.

Several members of the gallery started grumbling out loud about the leniency of her deal, prompting the registrar to call for silence.

Rosen then pointed out that Homolka would be eligible for day parole after serving just four years, a bid for freedom that she acknowledged the authorities would not oppose.

As the first day of her cross-examination wore on, Homolka gained strength in her responses, several times challenging Rosen's questions and telling him he was being too simplistic in his evaluation of her marriage. Some color returned to her face, and she sat up straighter and stared right back at him. Her answers were sharp, clear. It was as if she had discovered a new inner strength after reeling under his blistering opening attack. Crown psychiatrists had said that Homolka, as a battered woman, would see Rosen as Bernardo's agent, and would hate him as much as she did her former husband.

Her counter-assault on Rosen didn't faze the veteran lawyer in the least. On the contrary: by being so aggressive, she was playing right into his game plan, coming across as a strong-willed, emotionless woman. Though she came close to crying several times, she never once broke down. It was as if Rosen was drawing out her true character, one the courtroom never saw during her scripted answers to Ray Houlahan. How could such a forceful woman be so easily manipulated by her husband into committing such atrocious crimes? How could she watch and do nothing while he killed two women? Homolka's credibility was sinking faster than the setting sun.

In the following days Rosen described her relationship with Bernardo as one driven by sex. These were two people whose hormones had run wild. To prove his point, he read out a series of often crude cards she had sent Paul while they were courting, and from him to her.

Although Homolka had told the Crown that Bernardo had started beating her during their courtship, there was no mention of the abuse in her letters to friends. Rosen read one, to Debbie Purdie, aloud: " 'Our wedding plans are going great . . . Our relationship gets better every day. He'll make the perfect husband. I can't wait 'til it's official.'

"This is, of course," Rosen said to Homolka, holding up her letter, "all this, acting?"

"Part of it," she replied. "As I said, he was still nice, but still abusing me. There was abuse, but there was also good times."

Rosen was leading up to Tammy Lyn. The two of them were preoccupied with sex and needed to involve a third person to increase their pleasure. "The two of you fantasized about having sex with Tammy," Rosen told her.

She shot back: "That is a lie!"

Rosen also suggested that Homolka was jealous of the attention her sister paid to Bernardo.

"I had no reason to be jealous of my sister."

Rosen asked her about the first time Bernardo said he wanted to have sex with her sister. "We're not talking about a stranger here, but your baby sister. Your parents trusted you to look after your baby sister. It was a breach of trust by you."

"Yes," Homolka acknowledged.

"The first time he mentioned having sex with your sister I would have thought you'd spring out of bed and say, 'There's no way I'm going to let you touch my baby sister.' Wouldn't that be the right reaction?"

"Yes."

"But you didn't do that?"

"No, I didn't."

"You thought, knock her out and have some sex with her. What's the harm?"

"I didn't know her safety would be in danger," Homolka blurted. "I was afraid he would do it regardless. I was afraid he would just grab her off the street and rape her. This was the best way. I had no choice." This response, suggesting that the rape was inevitable, but that at least this way she could watch over her baby sister, left many in the courtroom shaking their heads in disbelief.

Less than two days into his cross-examination, Rosen had already elicited from Homolka her warped code of ethics. Here was a woman who handed her baby sister over to the man she loved, and then tried to justify her decision by cloaking it in a warped morality.

"Did you ever think that letting her get sexually molested was a violation of her body?" Rosen asked, barely able to contain his disgust.

"I didn't think her life would be in danger. That's all I'm saying. I did not know Tammy would die. I thought it would happen once and it would all be over."

But the worst for Homolka was yet to come as Rosen

moved on with his grilling. He read out several letters she had written to her friend Debbie Purdie, including the one in which she bragged about her new house.

" 'I finally have some good news in my life,' " he quoted. " 'Paul and I are moving in together. Yes, we'll be living in sin. We've got a beautiful house in Port Dalhousie … I fell in love with the house and so did Paul when we saw it.'

"This is someone," Rosen asked about the letter, "who claims to hate the man she's forced to live with? You couldn't wait to tell the world, your friends, how you and Paul were moving in together."

"I told them all, yes," Homolka agreed.

Rosen continued, slowly building to his next point. He asked about her parents' concern about a wedding coming so soon after her sister's death. "Your parents were starting to wonder about the wedding, right? They're still in mourning. But you, you've forgotten about your sister, haven't you?"

"That's not true," she shot back.

"Karla, we don't think the wedding is a good idea," Rosen said, quoting to her what her parents had said.

"Yes," she answered.

"They were short on cash, weren't they? They wanted you to let it go for another year, or go to city hall. Paul told them to mortgage the house if they didn't have the money."

She agreed it was true.

Rosen reached for another letter. Just as he did, Homolka's parents got up from their front-row seats and walked out of the courtroom.

"I guess after that meeting with your parents," Rosen continued, "you said things you shouldn't have said. You know what's coming next, don't you?"

"Yes."

Rosen read a second letter she had written to Purdie just before her marriage. In it she talked about wanting a dog, her new house, the color of her carpets, about how there were too many immigrants in Toronto, her upcoming wedding, and what gifts she wanted. And she had some advice for her friend: "The world will screw you in every way it can, Deb. So take as much as you can, while you can."

Then she started talking about her parents. Rosen read: " 'My wedding plans are great, except for my parents being such assholes. They pulled out half of the money from the wedding saying they couldn't afford it. Bullshit!!! Now Paul and I have to pay for seven or eight thousand dollars of the wedding. We've been compromising like crazy; a cash bar, no flowers on the table, etc. Finally Paul and I said fuck it! We're going to do everything we planned. Real flowers. No paying for the bar. Cocktails. Everything!!!

" 'Fucking parents. They are being so stupid. Only thinking of themselves. My father doesn't even want us to have a wedding. He thinks we should just go to the hall. Screw that! If he wants to sit at home and be miserable, he's welcome to it. He hasn't worked, except for one day, since Tammy died. He's wallowing in his own misery, and fucking me.

" 'It sounds awful on paper, but I know you really see what I'm saying. Tammy always said she wanted a Porsche on her sixteenth birthday. Now my dad keeps saying, "I should have bought it." Bull! If he really felt like that he'd be paying for my wedding because I could die tomorrow, or next year. He's such a liar.

" 'And for the real reason we moved out. My parents told Paul and I that they wanted him to stay at the house until the wedding. Then they said they wanted him to go after Tammy died because they needed their privacy. First they took away half the wedding money, and then they kicked us out. They knew how much we needed to be together, but they didn't care. What assholes!!!' "

The letter was a further contradiction of Homolka's earlier statements that she was numb after the death of her sister and didn't want to marry the man she later described as a monster. Taken at face value, the letter exposed her as a liar, not to mention cold-hearted, selfish, and insensitive to her parents' grief.

Rosen had effectively shown the jurors another side to the enigmatic woman, one in which she was the mirror image of the man on trial. Homolka was looking less and less a victim and more like the weak accomplice who was beaten up a lot by the dominant partner.

Despite the litany of abuse Homolka suffered, there wasn't much sympathy in the gallery, which was enjoying the public flogging of a confessed killer. Rosen was clearly reveling in his exposure of what he believed was Homolka's true character. In the process he was setting the groundwork for the final phase of his cross-examination: his theories on who really killed the two schoolgirls in the pretty pink house in Port Dalhousie that he labeled "the Venus Flytrap."

Taking Homolka through the abduction, rape, and murder of Leslie Mahaffy, Rosen asked her about her thoughts when Bernardo woke her up to say he had a girl in the house. "It must have crossed your mind that there was an abduction and you didn't want to be implicated. All you had to do was reach over and call 911, and the police would've found him with her?"

"Yes."

"Or you could have got dressed and left. Got out of the house because you were innocent?"

Again she agreed.

"But, in fact, you weren't so innocent. You were partners in this and it was just a question of time when the two-way sex would become three-way sex."

"I figured that was coming, but I didn't want to do it."

"It's a crime not to call the police when you know something is wrong. But you were an innocent victim."

"I don't like that phrase. I was involved. I was in the house and I didn't call the police."

"And did that bother your conscience?"

"I can't say. So many things have bothered my conscience."

"Instead of being concerned about what was going on, you sat upstairs and read a book. And then you started a second one."

"Books are a great way to escape reality, Mr. Rosen."

Rosen asked her why she had got so mad when she noticed Bernardo had used their fine crystal goblets to give Mahaffy some champagne after he raped her. "You were angry and you confronted Paul . . . and he said he was sorry. He wanted to avoid the wrath of Karla."

"It may be difficult to understand," she replied, using a line straight out of a textbook on battered women, "but one way to get through it was to act as normal as possible."

Rosen then played the tapes that showed Mahaffy on the toilet, taking off her clothes, having a shower, being anally raped, and having sex with Homolka, who smiled several times for the camera. The lawyer asked about the beatings she said Bernardo inflicted on the prisoner, so brutal, she had said to the police, that she had to turn away. "He beat her to the point where he wouldn't give up. He beat her so bad he didn't hear you asking him to stop."

"I didn't feel like I could do anything."

"That girl must have been black and blue all over.

Internally, she must have had bruises for every single place he hit her."

Rosen then read out parts of the autopsy report. The pathologists, he said, found no bruising on the body. Except for one place. "Two small circles almost side by side on her spinal column. The bruising is consistent with a pair of knees the size of your knees when you held her head down on a pillow and suffocated her."

That comment drew a denial from Homolka and an objection from Ray Houlahan. Rosen pressed on.

"You had a discussion about what to do with her, and Paul wanted to let her go."

"That's a lie!"

"I suggest to you that Paul said all you had to do was drive her back to Burlington and let her go."

"That's a lie!" she repeated.

"You had just as much motive to want her dead."

"I didn't want her to die."

"But you didn't want her in the house?"

"Yes."

"At this point, you must have really hated Paul."

"I hated him."

"He pushed you into sexually assaulting your sister. He brought this stranger home and forced you to participate in sex acts. And he's punishing you and beating you."

Rosen picked up one of her earlier statements to the police. He read back her words: " 'I was very upset because I didn't want him to go to jail. I didn't hate him that much at that point. I was really afraid of myself going to jail.' "

"I didn't want to marry him," Homolka said, repeating a familiar line from her time on the stand.

Rosen read some of the cards and letters Homolka had written to her husband after the murder of Mahaffy. "I love you so much," began one. "Once we were an unbeatable team, you and me against the world. Best friends to the end. I want our love back. People think that we are the perfect couple. We are! We've just gotten sidetracked. Even though we have our problems, I still want to be in love with you. I'm still so much in love with you. I want us to put our arms around each other and fall in love all over again. Some couples are meant to be, and we're one of those.

"The happiest days of my life were the day we met, and most of all the day we married. We still have a lot of love left for each other. Please honey, let's try to have a fairytale marriage like we were meant to. All my love, Karly Curls."

Rosen turned his questioning to the abduction of Kristen French. On his sixth day of cross-examination he wanted to know what was going through Homolka's mind as she watched Bernardo take another prisoner up to their bedroom. "My God, you must have thought. Another girl is going to be killed at my house."

"I don't know what I thought."

"Did you think of your dead sister? Did you think of Leslie Mahaffy? Did you call 911?"

"No, and I have to live with that for the rest of my life."

"Did you think of running from the house?"

"I felt helpless, very, very helpless."

"More helpless than Kristen French?"

"I can't say how she felt."

"But you did nothing to help the girl?"

"No . . . I didn't."

Rosen focused his questions on the time when French had a black cord around her neck that was tied to the hope chest in the master bedroom. "I suggest to you," he said, "that she was bound like that when he went out the second time to get the food."

"No," Homolka insisted, "that's wrong."

"She'd be in a rather dangerous position with a cord around her neck."

"Yes."

"There'd be a lot of friction on that cord."

"I don't know."

"If she were to struggle against the cord, she could strangle herself."

"I don't know how to answer that."

"Paul was attracted to her, wasn't he? He wanted to keep her longer."

"Yes."

"But you knew that was impossible."

"Yes."

"All weekend you had been getting calls from people who wanted to come over to the house."

"I'm not positive."

"You had to go to your parents' house for Sunday Easter dinner and Paul said just cancel it so he could stay home and play with the sex slave."

"He said something like that."

"And you had to go to work on Monday."

"Yes."

"And you knew that if she got away a short time later the police would be knocking on your door. You knew she had to die."

"I knew that was what Paul had planned to do from the beginning."

"And you knew that Paul wanted to keep her for a while longer and you didn't."

"I didn't want the girl in my house when I was at work."

"And when you were alone with her when he went for food she tried to get away."

"She never tried!"

"She asked if she could go to the bathroom and then she gave you a shove and you went after her with the mallet."

"That's not true."

"And you can't help us explain the deep bruises on both sides of her face. Bruises not from a fist, but more like a mallet."

"I didn't hit her."

"The reason you can't help us explain the bruises is that you're the one who hit her when she tried to escape."

"I never hit anyone."

"She's dead on the floor when he came back with the food and you said she died trying to escape and you had to hit her."

"No, that's a lie!"

Rosen turned to the day she left Bernardo. "There's evidence you had to be dragged from the house."

"I was terrified. I was staying with that marriage because he had stuff over my head. Until you've been in that situation, you'd never understand."

As Homolka was led from the courtroom and taken back to her prison cell in Kingston after 16 days on the witness stand, few people did understand her and her twisted sense of values. Though intelligent and seemingly aware of her crimes, she seemed unashamed of what she had done because she believed her former husband had forced her to do it. That left many wondering what would happen if she met another man like Bernardo when she got out of jail.

42
Crime and Punishment

For 47 days Bernardo had sat quietly in the prisoner's dock, listening attentively to each of the 85 prosecution witnesses, patiently waiting for his turn to take the stand. On the forty-eighth day, John Rosen told the court the first witness for the defense would be Bernardo himself.

"A trial is like a jigsaw puzzle," he told the jurors. "You take each piece and you get a feel for it, but you don't rush to put together a picture until you've seen all the different pieces. You've already heard from one of the two people in the house who's still alive. Why not call the other witness to the stand and hear what he has to say?"

Bernardo strode confidently up to the witness box, looking at each of the jurors as he passed by. Young Hype wore a dark blue suit, crisp white shirt and floral tie for his center-stage appearance.

Prosecutors had been frustrated in their efforts to get the writings of Paul Bernardo introduced as evidence. Judge LeSage had ruled the bookkeeper's personal thoughts inadmissible. Prosecutors had wanted to show the jurors that the man who penned the words: "A professional liar, with time to waste . . . You got no confession, you got no case" was really writing about himself and was not to be believed, no matter how convincing he sounded.

Bernardo chose to stand in the box and kept his back ram-rod straight, like a drill sergeant's. Yes, that was him on the tapes, he told Rosen, raping Kristen French and Leslie Mahaffy. Sure, he was a kidnapper and a rapist, he told the court, but he was no killer. A man had to have some moral principles.

"I know I've done some terrible things, and caused sadness and sorrow to many people," he said, coming as close to an apology as he ever would. "And I know I deserve to be punished. But I didn't kill those girls."

Karla Homolka had been vague and confusing during her 16 days in the box; Bernardo was just the opposite. In a firm voice he peeled back the thin veneer that had hidden his true character and gave the court a rare, if sketchy, insight into the forces that drove him. Sex was the primary force in his life with Homolka, he said. The couple who had gone to bed an hour after they met had later turned to bondage, then threesomes, when they became increasingly bored with each other's bodies. Tammy Lyn was an experiment, Bernardo claimed, and after they assaulted the unconscious child both "thought it was neat . . . and wanted to do it again."

According to Bernardo, the couple's passion for three-way sex increased dramatically after Tammy's death. "It was all we talked about," he said. And when he kidnapped the two young schoolgirls, he claimed he was doing it as much for his wife as for his own enjoyment — he never wanted to kill either one. In fact, he went on, he wasn't even in the room when Mahaffy died, possibly smothered to death by a pillow at the hands of Homolka, as Rosen had suggested. And French had died while trying to escape. Again he had been out of the house at the time.

All through his testimony it was "we" who did everything, as in "we liked having sex slaves in the house;" "we liked making the homemade pornographic videos." There was no reason the two girls had to die, he said. "What we did was just for the sex."

Whether he was talking about smuggling cigarettes, or about how the saw blade jammed up when he was slicing through Mahaffy's shoulder, Bernardo's voice had a breezy tone to it. Cutting up Mahaffy's body was the most disgusting thing he had ever done, he testified. But he was referring more to the grossness of the act than to its morality. The apparent absence of remorse was in keeping with one psychiatrist's evaluation:

"There is nothing I have seen in the evidence available that he has, or has had, a major illness of the psychotic type. That is, he is fully in touch with reality," wrote Dr. Stephen John Hucker in one court brief. "Everything that I have reviewed indicates that he was fully aware that his behavior was legally and morally wrong."

He didn't have to hit Mahaffy, Bernardo told the court, because she was "compliant . . . didn't cause any problems." Never mind that it was wrong to strike anybody, period. Mahaffy had co-operated with his fantasies and didn't have to be punished. He was saying that the fulfillment of his desires came first, and nothing else mattered. French, though, he had had to beat because she wasn't doing a good job of giving him oral sex. She failed to live up to his standards, and needed to be taught a lesson.

"How could you go through life with all these horrible things on your mind?" asked Rosen.

Bernardo had a ready answer. "We tried to block it out of our minds." Rather than agonize, Bernardo sought to ensure his positive mental health by simply forgetting about the unpleasant side effects of his fantasies.

"Why did you do this?" Rosen asked about the abduction of French.

His sex life with Homolka had evolved, Bernardo replied. It had run wild. The pair, he said, were out of control.

But even after raping and beating French, he still thought that perhaps they could be friends. One night he wanted the three of them to sleep together in the same bed. "Our fantasy," he said, "was to have three people together and love one another and be happy."

He wanted to keep French alive, and captive, for a long time, he said, because he was unemployed and didn't have much else to do with his time. Both he and Homolka were sad and upset when she died, he said. They hugged one another, and cried. And then they got rid of the body.

Bernardo thought the two deaths would bind him and Homolka together for the rest of their lives. But their marriage fell apart after French's death, he said. He beat his wife just before she left him, he said, because she didn't show enough emotion when they talked about her dead baby sister.

Rosen wanted to know if Bernardo had thought about his crimes while sitting in his jail cell.

"Yes, sir," he answered, "a lot. When I look back at how our sex fantasies hurt so many people I can't believe I was the same person."

When Crown Prosecutor Ray Houlahan got his chance to cross-examine Bernardo, he went through the Mahaffy videotapes again, frame by excruciating frame. And to assist Bernardo in hearing some dialogue — and no doubt to re-focus the minds of the jurors on who was the lead character — he had the sound cranked up.

Leslie Mahaffy's screams filled the cavernous courtroom, leaving many spectators wincing.

"I want to see my family, my friends again," she sobbed. "Please. Please!"

There was a phrase Houlahan asked Bernardo if he could hear. When he said he couldn't, Houlahan played the tape again with the sound even louder. It was the line, "Help me."

"She's pleading for her life," the prosecutor said, his voice heavy with the contempt he felt for Bernardo, "and you're raping her vaginally and anally. Who's she asking for help?"

"She's asking for help," Bernardo acknowledged. "She wants to go home."

At the start of his testimony Bernardo had often turned to the jurors, gesticulating and looking at each in turn while offering his detailed responses. But after several days in the box, Houlahan was beginning to wear him down by replaying the videos, tapes which clearly showed Bernardo — despite his repeated denials — obviously controlling the show. Eventually the cockiness disappeared from his voice and his posture didn't seem quite as erect. He didn't look at the jurors so often. Houlahan, while not flashy, was effective with his persistent, at times plodding, style. He was getting the job done, even if it wasn't as dramatic as Perry Mason courtroom TV.

Houlahan then went through every one of the French tapes. Slowly. Towards the end of the cross-examination some people in the gallery began covering their ears to avoid listening to French's cries. In one segment, French was heard to call Bernardo "the master" over and over.

"She's desperately trying to please you, trying to say the things you want her to hear?"

"Correct," Bernardo acknowledged.

Houlahan pointed out that in the segment Bernardo was getting anilingus from his wife, while he was raping French. Bernardo, trying to bring in Homolka as much as he could, astonished the gallery by saying, "I think we were both raping Kristen French, not just me."

"But she's calling you the king, isn't she?" Houlahan shot back.

"I liked, at the time, to be called that during sex," he answered, as if he wanted the jurors to believe he had suddenly rid himself of all his sexual dysfunctions.

"You're the dominant person here," Houlahan persisted.

"Both Karla and me are dominant," Bernardo responded. It just didn't sound believable.

In response to another series of questions, Bernardo attempted to explain the evolution of his six-year sexual relationship with Homolka, trying to incriminate her as much as he could: "It started off with Karla and me in handcuffs. Then Karla and me in the dog collar. Karla and me in the pictures. Then Karla and me with pictures of other women. And finally Karla and me with other women. If she wasn't happy, she would have left."

That answer enraged Houlahan.

"Did you ever wear handcuffs when having sex with women?"

"No sir, I can't recall."

"Did you ever wear a choke collar?"

"No sir, I can't recall."

"Were you ever tied or bound while having sex?"

"No sir, I can't recall."

"It's always the other way around, isn't it?" Houlahan asked pointedly. "That pretty well tells the story, doesn't it?"

Paul Bernardo, 31 was convicted of all nine charges against him in the kidnapping, rape, and murder of Kristen French and Leslie Mahaffy. He still faces the possibility of two more trials, one for a series of sexual assaults blamed on the Scarborough Rapist and for the assault on Jane, and a second on a charge of manslaughter in the death of Tammy Lyn Homolka.

Under recent changes in Canadian laws, he can start applying for parole after 25 years, in 2020, when he is fifty-six years old.

At 12:05 p.m. on Friday, September 1, 1995, the jury came back with its verdict after eight hours of deliberation. Bernardo, flanked by defense lawyers Tony Bryant and John Rosen, rose and faced the eight men and four women who were about to deliver his fate. The foreman stood. Judge LeSage asked him if the jurors had reached a decision.

"Yes," he replied.

And when asked the verdict on each of the nine counts he replied, "Guilty."

"First-degree murder."

"Guilty."

"First-degree murder in the death of Kristen French and Leslie Mahaffy."

"Guilty."

"First-degree murder in the kidnappings, confinement and aggravated sexual assaults."

"Guilty."

The families of the two girls were in the public gallery softly crying as the decision was read out. LeSage then sentenced Bernardo to life in jail with no parole for 25 years. When this book went to press, prosecutors were planning to make a motion to have Bernardo declared a dangerous offender, therefore keeping him in jail literally for life.

Epilogue
Loose Ends

Karla Homolka was never charged for her involvement in the rape of Jane. Whereas Paul Bernardo was eventually charged with sexual assault in the attack, Homolka avoided prosecution, although she was there when the woman was drugged with sleeping pills and stripped naked. The pair then assaulted Jane, and took turns videotaping their actions.

As part of her plea-bargaining deal, Homolka was to tell the authorities about any other crimes she and Bernardo might have committed, beyond their involvement in the deaths of French, Mahaffy, and Tammy Lyn. Under the terms of her deal, she was liable for further charges if the police ever found out — on their own — that she had committed other crimes and not told them.

Two months after signing the plea resolution, when Homolka went to court to face trial on the pre-arranged package, the Canadian journalists allowed to attend the trial — but not to report on it at the time — listened to all the evidence presented. But no mention was ever made at Homolka's trial about how the pair had drugged and sexually assaulted Jane.

And that was because the authorities didn't know about the attack at the time of Homolka's trial. They learned about it only *after* Homolka's trial, when she first revealed it. The victim had never reported the incident to the police.

In October 1993, three months after her trial, Homolka wrote a letter to her lawyer, George Walker, informing him of her possible involvement. Her recollections of the assault were hazy, she said, but she believed she had been lying with her back to Jane when Bernardo raped the unconscious teen in the living room of their home in 1992. It was an attack eerily similar to that on her sister Tammy Lyn.

The police later questioned Homolka about the incident, and she recalled taking Jane to their bedroom afterwards, where she watched over the teenager until she awakened, just to ensure she was okay. Some six months later, however, the police received a videotape that clearly showed that Homolka's role was far greater than what she had previously claimed.

Homolka was seen putting an ether-like substance over the teenager's mouth and then taking part in both oral sex with her and digital penetration. When police went back to question her again, she told them she was having dreams about her involvement in the attack, nightly visions that showed she was doing more to the girl than she had first believed. But she claimed her memories were still hazy, saying that some internal defense mechanism was preventing her from full recall. Although apparently caught in a lie, Homolka still wasn't charged in the attack.

Before they resigned from the case, Bernardo's defense team of Carolyn MacDonald and Ken Murray tried to find out about the Jane incident. They questioned Homolka in 1994, about a year after her trial, at the Prison for Women in Kingston.

"Are you currently facing any new charges?" MacDonald asked Homolka.

Also in the room were Murray, Crown prosecutor Ray Houlahan, and Niagara Region police detectives Scott Kenney and Robert Gillies.

"No," replied Homolka.

"Has there been any discussion about a charge being laid against you with respect to [Jane]?" MacDonald asked.

Again the answer was no.

"Have you received an undertaking that there won't be any charges with respect to [Jane]?" MacDonald pressed.

Once more, Homolka said no.

"Is that something you are concerned about?"

"No."

"Why?"

"I'm just not."

Later, MacDonald asked Homolka about the letter she had written to George Walker in October 1993, nearly five months after she had signed the deal with provincial law authorities, in which she discussed her involvement in the assault. When prosecutors Houlahan and Greg Barnett had talked to Homolka about Jane, they had made some notes of the interview. It was these notes that MacDonald now referred to.

"The [Barnett] notes say: 'Karla points out that she came forward about this' " — a reference to Jane. " 'She says she wants to tell what she knew, even though she might be charged with another offense.' Do you remember discussing that with Mr. Barnett and Mr. Houlahan?"

"No."

"Were you concerned about another charge when you revealed the information that is contained in that letter?" MacDonald pressed.

"It wasn't at the top of my mind."

"Was the issue of a charge something you discussed with your counsel?"

"No."

"Excuse me," Houlahan interrupted, "but it is my duty, as it is your duty under the rules of professional conduct, to advise the witness that any communication between herself and her lawyer is privileged, and she would have to consult her lawyer in order to obtain his advice as to whether or not she should waive that privilege."

During that interview, Homolka said she didn't want to disclose confidential communications between herself and her lawyer. At Bernardo's trial, however, she told the court she was going to waive privilege and would testify about the discussions with her lawyer. Her change of heart came after Bernardo's defense team subpoenaed Walker's file on her plea discussion with the Crown.

During Bernardo's trial, she admitted she was worried about "getting into trouble . . . getting punished" over her role in the assault on Jane. But she stuck to her story that she couldn't recall details of the attack.

"My mind won't let me remember," she said. "My mind does this to me."

And later: "I've told the truth from the beginning, with the exception of the first interview [at Calvin and Patti Seger's apartment] with the Metro police."

When MacDonald and Murray interviewed Homolka in jail, MacDonald read to her a section of the plea-bargaining deal where she agreed to co-operate with the authorities in their investigation of Bernardo: " 'She will provide all reasonable and lawful assistance in permitting the police to recover real evidence . . . relevant to the inquiries.' "

MacDonald then asked Homolka if she had authorized Walker to release her original letter about Jane to the authorities.

"Yes," she replied. Earlier she had said: "I put my trust and my faith in my lawyer to do all the negotiations, to do what he thought was right."

Also during that interview in 1994, MacDonald asked Homolka if the police had spoken to her about the unsolved murders of two other women, Lynda Shaw and Cindy Halliday.

"Are you attributing any criminal misconduct to Paul Bernardo in connection with the Lynda Shaw [murder]?" MacDonald asked her.

"No, I'm not."

Earlier, when detectives from the Ontario Provincial Police had interviewed Homolka on the same matter, her answer had been just as terse.

"Not his type," she had told them. If Bernardo murdered Shaw, he never bragged to her about it, Homolka had told the detectives. But Homolka also acknowledged that Bernardo had kept many secrets from her during their six-year relationship.

Shaw, an engineering student at the University of Western Ontario, had apparently been kidnapped late one evening in 1990, after she pulled off the highway to fix a flat tire. Weeks later, her burned and mutilated body was discovered near a Lovers' Lane, not far from where police found her abandoned car.

Although the OPP had put together a huge task force, the killer, or killers, were never found. Witnesses later said they saw at least two, and perhaps three, people near the spot where Shaw's charred remains were left.

Detectives were running out of leads when a man identifying himself as Jim Gold sent a letter to the police revealing details of the murder that only the killer could know. Several detectives tried to find the letter writer, without success. The case was then put on the back burner, until Bernardo's arrest in February 1993.

Investigators looked at Bernardo as a possible suspect. A duffel coat had been found near Shaw's body, and investigators had speculated that it probably belonged to the killer. At one time Bernardo had owned a similar coat. Bernardo also liked to cruise the highways on the lookout for victims. Shaw had also been abducted and murdered on an Easter weekend, as had Kristen French.

Even if Bernardo had nothing to do with Shaw's slaying, investigators still wanted to clear him as a possible suspect. To do that, they had gone to the Kingston prison to interview Homolka. But she wasn't much help to them. After looking at a picture of Shaw, she said the young woman didn't look like Bernardo's type. She admitted that she didn't know where Bernardo was the weekend that Shaw was murdered, but doubted he had anything to do with it. Bernardo, she said, liked them younger, and with long blond hair. Shaw's hair was short and dark. The interview ended any further speculation, detectives said later.

But had the investigators eliminated all the possible connections between Paul Bernardo and the murder of Lynda Shaw? At least one handwriting expert approached privately about the case has suggested that the printing in the Jim Gold letter is similar to the printing on some government documents Bernardo signed in 1990, the year of the Shaw murder. Another expert, however, says no.

Although it is in no way evidence of Bernardo's involvement in the Shaw murder, he did once tell Homolka about his plans to kidnap and rape a woman using a scheme that bore a remarkable resemblance to what may have happened in the Shaw murder. His plan was to look for lone female motorists at a shopping mall in St. Catharines, he told Homolka. When he found a suitable candidate, he would put a nail in a tire of her car and then follow her. When she pulled over to the side of the road to fix it, he would offer to help her and, if the conditions were right, would abduct her.

Detectives have speculated that this was a possible

scenario in the Shaw murder. She had pulled over to the side of the highway to fix a flat tire not long after leaving a burger stand. It was possible, detectives said, that someone, possibly her killer, could have jimmied her tire while she was at the highway rest stop, causing it to deflate soon after she was back on the road.

Homolka's responses to questions from MacDonald about the second unsolved murder, that of Cindy Halliday, were vaguely non-committal.

"Are you aware of any other force that wishes to interview you?" she was asked.

"Yes," she replied. "The Ontario Provincial Police in Barrie, regarding Cindy Halliday."

"Has that been arranged?"

"No, it hasn't."

"Will you be providing statements about any criminal activity associated with Paul Bernardo in the death of Cindy Halliday?"

"No, I won't."

Halliday disappeared near Barrie, a city north of Toronto, in April 1992, five days after Kristen French was abducted in St. Catharines. Bernardo's possible connection to her murder was bolstered by a story told by a man in jail. The inmate said to his cellmate that Bernardo knew Halliday, adding that he knew the man who had introduced Bernardo to the blond-haired teenager. But by the time police heard the story and went to check it out, the inmate had died from a drug overdose.

Halliday's murder had received little attention at the time, as police forces everywhere were focused on the French abduction. Halliday had last been seen hitching a ride on Easter Monday at the end of the bus line on Highway 27. Her dismembered remains were later found in a secluded area used by teenagers as a Lovers' Lane. She had been stabbed repeatedly.

A man picking mushrooms found the body, minus its head. That was found later, propped up on a rock. The area where the head was found had earlier been searched by police, and detectives believed the killer had returned later and put it there to mock the investigators.

The police checked the usual suspects in Halliday's death: boyfriends, acquaintances, known sex offenders who lived in the area. All were cleared. When Bernardo was arrested, the focus shifted onto him.

What investigators found was that Bernardo often traveled the highway where Halliday was last seen. He skied in the area, had friends who lived there, and sold cigarettes to bikers whose clubhouse was nearby.

Although investigators could put Bernardo in the area where Halliday vanished, they couldn't place him there specifically on the Monday afternoon she vanished. On the other hand, they knew that Bernardo had vanished from his home in Port Dalhousie on Monday, the day after he killed Kristen French. He simply drove off, Homolka told the police, and didn't return for about 24 hours, never telling Homolka where he went. That was more than enough time for him to drive to the Barrie area and abduct and murder Halliday.

But that's where the investigation ended. The police had their suspicions, but no proof. Detectives attempted to talk to Homolka about the Halliday murder, but government officials turned down requests for interviews. No reason was given. As with Lynda Shaw, the murder of Cindy Halliday has been put on the back burner, unsolved.

Appendix

Karla Homolka received what has been termed a "sweetheart deal" in exchange for her testimony against Paul Bernardo. At the time prosecutors desperately needed her evidence to put him behind bars. Although Homolka agreed to co-operate fully it later became clear that she was less than forthcoming about the extent of her involvement in the series of sex crimes that started with the death of her sister.

The following is a chronology of events in the signing of what with hindsight seems arguably the worst deal the Canadian system has ever made with a criminal:

January 5, 1993: Homolka leaves her husband after he beat her with a flashlight.

February 9: Her first interview with the police about her husband's involvement in a series of rapes in Scarborough. She keeps silent about her role in the murders of Kristen French and Leslie Mahaffy, the death of her sister, Tammy Lyn, and the rape of a woman known as Jane Doe.

February 17: After consulting a lawyer, Homolka asks for blanket immunity in exchange for her testimony in the French and Mahaffy murders. She still does not tell the authorities about her sister or Jane.

February 26: a tentative agreement is reached in which Homolka will get ten years in jail for manslaughter in the French and Mahaffy killings.

March 5: Homolka finally admits, in a letter to her parents, the truth about the death of her sister. When the authorities learn about this, they decide not to charge her in the death, but give her two extra years in prison.

May 14: Homolka signs the formal plea arrangement (see below). Her tab: 12 years for three killings. The authorities agree to tell parole officials that she co-operated with them when she applies for early release after serving four years. Under the terms of the deal, she is supposed to have told the police about any other crimes in which she was involved.

July 6: Homolka's closed-door trial, from which the public and American journalists are barred, begins. Canadian journalists are allowed to witness the trial, but cannot report on it until after Bernardo's day in court.

October 9: Homolka "remembers" her involvement in the rape of Jane, after having a dream about the assault while in prison. The police are notified, but are later given tapes that show Homolka's role in the assault was far more extensive than she originally described. When later asked for an explanation, Homolka says the attack was so traumatic she had blocked it from her mind.

September 22, 1994: The videotapes are handed over to prosecutors.

June 1, 1995: Two weeks before she takes the stand at Bernardo's trial, Homolka is assured that she will not be charged in the rape of Jane, even though she has apparently broken the terms of the deal by not telling the police about the assault before her agreement was signed.

Karla Homolka's deal:

Office of the Director

Ministry of the Attorney General

May 14, 1993

Mr. George F. Walker, Q.C.
Barrister and Solicitor

Dear Sir:

I am writing to confirm our mutual understanding respecting
a proposed resolution as between the Crown and Karla
Bernardo. It has been arrived at after lengthy discussions. If
you are in agreement I would be obliged if you would confirm
same in writing.

As I understand it, your client, after receiving legal advice,
has chosen to engage in a process that may lead to a resolution of certain investigations in her case. Your client's position
is that she is permanently estranged from her husband with no
interest nor prospect or reconciliation. She has received legal
advice regarding spousal immunity and is prepared to speak
to the police and to testify regarding certain matters as
described below.

The outline of the proposed resolution is that your client will
provide an induced statement. If the authorities are satisfied at
that stage, she will provide cautioned statements. At that point
your client will be charged, waive the preliminary inquiry,
plead guilty, and be sentenced to twelve years imprisonment,
subject to a judge's approval. I have now had the opportunity
to discuss, in general terms, the proposed resolution with the

families of the victims. I am totally satisfied that there exists admissible evidence respecting your client's involvement in the crimes for which pleas will be entered. I am in a position to proceed with the proposed resolution. The following represents the terms of our understanding.

A   Induced Statement

1.   Your client will attend upon the police.

2.   The induced statement will not be used against her in any criminal proceedings.

3.   She will give permission for audio and video taping.

4.   It will be forthright and truthful. It will be complete, bearing in mind it is an initial statement.

5.   No assurances can or will be given respecting derivative evidence.

6.   Upon completion, the Crown and the police will assess it to determine whether they are satisfied that it has been given in a forthright and truthful manner.

7.   The police may decide that a second induced statement is required if insufficient time is set aside for the initial one.

8.   If the authorities learn through any means that your client has caused the death of any person, in the sense of her stopping life, any proposed resolution will be terminated at the suit of the Crown, regardless of the state the process is at.

9.   If any of the above matters are not to the satisfaction of the Crown, resolution discussions will be terminated and if no cautioned statement has been taken, the induced statement will not be used against her.

10.   The statement and any subsequent statement will be a full, complete, and truthful account regarding her

knowledge and/or involvement or anyone else's
involvement in the investigations to the deaths of
Leslie Mahaffy; Kristen French; the death of Tammy
Homolka; and any other criminal activity she has
participated in or has knowledge of.

B   Cautioned Statement(s)

1.   They will be under caution.
2.   They will be under oath.
3.   Permission will be granted to audio and video tape.
4.   They will provide no protection for a prosecution if
      it is discovered that she lied, including a prosecution
      for obstruct justice, public mischief, fabricating evi-
      dence, perjury, inconsistent statements and/or false
      affidavits.
5.   The video taped statement(s) will be used at any
      criminal proceeding if she recants, or if the Crown
      otherwise tenders them, or if a judge permits their use.
6.   They will be complete, full, and forthright.
7.   She shall fairly set out the roles or knowledge of all
      parties and witness to the crimes under investigation,
      including her role and knowledge.

C   Other Assistance

1.   She will provide all reasonable and lawful assistance
      in permitting the police to recover real evidence, and
      providing written authority to police to recover real
      evidence relevant to the inquiries. She will assist the
      police in their inquiries relating to any real evidence
      in relation to anyone who is associated with the
      crimes under investigation.

2.   She will voluntarily provide fingerprints, handwriting, hair and blood samples and like matters.

3.   She will provide a witnessed, written consent to the seizure of all items from 57 Bayview Drive, St. Catharines from February 19 to April 30, 1993, and such other consents respecting real evidence and information as may be requested by the Crown.

D   **Charge, Plea, and Sentencing**

1.   Upon conclusion of the receipt of voluntary cautioned statements as such time as the police require, she will be charged.

2.   She will be charged with two counts of manslaughter in relation to the Mahaffy and French homicides. The defense will consent to the reading in of facts of any other crimes as the Crown deems appropriate, the sentence of twelve years and twelve years concurrent taking into account any such additional matters.

3.   She shall waive the preliminary inquiry when the Crown deems appropriate.

4.   An indictment shall be presented.

5.   A joint submission shall be made for a total sentence of twelve years, comprised of two terms of twelve years concurrent with each other. A s. 100 weapons order will be requested.

6.   It is not the intention of the Crown to seek an increase in parole eligibility, given all the circumstances of these matters, including the total sentence that will be sought.

7.   The Crown is prepared to agree that your client be remanded out of custody, subject to the court's approval, for three weeks, but on satisfactory sureties

and in an amount exceeding $100,000, and with such conditions as the Crown may require pending sentence.

8. The acceptance of the pleas of guilty, the charges, the sentences, the period of parole ineligibility, and remand out of custody pending sentence are subject to acceptance by the trial judge.

9. A refusal by a judge to accept the charges upon which pleas are to be entered, or the proposed sentences, will result in a trial being held on whatever charges the police and the Crown deem appropriate. In such circumstances, the admissibility of the cautioned statements is not affected.

10. The Crown's position on sentencing of twelve years, and no less, will take into account any assistance given and proposed, the early pleas, and like factors. The Crown may read in such facts as the Crown deems fit. The Crown is prepared to receive any reasonable suggestion respecting such facts. The Crown will fairly describe to the court the effect that the pleas and assistance will and may have respecting all participants in the crimes.

11. Her counsel will voluntarily provide at the first opportunity to Crown counsel, an opportunity to inspect a copy of any psychiatric, psychological, or other medical reports.

12. The Crown will in its discretion, supported by the defense, and subject to the approval of a judge, tender victim impact statements and related material, and/or move to call the parents of the victims at the sentencing hearing.

E   Post-Sentencing Matters

1. Your client need provide sworn testimony in any and all proceedings to which she is subpoenaed by the Crown arising from her cautioned statements and she will tell the truth.

2. The Crown, on behalf of the police, is prepared to write to Correctional Services Canada and/or the Parole Board, attaching a full transcript of all proceedings and making full reference to any assistance offered and received in relation to interviews, testimony, and like matters, all of which will be for the exercise of the discretion of Correctional Services Canada and/or the Parole Board. In the event the accused applies for transfer for purposes of psychiatric treatment while in custody, the Crown and the police will leave such matters to the discretion of Correctional Services Canada and/or the Parole Board.

3. Neither the Crown nor the police will make any other warranties respecting post-sentence custody or parole and like matters. The Crown and the police agree that such issues will be in the discretion of Correctional Services Canada and/or the Parole Board.

4. While in custody, she will continue to fully assist the authorities.

5. If released prior to the termination of all trials involving others implicated in the investigated crimes she will make herself available to be fully interviewed and to testify as required.

6. If the sentencing judge imposes a sentence greater than twelve years, nothing prevents the defense from appealing against sentence to seek a reduction to twelve years.

7. The Crown is prepared to confirm any aspect of this agreement to a court or any government agency for

the purposes of carrying out what is contained in this agreement.

F   Other Matters

1.   She will not give an account directly or indirectly to the press, media, or for the purpose of any book, movie, or like endeavor.

2.   She will not seek or receive, directly or indirectly, any compensation relating to the above, including any and all events and occurrences arising from the police investigations, criminal proceedings, or any statements given by her to the police.

Thank you.
Yours very truly,

Murray D. Segal
Director